Lecture Notes in Computer Scier

Commenced Publication in 1973
Founding and Former Series Editors:
Gerhard Goos, Juris Hartmanis, and Jan van Leeuwen

Tiziana Margaria   Bernhard Steffen (Eds.)

Leveraging Applications of Formal Methods, Verification and Validation

Applications and Case Studies

5th International Symposium, ISoLA 2012
Heraklion, Crete, Greece, October 15-18, 2012
Proceedings, Part II

 Springer

Volume Editors

Tiziana Margaria
Universität Potsdam, Institut für Informatik
August-Bebel-Straße 89, 14482 Potsdam, Germany
E-mail: margaria@cs.uni-potsdam.de

Bernhard Steffen
Technische Universität Dortmund, Fakultät für Informatik
Otto-Hahn-Straße 14, 44227 Dortmund, Germany
E-mail: steffen@cs.tu-dortmund.de

ISSN 0302-9743   e-ISSN 1611-3349
ISBN 978-3-642-34031-4   e-ISBN 978-3-642-34032-1
DOI 10.1007/978-3-642-34032-1
Springer Heidelberg Dordrecht London New York

Library of Congress Control Number: 2012948288

CR Subject Classification (1998): D.2.4-5, D.2.1-3, D.3.3-4, D.4.1, D.4.5, D.4.7, F.1.1, F.3.1-2, I.2, C.2

LNCS Sublibrary: SL 1 – Theoretical Computer Science and General Issues

Typesetting: Camera-ready by author, data conversion by Scientific Publishing Services, Chennai, India

Printed on acid-free paper

Springer is part of Springer Science+Business Media (www.springer.com)

Preface

Welcome to ISoLA 2012, the 4th International Symposium on Leveraging Applications of Formal Methods, Verification and Validation, that was held in Heraklion, Crete (Greece) during October 14–18, 2012, endorsed by EASST, the European Association of Software Science and Technology.

This year's event followed the tradition of its forerunners held 2004 and 2006 in Cyprus, 2008 in Chalkidiki, and 2010 in Crete, and the series of ISoLA Workshops in Greenbelt (USA) in 2005, Poitiers (France) in 2007, Potsdam (Germany) in 2009, and in Vienna (Austria) in 2011.

As in the previous editions, ISoLA 2012 provided a forum for developers, users, and researchers to discuss issues related to the adoption and use of rigorous tools and methods for the specification, analysis, verification, certification, construction, test, and maintenance of systems from the point of view of their different application domains. Thus, since 2004 the ISoLA series of events serves the purpose of bridging the gap between designers and developers of rigorous tools on the one hand, and users in engineering and in other disciplines on the other hand. It fosters and exploits synergetic relationships among scientists, engineers, software developers, decision makers, and other critical thinkers in companies and organizations. By providing a specific, dialogue-oriented venue for the discussion of common problems, requirements, algorithms, methodologies, and practices, ISoLA aims in particular at supporting researchers in their quest to improve the usefulness, reliability, flexibility, and efficiency of tools for building systems, and users in their search for adequate solutions to their problems.

The program of the symposium consisted of a collection of special tracks devoted to the following hot and emerging topics

- Adaptable and Evolving Software for Eternal Systems (R. Hähnle, I. Schäfer)
- Approaches for Mastering Change (M. Leucker, M. Lochau, I. Schäfer)
- Bioscientific Data Processing and Modeling (J. Kok, A.-L. Lamprecht, F. Verbeek, M. Wilkinson)
- Formal Methods for the Development and Certification of X-by-Wire Control Systems (A. Fantechi, F. Flammini, S. Gnesi)
- Handling Heterogeneity in Formal Development of HW and SW Systems (Y. Ait-Ameur, D. Mery)
- Learning Techniques for Software Verification and Validation (E.M. Clarke, M. Gheorghiu Bobaru, C. Pasareanu, D. Song)
- Model-Based Testing and Model Inference (K. Meinke, N. Walkinshaw)
- Processes and Data Integration in the Networked Healthcare (A. Braun v. Reinersdorff, T. Margaria, C. Rasche)
- Process-Oriented Geoinformation Systems and Applications (H. Asche)
- Quantitative Modeling and Analysis (J.-P. Katoen, K.G. Larsen)
- Runtime Verification: The Application Perspective (Y. Falcone, L. Zuck)

- Software Aspects of Robotic Systems (J. Knoop, D. Schreiner)
- Timing Constraints: Theory Meets Practice (B. Lisper, J. Nordlander, P. Quinton)

and of the following four events

- LearnLib Tutorial: From Finite Automata to Register Interface Programs (F. Howar, M. Isberner, M. Merten, B. Steffen)
- The RERS Grey-Box Challenge 2012: Analysis of Event-Condition-Action Systems (F. Howar, M. Isberner, M. Merten, B. Steffen, D. Beyer)
- Linux Driver Verification Workshop (D. Beyer, A. Petrenko)
- ITSy Day 2012 (T. Margaria, B. Steffen)

The ISoLA Symposium was itself part of the ISoLA Week, which signaled the steady growth of the community and included the following four co-located events:

- STRESS 2012 — International School on Tool-Based Rigorous Engineering of Software Systems (P.Chalin, J. Hatcliff, Robby, T. Margaria, B. Steffen)
- SEW 2012 — 35th IEEE Software Engineering Workshop (M. Hinchey, J. Bowen, H. Zhu)
- Graduate/Postgraduate Course on Soft Skills for IT Professionals in Science and Engineering (B. Floyd)
- FRCSS 2012 — 2nd Future Research Challenges for Software and Services (T. Margaria)

We thank the track organizers, the members of the Program Committee and their subreferees for their effort in selecting the papers to be presented, the Local Organization Chair, Petros Stratis, and the Easyconference team for their continuous precious support during the week as well as during the entire two-year period preceding the events, and Springer for being, as usual, a very reliable partner in the proceedings production. Finally, we are grateful to Horst Voigt for his Web support, and to Maik Merten, Johannes Neubauer, and Stephan Windmüller for their help with the online conference service (OCS).

Special thanks are due to the following organization for their endorsement: EASST (European Association of Software Science and Technology), and our own institutions — the TU Dortmund, and the University of Potsdam.

October 2012   Tiziana Margaria
                                                           Bernhard Steffen

Organization

Committees

Symposium Chair   Bernhard Steffen

Program Chair   Tiziana Margaria

Program Committee

Yamine Ait-Ameur
Hartmut Asche
Dirk Beyer
Mihaela Bobaru
Edmund Clarke
Ylies Falcone
Francesco Flammini
Stefania Gnesi
Reiner Hähnle
John Hatcliff
Falk Howar
Joost-Pieter Katoen
Joost Kok
Jens Knoop
Anna-Lena Lamprecht
Kim G. Larsen
Martin Leucker

Björn Lisper
Malte Lochau
Karl Meinke
Dominique Mery
Alessandro Moschitti
Johan Nordlander
Corina Pasareanu
Alexander K. Petrenko
Sophie Quinton
Ina Schaefer
Dietmar Schreiner
Dawn Song
Fons Verbeek
Neil Walkinshaw
Mark D. Wilkinson
Lenore Zuck

Table of Contents – Part II

Timing Constraints: Theory Meets Practice

Formal Methods for the Development and Certification of X-by-Wire Control Systems

Quantitative Modelling and Analysis

Software Aspects of Robotic Systems

Process-Oriented Geoinformation Systems and Applications

Handling Heterogeneity in Formal Development of HW and SW Systems

Table of Contents – Part I

Adaptable and Evolving Software for Eternal Systems

Approaches for Mastering Change

Runtime Verification: The Application Perspective

Model-Based Testing and Model Inference

Learning Techniques for Software Verification and Validation

LearnLib Tutorial: From Finite Automata to Register Interface Programs

RERS Grey-Box Challenge 2012

Linux Driver Verification

(Position Paper)

Dirk Beyer[1] and Alexander K. Petrenko[2]

[1] University of Passau, Germany
[2] ISPRAS, Moscow, Russia

Abstract. Linux driver verification is a large application area for software verification methods, in particular, for functional, safety, and security verification. Linux driver software is industrial production code — IT infrastructures rely on its stability, and thus, there are strong requirements for correctness and reliability. This implies that if a verification engineer has identified a bug in a driver, the engineer can expect quick response from the development community in terms of bug confirmation and correction. Linux driver software is complex, low-level systems code, and its characteristics make it necessary to bring to bear techniques from program analysis, SMT solvers, model checking, and other areas of software verification. These areas have recently made a significant progress in terms of precision and performance, and the complex task of verifying Linux driver software can be successful if the conceptual state-of-the-art becomes available in tool implementations.

1 Overview

The Linux kernel is currently one of the most important software systems in our society. Linux is used as kernel for several popular desktop operating systems (e.g., Ubuntu, Fedora, Debian, Gentoo), and thus, the seamless workflow of many users depends on this software. Perhaps even more importantly, the server operating systems that currently dominate the market are based on Linux. Almost all (90 % in 2010) supercomputers run a Linux-based operating system. Increasingly many embedded devices such as smart phones run Linux as kernel (e.g., Android, Maemo, WebOS). This explains an increasing need for automatic verification of Linux components.

Microsoft had identified the device drivers as the most important source of failures in their operating systems. Consequently, the company has significantly increased the reliability of Windows by integrating the Static Driver Verifier (SDV) into the production cycle. The foundations were developed in the SLAM research project [1]. The SDV kit is now included by default in the Windows Driver Kit (WDK).

For Linux, an industry-funded verification project of the size of SDV does not exist. But the development community is increasingly looking for automatic techniques for verifying crucial properties, and the verification community is using Linux drivers as application domain for new analysis techniques. During the

T. Margaria and B. Steffen (Eds.): ISoLA 2012, Part II, LNCS 7610, pp. 1–6, 2012.
© Springer-Verlag Berlin Heidelberg 2012

last years, three verification environments were build in order to define verification tasks from Linux drivers: the Linux Driver Verification project [1] [23], the AVINUX project [27], and the DDVERIFY project [2] [32].

The Linux code base is a popular source for verification tasks [17, 22, 24, 25]. Linux drivers provide a unique combination of specific characteristics that attract researchers and practitioners to challenge their tools. The most important benefits of using the Linux code as source for verification tasks are the following:

- the software is important – many people are interested in verification results;
- every bug in a driver is potentially critical because the driver runs with kernel privileges and in the kernel's address space;
- the code volume is enormously large (10 MLOC) and continuously increases;
- the verification tasks are difficult enough to be challenging, but not too complex to be hopeless; and
- most Linux drivers are licensed as open source and therefore easy to use in verification and research projects.

Although many new advancements in the area of software verification have been made, it requires a special effort to transfer them to practice and make them applicable to complex industrial code such as Linux device drivers. The recent competition on software verification (SV-COMP'12) [3] [3] showed that even modern state-of-the-art tool implementations have problems analyzing the problems in the category on device drivers.

2   Research Directions

Pointer Analysis and Dynamic Data Structures. Many safety properties of device drivers depend on a precise analysis of pointers and data structures on the heap. The analysis of pointers is well understood, but due to the low-level code that is used in system programming, the analysis concepts are difficult to implement. The LDV project has made a significant progress on this topic with implementing a more precise pointer analysis into the software model checker BLAST [29]. This improved version of the original software model checker BLAST [5] is the SV-COMP'12 winner on the verification tasks that were derived from the Linux kernel [28].

The analysis of data structures is still an ongoing research topic, with significant progress in the last years; however, there is no large set of open benchmark verification tasks to practically compare the different implementations. The tool PREDATOR is an example of a state-of-the-art static analyzer with the ability to check data structures and memory safety [16].

Symbolic Verification. Due to the progress in SMT solving, formula-based symbolic representations of abstract states are nowadays effective and efficient.

---

[1] http://linuxtesting.org/project/ldv
[2] http://www.cprover.org/ddverify
[3] http://sv-comp.sosy-lab.org

Microsoft's SDV and SLAM [1], and several current research tools are based on predicate abstraction [5, 8, 12, 18]. Several tool implementations integrate the concepts of counterexample-guided abstract refinement (CEGAR) [11], various kinds of shape analysis, abstract reachability trees [5], lazy abstraction [21], interpolation [20], and large-block encoding [4, 9]. Also bounded model checking [10] is a technique of practical relevance and with impressive results in the verification competition [14, 30].

Not yet sufficiently addressed in research projects are the problems of determining the interpolants (there is a wide range between weak and strong interpolants), block-sizes (which criterion should be used to determine the end of a block that is completely encoded in one post operation), and traversal orders (coverage-directed verification, BFS, DFS, etc.). Another important and promising technique that has been largely ignored in software verification is the possibility to encode abstract states and transition relations completely as binary decision diagrams (BDD). There was some progress on this topic, e.g., the extension of CPACHECKER and JAVA PATHFINDER to using BDDs to represent the state space that boolean variables span in code of product-line simulators [31].

Explicit-State Verification. Some explicit-state model checkers are successful in their application domain (e.g., SPIN and JAVA PATHFINDER). In order to apply this technology to the verification of driver software in a scalable manner, it would be interesting to incorporate state-of-the-art techniques that are successful in symbolic verification. For example, CEGAR should be used to automatically create an abstraction, and Craig interpolation for explicit-value domains could identify which parts of the state space are necessary to be analyzed.

Combination of Verification Techniques. In the past, several combination techniques have been proposed for assembling new analyses that are created by parallel combination of different existing analyses [7, 15]. This is extremely effective and should receive more attention and be used in practical applications. The practical application of parallel combinations is hindered by technical barriers: the two analyses have to use the same traversal algorithm, have to be implemented in the same programming language and in compatible tool environments, and need to run on the same machine at the same location (e.g., not distributed in a computing cloud).

Sequential combination using conditional model checking is an effective solution to this problem [6]. Different tools and techniques can be run one after the other, and try to solve the verification task using the various strengths. A conditional model checker is instructed when to give up (by an input condition). The input conditions represent a flexible way of bounding or restricting the verification process. Output conditions represent the state space that was successfully verified already. A successive verifier can use such conditions of previous runs to not perform the same verification work again, but concentrate on applying its strengths to the remaining task.

Termination Analysis. An area that needs more attention is termination analysis. There are a few tools for termination checking (most prominently, ARMC [26]) but the technology is not yet as wide-spread as it should be. The technology has been adopted and further improved by Microsoft's TERMINATOR project [13].

Concurrency. Due to the increasing availability of multi-core machines, the verification of multi-threaded software becomes an important research direction. Checking for race conditions and deadlocks is an essential quality assurance means that needs to be applied to Linux driver software as well. The verification community actively invents new concepts and implements new tools to approach this problem (for example, ESBMC [14], SATABS [2], THREADER [19]). It is interesting to observe that the best tool for checking concurrency problems in the last competition was a bounded model checker [14].

3 Conclusion

We outlined the motivation for considering Linux device drivers as application domain for verification research. It is important to develop verification tools that are efficient and effective enough to successfully check software components that are as complex as device drivers. The benefits are twofold: for the society it is important to get such crucial software verified; for the verification community it is important to get realistic verification tasks in order to tune and further develop the technology. We provided an overview of the state-of-the-art and pointed out research directions in which further progress is essential.

References

1. Ball, T., Rajamani, S.K.: The SLAM Project: Debugging System Software via Static Analysis. In: Proc. POPL, pp. 1–3. ACM (2002)
2. Basler, G., Donaldson, A., Kaiser, A., Kröning, D., Tautschnig, M., Wahl, T.: SatAbs: A Bit-Precise Verifier for C Programs. In: Flanagan, C., König, B. (eds.) TACAS 2012. LNCS, vol. 7214, pp. 552–555. Springer, Heidelberg (2012)
3. Beyer, D.: Competition on Software Verification. In: Flanagan, C., König, B. (eds.) TACAS 2012. LNCS, vol. 7214, pp. 504–524. Springer, Heidelberg (2012)
4. Beyer, D., Cimatti, A., Griggio, A., Keremoglu, M.E., Sebastiani, R.: Software Model Checking via Large-block Encoding. In: Proc. FMCAD, pp. 25–32. IEEE (2009)
5. Beyer, D., Henzinger, T.A., Jhala, R., Majumdar, R.: The Software Model Checker BLAST. Int. J. Softw. Tools Technol. Transfer 9(5-6), 505–525 (2007)
6. Beyer, D., Henzinger, T.A., Keremoglu, M.E., Wendler, P.: Conditional Model Checking: A Technique to Pass Information Between Verifiers. In: Proc. FSE. ACM (2012)
7. Beyer, D., Henzinger, T.A., Théoduloz, G.: Program Analysis with Dynamic Precision Adjustment. In: Proc. ASE, pp. 29–38. IEEE (2008)
8. Beyer, D., Keremoglu, M.E.: CPACHECKER: A Tool for Configurable Software Verification. In: Gopalakrishnan, G., Qadeer, S. (eds.) CAV 2011. LNCS, vol. 6806, pp. 184–190. Springer, Heidelberg (2011)
9. Beyer, D., Keremoglu, M.E., Wendler, P.: Predicate Abstraction with Adjustable-block Encoding. In: Proc. FMCAD, pp. 189–197. FMCAD (2010)

10. Biere, A., Cimatti, A., Clarke, E., Zhu, Y.: Symbolic Model Checking without BDDs. In: Cleaveland, W.R. (ed.) TACAS 1999. LNCS, vol. 1579, pp. 193–207. Springer, Heidelberg (1999)
11. Clarke, E.M., Grumberg, O., Jha, S., Lu, Y., Veith, H.: Counterexample-guided Abstraction Refinement for Symbolic Model Checking. J. ACM 50(5), 752–794 (2003)
12. Clarke, E., Kroning, D., Sharygina, N., Yorav, K.: SatAbs: SAT-Based Predicate Abstraction for ANSI-C. In: Halbwachs, N., Zuck, L.D. (eds.) TACAS 2005. LNCS, vol. 3440, pp. 570–574. Springer, Heidelberg (2005)
13. Cook, B., Podelski, A., Rybalchenko, A.: TERMINATOR: Beyond Safety. In: Ball, T., Jones, R.B. (eds.) CAV 2006. LNCS, vol. 4144, pp. 415–418. Springer, Heidelberg (2006)
14. Cordeiro, L., Morse, J., Nicole, D., Fischer, B.: Context-Bounded Model Checking with ESBMC 1.17. In: Flanagan, C., König, B. (eds.) TACAS 2012. LNCS, vol. 7214, pp. 534–537. Springer, Heidelberg (2012)
15. Cousot, P., Cousot, R., Feret, J., Mauborgne, L., Miné, A., Monniaux, D., Rival, X.: Combination of Abstractions in the ASTRÉE Static Analyzer. In: Okada, M., Satoh, I. (eds.) ASIAN 2006. LNCS, vol. 4435, pp. 272–300. Springer, Heidelberg (2008)
16. Dudka, K., Müller, P., Peringer, P., Vojnar, T.: Predator: A Verification Tool for Programs with Dynamic Linked Data Structures. In: Flanagan, C., König, B. (eds.) TACAS 2012. LNCS, vol. 7214, pp. 545–548. Springer, Heidelberg (2012)
17. Galloway, A., Lüttgen, G., Mühlberg, J.T., Siminiceanu, R.I.: Model-Checking the Linux Virtual File System. In: Jones, N.D., Müller-Olm, M. (eds.) VMCAI 2009. LNCS, vol. 5403, pp. 74–88. Springer, Heidelberg (2009)
18. Grebenshchikov, S., Gupta, A., Lopes, N.P., Popeea, C., Rybalchenko, A.: HSF(C): A Software Verifier Based on Horn Clauses. In: Flanagan, C., König, B. (eds.) TACAS 2012. LNCS, vol. 7214, pp. 549–551. Springer, Heidelberg (2012)
19. Gupta, A., Popeea, C., Rybalchenko, A.: Threader: A Constraint-Based Verifier for Multi-threaded Programs. In: Gopalakrishnan, G., Qadeer, S. (eds.) CAV 2011. LNCS, vol. 6806, pp. 412–417. Springer, Heidelberg (2011)
20. Henzinger, T.A., Jhala, R., Majumdar, R., McMillan, K.L.: Abstractions from Proofs. In: Proc. POPL, pp. 232–244. ACM (2004)
21. Henzinger, T.A., Jhala, R., Majumdar, R., Sutre, G.: Lazy Abstraction. In: Proc. POPL, pp. 58–70. ACM (2002)
22. Khoroshilov, A., Mutilin, V., Novikov, E., Shved, P., Strakh, A.: Towards an Open Framework for C Verification Tools Benchmarking. In: Clarke, E., Virbitskaite, I., Voronkov, A. (eds.) PSI 2011. LNCS, vol. 7162, pp. 179–192. Springer, Heidelberg (2012)
23. Khoroshilov, A., Mutilin, V., Petrenko, A., Zakharov, V.: Establishing Linux Driver Verification Process. In: Pnueli, A., Virbitskaite, I., Voronkov, A. (eds.) PSI 2009. LNCS, vol. 5947, pp. 165–176. Springer, Heidelberg (2010)
24. Mühlberg, J.T., Lüttgen, G.: BLASTing Linux Code. In: Brim, L., Haverkort, B.R., Leucker, M., van de Pol, J. (eds.) FMICS 2006 and PDMC 2006. LNCS, vol. 4346, pp. 211–226. Springer, Heidelberg (2007)
25. Penninckx, W., Mühlberg, J.T., Smans, J., Jacobs, B., Piessens, F.: Sound Formal Verification of Linux's USB BP Keyboard Driver. In: Goodloe, A.E., Person, S. (eds.) NFM 2012. LNCS, vol. 7226, pp. 210–215. Springer, Heidelberg (2012)
26. Podelski, A., Rybalchenko, A.: Transition Predicate Abstraction and Fair Termination. In: Proc. POPL, pp. 132–144. ACM (2005)

27. Post, H., Sinz, C., Küchlin, W.: Towards Automatic Software Model Checking of Thousands of Linux Modules — A Case Study with AVINUX. Softw. Test., Verif. Reliab. 19(2), 155–172 (2009)
28. Shved, P., Mandrykin, M., Mutilin, V.: Predicate Analysis with BLAST 2.7. In: Flanagan, C., König, B. (eds.) TACAS 2012. LNCS, vol. 7214, pp. 525–527. Springer, Heidelberg (2012)
29. Shved, P., Mutilin, V., Mandrykin, M.: Experience of Improving the BLAST Static Verification Tool. Programming and Computer Software 38(3), 134–142 (2012)
30. Sinz, C., Merz, F., Falke, S.: LLBMC: A Bounded Model Checker for LLVM's Intermediate Representation. In: Flanagan, C., König, B. (eds.) TACAS 2012. LNCS, vol. 7214, pp. 542–544. Springer, Heidelberg (2012)
31. von Rhein, A., Apel, S., Raimondi, F.: Introducing Binary Decision Diagrams in the Explicit-state Verification of Java Code. In: Proc. Java Pathfinder Workshop (2011)
32. Witkowski, T., Blanc, N., Kröning, D., Weissenbacher, G.: Model Checking Concurrent Linux Device Drivers. In: Proc. ASE, pp. 501–504. ACM (2007)

Bioscientific Data Processing and Modeling

Joost Kok[1], Anna-Lena Lamprecht[2], Fons J. Verbeek[1],
and Mark D. Wilkinson[3]

[1] Leiden Institute of Advanced Computer Science, Leiden University,
2300 RA Leiden, The Netherlands
{joost,fverbeek}@liacs.nl
[2] Chair for Service and Software Engineering, University of Potsdam,
14482 Potsdam, Germany
lamprecht@cs.uni-potsdam.de
[3] Centro de Biotecnología y Genómica de Plantas,
Parque Científico y Tecnológico de la U.P.M., Campus de Montegancedo, 28223
Pozuelo de Alarcón (Madrid), Spain
mark.wilkinson@upm.es

With more than 200 different types of "-omic" data [1] spanning from sub-molecular, through molecular, cell, cell-systems, tissues, organs, phenotypes, gene-environment interactions, and ending at ecology and organism communities, the problem and complexity of bioscientific data processing has never been greater. Often data are generated in high-throughput studies with the aim to have a sufficient volume to find patterns and detect rare events. For these high-throughput approaches new methods have to be developed in order to assure integrity of the volume of data that is produced. At the same time efforts to integrate these widely-varying data types are underway in research fields such as systems biology. Systems-level research requires yet additional methodologies to pipeline, process, query, and interpret data, and such pipelines are, themselves, objects of scientific value if they can be re-used or re-purposed by other researchers.

This ISoLA 2012 special track focuses at the various topics concerned with the discovery and preservation of knowledge in the biosciences. The track comprises four papers, of which three are concerned with algorithms for image analysis, and one with a new workflow management methodology. The following gives a brief overview of these two thematic areas and of all the papers in the track.

Algorithms for Image Analysis

Although imaging and bioinformatics are research fields in their own right, there exists a quite substantial overlap between these two areas. On the interface of these two fields we find typically with image analysis as well as with the study of interoperability of image information to other bio-molecular information resources. In the life-sciences image analysis spans quite an application area ranging from molecular biology to interpretation of areal imagery for ecology. Then there is medical imaging focussed on patients and health care. Here we focus on the imaging from the molecules to (small) organisms; the imaging device is the microscope and the field is pre-clinical research.

T. Margaria and B. Steffen (Eds.): ISoLA 2012, Part II, LNCS 7610, pp. 7–11, 2012.
© Springer-Verlag Berlin Heidelberg 2012

In microscopy imaging, at least, three issues are important, the first being obtaining and organizing the images, then analyzing the images and reducing the scene to numbers so that patterns can be found and analyzed, next, the information in the image needs to be represented properly. The analysis of images requires images to be acquired in large volumes so that patterns are statistically meaningful. Moreover, large volumes are required to detect rare events. A trend in life sciences research is, therefore, to approach problem with a high-throughput workflow. This puts demands in the acquisition phase, that need be largely automated but also on the processing phase. The latter requires algorithms that are robust and reproducible; here we present two examples on different levels of resolution, one on the organismal/tissue level [2,3] and one at the cellular level [4,5]; application of high-throughput to cellular systems is also referred to as cytomics. The specific algorithms that are presented here are designed and evaluated with the specific requirements for high-throughput analysis in mind.

Further processing of the features extracted from the images requires frameworks for pattern recognition specific to the data at hand [4,6,2]. However, we need to be able to integrate images as well as the resulting analysis in systems that include a reference model. Such systems are now being made on the level of the model system: e.g. mouse [7], the zebrafish [8,9], but also on the level of the organ. The brain is a good example for that, the rodent brain is used as a model for the human brain and specific reference systems for integration are being developed for the rodent brain [7]. The integration requires intelligent use of reference systems on the semantic level [4,10]. Therefore well maintained ontologies will be extremely important to maintain and disclose the large amounts of data that are currently produced. Ultimately, resources for genomic and molecular research will be integrated with image based resources. The challenge for the scientific community is to do this right.

The first paper of this ISoLA track, **Using multiobjective optimization and energy minimization to design an isoform-selective ligand of the 14-3-3 protein** (Hernando Sanchez-Faddeev, Michael T.M. Emmerich, Fons J. Verbeek, Andrew H. Henry, Simon Grimshaw, Herman P. Spaink, Herman W. van Vlijmen and Andreas Bender) [11], presents an approach for de novo design of protein ligands based on evolutionary multiobjective optimization. It shows that multiobjective optimization with evolutionary algorithms can be successfully employed in selective ligand design.

The paper **Segmentation for High-throughput Image Analysis: Watershed Masked Clustering** (by Kuan Yan and Fons J. Verbeek) [12] is concerned with high-throughput analysis of images of cells. It describes a new segmentation algorithm for high-throughput imaging, which is in particular suitable for image analyses in the fields of cytomics and high-throughput screening. The algorithm has been used with good results in a number of studies and is reported to perform better than previous algorithms for this task.

In **Efficient and Robust Shape Retrieval from Deformable Templates** (Alexander E. Nezhinski and Fons J. Verbeek) [13] an algorithmic framework for the automated detection of shapes in images through deformable templates is presented. For demonstration purposes, it is applied to a biological case study, namely to high-throughput screening images of zebrafish larvae, and the algorithm is reported to be particularly accurate and robust.

Workflow Management

In recent years, numerous software systems have been developed for specifically supporting the management of scientific workflows (see, e.g., [14,15] for surveys). Research in this comparatively new field is currently going into many different directions. At the previous ISoLA in 2010, we focused on workflow management for scientific applications in the scope of a symposium track on "Tools in scientific workflow composition" [16], which comprised papers on subjects such as tools and frameworks for workflow composition, semantically aware workflow development, and automatic workflow composition, as well as some case studies, examples, and experiences.

Particularly interesting and challenging in the field of scientific workflow management is currently the research concerned with the use of semantics-based methods for automating workflow composition (see, e.g., [17,18]). Some examples of concrete systems which have lately been applied for semantics-based, (semi-) automatic workflow composition in the bioinformatics domain are the Bio-jETI framework [19,20,21] that makes use of workflow synthesis techniques to translate abstract, high-level workflow specifications into concrete, executable workflow instances, the jORCA [22,23] system that automatically creates pipelines of web services given the desired input and output data types, the SADI and SHARE frameworks [24,25] that facilitate on-the-fly service discovery and execution based on OWL-annotated data, and the Wings (Workflow INstance Generation and Selection) [26] extension for the Pegasus [27] grid workflow system that provides functionality for (semi-) automatic workflow creation based on semantic representations and planning techniques. Some of these systems have also been presented in the scope of the ISoLA 2010 track.

In this context, and as a continuation of the ISoLA 2010 paper on semantics-guided workflow construction in the Taverna workbench [28], the fourth paper of our track addresses the problem of workflow sharing and re-purposing in bioinformatics: In **OWL-DL domain models as abstract workflows** (Ian Wood, Ben Vandervalk, Luke McCarthy and Mark D. Wilkinson) [29], the authors discuss the growing popularity of formal analytical workflows, and the associated difficulty in re-using these workflows due to their rigidity. To overcome these issues, they present an original approach where a domain-concept, modeled in OWL-DL and based on the SADI and SHARE frameworks, can be used dynamically as a workflow template, which is then concretized into a Web Service workflow at run-time. Moreover, the semantics inherent in these domain-models can act as a form of workflow annotation. The authors propose that, over time, these abstract workflows may be easier to share and repurpose than conventional "concrete" workflows. The paper demonstrates the approach by automatically reproducing a published comparative genomics analysis through creating an OWL-DL representation of the biological phenomenon being studied.

References

1. McDonald, D., Clemente, J., Kuczynski, J., Rideout, J., Stombaugh, J., Wendel, D., Wilke, A., Huse, S., Hufnagle, J., Meyer, F., Knight, R., Caporaso, J.: The Biological Observation Matrix (BIOM) format or: how I learned to stop worrying and love the ome-ome. GigaScience 1(1), 7 (2012)
2. Stoop, E., Schipper, T., Rosendahl Huber, S., Nezhinsky, A., Verbeek, F., Gurcha, S., Besra, G., Vandenbroucke-Grauls, C., Bitter, W., van der Sar, A.: Zebrafish embryo screen for mycobacterial genes involved in the initiation of granuloma formation reveals a newly identified ESX-1 component. Disease Model Mechanisms, 526–536 (2011)
3. Nezhinsky, A.E., Verbeek, F.J.: Pattern Recognition for High Throughput Zebrafish Imaging Using Genetic Algorithm Optimization. In: Dijkstra, T.M.H., Tsivtsivadze, E., Marchiori, E., Heskes, T. (eds.) PRIB 2010. LNCS, vol. 6282, pp. 301–312. Springer, Heidelberg (2010)
4. Larios, E., Zhang, Y., Yan, K., Di, Z., LeDévédec, S., Groffen, F., Verbeek, F.J.: Automation in Cytomics: A Modern RDBMS Based Platform for Image Analysis and Management in High-Throughput Screening Experiments. In: He, J., Liu, X., Krupinski, E.A., Xu, G. (eds.) HIS 2012. LNCS, vol. 7231, pp. 76–87. Springer, Heidelberg (2012)
5. LeDévédec, S., Yan, K., de Bont, H., Ghotra, V., Truong, H., Danen, E., Verbeek, F., van de Water, B.: A Systems Microscopy Approach to Understand Cancer Cell Migration and Metastasis. Journal Cellular and Molecular Life Sciences 67(19), 3219–3240 (2010)
6. Yan, K., Larios, E., LeDevedec, S., van de Water, B., Verbeek, F.J.: Automation in Cytomics: Systematic Solution for Image Analysis and Management in High Throughput Sequences. In: Proceedings IEEE Conf. Engineering and Technology (CET 2011), vol. 7 (2011)
7. Hawrylycz, M., Baldock, R.A., Burger, A., Hashikawa, T., Johnson, G.A., Martone, M., Ng, L., Lau, C., Larsen, S.D., Nissanov, J., Puelles, L., Ruffins, S., Verbeek, F., Zaslavsky, I., Boline, J.: Digital Atlasing and Standardization in the Mouse Brain. PLoS Comput. Biol. 7(2), e1001065+ (2011)
8. Belmamoune, M., Potikanond, D., Verbeek, F.: Mining and analysing spatio-temporal patterns of gene expression in an integrative database framework. Journal of Integrative Bioinformatics 7(3)(128), 1–10 (2010)
9. Verbeek, F., Boon, P., Sloetjes, H., van der Velde, R., de Vos, N.: Visualization of complex data sets over Internet: 2D and 3D visualization of the 3D digital atlas of zebrafish development. In: Proc. SPIE 4672, Internet Imaging III, pp. 20–29 (2002)
10. Slob, J., Kallergi, A., Verbeek, F.J.: Observations on Semantic Annotation of Microscope Images for Life Sciences. In: Marshall, M.S., Burger, A., Romano, P., Paschke, A., Splendiani, A. (eds.) SWAT4LS. CEUR Workshop Proceedings, vol. 559, CEUR-WS.org (2009)
11. Sanchez-Faddeev, H., Emmerich, M.T., Verbeek, F.J., Henry, A.H., Grimshaw, S., Spaink, H.P., van Vlijmen, H.W., Bender, A.: Using Multiobjective Optimization and Energy Minimization to Design an Isoform-Selective Ligand of the 14-3-3 Protein. In: Margaria, T., Steffen, B. (eds.) ISoLA 2012, Part II. LNCS, vol. 7610, pp. 12–24. Springer, Heidelberg (2012)
12. Yan, K., Verbeek, F.J.: Segmentation for High-throughput Image Analysis: Watershed Masked Clustering. In: Margaria, T., Steffen, B. (eds.) ISoLA 2012, Part II. LNCS, vol. 7610, pp. 25–41. Springer, Heidelberg (2012)

13. Nezhinsky, A.E., Verbeek, F.J.: Efficient and Robust Shape Retrieval from Deformable Templates. In: Margaria, T., Steffen, B. (eds.) ISoLA 2012, Part II. LNCS, vol. 7610, pp. 42–55. Springer, Heidelberg (2012)
14. Taylor, I.: Workflows for E-Science: Scientific Workflows for Grids. Springer (2007)
15. Wikipedia: Bioinformatics workflow management systems — Wikipedia, The Free Encyclopedia (2012) (Online; last accessed June 25, 2012)
16. Kok, J.N., Lamprecht, A.-L., Wilkinson, M.D.: Tools in Scientific Workflow Composition. In: Margaria, T., Steffen, B. (eds.) ISoLA 2010, Part I. LNCS, vol. 6415, pp. 258–260. Springer, Heidelberg (2010)
17. Chen, L., Shadbolt, N.R., Goble, C.A., Tao, F., Cox, S.J., Puleston, C., Smart, P.R.: Towards a Knowledge-Based Approach to Semantic Service Composition. In: Fensel, D., Sycara, K., Mylopoulos, J. (eds.) ISWC 2003. LNCS, vol. 2870, pp. 319–334. Springer, Heidelberg (2003)
18. Lord, P., Bechhofer, S., Wilkinson, M.D., Schiltz, G., Gessler, D., Hull, D., Goble, C.A., Stein, L.: Applying Semantic Web Services to Bioinformatics: Experiences Gained, Lessons Learnt. In: McIlraith, S.A., Plexousakis, D., van Harmelen, F. (eds.) ISWC 2004. LNCS, vol. 3298, pp. 350–364. Springer, Heidelberg (2004)
19. Lamprecht, A.L., Margaria, T., Steffen, B.: Bio-jETI: a framework for semantics-based service composition. BMC Bioinformatics 10(suppl. 10), S8 (2009)
20. Lamprecht, A.L., Naujokat, S., Margaria, T., Steffen, B.: Semantics-based composition of EMBOSS services. Biomedical Semantics 2(suppl. 1), S5 (2011)
21. Lamprecht, A.L., Naujokat, S., Steffen, B., Margaria, T.: Constraint-Guided Workflow Composition Based on the EDAM Ontology. In: Burger, A., Marshall, M.S., Romano, P., Paschke, A., Splendiani, A. (eds.) Proceedings of the 3rd Workshop on Semantic Web Applications and Tools for Life Sciences (SWAT4LS 2010), vol. 698, CEUR Workshop Proceedings (December 2010)
22. Martín-Requena, V., Ríos, J., García, M., Ramírez, S., Trelles, O.: jORCA: easily integrating bioinformatics Web Services. Bioinformatics 26(4), 553–559 (2010)
23. Karlsson, J., Martín-Requena, V., Ríos, J., Trelles, O.: Workflow Composition and Enactment Using jORCA. In: Margaria, T., Steffen, B. (eds.) ISoLA 2010, Part I. LNCS, vol. 6415, pp. 328–339. Springer, Heidelberg (2010)
24. Wilkinson, M.D., Vandervalk, B., McCarthy, L.: SADI Semantic Web Services - 'cause you can't always GET what you want! In: Proceedings of the IEEE Services Computing Conference, APSCC 2009, December 7-11, pp. 13–18. IEEE Asia-Pacific, Singapore (2009)
25. Vandervalk, B.P., McCarthy, E.L., Wilkinson, M.D.: SHARE: A Semantic Web Query Engine for Bioinformatics. In: Gómez-Pérez, A., Yu, Y., Ding, Y. (eds.) ASWC 2009. LNCS, vol. 5926, pp. 367–369. Springer, Heidelberg (2009)
26. Gil, Y., Ratnakar, V., Deelman, E., Mehta, G., Kim, J.: Wings for Pegasus: creating large-scale scientific applications using semantic representations of computational workflows. In: Proceedings of the 19th National Conference on Innovative Applications of Artificial Intelligence, vol. 2, pp. 1767–1774. AAAI Press (2007)
27. Deelman, E., Singh, G., Hui Su, M., Blythe, J., Gil, A., Kesselman, C., Mehta, G., Vahi, K., Berriman, G.B., Good, J., Laity, A., Jacob, J.C., Katz, D.S.: Pegasus: a framework for mapping complex scientific workflows onto distributed systems. Scientific Programming Journal 13, 219–237 (2005)
28. Withers, D., Kawas, E., McCarthy, L., Vandervalk, B., Wilkinson, M.: Semantically-Guided Workflow Construction in Taverna: The SADI and BioMoby Plug-Ins. In: Margaria, T., Steffen, B. (eds.) ISoLA 2010, Part I. LNCS, vol. 6415, pp. 301–312. Springer, Heidelberg (2010)
29. Wood, I., Vandervalk, B., McCarthy, L., Wilkinson, M.D.: OWL-DL Domain Models as Abstract Workflows. In: Margaria, T., Steffen, B. (eds.) ISoLA 2012, Part II. LNCS, vol. 7610, pp. 56–66. Springer, Heidelberg (2012)

Using Multiobjective Optimization and Energy Minimization to Design an Isoform-Selective Ligand of the 14-3-3 Protein

Hernando Sanchez-Faddeev[1], Michael T.M. Emmerich[1], Fons J. Verbeek[1], Andrew H. Henry[2], Simon Grimshaw[2], Herman P. Spaink[3], Herman W. van Vlijmen[4], and Andreas Bender[4]

[1] Leiden Institute of Advanced Computer Science, Leiden University, Niels Bohrweg 1, 2333 CA Leiden, The Netherlands
[2] Chemical Computing Group, St John's Innovation Centre, Cowley Road, Cambridge, United Kingdom, Cambridge CB40WS, United Kingdom
[3] Institute of Biology, Leiden University, Einsteinweg 55, 2333 CC Leiden, The Netherlands
[4] Medicinal Chemistry Division, Leiden / Amsterdam Center for Drug Research, Leiden University, Einsteinweg 55, 2333 CC Leiden, The Netherlands

Abstract. Computer simulation techniques are being used extensively in the pharmaceutical field to model protein-ligand and protein-protein interactions; however, few procedures have been established yet for the design of ligands from scratch ('*de novo*'). To improve upon the current state, in this work the problem of finding a peptide ligand was formulated as a bi-objective optimization problem and a state-of-the-art algorithm for evolutionary multiobjective optimization, namely SMS-EMOA, has been employed for exploring the search space. This algorithm is tailored to this problem class and used to produce a Pareto front in high-dimensional space, here consisting of 23^{22} or about 10^{30} possible solutions. From the knee point of the Pareto front we were able to select a ligand with preferential binding to the gamma versus the epsilon isoform of the *Danio rerio* (zebrafish) 14-3-3 protein. Despite the high-dimensional space the optimization algorithm is able to identify a 22-mer peptide ligand with a predicted difference in binding energy of 291 kcal/mol between the isoforms, showing that multiobjective optimization can be successfully employed in selective ligand design.

Keywords: protein design, ligand design, de novo assembly, SMS-EMOA, multiobjective optimization, 14-3-3, Pareto front, multiobjective selection, hypervolume indicator.

1   Introduction

Over vast timescales, nature has optimized the genetic material to account for survival of organisms that are better adapted to the immediate, local environment [1]. The interplay of genetic variation and natural selection is the driving force of DNA evolution that, for instance, determines the function of all proteins encoded by the genome.

T. Margaria and B. Steffen (Eds.): ISoLA 2012, Part II, LNCS 7610, pp. 12–24, 2012.

Evolutionary algorithms (EA) seek to mimic this process on an algorithmic level [2]. Starting from an initial population of candidate solutions, the application of variation (mutation and recombination) operators and selection operators adapts the solutions to its environment (the fitness function).

In EAs the adaptation to the environment is given by a user-defined fitness function, which determines the likelihood of new genotypes for survival recombination and/or selection; equivalent to reproductive fitness in nature [2]. The defining difference is that fitness functions can be used to optimize the same type of molecules that have been created in the process of evolution with a user-defined objective in mind.

Taking into consideration the complexity of molecular interactions and the promiscuity of those interactions observed in nature [3,4], it is often not sufficient to have only one optimization goal; rather, when designing a ligand for a protein, it is important to make sure it is selective for the target(s) of interest, relative to other, possibly very similar targets [3]. As in the natural environment multiobjective EAs can deal with several conflicting objective functions at the same time and select trade-off solutions that are better suited for both objectives; however, it will favor those solutions which are superior to all others in at least one way (they are the 'non-dominated' solutions) [5].

The desired activity profile for a set of targets is relevant both for efficacy of a compound in a biological system, as well as to avoid adverse side effects such as in case of drugs that are applied to humans [3]. Given the current huge amount of bioactive data we are becoming aware of the suitability of a ligands with a bioactivity profile of interest, with areas such as 'chemogenomics' and 'proteochemometrics' gaining increasing importance [6,7,8].

We have applied structure-based multiobjective ligand design to the family of 14-3-3 proteins, which are present in multiple isoforms in all eukaryotic organisms. Given that this protein is also of large biomedical interest such as in cancer research, and the requirement for a ligand to prefer some 14-3-3 isoforms over others, we chose this case study for the in silico design of isoform-selective peptide ligand design.

14-3-3 proteins participate in many biological processes including protein kinase signaling pathways within all eukaryotic cells, being involved in progression through the cell cycle, initiation and maintenance of DNA damage checkpoints, regulation of mitosis, prevention of apoptosis, and coordination of integrin signaling and cytoskeleton related dynamics [9]. Current studies have demonstrated the important role that 14-3-3 plays in cancer [10], particularly leukaemia as described by Dong et al.[11], and Alzheimer's disease as reported by Jayaratnam et al.[12]. The 14-3-3 proteins are intensively studied in many animal species such as zebrafish, mouse and human.

We recently reported on the 14-3-3 protein isoforms in zebrafish (*Danio rerio*) that are encoded by eleven genes named after their Homo sapiens homologues [13], while the human isoforms γ, β, ε and θ each possess two homologue isoforms in zebrafish. Zebrafish isoforms are the subject of this study due to their similarity to the human isoforms, as well as to be able to validate the predictions later directly by means of in vitro experiments.

The differential expression of various isoforms in different tissues and diseases suggests that different isoforms possess different functionality, which implies different binding preferences for particular ligands [14]. However, only little is known on the differences in the binding specificities to 14-3-3 proteins. Given the large number of isoforms of 14-3-3 and their different roles, the design of specific ligands is important to achieve; yet it is a task that is not trivial in practice. Given recent advances in molecular modeling as well as computational optimization techniques, this study now aims at merging the best of both worlds in order to establish advanced computational methods for 14-3-3 $\gamma 1$ isoform specific ligand design.

A recent review [15] outlines the opportunities and challenges in the application of computer tools to design peptide based drugs, an area of which we present an application of particular interest. Several previous studies have focused on in silico peptide screening for potential new therapeutic entities [16,17,18,19,20,21,22,23,24]; however, in those cases only existing peptides were screened virtually and evaluated with respect to their ability to bind to a protein of interest. The approach taken in this work is rather different, however: instead of screening a library of known peptides and scoring the best solutions, this study focuses on mutating the peptide in a step-wise optimization process, in order to achieve better affinity and to access novel chemical space, in a 'de novo' peptide design approach.

Relating this to previous work, Li et al. [25] analyzed peptide binding to the p53–MDM2/MDMX interface by randomly mutating and evaluating affinities using computational methods. Our random mutation process is similar, except for the fact that Li et al. [25] used a single objective function, so no other protein interactions other than the one with the intended target were taken into account.

However, in this work we emphasize both the de novo, as well as the multiobjective nature of peptide ligand design. We do so by trying to identify a peptide with high binding affinity for the $\gamma 1$ isoform, as compared to the $\epsilon 1$ isoform. $\epsilon 1$ and $\gamma 1$ isoforms have been selected as they have been suggested to have different biological functions, namely $\gamma 1$ has a specialized function in adult physiology, and $\epsilon 1$ is highly expressed during the embryonic stage [13,26,27].

Multiobjective optimization is meant to find good compromises (or "trade-offs"), rather than a solution that is optimal in a single objective function only. If the number of conflicting objectives is low, a well-established approach is to approximate the Pareto front of the problem, i.e., the set of non-dominated optimal solutions, or rephrasing the above a set of optimal "trade off" solutions [28,31]. With two objectives minimization the solution is "Pareto-optimal" if there exists no other solution which improves the one of the objective function values without causing a simultaneous deteriorating of the other objective function value. This is visualized in Figure 1A, which contains a Pareto-optimal set of solutions that were generated in this study.

Multi-objective optimization is not easy to perform in high-dimensional spaces due to the sheer size of the hypothesis space. EA, due to their population-based search concept and high number of generated solutions, lend themselves very well for the task of generating and maintaining Pareto-optimal solutions in higher-dimensional spaces [29]. Pareto optimization hence recently received increasing attention in drug design problems [19,20,30] and bioinformatics [31], besides other application fields.

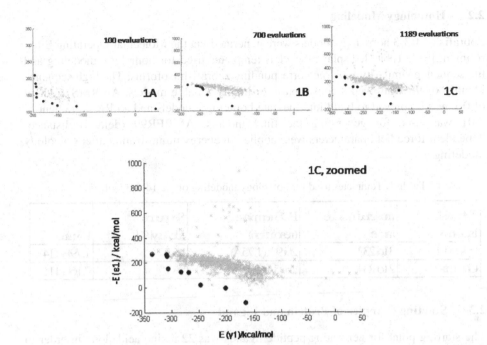

Fig. 1. Binding energy of peptides to the γ1 and ε1 isoforms of the 14-3-3 protein as a function of the number of optimization iterations using the SMS-EMOA algorithm. The X-axis shows the potential energy of interaction with γ1 (which was desired) while the Y-axis shows the inverse of the potential energy of interaction with ε1 (which we attempted to 'design out' of the peptide). The solutions that belong to the Pareto front are represented by circles. The intermediate solutions rejected during the SMS-EMOA run are represented by crosses. It can be seen that already after 100 iterations partially selective peptides are obtained, while after the full number of 1,189 iterations even peptides with no affinity to the ε1 isoform, but 335 kcal/mol binding energy to the γ1 isoform could be identified. Hence, our optimization can be considered successful even in this 22-dimensional search space.

This study intends to use EA with multiobjective optimization to find a binding peptide with relative high binding affinity for the γ1 isoform, as compared to the ε1 isoform [32]. We use multiobjective EA as implemented in SMS-EMOA [28,33], a state-of-the-art Pareto optimization algorithm for this purpose as described in the following.

2   Methods

2.1   Sequence Data

The nucleotide sequences of 14-3-3 isoforms in zebrafish were described by Besser et al. [13]. They performed a phylogenetic analysis of the 14-3-3 family together with microarray expression analysis; the results provided the basis for the choice of 14-3-3 isoforms analyzed in this study.

2.2   Homology Modeling

Zebrafish 14-3-3 homology models were generated via the Molecular Operating Environment [34]. Table 1 displays the PDB templates used for homology modeling and the sequence similarity with the corresponding zebrafish isoforms. The high sequence identity of 96% allowed a construction of highly reliable models. An RMS gradient of 0.1 was employed to build intermediate homology models and an RMS gradient of 0.01 was used for generating the final models. AMBER99 (default) distance-dependent force field parameters were applied in energy minimization after homology modeling.

Table 1. Templates used for homology modeling of the 14-3-3 isoforms

Zebrafish Isoforms	modeled residue range	PDB template (resolution)	Sequence Identity[%]	E-value
Epsilon-1	3 to 232	2br9A (1.75Å)	96.5	1.79E-114
Gamma-1	2 to 234	2b05A (2.55Å)	96.1	7.16E-111

2.3   Starting Complex of Protein and Ligand

The starting point for generating peptide ligands was 22 amino acids long in order to allow interaction both with the binding groove as well as the regions immediately outside to achieve selectivity. This length has also been chosen based on the location of variable regions of 14-3-3 as well as low energy desolvation sites identified previously [14]. 23 possible amino acids could be selected in each position, namely the 20 natural amino acids as well as phosphorylated tyrosine, serine and threonine. The reason for also including phosphorylated amino acids in the study was that in particular phosphorylated serines and threonines are known to be of relevance for peptides interacting with the 14-3-3 protein from previous work [14].

Homology models of both isoforms were aligned sequentially using the Blosum62 matrix and subsequently structurally aligned using the MOE protein alignment tool. The ligand template formed by 22 alanines in an extended conformation was positioned inside the binding groove, with sufficient space to prevent clashing at posterior mutation steps and optimization (the resulting structure can be found in the supporting material). In this orientation the peptide extends from the binding groove to the regions that have been identified as possible interaction sites due to their low desolvation energy to allow peptide selectivity to be achieved in the optimization step [14].

2.4   Estimation of Peptide Binding Energy

The MOE Protonate 3D function was used to assign ionization states and position hydrogen atoms in the macromolecular structure. Subsequently the MM function of MOE was employed to perform potential energy minimization by use of the AMBER99 force field. Finally, the Potential function was used to evaluate the resulting potential energy of the complex.

2.5   Molecular Search Space and Landscape Analysis

In combinatorial search correlated landscapes neighborhoods are typically induced by a set of small mutations. However, not all neighborhoods can be explored with an EA that uses consecutive mutations to find better fitness value. An important requirement for EA to work is the correlation between parent solutions and offspring solutions in fitness space, called the 'causality requirement'. Using landscape analysis it is possible to get indications on the causality of the search space and the difficulty for optimization [35]. This requirement was assessed empirically in a preliminary study.

In our case the set of configurations or solutions is the set of all sequences of a 22-mer peptide sequence that can be built from 23 possible amino acids, and neighbors are given by solutions that differ in only one amino acid. The correlation and other properties such as ruggedness of the molecular landscape was assessed with the MOE forcefield fitness function in combination with random walks on this surface, based on previous work [29,35]. This study indicated a positive correlation of the fitness function and the proximity of solutions in search space, measured as Hamming distance. A positive correlation was observed up to thirty random steps, which indicated a causal relation between parents and offspring fitness for the given mutation type. Hence it could be seen as promising to perform evolutionary optimization in this search space.

2.6   Multiobjective Optimization

The SMS-EMOA algorithm was used as a multi-objective evolutionary optimization algorithm [28,33]. The instantiation of this algorithm consisted of ten parents and one offspring ((10+1)-SMS-EMOA). A population of ten peptides was maintained throughout the run. In each of the iterations a new sequence was generated by mutating the least recently changed peptide from this population. The new peptide was generated by randomly replacing a residue of the peptide at a random position with a random new amino acid. The potential energy of the complex of the ligand with the $\gamma 1$ isoform was considered as a first objective function, and the inverse of the potential energy of the complex of the ligand with the $\varepsilon 1$ isoform was considered as the second objective function. The inverse was taken since binding against this isoform was not desired and the standard implementation of SMS-EMOA aims at minimization of objectives.

The acronym SMS-EMOA stands for **S**-Metric **S**election **E**volutionary **M**ultiobjective **O**ptimization **A**lgorithm. As indicated in the name, its selection is based on the S-Metric, a metric for measuring the quality of a Pareto front approximation which does not require a-priori knowledge of the true Pareto front. The S-Metric is nowadays more commonly referred to as the hypervolume indicator. It measures the size (area in two dimensions, hypervolume in higher dimensions) of subspace that is dominated by a Pareto front approximation and cut from above by a reference point. A high value of the hypervolume indicator corresponds to a good approximation to the Pareto front. The hypervolume contributions are also positively correlated with the distance between neighbors. Hence its maximization promotes diversity of solutions on the

Pareto front. In its selection, either a dominated solution or otherwise one with lowest hypervolume contribution is removed from the population [33]. While the SMS-EMOA specifies the algorithmic details for the selection step, it is generic in terms of search space representation and variation operators. SMS-EMOA is well suited for Pareto front approximation in large search spaces and small population sizes, where the goal is to find well spread Pareto front approximations with relatively few evaluations, such as in the present problem. The reason for this is that SMS-EMOA concentrates the distribution in the so-called 'knee-point' regions of the Pareto front, where good compromise solutions are found, while representing regions with an unbalanced trade-off with a decreased density of points.

The structural energy minimization and evaluation of potential energy of the isoform complexes with the mutated template took on average 4 minutes per complex (8 minutes per iteration for both isoforms). The computational overhead of the internal operations performed in SMS-EMOA is negligible in case of two and three objective functions. More precisely, all hypervolume computations for a single iteration require only subquadratic time. Hence the computational effort is essentially determined by the number of objective function evaluations.

3   Results

The SMS-EMOA implementation in the Molecular Operating Environment (MOE) (available from the authors on request) evaluated 1,089 random mutations (and evaluations of the objective function) after one week of processing time on four Xeon 2.5 GHz processors machine with Scientific Linux. 1,089 mutations correspond to $1,089 / 23^{\wedge}22 \times 100 \approx 1.19954208 \times 10^{\wedge}\text{-}25$ per cent of all possible solutions; however even with this small number of evaluations the Pareto front (X/Y axes: potential energy of interaction with $\gamma 1/ \varepsilon 1$) took its characteristic J-shape (a line bending towards the optimizing direction) after about 100 iterations (Figure 1A).

To evaluate the behavior of the algorithm properly it is important to present the development of peptide fitness as a function of time. Figure 1A hence visualizes the Pareto front obtained after 100 iterations of the algorithm. For the 10 peptides that formed part of the Pareto front the number of substitutions of the initial alanine amino acids varied from one to seven while the energy of the complex varied from the original -142 to -196 kcal/mol for the $\gamma 1$ isoform. The solution of the first Pareto front already shows considerable improvement over the starting point clearly a big advancement since already after eight replacements of alanine amino acids a difference in binding between the isoforms of 49 kcal/mol was obtained (detailed numbers regarding the evolution of the Pareto front are given in the supplementary material).

Figure 1B contains the corresponding Pareto front after 700 evaluations. At this point most of the alanine residues from the initial template were replaced. The potential energy difference of the complex with the 14-3-3 $\gamma 1$ isoform, compared to the $\varepsilon 1$ isoform, varied from 7 kcal/mol to 291 kcal/mol in this case while he best potential energy upon binding the $\gamma 1$ isoform has reached -282 kcal/mol.

Finally, at the end of our SMS-EMOA run, Figure 1C displays the potential energy along the Pareto front after a total of 1,189 iterations. We observe a set of 9 Pareto-optimal solution and 1 dominated solution with energy of the complex ranging from -138 to -335 kcal/mol for $\gamma1$ and 125 to -284 kcal/mol for $\varepsilon1$. Hence, the algorithm was successful in navigating a very high-dimensional (22-dimensional) search space to arrive to peptides of interest for both optimization criteria.

Figure 2 and Table 2 show the energy differences for $\varepsilon1$ and $\gamma1$ isoform binding for the final Pareto front. Throughout all solutions, at least an energy difference of about 40 kcal/mol is maintained, which grows to 291 kcal/mol in case of the most selective peptide listed at position 9. The solution at position 7 might be the one most relevant in practice, since it exhibits only minimal binding to the $\varepsilon1$ isoform (free energy of 23 kcal/mol), while binding relatively tightly to the $\gamma1$ isoform (free energy of 247 kcal/mol).

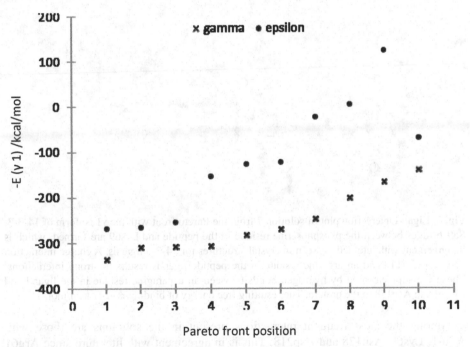

Fig. 2. Potential energy of peptide binding to the $\varepsilon1$ and $\gamma1$ isoforms of the 14-3-3 protein after 1,189 iterations of the SMS-EMOA algorithm. The x axis corresponds to the ligand position on the final Pareto front approximation from the leftmost to the rightmost solution in Figure 1C while the y axis represents the potential energy of the complex. It can be seen that multiple trade-offs between affinity and selectivity can be chosen, with solution 7 representing probably a solution of relevance in practice; high selectivity while at the same time high affinity to the $\gamma1$ isoform is maintained.

Table 2. Sequence and potential energy of the final solutions obtained after 1,189 iterations of the SMS-EMOA algorithm, optimizing the difference in the potential energy between the ε1 and γ1 isoforms. The ligand position corresponds to the order from the leftmost to the rightmost solution in Figure 1C on the final Pareto front, with all binding energies also visualized in Figure 2.

Aminoacid Sequence																						ligand #	gamma1	epsilon1	difference
PHE	ILE	TPO	ARG	SEP	GLY	TYR	SER	TPO	TRP	TRP	ASP	ASN	ARG	ARG	TYR	ARG	TYR	SEP	ASN	ASN	ALA ALA	1	-335	-269	67
PHE	ILE	TPO	ARG	SEP	GLY	GLY	SER	TPO	ALA	ASP	ASN	ARG	ARG	TYR	LEU	TYR	MET	ASN	ASN	ALA	ALA	2	-309	-266	43
PHE	ILE	TPO	ARG	SEP	GLY	TYR	SER	TPO	ALA	ASP	ASN	ARG	ARG	TYR	ARG	TYR	VAL	ASN	ASN	ALA	ILE	3	-308	-254	54
PHE	ILE	TPO	ARG	SEP	GLY	TYR	SER	TPO	ALA	ASP	ASN	ARG	ARG	TYR	LEU	TYR	MET	ASN	ASN	ALA	ALA	4	-306	-154	152
LEU	TRP	TPO	ARG	SEP	GLY	TRP	ASN	TPO	ALA	ASP	ASN	PRO	ARG	GLU	ARG	TYR	MET	ASN	ASN	ALA	ALA	5	-283	-126	157
LEU	PHE	TPO	ARG	SEP	GLY	TRP	ASN	TPO	ALA	ASP	ASN	PRO	ARG	GLU	ARG	TYR	MET	ASN	ASN	ALA	ALA	6	-269	-123	147
LEU	PHE	TPO	CYS	SEP	GLY	TYR	ASN	TPO	ALA	SER	ASN	LEU	GLN	GLU	ARG	ALA	MET	ASN	ASN	ALA	ALA	7	-247	-23	224
ALA	VAL	ALA	CYS	SEP	GLY	TRP	ASN	TPO	ALA	SER	ASN	ALA	ALA	GLU	ALA	ALA	MET	TPO	ASN	ALA	ALA	8	-202	5	207
LYS	TRP	ALA	ALA	ALA	TRP	ALA	ALA	ALA	ALA	ALA	PRO	ALA	ALA	LEU	ALA	ALA	ALA	ALA	ALA	ALA	ALA	9	-166	125	291
LYS	TRP	ALA	ALA	ALA	TRP	ALA	ALA	ALA	ALA	ALA	PRO	ALA	ALA	LEU	PHE	ALA	ALA	ALA	ALA	ALA	ALA	10	-139	-69	69

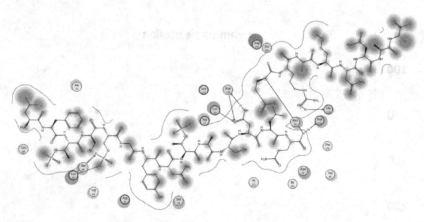

Fig. 3. Ligand interaction plot of solution 7 from the Pareto front with the γ1 isoform of 14-3-3. Salt bridges between the phosphoserine residue in the peptide and Lys69 are formed, which is in agreement with interactions seen in crystal structures for 14-3-3 ligands. A charge interaction between Glu118 and an arginine residue in the peptide ligands results in strong interactions. These are supplemented by hydrogen bonds between an asparagine residue in the ligand and Lys50 and Asn178 in the protein. The resulting free energy of binding is -247 kcal/mol.

Among the most frequent interactions present in the solutions are those with Arg61, Lys69, Asn178 and Asp218. This is in agreement with literature since Arg61 and Lys69 are located above the commonly accepted binding pocket, and Asp218 is located below the binding pocket at the sites predicted by other studies of human 14-3-3 [14]. Asn178 on the other hand is located very close to the binding pocket and may also be involved in recognition of natural ligands as well.

In order to understand ligand selectivity better, the interactions for solution 7 from the final Pareto front shall be discussed here in more detail.

As can be seen, in the ligand complexed with the γ1 isoform of 14-3-3 (displayed in Figure 3) salt bridges between the a phosphoserine residue in the peptide and Lys69 are formed, which is in agreement with interactions seen in crystal structures for 14-3-3 ligands, as well as a charge interaction between Glu118 and an arginine residue in the peptide ligands, resulting in strong interactions. These are supplemented by hydrogen bonds between an asparagine residue in the ligand and Lys50 and Asn178 in the protein, resulting in a free energy of binding of -247 kcal/mol. On the other hand, binding interactions with the ε1 isoform (Figure 4) are much weaker, leading only to a free energy of binding of -23 kcal/mol. While the salt bridge of Lys69 to the phosposerine is retained, Glu118 is not able to form an electrostatic interaction with the arginine residue of the ligand anymore. Additional hydrogen bonds such as the one to Asp216 are formed; however they are on average weaker than those in the γ1 complex, resulting in a decrease in binding affinity.

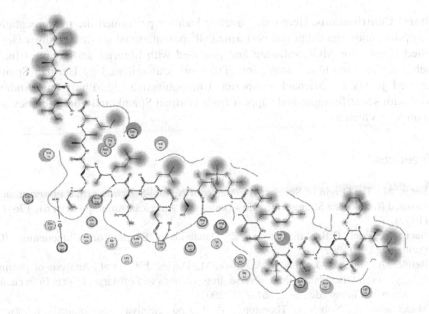

Fig. 4. Ligand interaction plot of solution 7 from the final Pareto front with the ε1 isoform of 14-3-3. As compared to the γ1 isoform (Figure 3) interactions are much weaker, leading only to a free energy of binding of -23 kcal/mol. While the salt bridge of Lys69 to the phosposerine is retained, Glu118 is not able to form an electrostatic interaction with the arginine residue of the ligand anymore. Additional hydrogen bonds such as the one to Asp216 are formed, but they are on average weaker than those in the γ1 complex, resulting in a decrease in binding affinity.

Hence, by analyzing binding interactions we can also rationalize peptide ligand selectivity, leading to an increase of the trustworthiness of the optimization algorithm applied in this work to design isoform-selective ligands for the 14-3-3 protein.

4 Conclusions

By employing evolutionary multiobjective optimization in the form of an SMS-EMOA algorithm we were able to design, de novo, peptide ligands of the γ1 isoform of the 14-3-3 protein with predicted selectivity over the ε1 isoform. Given the 22-dimensional nature of the search space, this is a practical application of this type of algorithm which will be experimentally validated in the near future.

Acknowledgements. We would like to thank Gerard van Westen (LACDR) for computational support. Andreas Bender thanks Dutch Top Institute Pharma (TI Pharma) for funding. Michael Emmerich thanks LIACS, Leiden University and the Foundation for Science and Technology (FCT), Portugal. Grant: Set-Indicator Based Multiobjective Optimization (SIMO), SFRH/BPD/65330/2009 for financial support. Hernando Sanchez Faddiev thanks Pieter de Knijf and Rudi Westendorp for their support.

Authors' Contributions. Hernando Sanchez Faddiev performed the implementation of the optimization algorithm and performed all computational studies. Andrew Henry supplied support for MOE software and provided with libraries and routines indispensable for the algorithm completion. The work was initiated by Herman Spaink, supervised jointly by Michael Emmerich (multiobjective algorithm) and Andreas Bender with scientific input and support from Herman Spaink and Fons Verbeek and Herman Van Vlijmen.

References

1. Bates, M.: The Origin of Species - by Means of Natural-Selection or the Preservation of Favored Races in the Struggle for Life - Darwin, C. American Anthropologist 61, 176–177 (1959)
2. Back, T., Fogel, D.B., Michalewicz, Z.: Handbook of Evolutionary Computation. IOP Publishing Ltd. (1997)
3. Bender, A., Scheiber, J., Bender, A., Glick, M., Davies, J.W., et al.: Analysis of pharmacology data and the prediction of adverse drug reactions and off-target effects from chemical structure. Chemmedchem 2, 861–873 (2007)
4. Macchiarulo, A., Nobeli, I., Thornton, J.M.: Ligand selectivity and competition between enzymes in silico. Nature Biotechnology 22, 1039–1045 (2004)
5. Kalyanmoy, D.: Multi-Objective Optimization using Evolutionary Algorithms (2001)
6. van der Horst, E., Peironcely, J.E., IJzerman, A.P., Beukers, M.W., Lane, J.R., et al.: A novel chemogenomics analysis of G protein-coupled receptors (GPCRs) and their ligands: a potential strategy for receptor de-orphanization. Bmc Bioinformatics 11 (2010)
7. Bender, A., Spring, D.R., Galloway, W.R.J.D., Overington, J.P., van Westen, G.J.P., et al.: Chemogenomics Approaches for Receptor Deorphanization and Extensions of the Chemogenomics Concept to Phenotypic Space. Current Topics in Medicinal Chemistry (2010)
8. van Westen, G.J.P., Wegner, J.K., IJzerman, A.P., van Vlijmen, H.W.T., Bender, A.: Proteochemometric Modeling as a Tool for Designing Selective Compounds and Extrapolating to Novel Targets (2010)
9. Fu, H.A., Subramanian, R.R., Masters, S.C.: 14-3-3 proteins: Structure, function, and regulation. Annual Review of Pharmacology and Toxicology 40, 617–647 (2000)
10. Wilker, E., Yaffe, M.B.: 14-3-3 Proteins - a focus on cancer and human disease. Journal of Molecular and Cellular Cardiology 37, 633–642 (2004)

11. Dong, S., Kang, S., Lonial, S., Khoury, H.J., Viallet, J., et al.: Targeting 14-3-3 sensitizes native and mutant BCR-ABL to inhibition with U0126, rapamycin and Bcl-2 inhibitor GX15-070. Leukemia 22, 572–577 (2008)

12. Jayaratnam, S., Khoo, A.K., Basic, D.: Rapidly progressive Alzheimer's disease and elevated 14-3-3 proteins in cerebrospinal fluid. Age Ageing 37, 467–469 (2008)

13. Besser, J., Bagowski, C.P., Salas-Vidal, E., van Hemert, M.J., Bussmann, J., et al.: Expression analysis of the family of 14-3-3 proteins in zebrafish development. Gene. Expr. Patterns 7, 511–520 (2007)

14. Yang, X., Lee, W.H., Sobott, F., Papagrigoriou, E., Robinson, C.V., et al.: Structural basis for protein-protein interactions in the 14-3-3 protein family. Proc. Natl. Acad. Sci. U S A 103, 17237–17242 (2006)

15. Audie, J., Boyd, C.: The Synergistic Use of Computation, Chemistry and Biology to Discover Novel Peptide-Based Drugs: The Time is Right. Current Pharmaceutical Design 16, 567–582 (2010)

16. Belda, I., Madurga, S., Llora, X., Martinell, M., Tarrago, T., et al.: ENPDA: an evolutionary structure-based de novo peptide design algorithm. Journal of Computer-Aided Molecular Design 19, 585–601 (2005)

17. Abe, K., Kobayashi, N., Sode, K., Ikebukuro, K.: Peptide ligand screening of alpha-synuclein aggregation modulators by in silico panning. Bmc Bioinformatics 8 (2007)

18. Zahed, M., Suzuki, T., Suganami, A., Sugiyama, H., Harada, K., et al.: Screening of SMG7-Binding Peptides by Combination of Phage Display and Docking Simulation Analysis. Protein and Peptide Letters 16, 301–305 (2009)

19. Gillet, V.J.: Applications of evolutionary computation in drug design. Applications of Evolutionary Computation in Chemistry 110, 133–152 (2004)

20. Nicolaou, C.A., Apostolakis, J., Pattichis, C.S.: De Novo Drug Design Using Multiobjective Evolutionary Graphs. Journal of Chemical Information and Modeling 49, 295–307 (2009)

21. Keijzer, M.: Genetic and evolutionary computation conference: GECCO 2006, vol. 2. Association for Computing Machinery, New York (2006)

22. Malard, J.M., Heredia-Langner, A., Cannon, W.R., Mooney, R., Baxter, D.J.: Peptide identification via constrained multi-objective optimization: Pareto-based genetic algorithms. Concurrency and Computation-Practice & Experience 17, 1687–1704 (2005)

23. Yagi, Y., Terada, K., Noma, T., Ikebukuro, K., Sode, K.: In: silico panning for a noncompetitive peptide inhibitor. Bmc Bioinformatics 8 (2007)

24. Fjell, C.D., Jenssen, H., Cheung, W.A., Hancock, R.E., Cherkasov, A.: Optimization of Antibacterial Peptides by Genetic Algorithms and Cheminformatics. Chem. Biol. Drug. Des. (2010)

25. Li, C., Pazgier, M., Li, C.Q., Yuan, W.R., Liu, M., et al.: Systematic Mutational Analysis of Peptide Inhibition of the p53-MDM2/MDMX Interactions. Journal of Molecular Biology 398, 200 213 (2010)

26. Satoh, J., Yamamura, T., Arima, K.: The 14-3-3 protein epsilon isoform expressed in reactive astrocytes in demyelinating lesions of multiple sclerosis binds to vimentin and glial fibrillary acidic protein in cultured human astrocytes. American Journal of Pathology 165, 577–592 (2004)

27. Roberts, M.R., de Bruxelles, G.L.: Plant 14-3-3 protein families: evidence for isoform-specific functions? Biochemical Society Transactions 30, 373–378 (2002)

28. Beume, N., Naujoks, B., Emmerich, M.: SMS-EMOA: Multiobjective selection based on dominated hypervolume. European Journal of Operational Research 181, 1653–1669 (2007)

29. Emmerich, M., Li, B.V.Y., Bender, A., Sanchez-Faddiev, H., Kruisselbrink, J., et al.: Analyzing molecular landscapes using random walks and information theory. Chemestry Central (2009)

30. Kruisselbrink, J.W., Aleman, A., Emmerich, T.M., IJzerman, A., Bender, A., et al.: Enhancing search space diversity in multi-objective evolutionary drug molecule design using niching. In: Proceedings of the 11th Annual Conference on Genetic and Evolutionary Computation, pp. 217–224. ACM, Montreal (2009)

31. Handl, J., Kell, D.B., Knowles, J.: Multiobjective optimization in bioinformatics and computational biology. IEEE-ACM Transactions on Computational Biology and Bioinformatics 4, 279–292 (2007)

32. Paul, A.L., Sehnke, P.C., Ferl, R.J.: Isoform-specific subcellular localization among 14-3-3 proteins in Arabidopsis seems to be driven by client interactions. Molecular Biology of the Cell 16, 1735–1743 (2005)

33. Emmerich, M., Beume, N., Naujoks, B.: An EMO Algorithm Using the Hypervolume Measure as Selection Criterion. In: Coello Coello, C.A., Hernández Aguirre, A., Zitzler, E. (eds.) EMO 2005. LNCS, vol. 3410, pp. 62–76. Springer, Heidelberg (2005)

34. Vilar, S., Cozza, G., Moro, S.: Medicinal Chemistry and the Molecular Operating Environment (MOE): Application of QSAR and Molecular Docking to Drug Discovery. Current Topics in Medicinal Chemistry 8, 1555–1572 (2008)

35. Vassilev, V.K., Fogarty, T.C., Miller, J.F.: Information Characteristics and the Structure of Landscapes. Evolutionary Computation (2000)

Segmentation for High-Throughput Image Analysis: Watershed Masked Clustering

Kuan Yan and Fons J. Verbeek

Section Imaging and Bioinformatics
Leiden Institute of Advanced Computer Science, Leiden University
Niels Bohrweg 1, 2333 CA Leiden, The Netherlands
{kyan,fverbeek}@liacs.nl

Abstract. High-throughput microscopy imaging applications represent an important research field that is focused on testing and comparing lots of different conditions in living systems. It runs over a limited time-frame and per time step images are generated as output; within the time-range a resilient variation in the images of the experiment is characteristic. Studies represent dynamic circumstances expressed in shape variation of the objects under study. For object extraction, i.e. the segmentation of cells, aforementioned conditions have to be taken into account. Segmentation is used to extract objects from images and from objects features are measured. For high-throughput applications generic segmentation algorithms tend to be suboptimal. Therefore, an algorithm is required that can adapt to a range of variations; i.e. self-adaptation of the segmentation parameters without prior knowledge. In order to prevent measurement bias, the algorithm should be able to assess all inconclusive configurations, e.g. cell clusters. The segmentation method must be accurate and robust so that results that can be trustfully used in further analysis and interpretation. For this study a number of algorithms were evaluated and from the results a new algorithm was developed; the watershed masked clustering algorithm. It consists of three steps: (1) a watershed algorithm is used to establish the coarse location of objects, (2) the threshold is optimized by applying a clustering in each watershed region and (3) each mask is reevaluated on consistency and re-optimized so as to result in consistent segmented objects. The evaluation of our algorithm is realized by testing with images containing artificial objects and real-life microscopy images. The result shows that our algorithm is significantly more accurate, more robust and very reproducible.

Keywords: High-Throughput Imaging, Segmentation, Watershed, Fuzzy C-means clustering, Fluorescence Microscopy, Systems Biology.

1 Introduction

Image segmentation is an image analysis method that separates pixels into characteristic groups. For high-throughput image analysis, image segmentation is quintessential in obtaining precise per-object information that need be analyzed. Generic segmentation methods cannot always obtain optimal results. Often we have to tune

T. Margaria and B. Steffen (Eds.): ISoLA 2012, Part II, LNCS 7610, pp. 25–41, 2012.
© Springer-Verlag Berlin Heidelberg 2012

the generic segmentation method with heuristics to get the result with which further processing will be possible. The methodology described in this paper is used in a biomedical setting; i.e., in a workflow which measurements are extracted from images to support the understanding of indigenous phenomena in the images. Segmentation is but one step in this workflow towards the understanding of the image content by means of pattern recognition. Notably, such understanding can only be retrieved in the context of the application; often in the process of image segmentation, heuristics from the domain at hand are included. Thus, assuring that the understanding is based on correctly measured features makes the segmentation step crucial.

In this paper, we focus on segmentation in the high-throughput (HT) imaging as applied to the study of cell systems. High-throughput applications are often related with high-content applications, here we restrict to high-throughput as for the understanding of the development of our algorithm it suffices. This study is motivated by the consideration that in the field HT-imaging the current segmentation algorithms perform inadequate. In order to explain the development of a new algorithm we briefly introduce the application field. Subsequently, we introduce typical pitfalls of HT-imaging and thereby formulate requirements that are important to the development of our algorithm. Underlying this introduction is the workflow in HT-imaging that starts with image acquisition and through a pipeline of image processing ends with image understanding achieved through pattern recognition.

1.1   High-Throughput Cell Imaging

The application of HT-imaging is of increasing importance in the study of cell systems. In the past decades, there has been a considerable progress in imaging techniques and molecular engineering. Consequently, this progress has been addressed to make the study of cell systems feasible. Starting point for the imaging is the compound microscope that is adapted to study cell systems *in vitro*. That is, as cell cultures in small containers specifically suitable for microscopy imaging. These systems are studied under a range of different conditions including duplicates and controls in the same experiment. This requires a specific setup which is commonly referred to as a high-throughput screening (HTS) [6, 20, 31]. The aim of a screen is to capture and quantify the unique cellular and/or molecular phenotype of a particular cell line under different conditions. The cells are cultured in a 96-well culture plate [20, 31] in which each well represents an experimental condition; some wells are used for duplicates and control groups.

In order to accomplish a quantification of the phenotype by accurate descriptors, a robust image analysis pipeline must be configured. This pipeline receives time-lapse image sequences as input. These time-lapse sequences are captured with a microscope/camera setup and comprehend a complete HTS experiment. The pipeline includes acquisition, preprocessing, segmentation, object labeling, tracking, measurement and classification [4, 5, 28]. From the results of machine learning, conclusions can be formulated that are meaningful and comprehensive in the context of biology. The critical step in the processing pipeline, however, is the extraction of individual objects, i.e. cells, as precise as possible. This requires a robust segmentation algorithm that produces accurate and reproducible results over the large amounts of images from the HTS. A typical screen requires large volumes of data to be processed; e.g. an experiment for drug-target discovery produces more than ten 96-well plates. Assuming acquisition of three time-lapse image sequences per well, with a length of 150 frames (5 min/frame over 12 hrs), will then result in over 400K images per experiment. Each image contains 50-200 objects (cells), which, normally, cover approximately 10% of the cell population in a well. So, in the application domain of HTS, we have to take into account the conditions under which images of the objects are acquired. There are limitations that need be accounted for in terms of heuristics in the algorithm that is devised for such applications.

Typically, fluorescence microscopy [26, 29] is the microscope modality in HTS imaging and it requires the application of fluorophores to the object under study, a.k.a. fluorescent staining or 'labeling'. Fluorescent staining is based on a class of dyes that have the capacity to emit light under excitation [26]. The major advantage of fluorescence microscopy, over phase contrast or bright field microscopy is that different stains can be simultaneously applied to functional components or protein complexes within the cell, which may reveal underlying phenotypic correlations between cell migration and protein complex localization. Each specific staining can be visualized in a separate channel of the microscope through the use of bandpass filters. The image capture is achieved with a CCD camera mounted on the microscope [4, 5, 28]. The CCD characteristic of a linear response to the amount of light, even at low doses [29], is important in fluorescence microscopy. The amount of fluorophore, through specific binding per object, however, is subject to per-object variation and experimental bias (cf. Fig. 1).

In the 96-well plate, the substrate of each well to which the cells are adhered, is slightly concave toward the center of the well. This complicates the imaging, and contributes in uneven density distribution in the cells. The lens cannot correct for this, it is a trade-off between higher numerical aperture, i.e. resolution [29], and focal depth. As accuracy in the description of the shape is required, a sufficient numerical aperture needs to be chosen for the imaging thus compromising in focal depth. We have to acknowledge these conditions to contribute to the quality of imaging and henceforth might affect the quality of the segmentation result.

1.2   Evaluation of Segmentation Algorithms in HT-Imaging

As indicated, HTS experiments cover dynamic events and therefore images are acquired in time-lapse. This result in large amounts of images, a typical experiment can account for 100K to 500K images per screen; consequently, computational load has to be considered. Moreover, as conditions may differ, the parameters for segmentation cannot be applied over a global set but have to be determined in local environments. In addition, over all images the algorithm needs to cope with situations that may result in erroneous outcome of the features. The crux of the segmentation algorithm is therefore to prevent errors in the measurements that would otherwise introduce misclassification and misinterpretation. The objective is to find all objects and extract morphological features/descriptors from these objects. A major complication is that the signal, i.e. the fluorescent labeling, is not evenly strong in all objects (cf. Fig. 1b). This is an experimental flaw that needs to be taken into account.

Given the consideration on the segmentation algorithms, a possible candidate is the fuzzy C-means segmentation algorithm, which is derived from the fuzzy C-means clustering algorithm [3]. Similar to Otsu [23], it provides an intensity threshold that is used to separate background and foreground pixels. The disadvantages are similar to those found in the Otsu algorithm. Therefore, we aim at a local approach of a clustering application and we need to consider methods to regionalize the image. Finding such regions can be dealt with through a seeded watershed approach [2, 14]. Via the combination of fuzzy C-means algorithm and watershed algorithm, we derive an innovative form of segmentation, namely watershed masked clustering (WMC).

The WMC algorithm consists of three steps and at each step the segmentation result is further refined. It first finds several coarse regions; each region is considered a rough mask that requires further optimization. Next, a more precise mask is obtained from each coarse region. In the final step, the masks are assessed and, if necessary, corrected using multiple criteria. Following this principle, the WMC algorithm converts a multimodal optimization problem into a simpler collection of several optimization problems while each is guaranteed unimodal.

The WMC is designed to be a robust and dedicated solution to the particular application of the image segmentation in large high-throughput screens to study cell systems. Compared to currently used segmentation approaches, WMC is very sensitive to regional variation of intensity values in images (cf. Fig. 1b); specifically for images of cells with fluorescent labeling.

The remainder of this paper is organized as follows; in section 2, the structure of the WMC algorithm is explained in detail. Subsequently, the performance of the WMC algorithm is illustrated, at the same time the algorithm is compared to a number of other segmentation approaches, i.e. Otsu [23], Bernsen local adaptive thresholding [13], hysteresis edge-based thresholding [9] and level-set methods [30]. Finally, we present our conclusions and discuss our developments and results in broader context.

2   Watershed Masked Clustering Algorithm

In Figure 2, the outline of the algorithm is depicted. In the discussion of the algorithm, we will refer to this figure and its corresponding details for each of the subparts of the algorithm. For an algorithm to be suitable for high-throughput screening the following requirements must be satisfied:

1. Adaptive to local variations in intensity
2. Capable of processing large amount of images without parameter recalibration
3. Capable of finding a separation between objects
4. Computationally efficient

This can be translated to the three main features of the segmentation approach that we propose:

1. Divide the image in intensity regions
2. Find object(s) in each intensity region
3. Check integrity of each object

The intensity regions in the image are established using watershed segmentation. For our algorithm, this is a preprocessing step, as it will not sufficiently separate all objects. Next, in each of the regions a clustering is applied to find the objects with a highest possible precision. In the case, that the preprocessing has split objects that actually should be considered as one object, a correction will follow in the last step of the algorithm. In this step re-evaluation over the objects is applied to get the best possible output. For this re-evaluation, a special form of watershed object segmentation is designed. In Figure 2 the overall pseudo code is given. In the next sections, each of the steps of the algorithm is described in detail.

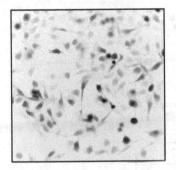
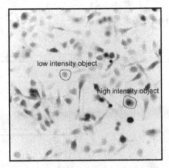

(a) Fluorescence microscope image of cancer cells with fluorescent label (GFP)

(b) Indication of typical variation in the intensity of the fluorescence in one image

Fig. 1. Image (512x512) from a HTS of cancer cells visualized with a fluorescence microscope (20x). In order to better render intensity differences the inverse LUT of image 1a is used in 1b.

2.1   Region Selection

The implementation of the maxima-seeded watershed masking is based on research by Pinidiyaarachchi [2]. In this flavor of the watershed algorithm, the growing of the watershed region is initialized from a pixel with the highest intensity compared to its neighboring pixels: this particular pixel is referred to as the local maximum. In order to define a valid local maximum, the intensity of such a pixel must exceed the surrounding pixel intensities by a threshold value h, where h is an estimated level of noise tolerance in terms of intensity (cf. Fig. 3); h is commonly referred to as the h-maximum [2]. A higher value of h provides a less sensitive watershed separation and *vice versa*. In practice, a higher value of h often leads to incomplete separation of the objects in the image and moreover, objects that occur in clusters are often not sufficiently separated (cf. Fig. 3b). We can derive the range for the value of h, since the h-maximum is considered a reference relative to the intensity value of the pixels. Let I_M be the maximum intensity in the dynamic range of the sensor, and I_{max} the maximum intensity in the region under study, the h-maximum is typically in $[1, (I_M-I_{max})]$. In

Figure 3, the results of the maxima-seeded watershed for different values of h are depicted. From empirical observations in HTS images (I_M=255), a value h=20 provides satisfactory watershed regions.

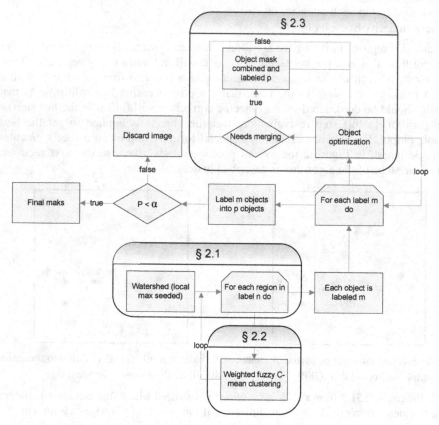

Fig. 2. A workflow diagram illustrates of the three main steps of the Watershed Masked Clustering Algorithm. As part of the automation process, at completion of the loop there is always a quality check Q to prevent wrongly processed images to be part of the analysis.

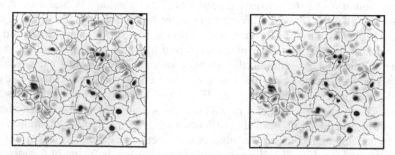

(a) Original image with watershed lines, h=20   (b) Original image with watershed lines, h=50

Fig. 3. It contains results from the watershed algorithm illustrating the effect of the value of h. The (a) and (b) illustrate the watershed cutting lines of Fig. 1b for h=10.

2.2   Object Segmentation

The application of the watershed method provides coarse regions. Given these coarse regions, starting point for the next step in our algorithm follows from the intrinsic features of the watershed method; it is guaranteed that:

1. In each watershed region, the intensity landscape is always unimodal [2, 14].
2. Seeded watershed implements a restriction on the possible starting point of path searching. An empty region usually does not contain valid seed, thus no watershed region will be formed in an empty region.

In order to find the object in each region, an approach is required that is capable of establishing a local adaptive threshold while being computational finite. Such can be accomplished by a weighted fuzzy C-means clustering algorithm (WFCM). This clustering is applied sequentially in each of the regions to search an optimal value for thresholding in the region. Consequently, each region has its own threshold value taking into account local conditions, i.e. the local variation in image intensity.

In addition, the WFCM method has a set of weighting factors ω that allows the introduction of prior probability of the pixel membership in clusters. The definition of such a weighting factor is similar to the reversed version of the prior probability in Bayesian theory. A smaller weighting factor is assigned to the cluster having, potentially, a larger standard deviation and vice versa. The sum of all weighting factors is always one. The weighting factor ω can be directly derived from the data [15, 21] however, with a known type of image data, commonly, a preset value is used. The WFCM method is formalized as:

$$u_{ij} = \left(\sum_{c}^{k=1} \left(\frac{\omega_j \cdot \|x_i - c_j\|}{\omega_k \cdot \|x_i - c_k\|} \right)^{\frac{2}{m-1}} \right)^{-1}, \tag{1}$$

where u_{ij} denotes the membership matrix, c_j is the jth cluster, x_i is the data vector i and ω_j is the weighting factor for cluster j. Empirically, it has been established that for cell imaging a value of $\omega = 0.2$ for the foreground and a value of $\omega = 0.8$ for the background is sufficient. This should be interpreted as: (1) there is an 80% chance a certain pixel is belongs to the foreground and (2) there is a 20% chance that a certain pixel is belongs to the background. By increasing the weighting factor for the foreground, less intense structures, such as cell protrusions or objects with a low overall intensity, will be discarded. In this manner, the weighting factor works similarly to the parameter for the degree of sensitivity in the fuzzy c-means clustering algorithm [21]. Along with eq.1, the clusters are formalized as:

$$c_j = \frac{\sum_{N}^{i=1}\left(u_{ij}^m \cdot x_i\right)}{\sum_{N}^{i=1}\left(u_{ij}^m\right)}, \tag{2}$$

where u_{ij} denotes is the membership matrix at step k and m is the, so called, fuzzy coefficient that expresses the complexity of the model, by default $m=2$. In our algorithm, we strive at a quick convergence of the WFCM and therefore the initial seeds for c are defined as follows:

$$c_{Foregroundseed} = \bar{I} + (2^{nb} - 1) \cdot \frac{I_{max} - \bar{I}}{\sigma(I)}, \tag{3}$$

$$c_{Backgroundseed} = \bar{I} - (2^{nb} - 1) \cdot \frac{\bar{I} - I_{min}}{\sigma(I)}, \tag{4}$$

where I_{min}, I_{max} denote the minimum/maximum intensity in the image I, $\bar{I}$ denotes the mean of the intensities in image I, $\sigma(I)$ denotes the standard deviation in the intensities of the image I and nb denotes the dynamic range of the intensity expressed in number of bits. In the standard case of unsigned 8-bit images $nb=8$.

This approach provides a robust solution to address the complexity in the HTS images regarding variation in foreground and background intensities. The application of this step results in a binary object in each of the regions of step 1 (cf. §.2.1), if correct, shape features can be derived. However, the watershed method might have introduced some irregularities in the establishment of the coarse regions, which requires an additional evaluation; this evaluation is elaborated in the next section. Examples of the application of this step of the WMC algorithm are worked out in the section 3.

2.3   Object Optimization

At onset of our algorithm, the watershed segmentation is applied resulting in regions that are individually processed. Depending on the variation in the data, the watershed algorithm is known to result in an overcut of the segmentation; overcut is referred to as the situation in which the watershed segmentation produces more regions than actually present in the image [12]. This overcut might affect the individual objects, because of which the objects need be split or merged (cf. Fig. 4). Therefore, the last step in our algorithm is to compensate for the possible overcut caused by the watershedding. This process is an object optimization as we evaluate the results obtained in the object segmentation. In this procedure, only the objects that share a border with a watershed line are evaluated, as these objects are the candidates for overcut.

The solution for the object optimization is a merging mechanism that uses multiple criteria; currently, two criteria are implemented, i.e.:

1. Evaluation of the strength of watershed line; the objects are merged based on a local difference in maximum and average intensity in the object.
2. Evaluation of the orientation of the objects; the object are merges based on assessment of the difference in orientation of their principal axes.

For criterion 1, we implemented an intensity-based merging algorithm so as to estimate the necessity of merging the objects through the evaluation of the strength of the watershed lines. In this function all watershed lines are evaluated. This criterion can be generalized with the evaluation function K:

$$K\,(l_i) \rightarrow min\left(\frac{\delta_1}{\tau_1}, \frac{\delta_2}{\tau_2}\right) > T_k, \tag{5}$$

where the l_i denotes the ith watershed line, δ_1 denotes the difference between the average intensity under the watershed line and maximum intensity of object on one side of the watershed and similarly, δ_2 represents the object on the other side of the watershed line; where τ_1 and τ_2 denote the difference between the maximum and minimum intensity value within one object on either side of the watershed line l_i. A valid watershed line should fulfill the condition given in eq. 5. If $K(l_i)$ exceeds a threshold T_k then the objects on either side of the line are merged to one and the watershed is neglected. In Figure 4a the intensity-based merging criterion is illustrated.

For criterion 2, we implemented an orientation-based merging algorithm [10, 11, 25], which provides a unique possibility to split/merge large structure complexes or elongated objects. At watershed line l_i we consider the principal axis of the objects on either side of the line. A two component Boolean function is designed so that, when true, i.e. both components are true, the objects will be merged and the watershed line will be neglected. This function P is written as:

$$P(l_i) \rightarrow \begin{cases} |\theta_1 - \theta_2| < T_p \\ |\theta_1 - \theta_m| + |\theta_2 - \theta_m| < T_p' \end{cases} \quad (6)$$

where θ_1 denotes the angle between the horizontal image axis (x-axis) and the principle axis of object 1, similarly θ_2 is defined for the object on the other side of watershed line l_i. The θ_m is the angle between the horizontal image axis and the line crossing the centers of mass of the two objects (cf. Fig. 4b). The components in $P(l_i)$ are separately evaluated; so, if the principle axis of each individual object spans a minimum angle T_p while the line crossing the centers of mass of the two objects lies within the angular wedge T_p of the two principle axes, only then these two objects will be merged. In Figure 4b, the orientation-based merging is illustrated by two cases.

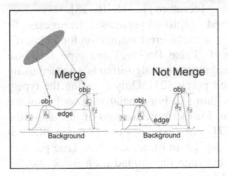

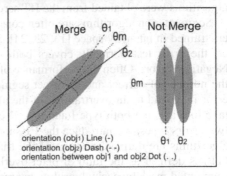

(a) Two typical cases of intensity based merging; (left) merge realized and (right) merge not realized using K(li) (eq. 5)

(b) Two typical examples of orientation based merging; (left) merge realized and (right) merge not realized using P(li) (eq. 6)

(c) Sample object   (d) Overcutting from step 1   (e) Merging from step 3

Fig. 4. Illustration of the merging of objects based on a combination of criteria; in (c,d,e) a specific case for one object (cell) is illustrated

Once the object optimization is applied, one can be certain that all objects are correctly extracted and these can be subject to a shape characterization. For the specific case of HTS time-lapse images, both shape and intensity profile of the object are measured. The intensity profile of an object is derived by applying the binary mask to the original image. A large range of features can be used [25] so that features can be used to discriminate between experimental conditions that are applied [18, 19, 31].

3   Performance of the WMC Algorithm

In this section the performance of our segmentation algorithm will be addressed. In order to get a good impression of its robustness, we employed two tests: i.e., a test with artificially generated images and a test with images from real HTS experiments. Each artificial image contains a number of generated ellipsoid objects. Each HTS image contains in vitro cells that are fluorescently labeled. The performance estimation for each algorithm is derived from the comparison between the binary mask obtained by the algorithm and the corresponding ground-truth binary mask for each image. In the generation of the test images, the ground-truth masks are for the artificial test images are explicitly constructed. The usage of such artificial image provides an image test set with an unbiased ground-truth and controllable noise, allowing the emulation of a worst scenario in fluorescence microscopy imaging.

The pixel-level mismatch of the comparisons is calculated for all algorithms. The rationale behind this test is to simulate the typical data processing workflow for HTS, therefore the parameters used for each of the algorithms are optimized only once and henceforth applied to the whole image set in the experiment. For none of the algorithms in the experiment an individual tuning is applied. The parameters for all algorithms were obtained from the HT screening literature [1, 4, 5, 16, 28].

Segmentation algorithms are often considered simplified versions of linear classifiers trained in intensity space [13, 23, 24]. Similar to the error estimation for a classifier, the error test normally covers both type I (False Positive) and type II (False Negative) errors. Often the performance of a segmentation algorithm is assessed using the number of correct and incorrect segmented pixels [21]. Only covering the type I error may lead to an overtraining of the algorithm [3]. For a balanced conclusion we take into account both type I and type II error. Furthermore, instead of just using the two errors types, we introduce the F1-score [7]. The two types of errors for different algorithms are defined in terms of the true positive and true negative. True positive (TP) is defined as the ratio of pixel overlap between the ground-truth mask and the segmented mask by each algorithm, expressed as:

$$TP = \frac{M \cap M'}{M'}, \tag{7}$$

where M' is the set of pixels belonging to the foreground of binary mask provided by the algorithm and M is the set of pixels belonging to the foreground of the ground-truth mask. In similar fashion, the true negative (TN) is calculated from:

$$TN = \frac{\bar{M} \cap \bar{M}'}{\bar{M}'}. \tag{8}$$

In this way, TP represents the percentage of correctly segmented foreground pixels whereas TN represents the percentage of correctly segmented background pixels. Form the values of TP and TN, the false positives (FP) are derived, i.e. FP = 1-TP (percentage of incorrectly segmented foreground pixels), and likewise the false negatives (FN) are derived, i.e. FN = 1-TN (incorrectly segmented background pixels). From these values, the sensitivity and specificity the [8] are calculated by:

$$sensitivity = \left(\frac{TP}{TP + FN}\right) \tag{9}$$

$$specificity = \left(\frac{TN}{FP + TN}\right) \tag{10}$$

Given the results, the specificity and the sensitivity for all of algorithms of a particular set of test images can be computed. The results are shown in Table 3. In addition, from the specificity and sensitivity, the F1-score is derived by:

$$F1 = 2 \cdot \frac{specificity \cdot sensitivity}{specificity + sensitivity}. \tag{11}$$

An ideal segmentation algorithm should yield the highest F1-score but this only occurs when both specificity and sensitivity are approaching 100%.

In the next sections, we tested for 5 algorithms, i.e. Bernsen local adaptive thresholding, Otsu thresholding, Level-set segmentation, Hysteresis edge-based segmentation, and our WMC algorithm. We have included Fuzzy C-means clustering (FCM) to the tests to illustrate the enhanced performance of our approach. All algorithms have claimed the intrinsic capacity of performing well under noisy conditions typical to HTS imaging [4, 5, 16, 25, 28]. For the algorithms, open-source plug-ins implementations available in ImageJ [32] and CellProfiler [1] have been used without modifications.

3.1 Artificial Objects and Test Images

The intended application for our segmentation algorithm is high-throughput cell imaging. In order to understand and verify the behavior and performance of our algorithm, ground-truth images with objects resembling the shapes which are normally found in time-lapse cell imaging, are constructed (cf. Fig. 5a). Each image consists of a number of ellipsoid objects and each object has a unique intensity profile. The intensity profile (landscape) is generated through an exponential decay function that is initiated at the centre of each object. The minimum and maximum value of an intensity profile of an object is generated using a uniform distributed random generator and scaled in the range of [20, 255] – in this way sampling to an 8-bit image is simulated. In addition, the orientation of each of the objects is varied by applying a rotation to each of the object in the range of [-30°, 30°] using the center of mass as the pivot; the rotation angle is selected from a uniform random generator. The original binary image with all the objects is kept as the absolute ground-truth mask for the segmentation so that error estimation can be applied over a range of test images that are subjected to a range of different conditions of noise. In this test, a total amount of 30 images is generated. To simulate image noise typical to HTS and fluorescence microscopy, Poisson noise is generated and applied to the images.

3.2 Performance Test with Artificial Images

All algorithms are applied over the same 30 test images (cf. Fig. 5). The F1-scores are listed in Table 1. The object merging accuracy in WMC is also tested using the same image set. An overcut object is defined as a group of objects obtained by segmentation algorithm share the same object in ground truth mask. A total amount of 238 overcut objects are detected in this image set. Using object optimization, the WMC recovers 202 out of 238 overcut objects, i.e. approximately 85%.

3.3   Microscope Images

In order to test the performance of the WMC in the images it is designed for, we have selected two sets of images from the application domain. The intention of the test is to illustrate the performance in a typical setting and compare the performance with respect to the same selection of segmentation algorithms used in the artificial test images; the test is completely similar to the test with the artificial test images. We will make use of two different image sets. The first image set is known as the "Human HT29 Colon Cancer" dataset [16] (cf. Fig. 6) containing 12 images of human HT29 colon cancer cells. The samples were stained for the nucleus (Hoechst) and the cytoplasm (phalloidin) in two separate channels. The second image set is a time-lapse image sequence, i.e. a dynamic process, which is an MLTn3 cell line [17, 19] used to study migration in live cancer metastasis processes (cf. Fig. 7). It consists of 96 time-lapse image sequences, each of 75 frames. Each sequence portrays an *in vitro* cell migration pattern typical in HTS experiments. The cytoplasm is stained through green fluorescent protein (GFP). For the performance tests, we will only use the first 14 images of the sequence to reduce the size of the image set to reasonable for proportions for this test. In addition, for this image set also a ground-truth image is required. The MTLn3 ground-truth images were obtained by manual segmentation performed by biologists through tracing on a digitizer tablet (WACOM Cintiq). In contrast to the artificial image set, manual segmentation may contain observation bias between and within observers. To that end the manual segmentation is replicated a few times to reduce observer effects.

We will further refer to the first image set as the HT29 set and the second set as the MTLn3 set. The HT29 set is captured at significant higher resolution compared to the MTLn3 set. These two sets are considered a reasonable representation of the scope of the images which are typical input for the WMC algorithm.

3.4   Performance Test with Microscope Images

For the two sets the results are presented in two tables and examples of the segmentation are given in two figures. In Table 2 and 3, the results of the experiment for this set are presented. The sensitivity and specificity are used as the performance indicators. From the result we can conclude that WMC has the best overall performance. It produces stable and robust results for the HT29 set (cf. Table 2). Compared to WMC, the standard FCM algorithm is similar in sensitivity but lower in specificity; the Otsu segmentation is higher in specificity but significantly lower in sensitivity; the Hysteresis segmentation has a similar performance as the WMC. At this point, it is important to realize that the quality of the HT29 set (cf. Fig. 6) is not, in all case, representative for the real high-throughput screens, especially if we consider the dynamic behavior common to live-cell imaging (cf. Fig. 7).

Table 1. Specificity and sensitivity of segmentation efficiency using artificial images

Performance	WMC	FCM	Bernsen	Otsu	Level-set	Hysteresis
Specificity	95.40%	98.11%	78.42%	86.02%	98.38%	79.78%
Sensitivity	96.62%	91.73%	90.14%	98.22%	71.52%	85.16%
F1 Score	95.99%	94.50%	84.60%	91.83%	74.98%	82.95%

Table 2. Specificity and sensitivity of the segmentation algorithms in the HT29 image set

Performance	WMC	FCM	Bernsen	Otsu	Level-set	Hysteresis
Specificity	98.59%	97.81%	99.84%	98.75%	70.68%	97.57%
Sensitivity	98.78%	98.64%	83.10%	89.67%	53.43%	97.88%
F1 Score	98.68%	98.23%	92.11%	93.40%	31.29%	97.73%

Table 3. Specificity and sensitivity of segmentation algorithms in MTLn3 image set

Performance	WMC	FCM	Bernsen	Otsu	Level-set	Hysteresis
Specificity	84.80%	95.76%	99.63%	90.60%	59.10%	82.82%
Sensitivity	91.45%	74.16%	59.25%	80.64%	56.35%	88.13%
F1 Score	88.05%	78.27%	47.63%	83.79%	53.33%	85.81%

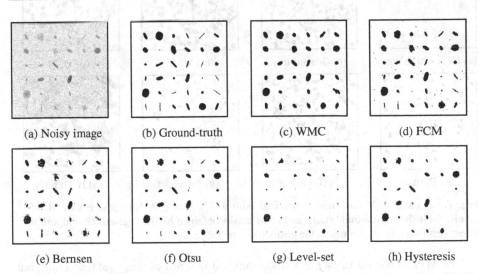

(a) Noisy image   (b) Ground-truth   (c) WMC   (d) FCM

(e) Bernsen   (f) Otsu   (g) Level-set   (h) Hysteresis

Fig. 5. (a) noise-added artificial test image, (b) ground-truth masks for the object, (c) to (h) are binary images obtained by corresponding segmentation algorithms. These results are used to compute the errors listed in Table 1.

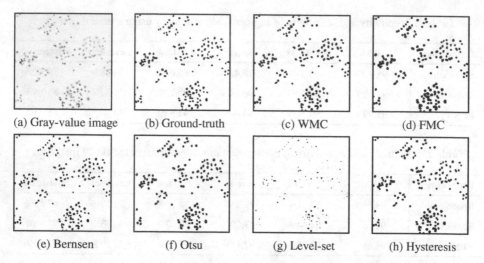

Fig. 6. (a) Original HT29 image acquired with a 10x lens; image size is 512x512 pixels, 8 bit. (b) Ground-truth masks and (c-h) masks obtained by the segmentation algorithms. These results are used to compute the errors listed in Table 2.

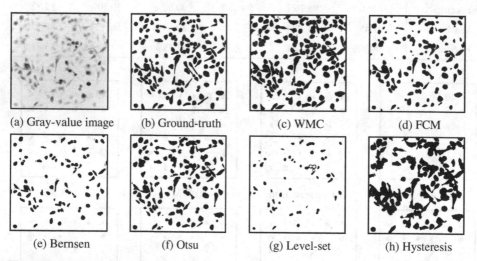

Fig. 7. (a) Original MTLn3 image acquired with a 20x lens (NA 1.4), image size 512x512 pixels, 8-bit (b) ground-truth masks and (c-h) masks obtained by the segmentation algorithms. These results are used to compute the errors listed in Table 3.

The MTLn3 test set is, *de facto*, undersampled in terms of temporal resolution, but a good representation of a HTS with *in vitro* cell migration (cf. Fig. 7a). When finding ground-truth segmentation through manual methods, the variance of the intensities over the whole image set is indicative for the complications that will be faced in automated methods. In Table 3, the results of the experiment with the MTLn3 set are shown. It is immediately clear that the overall performance is much lower compared to the other test set. However, also in this test the WMC still shows the highest performance. Compared to the WMC algorithm, the FCM algorithm is higher in specificity but significantly lower in the sensitivity. Hysteresis still portrays a good and stable performance. Compared to the previous experiment (cf. Table 2), the WMC algorithm performs quite stable under the different circumstances. In conclusion, from Table 2 and 3 it can be established that the WMC algorithm outperforms the other algorithms, which confirms its applicability for this area of bio-imaging research.

4   Conclusions and Discussion

We have proposed a segmentation algorithm for high throughput imaging that performs better than algorithms that have been used for this purpose so far. The algorithm consists of three steps, a watershed region selection followed by a fuzzy C-means clustering and if necessary followed by a correction for oversegmentation. The algorithm is particularly suitable for imaging in the domain of functional cytomics and high-throughput screenings. We have compared the WMC algorithm with five others and the results of the evaluation convincingly demonstrate the performance WMC algorithm. Over all tests, the WMC algorithm has the best recall (F1-score) without excessive increase in computation time. In the domain of cytomics, analysis is performed *post hoc*; and thus computation time is not a critical component of the analysis but segmentation robustness is. In practice, WMC is now used and we are obtaining high precision results that are understood in biological context [19, 20, 31].

The major advantage of the WMC algorithm is that it can deal with variations in staining intensity typical for bio imaging and specific to high-throughput *in vitro* experiments. The local intensity variations in the image limit application of Otsu segmentation; it requires a global optimum for the threshold, which may not be possible. Along the same line, the level-set method is not suitable as it presumes a consistent intensity for the objects in the image. The regional approach in WMC followed by a local clustering transforms the segmentation to a local problem so that threshold levels can be found efficiently. For segmentation in cytomics edge based methods are noise susceptible, therefore intensity variations necessitate region based approaches. This is confirmed from our findings comparing Hysteresis segmentation to WMC, especially with more artificial noise (cf. Table 1) or staining variations in the image (cf. Table 3).

The WMC consists of three independent steps and if we consider these individually further improvements can be formulated. In step 1, the watershed algorithm, the initialization of the watershed algorithm is currently based on local maxima; other schemas must be investigated to render a better initialization. Now, *a priori* knowledge is not used whereas this might facilitate a better estimate for the initialization. In step 2, fuzzy weighted C-means clustering is used, however, other clustering approaches can be probed; similarly to step 1, *a priori* knowledge on the intensity distribution might be supportive in finding a better clustering approach. Regarding step 3, we implemented only a few of situations of oversegmentation (cf. §.2.3). This particular step of the algorithm can be adapted to experimental conditions, i.e. *a priori* knowledge can be tuned with respect to the experiment so as to overcome certain imperfections of earlier steps. In future research this will be elaborated, however, the global idea of the WMC algorithm will stand its case (cf. Table 2 & 3).

The WMC has been successfully applied to other experiments in the domain of bio-imaging, e.g. detection of small vessels [18] and chromosomes. With further generalization, the algorithm can be engaged in a broader scale of imagery. The future research on the tuning of the subsequent steps of the WMC algorithm will contribute to this generalization.

Acknowledgements. This work has been partially supported by the Netherlands' Bioinformatics Centre (NBIC), BioRange Project. The authors like to express their gratitude to our collaborators Dr. S. Le Dévédec, Dr. S. Zovko and Prof. B. van de Water, for making available the MTln3 set. The MTLn3 ground-truth masks are obtained in collaboration with Toxicology/LACDR, Leiden University, the Netherlands. The HT29 was publically made available by the Broad Institute/MIT, USA.

References

1. Carpenter, A., Jones, T., Lamprecht, M., Clarke, C., Kang, I., Friman, O., Al, E.: CellProfiler: Image Analysis Software for Identifying and Quantifying Cell Phenotypes. Genome Biology 7(10) (2006)
2. Pinidiyaarachchi, A., Wählby, C.: Seeded Watersheds for Combined Segmentation and Tracking of Cells. In: Roli, F., Vitulano, S. (eds.) ICIAP 2005. LNCS, vol. 3617, pp. 336–343. Springer, Heidelberg (2005)
3. Webb, A.: Statistical Pattern Recognition, 2nd edn. Wiley, UK (2005)
4. Neumann, B., Held, M., Liebel, U., Erfle, H., Rogers, P., Pepperkok, R., et al.: High-throughput RNAi screening by time-lapse imaging of live human cells. Nature Methods 3(5), 385–390 (2006)
5. Neumann, B., Walter, T., Hériché, J.K., Bulkescher, J., Erfle, H., Conrad, C., et al.: Phenotypic profiling of the human genome by time-lapse microscopy reveals cell division genes. Nature 464(7289), 721–727 (2010)
6. Huang, C., Rajfur, Z., Borchers, C., Schaller, M., Jacobson, K.: JNK Phosphorylates paxillin and Regulates Cell Migration. Nature 424, 219–223 (2003)
7. van Rijsbergen, C.: Information Retrieval. Butterworth-Heinemann, UK (1979)
8. Altman, D.G., Bland, J.M.: Statistics Notes: Diagnostic Tests 1: Sensitivity and Specificity. BMJ 308(1552) (1994)
9. Hancock, E., Kittler, J.: Adaptive Estimation of Hysteresis Thresholds. In: Proc. of Computer Vision and Pattern Recognition, pp. 196–201 (1991)
10. Verbeek, F.J.: Three Dimensional Reconstruction from Serial Sections Including Deformation correction. PhD Thesis, Delft University of Technology, The Netherlands (1995)
11. Verbeek, F.J.: Theory & Practice of 3D-reconstructions From serial Sections. In: Baldock, R.A., Graham, J. (eds.) Image Processing, A Practical Approach, pp. 153–195. Oxford University Press, Oxford (1999)
12. Angulo, J., Schaack, B.: Morphological-Based Adaptive Segmentation and Quantification of Cell Assays in High Content Screening. In: Proc. of the 5th IEEE International Symposium on Biomedial Imaging, pp. 360–363 (2008)

13. Bernsen, J.: Dynamic Thresholding of Grey-Level Images. In: Proc. of the 8th Int. Conf. on Pattern Recognition (1986)
14. Roerdink, J.B., Meijster, A.: The Watershed Transform: Definitions, Algorithms and Parallelization Strategies. Fundamenta Informatica, 187–228 (2000)
15. Fan, J., Han, M., Wang, J.: Single Point Iterative Weighted Fuzzy C-means Clustering Algorithm for Remote Sensing Image Segmentation. Pattern Recognition 42(11), 2527–2540 (2009)
16. Moffat, J., Grueneberg, D.A., Yang, X., Kim, S.Y., Kloepfer, A.M., Hinkle, G.: A lentiviral RNAi library for human and mouse genes applied to an arrayed viral high-content screen. Cell 124(6), 1283–1298 (2006)
17. Pu, J., McCaig, C.D., Cao, L., Zhao, Z., Segall, J.E., Zhao, M.: EGF receptor Signaling is Essential for Electric-field-directed Migration of Breast Cancer Cells. Journal of Cell Science 120(19), 3395–3403 (2007)
18. Yan, K., Bertens, L., Verbeek, F.J.: Image Registration and Realignment using Evolutionary Algorithms with High resolution 3D model from Human Liver. In: Proc. CGIM 2010 (2010)
19. Yan, K., Le Dévédec, S., van de Water, B., Verbeek, F.J.: Cell Tracking and Data Analysis of in vitro Tumour Cells from Time-Lapse Image Sequences. In: Proc. VISAPP 2009, pp. 281–287 (2009)
20. Damiano, L., Le Dévédec, S.E., Di Stefano, P., Repetto, D., Lalai, R., Truong, H., Xiong, J.L., Danen, E.H., Yan, K., Verbeek, F.J., Attanasio, F., Buccione, R., van de Water, B., Defilippi, P.: p140Cap Suppresses the Invasive Properties of Highly Metastatic MTLn3-EGFR Cells via Paired Cortactin Phosphorylation. Oncogene 30(2) (2011) (in Press)
21. Ma, L., Staunton, R.: A modied fuzzy C-means image segmentation algorithm for use with uneven illumination patterns. Pattern Recognition 40(11), 3005–3011 (2007)
22. Sezgin, M., Sankur, B.: Survey over Image Thresholding Techniques and Quantitative Performance Evaluation. Journal of Electronic Imaging 13(1), 146–165 (2004)
23. Otsu, N.: A Threshold Selection Method from Gray-level Histogram. IEEE Transactions on Systems, Man and Cybernetics 9, 62–66 (1979)
24. Venkateswarlua, N., Raju, P.: Fast Isodata Clustering Algorithms. Pattern Recognition 25(3), 335–342 (1992)
25. van der Putten, P., Bertens, L., Liu, J., Hagen, F., Boekhout, T., Verbeek, F.J.: Classification of Yeast Cells from Image Features to Evaluate. Pathogen Conditions. In: SPIE 6506, MultiMedia Content Access: Algorithms & Systems, vol. 6506, pp. 65060I-1–65060I-14 (2007)
26. Goldman, R., Swedlow, J., Spector, D.: Live Cell Imaging: A Laboratory Manual. Cold Spring Harbor Laboratory Press, USA (2005)
27. Medina-Carnicer, R., Madrid-Cuevas, F., Carmona-Poyato, A., Muñoz Salinas, R.: On candidates selection for hysteresis thresholds in edge detection. Pattern Recognition 42(7), 1284–1296 (2008)
28. Pepperkok, R., Ellenberg, J.: High throughput Fluorescence Microscopy for Systems Biology. Nature Reviews Molecular Cell Biology 7(9), 690–696 (2006)
29. Inoue, S.: Video Microscopy: the Fundamentals, 2nd edn. Springer, USA (1997)
30. Osher, S.J., Fedkiw, R.P.: Level Set Methods and Dynamic Implicit Surfaces. Springer, USA (2002)
31. LeDévédec, S., Yan, K., de Bont, H., Ghotra, V., Truong, H., Danen, E., Verbeek, F.J., van de Water, B.: A Systems Microscopy Approach to Understand Cancer Cell Migration and Metastasis. Cellular and Molecular in Life Science 67(19), 3219–3240 (2011)
32. Collins, T.: Image J for microscopy. Bio Techniques 43, 25–30 (2007)

Efficient and Robust Shape Retrieval
from Deformable Templates

Alexander E. Nezhinsky and Fons J. Verbeek

Section Imaging and Bioinformatics,
Leiden Institute of Advanced Computer Science, Leiden University,
Niels Bohrweg 1, 2333CA, Leiden, The Netherlands
{anezhins,fverbeek}@liacs.nl

Abstract. Images with known shapes can be analyzed through template matching and segmentation; in this approach the question is how to represent a known shape. The digital representation to which the shape is sampled, the image, may be subject to noise. If we compare a known and idealized shape to the real-life occurrences, a considerable variation is observed. With respect to the shape, this variation can have affine characteristics as well as non-linear deformations. We propose a method based on a deformable template starting from a low-level vision and proceeding to high-level vision. The latter part is typically application dependent, here the shapes are annotated according to an ideal template and are normalized by a straightening process. The underlying algorithm can deal with a range of deformations and does not restrict to a single instance of a shape in the image. Experimental results from an application of the algorithm illustrate low error rate and robustness of the method. The life sciences are a challenging area in terms of applications in which a considerable variation of the shape of object instances is observed. Successful application of this method would be typically suitable for automated procedures such as those required for biomedical high-throughput screening. As a case study, we, therefore, illustrate our method in this context, i.e. retrieving instances of shapes obtained from a screening experiment.

Keywords: Content-based Indexing, Search, and Retrieval, Object detection and Localization, Object Recognition.

1 Introduction

In this paper we focus on the problem of object detection and localization in digitized images for structures that are deformed instances of an archetypal shape (Verbeek, 1995); as an extension to the case of single instance we have investigated the effect of the presence of more than one instance, intersecting or otherwise obscured. In all cases instances need be properly separated from the other content in the digital image.

In order to accomplish the detection in a robust and reproducible manner, we present a framework consisting of two steps for the recognition and annotation of the deformed instances of a predefined shape. Annotation is required so as to be able to compare different instances of objects in a comparable (reproducible) manner.

T. Margaria and B. Steffen (Eds.): ISoLA 2012, Part II, LNCS 7610, pp. 42–55, 2012.
© Springer-Verlag Berlin Heidelberg 2012

Therefore as part of our solution we also elaborate a straightening normalization of the shape according to a predefined template. Our framework will be applied to a case study in biology, i.e. high throughput screening of zebrafish larvae.

A large number of context based image retrieval systems have been described (Zhong *et al.*, 2000). These can be divided in the *free-form* and the *parametric* approaches. A popular approach for shape retrieval is the Active Contour, a.k.a. the active snake, (Kass *et al.*, 1987) which is a typical *free-form* model (Jain *et al.*, 1996). Free form models require a correct global initialization in the image and optimize the local shape. Free-form class models do not have global shape limitation, but focus mainly on attraction towards certain image features (Jain *et al.*, 1996). In our approach we focus on the cases in which a global shape is known and therefore we do not consider active snake as a possibility.

In research dealing with recognition of known shapes (Garrido *et al.*, 2000; Ng *et al.*, 2006; Felzenswalb, 2003(1,2)) the use deformable templates is emphasized. Deformable templates typically, are *parametric class* models; they start from a set of predefined parameters. The representation of the parameters might differ, but often a template is used, consisting of a set of contour points to which the basic shape outlineis approximated. So, if the basic shape that is looked for is known, it still needs be localized in the images. Therefore the prior knowledge can be exploited by choosing the parametric deformable shape template matching method as a basic approach (Bronkorsta *et al.*, 2000, Jain *et al.*, 1996, Zhong *et al.*, 2000, Felzenswalb, 2003(1)).

Such approach is used in the segmentation of cells in a microscope images (Garrido *et al*, 2000). In this application the Hough transform approach is reformulated to be used as a deformable template. However, if the shapes are more complex than a circular shape like object, it is difficult to adapt to this approach.

An example of a more complex shape is the segmentation of the masseter on the basis of a predefined template (Ng *et al.*, 2006); locally deformed instances of the template can be successfully extracted from input images.

On the basis of this approach we propose a further generalization with which it is also possible to deal with multiple objects in one image as well as with global deformations; e.g. bending of the entire object.

Based on silhouettes or boundary representations of prototype templates a considerable amount of research has been completed (Felzenswalb, 2003). Usually the silhouettes are defined by contour points and make up the template. These templates can then be deformed by a set of parametric transformations, including both local and global transformations (Zhong *et al*, 2000). We have taken this traditional representation as a starting point; however, we have replaced the contour points in the silhouette by a contour area (cf. Figure 2). The reason for using this representation is that we would like to allow multiple overlapping instances of the object in one input image and therefore we have to accommodate for missing contour points.

In addition to the template matching, we also address the problem of shape normalization; in particular for applications of biological objects. The combination of shape localization and normalization has been successfully applied for the round worm, i.e. *C.elegans* (Peng *et al.*, 2007). It is known as the BDB+ method. On the basis of the object boundary a straightening is applied so as to ease the further analysis of the objects. In our application, however, this method cannot be used; it starts from a pre-defined shape and then straightens the shape assuming the boundary has already been extracted. We want to investigate the recognition and straightening of more complex elongated shapes and, as indicated, account for the presence of multiple instances in one image.

The framework that we have elaborated consists of two steps. First, a preprocessing step including a segmentation of an input image in order to separate the object(s) of interest from the background is applied. Segmentation alone, however, does not give satisfactory results, as we are not only interested in separating background from foreground, but we also want to recognize position and best possible representation of the object. This is realized in the second step consisting of a matching of a deformable template to the segmented image. This step is the main focus of this paper. Finally, a post-processing step includes shape normalization through straightening of the ex-tracted shape. Such is possible from contextual information about the object in the image that we have gained. Deformations are known and therefore deformations can be normalized according to the template. The framework was implemented in C++ using the OpenCV graphics library (http://opencv.willowgarage.com).

2   Method

The starting point of our algorithm is variation; i.e. a shape has variation, it can be inflicted with noise and it can be deformed or partially occluded. Our framework detects deformed instances of a predefined structure by means of Deformable Template Matching and these are subsequently extracted from an input image. In Figure 1, an overview of the process is presented.

The method consists of two steps: the preprocessing step and the template matching step. First, during the preprocessing step, the input image is converted to a strict binary representation. In the main process the deformable template matching is applied in the binary image obtained from the preprocessing. This entails looking for the best match of a prototype template in the image. If a match is found the result is annotated according to the prototype template and henceforth, straightened.

2.1   Pre-processing

The first step in the analysis is retrieving foreground and background: i.e. an operation that converts an input image to a binary representation by marking the pixels which belong to foreground objects 1 and the background pixels 0. Different binarization methods are described in the literature; i.e. based on the usage of global or adaptive threshold methods, color or edge based segmentation. The choice of the method depends on the input image at hand, its properties and quality (Gonzales *et al.*, 2001). In the cases where prior spatial information is known this given can be exploited and the threshold value set can be based on this given.

A contour location area represents the region of interest within which the local template contour can exist and may change. In doing so, local deformations become limited by evaluating only at the pixels that are located within the contour location area (depicted in grey in Figure 2). Introducing a limitation to the template boundary location of the deformed template is necessary to predict image boundary location in cases where it is missing, incomplete or overlapping. As a result of this representation only global deformations are remaining, which will be described in the next subsection.

Parametric Transformation. Biological shape instances are often bended and rotated. In order to cope with these global deformations T_0 is distributed in n smaller sub-templates; these are hereafter referred to as slices t (Nezhinsky and Verbeek, 2010):

$$T_0 = t_0, t_1, ..., t_n \qquad (1)$$

A single slice can be seen as a rectangular matrix $t(i, j)$, consisting of binary values. This is shown in Figure 3.

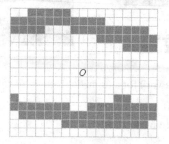

Fig. 3. An example of matrix $t(i, j)$ representing a template slice. Fields with value 1 are marked with grey color. Other fields have the value 0.

The horizontal medial axis of the slice $O_{horizontal}$, is defined at [i/2,*], and the slice origin as O at [i/2, j/2]. Within the whole template the slices can rotate around their origin O to allow matching against a rotated shape. The origins are linked together as a chain (Figure 4); at any deformation of the total shape the distance between sequential slice origins remains the same.

Fig. 4. A prototype template as a chain of slices and a deformed instance. All shape boundaries that fit in the grey area fit the template. Black lines represent two example shapes that fit these templates.

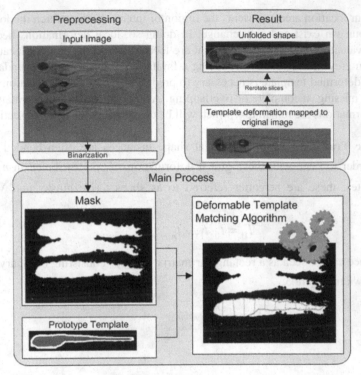

Fig. 1. Proposed framework for automatic shape retrieval and straightening

2.2   Deformable Template Matching

After separation of foreground and background in the image, the contextual information still needs to be retrieved in order to recognize the objects of interest.

Prototype Template. The initial contour sketch of the object of interest is defined by
the prototype template T_0. The construction of T_0 is based on prior knowledge and is
an approximate representation of how a typical object contour should look like and
represents a contour location area. In Figure 2 a few examples are shown.

Fig. 2. Some examples of prototype templates of different objects. Gray area represents the
space where connected component boundaries might be located.

A deformed template T' is derived from T_0 and is represented as:

$$T'(T_0, \underline{\xi}) \tag{2}$$

A deformation $\underline{\xi}$ of the slice chain is encoded by the following state-sequence:

$$\underline{\xi} = (x, y, \alpha_0, \alpha_1, .., \alpha_n) \tag{3}$$

x is the shift in the X-axis, y the shift in the Y-axis direction of the first slice t_0 and α_i the angle of rotation of each slice t_i. Due to the proposed slice based representation our deformable template approach is very suitable for use with elongated shapes.

Objective Function. The fitness of a template matching of an input image is measured by an objective function (Jain *et al.*, 1996). In the *C.elegans* application (Peng *et al.*, 2008) a parametric representation is used in which the algorithm marches along the backbone of a representation to calculate the objective function.

A similar approach is applied, by comparing simultaneously the matrix $S(i, j)$ of binary slices to a selected image region of the same size, i.e. the binary matrix $R(i, j)$ (Figure 5a,b). First, the matrix is considered in which both the template and the image region have overlapping foreground pixels, which are the result of $R(i, j) \cdot S(i, j)$ (Figure 5c).

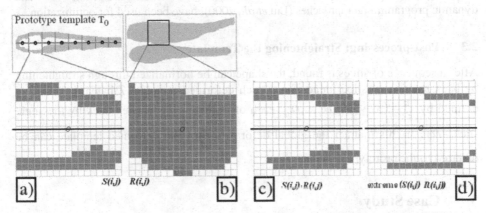

Fig. 5. An example of template matching of a template slice *S(i,j)* and a region *R(i,j)*

During this step the shape is a filled binary object, therefore matches that are farthest from the slice center but still in the silhouette contour area, are assumed to define the object. In order to get the actual border, the algorithm then marches along the horizontal medial axis of $R(i, j) \cdot S(i, j)$ iterating over 0 till j. Each orthogonal image plane pixel columns p_i (iterating from 0 to i) is compared to the template. It is assumed that the silhouette has only one silhouette pixel in the top and the bottom of each column. Therefore, per column, the two extreme points that are of value 1 (as measured from the horizontal medial axis) remain 1, all other values are set to 0 (Figure 5d). The result thus obtained is considered an intermediate result. The quality, i.e. the objective function, of this result is then measured by the length of the retrieved border. Objective function is 1 if all pixels of the silhouette have been retrieved. To that end the objective function for a slice $S(i, j)$ is defined as:

$$\phi(S(i, j)) = \frac{0.5}{j} \left(\sum (S(i, j) \cdot R(i, j)) \right) \qquad (4)$$

A template consists of n slices of the same size, and therefore $F(T, \underline{\xi})$ depends on the fitness function of each slice:

$$F(T, \underline{\xi}) = \frac{1}{n} \sum_{k=0}^{n} \phi_k (S(i, j)) \qquad (5)$$

Matching the Template to the Input Image. In order to check all possible occurrences, T_0 must be transformed, rotated and deformed by all possible parameters. To find the best solution there is a need to retrieve the global maximum of the fitness function (cf. Eq. 5) for the input image. That is, to compare each $S(i, j)$ to all possible regions $R(i, j)$ within the image.

A global search is computationally complex (Kim *et al.*, 2007), especially when the search space image is large. To that end Genetic algorithms (Tagare *et al.*, 1997) and dynamic programming approaches (Liu *et al.*, 2000), have been used for optimization.

2.3   Post-processing: Straightening the Template

After a sequence of slices is found, the shape can be normalized through straightening by back-rotation of slice found. Since each deformed template T has a deformation defined by $\underline{\xi} = (x, y, \alpha_0, \alpha_1, .., \alpha_n)$ each of its slices t_i is rotated back by the angle slice - α_i. In this manner the global deformation of the deformed template can be reverted to the prototype template T_0.

3   Case Study

The framework was developed in the context of high throughput imaging applications. Therefore, as a case study we will elaborate on shape analysis and retrieval of the zebrafish larvae (Stoop *et al.*, 2011). Typically, zebrafish are employed in high throughput studies to investigate new factors for mycobacterial infection. Such approach requires a screening of thousands of larvae.

The shapes of zebrafish larvae are similar, yet each individual (instance) is little different. Moreover, shapes are often slightly bent and rotated. Without proper localization and annotation of the regions in the shapes, the measurement of features within each instance is severely hampered.

The framework that we present fulfills the need for solutions in high-throughput applications in which shapes can be recognized in images and subsequently annotated in such way that these can be compared to other retrieved shapes.

The images for this case study were acquired using Leica MZ16FA light microscope as 24-bit color images with a size of 2592×1944 pixels. On average, each image contains up to 3 larvae. The orientation of the instances in the images is random; however they are not touching the image border. Given the experimental set-up we can assume that the images only contain zebrafish larvae and some incidental noise/debris.

3.1   Pre-processing

Because of uneven illumination, global threshold methods applied on gray-scale converted images of the zebrafish larvae will not produce satisfactory results. We, therefore, employ an edge map based method to the input image. Edges define the boundaries between objects and background without strong dependency to flaws in the illumination. There exist several algorithms to create an edge map. After creation of the edge map a threshold is applied to select for the strong edges.

The determination of the threshold value of an edge map can be a cumbersome task. To set the threshold automatically without prior spatial relationship knowledge of the image, the Otsu segmentation (Otsu, 1979) might be applied.

However, as we have prior spatial relationship knowledge of our particular dataset, we can exploit this for our *border based* method; i.e. the objects in the image are always located at some minimal distance d from image border. This characteristic is utilized. We can assume that a sheet of thickness d on the outside of an image contains only background pixels and some incidental noise. Of this sheet we retrieve a number of local maximal pixel values. Of all the collected values we take the median value to determine the threshold value for the edge map.

In order to select the best preprocessing approach we compare the performance of different simple edge detectors, i.e. Sobel gradient, Roberts gradient (Gonzales & Woods, 2001) in combination with Otsu segmentation (Otsu, 1979) and our *border based* method on 233 images. We count the number of objects in the segmented image. If the number of objects equals the number of objects in the original image we mark the prediction as correct. Both gradient methods in combination with our border method outperformed thresholding based on Otsu segmentation. Out of the images incorrectly segmented in 17 cases the zebrafish shapes were touching each other and thus connected. In all of these cases both edge detectors predicted 1 or 2 fish instead of 3 due to this connection.

After basic segmentation is completed, mathematical morphology operations are applied to get rid of noise and close up unwanted gaps. The closing operator is applied to connect small regions and close holes, then connected components labeling (with filling up holes) is applied to obtain the closed shapes. In order to eliminate remaining noise we use the fact that we know the minimal area covered by a zebrafish. This area size can be automatically retrieved from the template size. Thus we remove all objects smaller then this minimal area. We do not remove objects that are larger than the maximal area, since larger object might be intersecting zebrafish shapes.

3.2 Main Process: Deformable Template Matching

Prototype Template. Our initial zebrafish template (cf. Figure 6) is created from averaging a test set of training shapes (Cootes *et al.*, 1994); here the template is created by averaging a set of 20 zebrafish larvae shapes.

Zebrafish larvae tend differ in length. Therefore, the length of the template is not fixed, but can vary between some minimal (*min*) and maximal (*max*) number of slices t_{min} and t_{max}. If the number of found slices is smaller than *min* or larger then *max* we assume the shape is not found. All the slices t_x with *min* < *x* < *max* are thus optional slices. In Figure 6 this is depicted. The *max* and *min* are set based on the length of the longest and shortest encountered zebrafish.

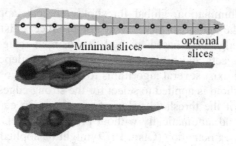

Fig. 6. Minimal slices and optional slices in a prototype template. The template is compared to an example of a short and a long larvae shape.

Objective Function for the First Slice. The described objective function is applicable for slices in which the important information is located above and below the slice center. While most of the zebrafish larvae template applies to this condition the very first slice, in which the head is located, does not. This is due to the fact that its shape is close to half circular. This is depicted in Figure 7. To cope with this case, instead of retrieving extreme values above and below the median axis extreme values are retrieved in a circular way as shown in Figure 7.

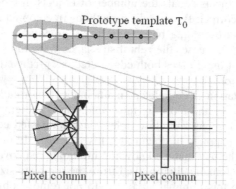

Fig. 7. Marching direction for the first slice depicted in the image pixel matrix

Matching the Template to the Shape. In order to obtain a global optimum a top-down dynamic programming approach is applied with a hash table saving for intermediate result. In our case study the larvae shapes are located in approximately vertical positions in the input image. This fact is used to reduce the search space by assuming that each slice can rotate between -45 to 45 degrees as measured from the image horizontal axis. Additionally, a discrete set of deformation angles for each slice is used.

To further reduce the search space a *Multi resolution* algorithm (Leroy, 1996) is used. First the solution is located on a low resolution template and a low resolution input image. Then, the solution is used for initialization in a higher resolution.

4 Experiments and Results

An evaluation of our algorithm is performed on a dataset consisting of 233 images which were obtained from a running experiment. Out of the images 177(76%) contained 3 larvae, 33(14%) contained 2 larvae and 23(10%) 1 larva.

A first basic test is to check for how many of the tested images the number of larvae is predicted correctly: for all images (100%) the number of the larvae shapes (1,2 or 3 larvae, even if overlapping) with in the image was correctly retrieved.

The correct prediction of the number of shapes in an image is promising, however only retrieving the number of shapes is not sufficient for a proper analysis. To that end we also tested the accuracy of the algorithm, that is, how precise the shapes were retrieved. In Figure 8 representative results of retrieved shapes are depicted. We show shapes that are deformed in different way as well as shapes touching each other. The template in Figure 6 was used for the creation of all these images.

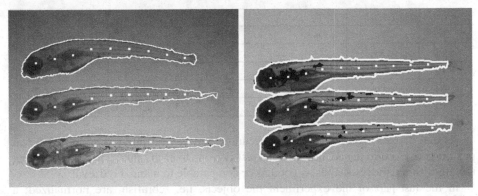

Fig. 8. Automatic localization of the zebrafish shapes using deformable template matching. The white line defines the shape as found by the algorithm. The white dots represent the slice centers found. In the right image the shapes are slightly touching each other, which complicates the recognition. These result were created using the same template as the left image; the black regions in each larva depicts a bacterial infection.

Methods that can be used for automated retrieval predefined shapes from images without an initialization have not been described, and therefore we have compared the resulting shapes of each retrieved zebrafish larva shape against ground truth images of the same shapes as annotated by experts. A comparison of human to automatic retrieval is regularly used for validation procedures (Peng *et al.*, 2008).

In order to have manageable proportions in the evaluation, we reduced our test set to a total of 104 zebrafish shapes (distributed over in 35 images, containing up to 3 shapes per image). Four experts (test-persons T1, T2, T3, T4) were asked to delineate the outline of the zebrafish larva. Drawing the shapes was realized with an LCD-tablet (Wacom) using the TDR software (Verbeek *et al.*, 2002).

Next, the precision of our method is compared by applying it to the same input data (algorithm output A). The accuracy of our shape retrieval algorithm is measured by the equation proposed in (Ng *et al.*, 2006):

$$accuracy = 2 \times \left(\frac{N(M_{area} \cap S_{area})}{N(M_{area}) + N(S_{area})} \right) \times 100\% \tag{6}$$

We have compared the accuracy of our algorithm to T1, T2, T3 and T4. The average accuracy was established as 96.71 (σ= 1.27). Note, that this accuracy could not be achieved by the segmentation step alone, as 35 (of the 104) shapes used for this test were touching each other and their boundary could only be derived through the template matching.

Table 1 presents the results of the comparison of the accuracy of our algorithm with the test persons. In addition the inter-observer variation is analyzed.

Table 1. Accuracy comparison of our algorithm T0 and the test subjects T1, T2, T3, T4. The matrix is symmetrical, yet we have shown all the values for viewing convenience

	T0	T1	T2	T3	T4
T0	-	96.85	97.19	96.29	96.47
T1	96.85	-	97.61	97.21	96.81
T2	97.19	97.61	-	97.17	97.46
T3	96.29	97.21	97.17	-	96.68
T4	96.47	96.81	97.46	96.68	-

As can be seen from the table the accuracy between our algorithm and each test person is as close to the accuracy of the test persons to each other. This indicates that the algorithm retrieves shapes as good as or comparable to manual retrieval.

In the last part of the experiment the objects, i.e. zebrafish, are normalized; a straightening operation. This is accomplished using a template with a straight top border in order to align the slices found with their top to a horizontal line. In Figure 9 and Figure 10 the results are shown.

To retrieve and straighten a single zebrafish shape from a 2592×1944 image took our application about 35s CPU time on an Intel Dual Core 2.66 Ghz, 1.00 Gb.

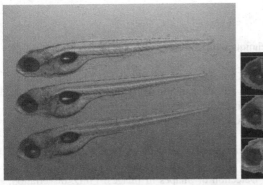
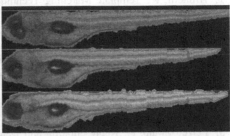

Fig. 9. Results showing the automated straightening of zebrafish larvae. Image (left) is the input image. Image (right) is the normalization result.

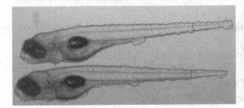
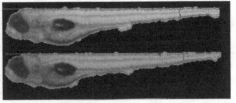

Fig. 10. Results of the automated straightening zebrafish larvae. Image (a) shows the retrieved shapes projected on the input image. Image (b) shows the automated normalization result.

5   Conclusions

In this paper we have described a framework for automated detection of archetypal object shapes in an image. Once detected a post-processing by straightening of each object on the basis of a predefined template is applied.

In our framework, the prototype template is represented as a bitmap and can easily be adapted to the needs of the application while the same algorithm is used.

The algorithm we propose does not rely on initial localization of the shape and therefore does not require any manual intervention or analysis.

The framework was applied in an experimental set-up for high throughput screening with a read-out in images. In the application to zebrafish screening average accuracy of about 96 percent has been achieved.

The framework can be easily adapted to work with other shapes, be in the life sciences or in other fields that require accurate and robust shape retrieval.

Further analysis of the validation and the precision in object straightening is part of the future work.

Acknowledgements. This work is partially supported through the Smartmix program.

References

1. Brunelli, R.: Template Matching Techniques in Computer Vision: Theory and Practice. John Wiley & Sons, Ltd. (2009)
2. Cootes, T.F., Taylor, C.J., Cooper, D.H., Graham, J.: Active shape models: their training and application. Computer Vision and Image Understanding 61(1), 38–59 (1995)
3. Cootes, T.F., Taylor, C.J., Lanitis, A.: Active Shape Models: Evaluation of a Multiresolution Method for Improving Image Searches. In: Proceedings of the British Machine Vision Conference, vol. 1, pp. 327–336 (1994)
4. Dormand, J.R., Prince, P.J.: A family of embedded Runge–Kutta formulae. J. Comp. Appl. Math. 6(6), 19–26 (1980)
5. Felzenszwalb, P.: Representation and Detection of Shapes in Images. Ph.D. dissertation, Massachusetts Institute of Technology (2003)
6. Felzenszwalb, P.: Representation and Detection of Deformable Shapes. In: 2003 IEEE Computer Society Conference on Computer Vision and Pattern Recognition (CVPR 2003), vol. 1, p. 102 (2003)
7. Garrido, A., Perez de la Blanca, N.: Applying deformable templates for cell segmentation. Pattern Recognition 33 (2000)
8. Gonzales, R., Woods, R.: Digital Image Processing, 2nd edn. Addison-Wesley, London (2001)
9. Jain, A.K., Zhong, Y., Lakshmanan, S.: Object matching using deformable templates. IEEE Tran. on Pattern Analysis and Machine Intell. 18(3) (1996)
10. Jain, A.K., Zhong, Y., Dubuisson-Jolly, M.: Deformable Template Models: a Review. In: Signal Processing - Special Issue on Deformable Models and Techniques for Image and Signal. Elsevier (1998)
11. Zhong, Y., Jain, A.K.: Object localization using color, texture and shape. Pattern Recognition 33 (2000)
12. Kass, M., Witkin, A., Terzopoulos, D.: Snakes: Active contour models. Int. Journal of Comput. Vision 1(4) (1987)
13. Kim, H.Y., de Araújo, S.A.: Grayscale Template-Matching Invariant to Rotation, Scale, Translation, Brightness and Contrast. In: Mery, D., Rueda, L. (eds.) PSIVT 2007. LNCS, vol. 4872, pp. 100–113. Springer, Heidelberg (2007)
14. Leroy, B., Herlin, I., Cohen, L.D.: Multi-resolution algorithms for active contour models. In: Proceedings of the 12th International Conference on Analysis and Optimization of Systems Images, Wavelets and PDE'S, Rocquencourt (1996)
15. Liu, Z., Wang, Y.: Face detection and tracking in video using dynamic programming. In: Proceedings of International Conference on Image Processing (2000)
16. Nezhinsky, A.E., Verbeek, F.J.: Pattern Recognition for High Throughput Zebrafish Imaging Using Genetic Algorithm Optimization. In: Dijkstra, T.M.H., Tsivtsivadze, E., Marchiori, E., Heskes, T. (eds.) PRIB 2010. LNCS (LNBI), vol. 6282, pp. 301–312. Springer, Heidelberg (2010)
17. Ng, H.P., Ong, S.H., Goh, P.S., Foong, K.W.C., Nowinski, W.L.: Template-based Automatic Segmentation of Masseter Using Prior Knowledge. In: Proceeding SSIAI 2006 Proceedings of the 2006 IEEE Southwest Symposium on Image Analysis and Interpretation (2006)
18. Peng, H., et al.: Straightening Caenorhabditis elegans images. Bioinformatics 24, 234–242 (2008)
19. Ren, M., Yang, J., Sun, H.: Tracing boundary contours in a binary image. In: Image and Vision Computing (2002)

20. Ridler, T.W., Calvard, S.: Picture thresholding using an iterative selection method. IEEE Trans. System, Man and Cybernetics SMC-8, 630–632 (1978)
21. Stoop, E.J.M., Schipper, T., Rosendahl Huber, S.K., Nezhinsky, A.E., Verbeek, F.J., Gurcha, S.S., Besra, G.S., Vandenbroucke-Grauls, C.M.J.E., Bitter, W., van der Sar, A.M.: Zebrafish embryo screen for mycobacterial genes involved in the initiation of granuloma formation reveals a newly identified ESX-1 component. Dis. Model. Mech. 4(4), 526–536 (2011)
22. Tagare, H.D.: Deformable 2-D template matching using orthogonal curves. IEEE Transactions on Medical Imaging 16(1), 108–117 (1997), http://www.ncbi.nlm.nih.gov/pubmed/9050413
23. Otsu, N.: A threshold selection method from gray-level histogram. IEEE Transactions on Systems Man Cybernet (1978)
24. Verbeek, F.J.: Three-dimensional reconstruction from serial sections including deformation correction Delft University of Technology, Delft (1995)
25. Verbeek, F.J., Boon, P.J.: High-resolution 3D reconstruction from serial sections: microscope instrumentation, software design, and its implementations. In: Three-Dimensional and Multidimensional Microscopy: Image Acquisition and Processing IX (2002)

OWL-DL Domain-Models as Abstract Workflows

Ian Wood[1], Ben Vandervalk[1], Luke McCarthy[1], and Mark D. Wilkinson[2]

[1] Institute for Heart + Lung Health, St. Paul's Hospital,
University of British Columbia, Vancouver, BC, Canada
`ian.wood@alumni.ubc.ca`, `luke@elmonline.ca`,
`ben.vvalk@gmail.com`
[2] Centro de Biotecnología y Genómica de Plantas,
Universidad Politécnica de Madrid, Madrid, España
`markw@illuminae.com`

Abstract. Workflows are an increasingly common way of representing and sharing complex *in silico* analytical methodologies. Workflow authoring systems such as Taverna and Galaxy precisely capture the services and service connections created by domain experts, and these workflows are then shared through repositories like myExperiment, which encourages users to discover, reuse, and repurpose them. Repurposing, however, is not trivial: ostensibly straightforward modifications are quite troublesome in practice and workflows tend not to be well-annotated at any level of granularity. As such, a "concrete" workflow, where the component services are explicitly declared, may not be a particularly effective way of sharing these analytical methodologies. Here we propose, and demonstrate, that a domain model for a given concept, formalized in OWL, can be used as an abstract workflow model, which can be automatically converted into a context-specific, concrete, self-annotating workflow.

Keywords: OWL-DL, ontologies, workflow, workflow modeling, SPARQL, Semantic Web, Semantic Web Services.

1   Introduction

Scientific workflows represent important "units of thought" that contain, implicitly or explicitly, both the detailed hypothesis of the researcher as well as the precise materials they utilized and methodology they undertook throughout their investigation. Unfortunately, these core elements of repeatable and reproducible science are, to date, still primarily shared as blocks of sometimes unclear narrative [1]. Though still quite rare, even for *in silico* science, formal workflows are starting to be adopted as an accepted unit of both publication and collaboration, allowing the precise representation of both resources and processes underlying complex *in silico* analytical methodologies [2].

Workflow authoring systems such as Taverna [3] and Galaxy [4] are used, usually by bioinformaticians or other technically-oriented personnel, to precisely capture the services and service connections that represent the evaluation of a biological hypothesis of a domain expert. The resulting workflow is then captured in some standard language. As of this writing, >76% of the 1839 workflows in myExperiment

T. Margaria and B. Steffen (Eds.): ISoLA 2012, Part II, LNCS 7610, pp. 56–66, 2012.

[2] are in some version of Taverna's SCUFL language, with the other 24% being spread over 8 other workflow languages, with the second most-common language being RapidMiner (198 Workflows). Importantly, because these workflows are designed to be used directly by some Orchestration Engine (e.g. Taverna) they are rigidly tied to specific web services (or other components).

Such workflows may then be shared through repositories like myExperiment which encourages users to discover, reuse, and repurpose them. Repurposing, however, is not trivial [28] specifically because the workflows are so tightly tied to a specific set of services and resources. Ostensibly straightforward modifications, such as executing a bioinformatics analysis, functionally unaltered, between one species or another, may be quite troublesome in practice as many of the underlying databases and algorithms for different model organisms will not expose the same interface, despite the overall analytical process being effectively identical. Moreover, scientific workflows tend not to be well-annotated at the macro level, and tend not to be annotated at all at even a modest level of granularity. This makes repurposing even more difficult as the workflow editor must divine the intent of each inter-service connection created by the original author, and what data element(s) that connection will contribute to the final output.

For these reasons, and others, a "concrete" workflow, where the component services are explicitly declared, may not be a particularly effective way of sharing analytical methodologies. What is required is a layer of abstraction, where the overall objectives of the workflow are described, without being tied to a specific concrete set of resources until such time as the context of the Workflow execution is known.

The workflow orchestration language BPEL [5] could, in principle, act as a type of abstraction by making sharable, functionally-meaningful combinations of internally-interoperable services, which then might be easier to interchange in a modular manner; however in practice BPEL is not widely used by the scientific community [6]. Scientific workflows are composed of (mainly) scientific services, and these are known to be, by and large, stateless and data-centric [6-9]. BPEL, on the other hand, is primarily a process-centric description language, and thus modeling scientific workflows in BPEL is somewhat un-natural and, moreover, provides little value to the workflow author. As such, it does not seem a promising approach to the abstraction we are trying to achieve.

GenePattern [10], a popular application for building genomics analysis workflows, provides a certain amount of abstraction in that their algorithms are organized hierarchically. For example, under the "Clustering" node are such values as "KMeans", and "Consensus", which may have a variety of concrete instantiations as services. To date, however, GenePattern has not expanded beyond the scope of genomics, and provides access only to the ~150 analytical tools in its repository. Thus it is not immediately suitable for the wider ecosystem of web services.

A considerable amount of effort has been invested in the creation of a semantic workflow abstraction/templating layer for the Wings [11] workflow system, which has resulted in a highly expressive set of OWL axioms and concepts [12] that enable the creation of linked-data documents that explicitly describe an abstract workflow. This includes the ability to enumerate both datasets and the analytical resources that make-up the workflow and the connections between them; to semantically type data, datasets, and tools in the abstraction; and to describe how to handle "sets-of-sets" (e.g. the cross-product of two datasets) at any point in the workflow. These abstract workflows have been demonstrably capable of being concretized (by the Wings orchestration engine) under a variety of conditions and, importantly, concretized by non-expert users, for example in the domain of text-mining [11,13].

A significant amount of research on the abstract specification of workflows has also been done outside of the biology domain. In particular, several frameworks [21-23] have been developed to specify workflows using constraints expressed in Linear Temporal Logic (LTL) or some variant thereof. While these systems are often designed to guide human processes, such as the activities of a hotel customer service clerk [21], the work can be readily adapted to web service workflows, as demonstrated by [23]. A key strength of the LTL-based workflow systems is that they are able to leverage existing algorithms for *model-checking* [24]. Model-checking algorithms allow automated detection of workflow errors such as dead activities (unreachable nodes), deadlocks, or any other type of error condition that can be expressed in LTL.

Of importance to this work are two inter-related observations about the Wings /LTL workflow abstractions which differentiate their approaches from what we describe here. First, both of these workflow abstractions take the form of distinct documents that describe *only* the workflow, and the semantics of that workflow. Second, the abstractions are *constructed* independently -as a separate engineering event -from the expert domain-knowledge (e.g. biological question) that the workflow relates to. While neither of these issues are negative or detrimental, they result in a slightly higher curatorial burden due to the need to maintain an additional resource (the abstraction) in parallel with changes in the domain knowledge. Thus, in light of our development of the SADI Semantic Web Service design patterns [14] and the SHARE system for resolving queries over SADI services [15], we have pursued an investigation of whether the posing of a domain-model, and the construction of a corresponding workflow to evaluate that model, can be more tightly linked -perhaps into a single, unified event.

We propose that a domain model for a given concept, formalized in OWL (i.e. an ontological Class), can itself be used as an abstract workflow model, which can be automatically converted into a context-specific concrete workflow as-needed by a semantic orchestration engine (SHARE [15]). Similar to the Wings abstraction, this has the advantage that the concrete representation of the workflow is constructed at run-time, based on the nature of inputs and other metadata, and does not require difficult and error-prone manual re-wiring of workflow components. Second, and unique to this approach, is that the metadata that explains each service and service connection is inherent in the semantics of the OWL domain model itself, making this representation largely self-annotating. We demonstrate our proposal by duplicating an existing, published bioinformatics analysis which we model as a domain concept in OWL. We use this OWL model to show how a variety of valid workflows can be automatically generated by simply changing the species of interest.

2   Materials and Methods

2.1   Technologies Used

SADI: Semantic Automated Discovery and Integration

SADI is a set of design patterns for Semantic Web Service publishing that differs from other projects in that it requires Web Service publishers to (a) consume and produce RDF natively; (b) model their input and output as OWL-DL classes, fully elaborated with the property-restrictions expected of incoming and output data; and (c) explicitly model the semantic relationship between input and output data through properties in the output class.

SHARE: Semantic Health And Research Environment.

SHARE is a specialized SPARQL-DL query engine that finds instances of an OWL class by recursively mapping property restrictions to SADI service invocations. For example, if a class called Homolog is defined using the value restriction ('is homologous to', uniprot:Q9UK53), SHARE will discover instances of Homolog by invoking SADI services that i) make 'is homologous to' statements about their input URIs, and ii) have an input OWL class matches an rdf:type of uniprot:Q9UK53. Building on this example, a class called InteractorOfHomolog could be defined using the value restriction ('interacts with', Homolog), and SHARE would resolve this class by i) finding instances of Homolog, then ii) using the discovered instances of Homolog as input to SADI services that make 'interacts with' statements. It is important to note that SHARE can only find instances of OWL classes that are defined using necessary and sufficient conditions. In addition, as SHARE currently utilizes reasoners that operate under the Open World Assumption (OWA) [29], certain types of property restrictions are not 'discoverable'. For example, SHARE cannot find instances of a OneHomolog class defined using the maximum cardinality restriction ('is homologous to' max 1), because it is not possible to prove the truth of a maximum cardinality restriction under the OWA, only the falsehood.

2.2   Target, Peer-Reviewed and Published Workflow

We selected the comparative genomics analysis and workflow of [16] as our target for abstraction, as diagrammed in Figure 1. The overall purpose of the workflow is to predict previously unknown protein-protein interactions [25], which are valuable for understanding the structure, signaling, and metabolic processes that occur within cells. The workflow predicts protein interactions by mapping known or probable interactions in one or more comparator species to a target species. The general principle is that if a particular pair of proteins is known to interact in one species, and two homologous (evolutionarily related) proteins exist in another species, then the latter pair of proteins is likely to interact as well. If homologous pairs of proteins exist in more than one comparator species, then the confidence of the prediction increases. In biology, homology is usually inferred from sequence similarity, and thus sequence comparison tools such as BLAST [26] or HMMer [27] represent important components of the workflow.

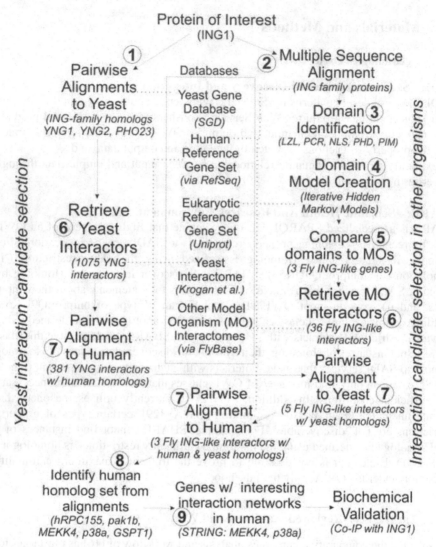

Fig. 1. Diagram of the conceptual workflow underlying the comparative genomics analysis of Gordon et al., taken directly from their publication (with permission) [16]. The workflow describes a bioinformatics analysis aimed at predicting protein-protein interactions in a lesser-characterized species based on comparison of protein sequences and interactions in a well-characterized species.

The workflow of Figure 1 was constructed by the original authors specifically for predicting interactors of the ING family of human proteins, but is generalizable for use with other proteins and species. In the first step, the human ING proteins are mapped to homologous proteins in the comparator organisms, yeast and fruitfly, which represent the two vertical branches of the diagram. In the left branch (yeast), the mapping of human proteins to homologs occurs in Step 1, whereas in the right branch (fruitfly) the mapping occurs in Steps 2-5. A detailed description of the semi-automated methods used for identifying homologs in each species is beyond the scope of this paper; however, for the purposes of this study, we will consider BLAST to be a suitable substitute, though likely at the cost of some sensitivity. After identifying homologs in the comparator species, probable interactors for the homologs are obtained from existing experimentally-derived interaction datasets for yeast and fruitfly (Step 6). Finally, the human homologs of the probable interactors are identified by sequence similarity (Steps 7 and 8), producing the predicted interactors for the human ING proteins. Step 9 is an optional filter step in which the scientist manually explores existing literature about the predicted interactors in order to select the best candidates for experimental validation.

In the following sections, the authors describe how the experimental environment was set-up to ensure that all necessary resources would be available to the automated workflow generation system (SHARE). We also ensure that the environment is generalized such that the workflow described above could be executed on any choice of input protein, target species, and two comparator species.

2.3   Selection and Deployment of Services

We first, in discussion with the author, delimited which analytical tools/algorithms were used in their original analysis with the goal of ensuring that corresponding SADI services were available. For those steps that did not exist as SADI services, services were written, deployed, and registered in the public SADI registry.

Figure 2A diagrams our hypothetical workflow for each comparator species; i.e., the workflow we anticipate our automated system will have to create. Each box represents a type of data, and each edge represents an algorithm and/or data source/species from or through which that data will be derived. Note that this workflow diagram does not simply describe the data-type based on its "nature" (e.g. "protein sequence", "dna sequence") but rather describes the data based on its "semantics" -its *role* in the overall workflow from the perspective of the domain-expert. This is important because we will now go on to explicitly model the semantics of each of these data elements -an undertaking that makes our approach to workflow abstraction distinct from any prior work of which we are aware.

Figure 2B shows the semantic model for the concept of a "Potential Interactor" -the semantic data-type that would result if the hypothetical model workflow in 2A were executed. This semantic model is then formalized into OWL-DL. The model shown in 2B is highly schematized for readability, as concepts within the model (e.g. homology) are extremely difficult to represent compactly (the OWL-DL model for BLAST-based homology was designed during the 2011 BioHackathon [17] as a collaboration between the SADI, SIO, and UniProt participants and can be viewed in its entirety here: [18,19]). Each component of the workflow was modeled in OWL-DL, and as such, at each step in the model it is only necessary to describe the relationship between the newly derived concept, and the concepts upon which it is based -as is typical in well-formed OWL, individual concepts are "modular" and "layered" [20]. In Figure 2B, however, we expand these more modular definitions somewhat to assist in showing the full semantics of the concept being modeled. Importantly for our discussion, the class-names are chosen to be familiar and meaningful to a biologist end-user, thus carrying semantics both in their class-names as well as in their more formal logical definition.

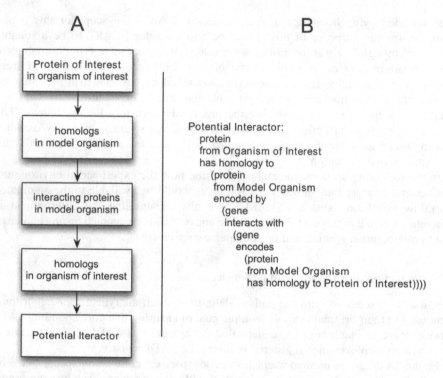

Fig. 2. The generalized workflow and (simplified) logical model. The generalized workflow in (A) describes how we migrate into, and out-of, each comparator species to determine likely interactors in the species of interest based on interactors in the comparator species. In (B) we show a highly simplified logical model that describes what a "Potential Interactor" is. It is a protein from a given organism that has homology to a protein in another organism, where the gene that codes for that protein has been annotated as interacting with the protein product of another gene, which has homology to a protein of interest.

```
ProbableInteractor:
has homology to (
      protein from ModelOrganism1... # similarly to Potential Interactor above
      protein from ModelOrganism2... # similarly to Potential Interactor above
)
```

Fig. 3. A subclass of **Potential Interactor** (Fig. 2) that requires homologous pairs of interacting proteins to exist in *both* **ModelOrganism1** and **ModelOrganism2**.

To achieve the comparative workflow from Gordon et al, it would be necessary to take the intersection of two "runs" of the workflow in Figure 2A to obtain only those results common to both comparator species, since this was a filtering step in the original analysis. In our study, we accomplish this by defining an OWL class called ProbableInteractor that is the intersection of two versions of the abstract Potential Interactor class, each referencing its own symbolic ModelOrganism class

(ModelOrganism1 and ModelOrganism2), but both referencing the same symbolic OrganismOfInterest class (Figure 3).

The components of our experiment, therefore, include an OWL model describing "the biology" of a Potential Interactor, in a generalized manner; and a set of SADI Semantic Web Services capable of generating the properties that define Potential Interactors.

3   Results and Discussion

To run the experiment, we created a small data-file containing the name of a protein of interest, and a set of target species, and the SPARQL query shown in Figure 4.

```
PREFIX interactions: <http://sadiframework.org/ontologies/InteractingProteins.owl#>
SELECT ?protein
FROM <file:/local/directory/workflow.input.n3>
WHERE {
    ?protein a interactions:MyPotentialInteractor .
}
```

```
@prefix interactions: <http://sadiframework.org/ontologies/InteractingProteins.owl#>.
@prefix uniprot: <http://purl.uniprot.org/uniprot/> .
@prefix sio: <http://semanticscience.org/resource/> .
@prefix taxon: <http://lsrn.org/taxon:> .

taxon:9606 a interactions:OrganismOfInterest . # human
uniprot:Q9UK53 a interactions:ProteinOfInterest . # ING1
taxon:4932 a interactions:ModelOrganism1 . # yeast
taxon:7227 a interactions:ModelOrganism2 . # fly
```

Fig. 4. The SPARQL query (top) that results in the workflow shown in Figure 5 and the local RDF/N3 data file referenced in the query (below), which specifies the organism and protein of interest and the 2 comparator model organisms

This SPARQL query was introduced to the SHARE client, and it was allowed to automatically build a workflow to resolve that query. SHARE finds instances of **ProbableInteractor** by loading data that binds the symbolic classes **OrganismOfInterest**, **ProteinOfInterest**, **ModelOrganism1**, and **ModelOrganism2** to the desired values via the SPARQL FROM clause (Figure 4). The result of SHARE execution is the workflow shown in Figure 5, which was synthesized automatically, and then executed by SHARE, populating a transient triple store, which was then used to resolve the SPARQL query itself. Of particular interest are the two distinct BLAST services selected near the beginning of the workflow -these were selected by SHARE based on precisely the same OWL model.   The difference in selection for each branch of the automatically-synthesized workflow is the result of the data-set loaded at run-time. The ability of SHARE to derive distinct workflows from the same OWL class is based on its perception of the value of ModelOrganism1 and ModelOrganism2 in the query, and the relationships in the ProbableInteractor class. For example, when ModelOrganism1 has the value taxon:7227, the look-up in the SADI registry becomes contextually constrained to only finding services related to *Drosophila*. In this way,

OWL has acted as an abstract workflow model, where the concretization of that workflow is decided depending on the context in which that Class finds itself at run-time; all that is required to adapt the workflow to a different protein of interest or a different model organism is to change the starting data.

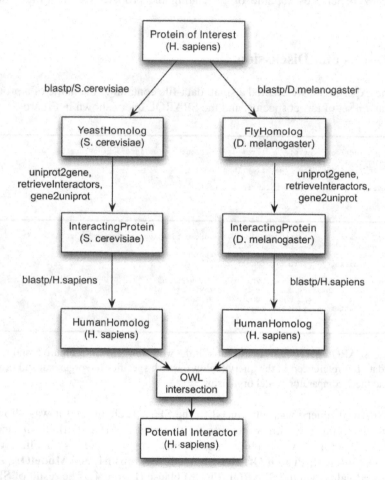

Fig. 5. The resulting workflow after SHARE has broken-down the OWL classes presented to it in the SPARQL query and mapped them, in context, on to relevant SADI Web Services

4   Conclusions

We have attempted to show that (a) OWL-DL domain-models can be used as abstract workflow templates, where the resulting workflow is capable of generating OWL individuals of that particular class (if such can exist), and (b) that that the semantics inherent in these domain-models can act as a form of annotation, such that the objectives, and the "purpose" of the data at any given step can be determined more intuitively through either the semantics of the class-name, or if necessary, the deeper semantics of the property restrictions that define that class. Our demonstration that, by changing the context of the Class (i.e. by presenting it with a different taxonomy identifier), we are able to derive a different workflow, provides strong evidence that, when the underlying resources are exposed as SADI Services, OWL descriptors carry sufficient semantics to act as *concretizable* workflow abstractions. Effectively, we achieved re-purposing of a workflow model (the OWL class itself) simply by putting that class into a new context. Since OWL classes are demonstrably sharable over the web, we believe that sharing workflows at this more abstract level might be more useful than the current paradigm of sharing the concretized workflow itself. Moreover, if the OWL is modeled in a modular and layered manner, the class-names and definitions at every depth provide the semantic meaning necessary to understand how each component of the workflow fits into the overall concept.

While we have not demonstrated that either of these successes improve the ability of end-users (in this case, biologists) to ask and answer complex domain questions through workflow re-use, we believe that additional tooling around such semantic abstractions might bring us considerably closer to achieving that goal.

References

1. Garijo, D., Gil, Y.: A New Approach for Publishing Workflows: Abstractions, Standards, and Linked Data. To appear in Proceedings of the Sixth Workshop on Workflows in Support of Large-Scale Science 2011, Held in Conjunction with SC 2011, Seattle, Washington (2011)
2. Goble, C.A., Bhagat, J., Aleksejevs, S., Cruickshank, D., Michaelides, D., Newman, D., Borkum, M., Bechhofer, S., Roos, M., Li, P., De Roure, D.: myExperiment: a repository and social network for the sharing of bioinformatics workflows. Nucleic Acids Research 38, W677–W682 (2010)
3. Oinn, T., Addis, M., Ferris, J., Marvin, D., Senger, M., Greenwood, M., Carver, T., Glover, K., Pocock, M.R., Wipat, A., Li, P.: Taverna: a tool for the composition and enactment of bioinformatics workflows. Bioinformatics 20, 3045–3054 (2004)
4. Goecks, J., Nekrutenko, A., Taylor, J.: Galaxy: a comprehensive approach for supporting accessible, reproducible, and transparent computational research in the life sciences. Genome Biology 11, R86 (2010)
5. Wohed, P., van der Aalst, W.M.P., Dumas, M., ter Hofstede, A.H.M.: Analysis of Web Services Composition Languages: The Case of BPEL4WS. In: Song, I.-Y., Liddle, S.W., Ling, T.-W., Scheuermann, P. (eds.) ER 2003. LNCS, vol. 2813, pp. 200–215. Springer, Heidelberg (2003)
6. Goderis, A., Sattler, U., Lord, P., Goble, C.A.: Seven Bottlenecks to Workflow Reuse and Repurposing. In: Gil, Y., Motta, E., Benjamins, V.R., Musen, M.A. (eds.) ISWC 2005. LNCS, vol. 3729, pp. 323–337. Springer, Heidelberg (2005)
7. Wilkinson, M., Links, M.: BioMOBY: an open source biological web services proposal. Briefings in Bioinformatics 3, 331–341 (2002)
8. Wilkinson, M.D., Senger, M., Kawas, E., Bruskiewich, R., Gouzy, J., et al.: Interoperability with Moby 1.0–it's better than sharing your toothbrush! Briefings in Bioinformatics 9, 220–231 (2008)

9. Lord, P., Bechhofer, S., Wilkinson, M.D., Schiltz, G., Gessler, D., Hull, D., Goble, C.A., Stein, L.: Applying Semantic Web Services to Bioinformatics: Experiences Gained, Lessons Learnt. In: McIlraith, S.A., Plexousakis, D., van Harmelen, F. (eds.) ISWC 2004. LNCS, vol. 3298, pp. 350–364. Springer, Heidelberg (2004)
10. Reich, M., Liefeld, T., Gould, J., Lerner, J., Tamayo, P., Mesirov, J.: GenePattern 2.0. Nature Genetics 38, 500–501 (2006)
11. Gil, Y., Ratnakar, V., Kim, J., González-Calero, P.A., Groth, P.T., Moody, J., Deelman, E.: Wings: Intelligent Workflow-Based Design of Computational Experiments. To appear in IEEE Intelligent Systems (2011)
12. Gil, Y., Groth, P., Ratnakar, V., Fritz, C.: Expressive Reusable Workflow Templates. In: Proc. 5th IEEE Int'l Conf. E-Science, pp. 344–351. IEEE Press (2009)
13. Hauder, M., Gil, Y., Sethi, R., Liu, Y., Jo, H.: Making Data Analysis Expertise Broadly Accessible through Workflows. To appear in Proceedings of the Sixth Workshop on Workflows in Support of Large-Scale Science, Held in Conjunction with SC 2011, Seattle, Washington (2011)
14. Wilkinson, M.D., Vandervalk, B., McCarthy, L.: The Semantic Automated Discovery and Integration (SADI) Web service Design-Pattern, API and Reference Implementation. Journal of Biomedical Semantics 2, 8 (2011)
15. Vandervalk, B.P., McCarthy, E.L., Wilkinson, M.D.: SHARE: A Semantic Web Query Engine for Bioinformatics. In: Gómez-Pérez, A., Yu, Y., Ding, Y. (eds.) ASWC 2009. LNCS, vol. 5926, pp. 367–369. Springer, Heidelberg (2009)
16. Gordon, P.M.K., Soliman, M.A., Bose, P., Trinh, Q., Sensen, C.W., Riabowol, K.: Interspecies data mining to predict novel ING-protein interactions in human. BMC Genomics 9, 426 (2008)
17. BioHackaton (2011), http://2011.biohackathon.org/
18. BLAST RDF Model, https://github.com/dbcls/bh11/wiki/BLAST-output-as-RDF
19. http://sadiframework.org/ontologies/blast.owl
20. ODP - semanticscience - SIO Ontology Design Principles, Scientific Knowledge Discovery, http://code.google.com/p/semanticscience/wiki/ODP
21. Pesic, M., Schonenberg, H., van der Aalst, W.M.P.: DECLARE: Full Support for Loosely-Structured Processes. In: 11th IEEE International Enterprise Distributed Object Computing Conference (EDOC 2007), p. 287 (2007)
22. Lamprecht, A.-L., Naujokat, S., Margaria, T., Steffen, B.: Synthesis-Based Loose Programming. In: 2010 Seventh International Conference on the Quality of Information and Communications Technology, pp. 262–267 (2010)
23. Montali, M., Pesic, M., van der Aalst, W.M.P., Chesani, F., Mello, P., Storari, S.: Declarative Specification and Verification of Service Choreographies. ACM Transactions on the Web 4, 1 (2009)
24. Clarke, E.M., Grumberg, O., Peled, D.: Model Checking. MIT Press (1997)
25. De Las Rivas, J., Fontanillo, C.: Protein-protein interactions essentials: key concepts to building and analyzing interactome networks. PLoS Computational Biology 6, 6 (2010)
26. Altschul, S.F., Gish, W., Miller, W., Myers, E.W., Lipman, D.J.: Blast local alignment search tool. Journal of Molecular Biology 215(3), 403–410 (1990)
27. Finn, R.D., Clements, J., Eddy, S.R.: HMMER web server: interactive sequence similarity searching. Nucleic Acids Research 39, W29–W37 (2011)
28. Goderis, A.: Workflow Re-use and Discovery in Bioinformatics. PhD Thesis, School of Computer Science, The University of Manchester (2008)
29. Baader, F.: The Description Logic Handbook: Theory, Implementation, and Applications, 2nd edn. Cambridge University Press (2003)

Processes and Data Integration
in the Networked Healthcare

Andrea Braun von Reinersdorff[1], Tiziana Margaria[2], and Christoph Rasche[3]

[1] Chair of Management in Healthcare Systems, Hochschule Osnabrück, Germany
Braun@wi.hs-osnabrueck.de
[2] Chair of Service and Software Engineering, University Potsdam, Germany
margaria@cs.uni-potsdam.de
[3] Chair of Management, Professional Services and Sports Economics, University
Potsdam, Germany
christoph.rasche@uni-potsdam.de

In the past decade, state-of-the-art Information and Communication Technology
(ICT) has gained a strong standing in all aspects of healthcare provision and
management. As already discussed in the ISoLA-Med workshop in Potsdam in
June 2009 [1], a set of innovative research topics related to the future of healthcare systems hinge on the notion of simplicity as a driving paradigm in ICT
development, maintenance and use. We believe that the philosophy of *consis-
tently applied simplicity* is strategically important to make advanced healthcare
provision accessible ad keep it affordable to patients and to society, yet the discipline of simplicity is still poorly understood and rarely systematically applied.

Instead, design principles attempt to focus on increased functionality within
thinly disguised complexity, often at the expense of life cycle costs and total cost
of ownership issues (e.g., training, system malfunctions, system upgrades). Often
designers are unaware of the tradeoffs and impacts. With the increased use of ICT
in such socially critical areas such as Health Care, society can no longer afford
systems that do not perform as specified. We believe that an understanding of
simplicity is the key. Simplicity is foundational, its essence fundamental to many
desired characteristics of ICT systems such as reliability, usability and trust.
This has been studied in the course of the ITSy project [6], a EU FET Support
Action that in 2010-2011 conducted a community-oriented research that involved
multidisciplinary experts to assist in surveying key research communities about
their understandings and vision of the philosophy of simplicity.

In order to illustrate the economic and business perspective in both of the
above described dimensions, in this track we consider several facets of the healthcare sector with their high potential for IT-based process optimization - a must
under the increasingly tight budget conditions. It spans standard office functionality (accounting, human resources, communication, . . .), as well as more
critical control scenarios as they appear in Assisted Living Environments, like
remote health control, detection of accidents, finding of lost patients, etc. - typical scenarios for our investigations in the Potsdam Ambient Assisted Living
initiative.

At the EU as well as at the national level, several initiatives concentrate
around the two central sectors: healthcare and the ageing population. For

T. Margaria and B. Steffen (Eds.): ISoLA 2012, Part II, LNCS 7610, pp. 67–69, 2012.
© Springer-Verlag Berlin Heidelberg 2012

example, in the German Theseus Initiative [7] that recently terminated and mobilized over 300 Mio Euro in the past 3 years, the choice of the first integrated application was in the health care sector. This choice was selected due to the problem of rapidly expanding healthcare costs. It also was innovative by using a remote medical expert consultation scenario. This domain is particularly suitable for investigation because it is centrally positioned within the so called TIME-value chain, that originates from the convergence of the Telecommunication, Information, Media and Entertainment industries. These four core industries lie at the heart of the information age (the fifth Kondratieff cycle) and trigger the sixth Kondratieff cycle (the coming age of healthcare and wellness) in terms of pioneering digital healthcare solutions to promote telemedicine and assisted ambient living concepts. The acceptance and market penetration of the latter are highly dependent on smart, simple, intuitive and appealing customer solutions contributing to life quality, self empowerment and cost efficiency. Simplicity is here core to knowledge and competence building, resulting in sustainable competitive advantages. Corporate staff must be enabled and empowered to design, engineer, implement and adapt their knowledge process in an agile, robust and smart way without being prisoners of overarching over-engineered systems and of IT lock-in philosophies.

Current hot issues that will shape the competitiveness of the European ICT in the next few decades and which require investigation from the perspective of *simplicity in IT* at the networked system level revolve around the notion of simplicity and its elevation to a design paradigm including:

- Balancing IT-aspirations with user demands: How to bridge the widening gap between software engineers and front-end clients.
- From sophisticated to smart technologies: User empowerment through simplicity, manageability, adaptability, robustness, and target group focus.
- Handing-over IT power to the co-value creating customers: Users as process designers, owners and change agents.
- Competing for the future: Sketching-out viable IT-roadmaps for multiple strategy.

Thinking in processes starts more easily in those sectors of medicine that are under the highest pressure of complexity and urgency: the emergency room and the surgical theater. There we see the technologically most advanced systems help the medical staff to cope with the parallel and heterogeneous needs they continuously face. As a successful prominent example we refer to the new thinking about processes in the emergency department proposed by Dr. Barbara Hogan, President elect of EuSEM, the European Society for Emergency Medicine [3] with her "First View" concept.

In the age of an upcoming service-based economy, many traditional questions take new shades due to the new possibilities offered by the modern IT and to the legal and ethical issues that the handling of data and knowledge in a networked world bears. How can we efficiently and legally manage and share the medical and diagnostic knowledge, the patients' data? How to manage the handling of administered treatments on the medical side, as well as under their aspect of an economic transaction that includes a supply chain and complex billing and clearing operations that span a network of stakeholders?

The papers and the panel in this track address exactly these needs, with a special attention to the process integration and simplification needed in the different aspects of diagnosis as in policlinic processes for outpatients [5], healthcare management and provision in the cloud [4], and manageable accounting and billing systems at the border between preventive and rehabilitative professional training [2].

References

1. ISoLA-Med 2009: 1st International isola Symposium on Structural Changes and Market Dynamics in the Healthcare Sector, Potsdam, Germany (June 2009), http://www.cs.uni-potsdam.de/isola-med-2009/?id=home
2. Doedt, M., Göke, T., Pardo, J., Steffen, B.: Reha-Sports: The Challenge of Small Margin Healthcare Accounting. In: Margaria, T., Steffen, B. (eds.) ISoLA 2012, Part II. LNCS, vol. 7610, pp. 75–77. Springer, Heidelberg (2012)
3. Hogan, B.: Leading an ed using industrial lean management and intelligent management technology to speed up emergency department procederes, http://www.ecare.be/images/stories/downloads/DrHogan_leading_an_ED.pdf
4. Holubek, A., Metzger, C.: Considerations for Healthcare Applications in a Platform as a Service Environment. In: Margaria, T., Steffen, B. (eds.) ISoLA 2012, Part II. LNCS, vol. 7610, pp. 73–74. Springer, Heidelberg (2012)
5. Margaria, T., Boßelmann, S., Kujath, B.: Simple Modeling of Executable Role-Based Workflows: An Application in the Healthcare Domain. In: Margaria, T., Steffen, B. (eds.) ISoLA 2012, Part II. LNCS, vol. 7610, pp. 70–72. Springer, Heidelberg (2012)
6. Project. Itsy - it simply works! http://www.cs.uni-potsdam.de/sse/ITSy/
7. Project. Theseus, new technologies for the internet of services. funded by the Federal Ministry of Economics and Technology, http://theseus-programm.de/en/about.php

Simple Modeling of Executable Role-Based Workflows: An Application in the Healthcare Domain

Tiziana Margaria, Steve Boßelmann, and Bertold Kujath

Institut für Informatik, Universität Potsdam
August-Bebel-Str. 89, 14482 Potsdam, Germany
{margaria,bossel,kujath}@cs.uni-potsdam.de

Abstract. Process modeling has developed to an established technique facilitating and supporting the documentation, analysis and automation of workflows. As in common practice workflow modeling requires immediate contribution of participants that lack broad knowledge of formal models as well as software engineering skills, simplicity of the selected modeling approach throughout each step of the design phase is a key factor for the success of a workflow management project. We present an approach that combines simplicity in the modeling phase with the feasibility of immediate evaluation via execution to rapidly develop systems supporting role-based workflows. Finally, we discuss practicability and benefits of this approach based on an exemplary case study of processes in the healthcare domain.

Keywords: process modeling, healthcare clinical processes workflow management, business process management, model-driven software development, simplicity, rapid prototyping.

1 Introduction

The core of any workflow are the people living it, i.e. carrying out each single task by means of everyday work. Hence, in order to capture the logic of a domain-specific workflow and in order to develop a system that supports we propose an approach that privileges *simplicity*: if it is easy to understand, even non-IT experts can contribute. A model-driven process-oriented approach has immediate benefits ranging from the possibility of simulation and verification to rapid prototyping of custom-tailored solutions. Although this seems to be obvious, this approach has not been widely adopted so far. Despite the rise of a Business Process Management (BPM) school of thought in organizations, the majority of their processes are not supported by systems relying on explicit process models. Although most of the adopted information systems are process-aware in some manner, they focus on common, generic enterprise processes and most of their functionality is buried within the hard-coded core of the application. At the same time, the adoption of enterprise systems has increasingly attracted attention in the healthcare domain in recent years [1].

T. Margaria and B. Steffen (Eds.): ISoLA 2012, Part II, LNCS 7610, pp. 70–72, 2012.
© Springer-Verlag Berlin Heidelberg 2012

In contrast, we present an approach that focuses on simplicity but is yet powerful enough to allow for rapid creation of solutions that support domain-specific processes. Recently, the notion of simplicity as a driving paradigm in information system development has been explicitly identified as an important research topic, yet poorly understood [2]. In the workflow context we aim at keeping the design simple in order to involve those people that best know the observed workflow and to achieve consistency between the created process model and reality. In fact, this means preserving simplicity throughout each of the design steps spanning process modeling as well as testing and evaluation, which as a whole support a step-by-step ripening of the workflow model.

We live up to this claim by leveraging the jABC Framework [3] and the advantageous characteristics of its architecture following the eXtreme Model Driven Design (XMDD) approach [4]. The jABC facilitates workflow modeling by designing processes as a composition of configurable domain-specific components, so called Service Independent Building Blocks (SIBs). In a workflow context, these SIBs represent discrete tasks familiar to the users, to be arranged along the process' control flow. Furthermore the framework supports immediate testing and evaluation, as the models specified this way are executable by means of service calls along the modeled control flow. Hence, any workflow system or role-based task list that provides an adequate service interface might be used as the service providing system to be interacted with during execution.

2 Case Study: Diabetes Day-Care Clinic

We present a case study of our approach by means of its application on healthcare processes of a diabetes day care clinic at a large hospital in Berlin. Here we focus on policlinical workflows as they are best structured and have a high repetition rate. They cover a patient's sequential pass through three discrete operational stages of the clinic, which are the outpatient reception, patient care, and medical examination. The clinic management has already used ARIS [5] for creating workflow models based on the syntax of Event-driven Process Chains (EPCs) [6] in previous projects and decided to stick with this approach in order to preserve consistency. Hence we are able to present a comparison of ARIS models and jABC models based on the same workflows. We thereby focus on simplicity in the design phase as well as readability of the models by means of typical users. Finally, we show that by focusing on core requirements the rapid creation of solutions supporting domain-specific processes does not need to be complex. In particular, the initial design step as well as the evaluation via execution following our approach is simple for any workflow practitioner without knowledge of formal models.

References

1. Li, L., Ge, R.-L., Zhou, S.-M., Valerdi, R.: Guest editorial integrated healthcare information systems. IEEE Transactions on Information Technology in Biomedicine 16(4), 515–517 (2012)

2. Margaria, T., Steffen, B.: Simplicity as a Driver for Agile Innovation. Computer 43(6), 90–92 (2010)
3. Steffen, B., Margaria, T., Nagel, R., Jörges, S., Kubczak, C.: Model-Driven Development with the jABC. In: Bin, E., Ziv, A., Ur, S. (eds.) HVC 2006. LNCS, vol. 4383, pp. 92–108. Springer, Heidelberg (2007)
4. Margaria, T., Steffen, B.: Service-Orientation: Conquering Complexity with XMDD. In: Hinchey, M., Coyle, L. (eds.) Conquering Complexity. Springer (2012)
5. Scheer, A.-W.: ARIS. Vom Geschäftsprozess zum Anwendungssystem, p. 20. Springer (2002)
6. van der Aalst, W.: Formalization and Verification of Event-driven Process Chains. Information & Software Technology 41(10), 639–650 (1999)

Considerations for Healthcare Applications in a Platform as a Service Environment

Andreas Holubek and Christian Metzger

Arlanis Software AG, Potsdam, Germany
{andreas.holubek,christian.metzger}@arlanis.com

Abstract. With the introduction of software as a service projects a fundamental change for the world of the IT services and also for the development of software systems goes on. One of the major challenges for today's companies is to detect and manage this change and business development. This are not only IT provided internal considerations, but must also be considered for business processes. Software as a service and platform as a service seems at first glance to have only advantages. Users do not need to install software anymore and also the maintenance is eliminated. Developers do not have to worry longer about infra-structure, software requirements and distribution of the results. It seems the perfect world for everyone. But special considerations must be taken into account when developing software for health care and medical solutions. Not only must such software meet highest security standards patient data must never be compromised or altered unobserved. The primary example under discussion consists of a clinic portal with numerous collaboration possibilities for surgeons.

The first question in traditional system development is for the components to be used. This means both hardware and software. This includes for example the question according to the database, the operating system, application server, or also the programming language. All this requires many decisions and a high risk, which affect the development process of the application much later already in advance.

With the introduction of the cloud and service platforms all of these decisions are moved to the operator of the platform. The selection of the appropriate platform remains for us as system architects, and application developers. This means a comfortable situation for the projects decision maker. However, a later change between platforms is not easily possible.

One of the advantages of a service platform is that infrastructure and platform are provided globally for all users. Modifications allow for adaptations to special requirements. Accordingly, a considerable part of software development consists of the definition of required components in the platform metadata.

To develop healthcare applications on a platform, special challenges are faced for the architecture. A big difference is added in the health sector. Here, security issues and the location of the data play a larger role. In the full paper we will discuss this in more detail. A first insight is that it requires not only a single platform. Due to the still existing, identifiable specialization of the platforms we need to connect the strengths from multiple platforms together. In addition, we must comply with common international standards such as HIPAA compliance and FDA compliance.

T. Margaria and B. Steffen (Eds.): ISoLA 2012, Part II, LNCS 7610, pp. 73–74, 2012.
© Springer-Verlag Berlin Heidelberg 2012

In the case study we consider, the client is one of the leading companies in the development of integrated medical software systems. The client at its sites already deploys salesforce.com. An exclusive portal for doctors, especially neurosurgeons, should be developed on this basisfor the professional exchange of experience. It should work similar to a social network (see Fig. 1).

Salesforce.com is by default suitable for the management of users and their rights. The platform comes in the handling of large medical image data sets to the borders. For this reason, Amazon's simple storage services (S3) and Amazon Elastic cloud computing (EC2) for these aspects are involved. The use of a Microsoft Silverlight component in the force.com platform is introduced for the integration of the two platforms in the same project. Silverlight in turn should then communicate by exchanging SOAP messages with S3 and the user interface, as well as processing of image sequences.The architecture of the final system is shown in Fig. 2.

Fig. 1. Home screen after successful login of a doctor

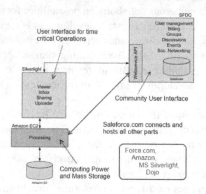

Fig. 2. Architecture of the project at a glance: community for doctors

Reha-Sports: The Challenge
of Small Margin Healthcare Accounting

Markus Doedt[1], Thomas Göke[2], Jan Pardo[1], and Bernhard Steffen[1]

[1] TU Dortmund University,
Dortmund, Germany
{markus.doedt,jan.pardo}@tu-dortmund.de,
steffen@cs.tu-dortmund.de
http://www.tu-dortmund.de
[2] sysTeam GmbH,
Dortmund, Germany
thomas.goeke@systeam-gmbh.com
http://www.systeam-gmbh.com

Abstract. The paper presents the development of a Web-based accounting system for rehabilitation sports, which, due to the small margins, requires a very economical approach, both for its development and for its later use. The development process was therefore driven by simplicity in two dimension: the accounting process itself was reduced to the minimum under the given legal circumstances, and the software development was clearly guided by total cost of ownership concerns. In particular, standards where taken and artifacts reused wherever possible.

Keywords: Simplicity, Software reuse, Web applications, Accounting, Healthcare, Rehabilitation sports.

1 Introduction

It is a new trend in the German healthcare system to actively involve the patients themselves and to try to improve their health conditions by changing their lifestyles. Reha-sports is one such initiative. It has the goal to educate disabled people or people with a risk of suffering from disability (i.e. everybody in fact) to be more active and to regularly exercise their bodies. This way Reha-ports participants should experience the impact of their own contribution to their health, be it for rehabilitation or simply to preserve/improve their health by regular sports exercises. Ideally, they should achieve a better feeling for their body and improve the quality of their lives in the long term. Due to the Code of Social Law ("Sozialgesetzbuch") every German individual has a right to benefit from rehasports if certain indications are given. The expenses of rehasports have to be borne by the statutory health insurances.

A general specification of Reha-sports has been set up by the German association of statutory health insurances together with various associations of Reha-sports providers. This general agreement describes for example how and

T. Margaria and B. Steffen (Eds.): ISoLA 2012, Part II, LNCS 7610, pp. 75–77, 2012.

how often Reha-sports sessions have to be exercised, who might be certified as a Reha-sports provider, and which basic accounting process has to be followed[1].

For patients with neck or back pain, too weak muscles or too high percentages of body fat, a typical prescription consists of about 50 sessions of Reha-sports. The Reha-sports patient may take this description to any certified Reha-sports provider in order to exercise there free of charge. (S)he only has to confirm participation by signing a special signature form. The Reha-sports provider can then send an invoice to the corresponding statutory health insurance together with this signature form and the description in order to get refunded. Organizing this process of accounting for their typically 300-600 patients is quite painful for Reha-sports providers, as there are almost 200 different statutory health insurances which need to be treated individually. In fact, due to the various frame conditions it is almost impossible without computer support: e.g., accounts can be sent only if a certain number of exercising sessions have been taken, and for economical reason it would be beneficial to bundle accounts for one and the same health insurance.

In this paper we present the development of a web-based accounting system for rehabilitation sports, which, due to the small margins, requires a very economical approach, both for its development and for its later use. The development process was therefore driven by simplicity in two dimension: the accounting process itself was reduced to the minimum under the given legal circumstances, and the software development was clearly guided by total cost of ownership concerns. In particular, standards where taken and artifacts reused wherever possible.

In particular, the paper sketches how the experience with an existing web application called "Rehasportzentrale" influenced the development of the new web application in its goal to simplify the accounting process. Not only was it possible to profit from the knowledge about the current bottlenecks of "Rehasportzentrale", but also from the wealth of already collected data concerning the rehasports participants, statutory health insurances, prescriptions, and also date, time and signatures for every rehasports session. As one of its important process optimizations, the new application automates the secure transfer of these data between the involved participants based on a clean roles, rights, and access management. This does not only simply the communication process itself, but it also the corresponding bookkeeping. It is now easy to reliably track, who got which information at what time, which is important in case something went wrong.

The development of the new web application was driven by simplicity as a major concern. Of course, the new application should simplify the life of its users, but simplicity of the software itself was also very important:

- The small margins did not allow any fancy development, and require a strictly cost cost of ownership-oriented. approach.
- Time to market war very essential, to exploit the early mover advantage in a new business area.
- Agility of a simple solutions war rated higher than perfectionism, concerning coverage issues and beauty. In particular, being able to cover potential future request was rated higher than a 100% match of today's requirements.

Throughout the paper we will emphasize simplicity as an essential and currently more and more prominent design principle (cf. [2, 4, 6]). Its impact on the user side is evident e.g. from Apple's enormous success with products like iMac, iPod, iPhone, iPad, ..., and it gradually enters system development, in particular in cases where fast results and flexibility are in the foreground. Here, the so-called 80/20 approach is central, meaning that often 80% of the requirements can be achieved with only 20% of effort. In fact, in system development, the numbers are even more striking, and one could easily speak of 90/10 approaches, as solutions close to current standards can often be realized in very short time, whereas deviations from those standards may be extremely costly. The project described here illustrates the success of such a KISS ("Keep it simple, stupid") approach.

In order to implement the software product in a simple way the eXtreme Model Driven Design (XMMD) approach has been followed, which achieves simplicity by combining service-orientation [5] with the "One Thing Approach" [3]. This supports strict separation of concerns while enforcing consistency between the design steps of the various involved roles.

References

[1] BAR - Bundesarbeitsgemeinschaft für Rehabilitation: Rahmenvereinbarung über den Rehabilitationssport und das Funktionstraining (2011), http://www.kbv.de/rechtsquellen/2610.html

[2] Margaria, T., Floyd, B., Steffen, B.: It simply works: Simplicity and embedded systems design. In: 2011 IEEE 35th Annual Computer Software and Applications Conference Workshops (COMPSACW), pp. 194–199 (July 2011)

[3] Margaria, T., Steffen, B.: Business Process Modelling in the jABC: The One-Thing Approach. In: Handbook of Research on Business Process Modeling. IGI Global (2009)

[4] Margaria, T., Steffen, B.: Simplicity as a driver for agile innovation. Computer 43(6), 90–92 (2010)

[5] Margaria, T., Steffen, B., Reitenspiess, M.: Service-Oriented Design: The Roots. In: Benatallah, B., Casati, F., Traverso, P. (eds.) ICSOC 2005. LNCS, vol. 3826, pp. 450–464. Springer, Heidelberg (2005), http://dx.doi.org/10.1007/11596141_34, 10.1007

[6] Merten, M., Steffen, B.: Simplicity driven application development. In: Proceedings of Society for Design & Process Science, SDPS 2012 (2012)

Timing Constraints: Theory Meets Practice

Björn Lisper[1], Johan Nordlander[2], and Sophie Quinton[3]

[1] School of Innovation, Design, and Engineering, Mälardalen University,
SE-721 23 Västerås, Sweden
[2] Department of Computer Science, Electrical and Space Engineering,
Luleå University of Technology, SE-971 87 Luleå, Sweden
[3] Institute of Computer Network and Engineering, TU Braunschweig, Germany

Many embedded systems must satisfy *timing requirements*, which describe how these systems should behave with respect to timing. Such requirements must be dealt with throughout the system development process: from their initial specification, expressed at an abstract level, through the increasingly concrete layers, to the final implementation level. There is a growing awareness that this process needs support from languages, tools, and methodologies.

The term "timing constraint" encompasses timing requirements, which describe how a system should behave, as well as timing properties which describe how the system really behaves. Languages for defining timing constraints allow checking the consistency of specifications and verifying the correctness of implementations with respect to requirements, by both formal means and testing. The AUTOSAR timing extensions provide an example of a domain-specific timing constraint language for automotive systems, but general principles for the design of suitable timing constraint languages are sorely needed.

This track aims to bring together researchers and practitioners who are interested in all aspects of timing constraint languages, including their syntactic and semantic formulation, probabilistic or weakly-hard variants, industrial case studies using timing constraints, tools and methods for verification of properties expressed in timing constraint languages, and methodologies for the use of such languages and tools in the system development process.

Three of the track contributions deal with the Timing Augmented Description Language (TADL) [3], which has been adopted by EAST-ADL and forms the basis for the timing extensions of AUTOSAR. In [5], a small first-order logic is defined. This logic can express timing constraints very succinctly, and it can be used to describe the semantics for timing constraint languages like TADL. [8] develops *generalized weakly-hard constraints*: such timing constraints specify that a condition on the timing is to hold at least n out of m times. An extension of TADL with such timing constraints is proposed. In [7], proposed novel features of TADL such as symbolic timing expressions and multiple time bases are demonstrated on an industrial case study.

Two track contributions consider the formal verification of timing constraints. In [6], Timed Observational Transition Systems are used to model and verify the TESLA source authentication protocol. [2] proposes to translate timing constraints expressed in the MARTE RTS modeling language into Timed Petri Nets for verification by model checking.

T. Margaria and B. Steffen (Eds.): ISoLA 2012, Part II, LNCS 7610, pp. 78–79, 2012.

Finally, two track contributions consider code-level timing analysis. [4] describes the Worst-Case Execution Time (WCET) analysis tool CalcWcet167, which has been extensively used in WCET analysis research at TU Vienna. In [1], the abstract-interpretation based WCET analysis technique of *abstract execution* is extended to a class of event-driven, concurrent programs.

In conclusion, this track presents contributions focusing on various aspects of timing constraints, from expressiveness issues to verification methods. This illustrates some of the current research directions in the domain.

References

1. Birken, K.: Abstract Execution for Event-Driven Systems – An Application from Automotive/Infotainment Development. In: Margaria, T., Steffen, B. (eds.) ISoLA 2012, Part II. LNCS, vol. 7610, pp. 173–186. Springer, Heidelberg (2012)
2. Ge, N., Pantel, M., Crégut, X.: Formal Specification and Verification of Task Time Constraints for Real-Time Systems. In: Margaria, T., Steffen, B. (eds.) ISoLA 2012, Part II. LNCS, vol. 7610, pp. 143–157. Springer, Heidelberg (2012)
3. Johansson, R., Frey, P., Jonsson, J., Nordlander, J., Pathan, R.M., Feiertag, N., Schlager, M., Espinoza, H., Richter, K., Kuntz, S., Lönn, H., Kolagari, R.T., Blom, H.: TADL: Timing augmented description language, version 2. Technical report (October 2009)
4. Kirner, R.: The WCET Analysis Tool CalcWcet167. In: Margaria, T., Steffen, B. (eds.) ISoLA 2012, Part II. LNCS, vol. 7610, pp. 158–172. Springer, Heidelberg (2012)
5. Lisper, B., Nordlander, J.: A Simple and Flexible Timing Constraint Logic. In: Margaria, T., Steffen, B. (eds.) ISoLA 2012, Part II. LNCS, vol. 7610, pp. 80–95. Springer, Heidelberg (2012)
6. Ouranos, I., Ogata, K., Stefaneas, P.: Formal Analysis of TESLA Protocol in the Timed OTS/CafeOBJ Method. In: Margaria, T., Steffen, B. (eds.) ISoLA 2012, Part II. LNCS, vol. 7610, pp. 126–142. Springer, Heidelberg (2012)
7. Peraldi-Frati, M.-A., Goknil, A., Adedjouma, M., Gueguen, P.-Y.: Modeling a BSG-E Automotive System with the Timing Augmented Description Language. In: Margaria, T., Steffen, B. (eds.) ISoLA 2012, Part II. LNCS, vol. 7610, pp. 111–125. Springer, Heidelberg (2012)
8. Quinton, S., Ernst, R.: Generalized Weakly-Hard Constraints. In: Margaria, T., Steffen, B. (eds.) ISoLA 2012, Part II. LNCS, vol. 7610, pp. 96–100. Springer, Heidelberg (2012)

A Simple and Flexible Timing Constraint Logic

Björn Lisper[1] and Johan Nordlander[2]

[1] School of Innovation, Design, and Engineering, Mälardalen University,
SE-721 23 Västerås, Sweden
[2] Department of Computer Science, Electrical and Space Engineering,
Luleå University of Technology, SE-971 87 Luleå, Sweden

Abstract. Formats for describing timing behaviors range from fixed menus of standard patterns, to fully open-ended behavioral definitions; of which some may be supported by formal semantic underpinnings, while others are better characterized as primarily informal notations. Timing descriptions that allow flexible extension within a fully formalized framework constitute a particularly interesting area in this respect.

We present a small logic for expressing timing constraints in such an open-ended fashion, sprung out of our work with timing constraint semantics in the TIMMO-2-USE project [15]. The result is a non-modal, first-order logic over reals and sets of reals, which references the constrained objects solely in terms of event occurrences. Both finite and infinite behaviors may be expressed, and a core feature of the logic is the ability to restrict any constraint to just the finite ranges when a certain system mode is active.

Full syntactic and semantic definitions of our formula language are given, and as an indicator of its expressiveness, we show how to express all constraint forms currently defined by TIMMO-2-USE and AUTOSAR. A separate section deals with the support for mode-dependencies that have been proposed for both frameworks, and we demonstrate by an example how our generic mode-restriction mechanism formalizes the details of such an extension.

1 Introduction

Timing behavior descriptions exist in many different forms. Classical real-time scheduling theory defines the basic *periodic* and *sporadic* patterns to describe task activations, along with the simple notion of *relative deadlines* for capturing the desired behavior of a system's response. Digital circuits are often accompanied by *timing diagrams* [4], where selected scenarios from an infinitely repeating behavior are depicted graphically, specifically indicating the minimum and maximum distances between key events. In the automotive domain, the model-based development frameworks of AUTOSAR [6] and EAST-ADL [8] offer a rich palette of *built-in timing patterns* and constraints, commonly specified in terms of typical-case timing diagrams. On the theoretical side, *temporal* and *real-time logics* concentrate on a few basic building blocks, from which more complex timing formulae can be constructed using logical connectives.

T. Margaria and B. Steffen (Eds.): ISoLA 2012, Part II, LNCS 7610, pp. 80–95, 2012.
© Springer-Verlag Berlin Heidelberg 2012

The timing models of classical scheduling theory are well-understood, but limited in expressiveness and essentially closed — even though they have been successfully extended with notions such as jitter and release offsets, every extension has to show that it also can be understood and analyzed in ways that mirror the original theory. As a contrast, graphical timing diagrams appear inherently open-ended, but this is primarily the consequence of a lack of rigor in this informal notation. AUTOSAR and EAST-ADL can express some very complex timing behaviors, but pay the price of being both informal as well as closed to extension. A formal foundation for the timing constructs of both languages has previously been defined by the TIMMO-2-USE project, but extensibility of this foundation has so far not been addressed.

This paper contributes a retake on the TIMMO-2-USE formalization effort, by means of a *timing constraint logic* that is able to express all existing constraints, while also acting as a toolbox for building new and open-ended forms of well-defined timing behaviors. The logic, called *TiCL* (Timing Constraint Logic), is similar to existing real-time logics in this respect, but differs in the following important ways:

- TiCL is a logic of *pure timing constraints*. It does not attempt to express any functional properties of the systems it constrains, and it only interfaces to the latter via the notion of *event occurrences*. This separation of concerns is central to the ability to blend with EAST-ADL and AUTOSAR, whose complex semantics does not yet allow full formalization of functional behavior.
- TiCL is not a modal logic. In fact, TiCL just represents a carefully chosen selection of operators from a standard first-order logic over the real numbers and real number sets.
- TiCL is not restricted to infinite behaviors only. Finite behaviors can be expressed with ease, and one of the strengths of TiCL is a mechanism for restricting a generic constraint to just the finite ranges when a certain system *mode* is active.

In Section 2 we introduce introduce TADL, a language for timing constraints that was defined in the TIMMO project and has influenced the AUTOSAR Timing Extensions. We then define the syntax and semantics of TiCL in Section 3, establish some convenient notational short-hands (Section 4), and show how current TADL and AUTOSAR constraints are captured (Section 5). The mechanism for interpreting mode-dependencies is explained in Section 6. We discuss related work in Section 7. Verification and analysis issues are beyond the scope of the current paper, but the topic will be returned to in the concluding discussion (Section 8).

2 TADL

The *Timing Augmented Description Language* (TADL) [10] is a constraint language for describing timing requirements and properties within the automotive domain. It was originally defined in the TIMMO project, and is now being revised and formalized within the TIMMO-2-USE project: TiCL is an outcome of this work. The syntax of TADL is compliant to the AUTOSAR meta-model, but the TADL constraints can also be understood through a textual syntax.

TADL defines constraints on *events*, which are simply (finite or infinite) sequences of strictly increasing times. The definition does not specify whether times are integers or reals: the constraints have meaningful interpretations in both cases. An element in an event is an *occurrence* of the event.

TADL's constraints, as defined in [10], can be divided into three groups: *repetition rate constraints*, which concern single events, *delay constraints*, which concern the timing relation between *stimuli* and *responses*, and *synchronization constraints*, that require that corresponding occurrences of a group of events appear in sufficiently tight clusters.

All repetition rate constraints can be seen as instances of a *generic repetition rate constraint*. Such a constraint is specified by four parameters *lower*, *upper*, *,jitter*, and *span*. An event $\langle t_1, t_2, \ldots \rangle$ satisfies a generic repetition rate constraint iff there exists an sequence of times $\langle x_1, x_2, \ldots \rangle$ such that for all $i > 1$,

$$x_i \leq t_i \leq x_i + jitter$$

and for all $i \geq span$,

$$lower \leq x_i - x_{i-span} \leq upper$$

Now, a *periodic* repetition constraint is a generic repetition rate constraint where $span = 1$, and $lower = upper$. A *sporadic* repetition constraint has $span = 1$, and $upper = \infty$. TADL also defines more complex *pattern* repetition constraints, and *arbitrary* repetition constraints, see [10].

Delay constraints relate two events, called stimulus and response, by demanding that each occurrence of one event is matched by at least one occurrence of the other within some time window. Depending on whether these time windows are achored at the stimulus or response occurrences, TADL names the delay constraints *reaction* or *age*, respectively.

Both the *reaction* and *age* constraints are characterized by the parameters *lower*, and *upper*. A stimulus event $\langle s_1, s_2, \ldots \rangle$ and a response event $\langle r_1, r_2, \ldots \rangle$ satisfy a reaction constraint with parameter *lower*, *upper* iff for all s_i there exists r_j such that

$$s_i + lower \leq r_j \leq s_i + upper$$

The same events satisfy an age constraint with the same parameters, iff for all r_j there exists an s_i such that

$$r_j - upper \leq s_i \leq r_j - lower$$

Synchronization constraints were originally defined as rather complex constructs in both TADL and AUTOSAR, being syntactic (but notably not semantic) extensions of the delay constraints [10]. Both language have since then simplified the notion of synchronization considerably, and the upcoming release of TADL v2 defines synchronization as a constraint on a group of events S, characterized by a single parameter *tolerance*. Such a constraint is satisfied iff there is a sequence of times $\langle x_1, x_2, \ldots \rangle$ such that for all x_i and all events $\langle s_1, s_2, \ldots \rangle \in S$ there exists at least one s_j such that

$$x_i \leq s_j \leq x_i + tolerance$$

The TADL v1 definition of synchronization will be further discussed at the end of Section 5.

A common theme in the definitions above is that they all rely on an infinite number of indexed event occurrences, which excludes their use in scenarios that span only finite intervals (as in mode-switching systems, for example). They are also practically closed, due to the fact that the logic in which the definitions are expressed is left unspecified in the current TADL. Both these deficiencies will be addressed by the introduction of TiCL.

3   TiCL

The basic purpose of the timing constraint language TiCL is to express truth statements about the points in time when *events* occur. Points in time are interpreted as real values, and since such values are totally ordered, events can simply be understood as sets of reals (infinite or finite). We make the choice to also represent *time intervals* as sets of time values; such sets are however always infinite. Three different sets of variables form the basis of TiCL: one denoting time values (**Tvar**), one ranging over sets (**Svar**), and yet another form standing for arbitrary arithmetic values not denoting points in time (**Avar**). The syntax of TiCL is given in Fig. 1.

Syntactic categories

$r \in \mathbb{R}$ (arithmetic constants)

v	$\in$	**Avar** (arithmetic variables)	e, f	$\in$	**AExp** (arithmetic expressions)
X, Y	$\in$	**Svar** (set variables)	E, F	$\in$	**SExp** (set expressions)
x, y	$\in$	**Tvar** (time variables)	c, d	$\in$	**CExp** (constraint expressions)

Abstract syntax

$$e \;\rightarrow\; r \mid v \mid e+f \mid e-f \mid e*f \mid e/f \mid |E| \mid \lambda(E)$$

$$E \;\rightarrow\; X \mid \{x : c\}$$

$$c \;\rightarrow\; e \leq f \mid x \leq y \mid x \in E \mid c \wedge d \mid \neg c \mid \forall v : c \mid \forall x : c \mid \forall X : c$$

Fig. 1. TiCL syntax

TiCL distinguishes between three kinds of terms. **AExp** is the set of arithmetic expressions formed from constants, variables, arithmetic operators, as well as the size $|E|$, or the *measure* $\lambda(E)$, of a set expression E. By measure we mean the total length of all continuous intervals in E (that is, the *Lebesgue* measure of E). The set expressions **SExp** take the form of a set variable X, or a set comprehension $\{x : c\}$ – the set of all times x such that constraint c (which may reference x) is true. **CExp**, finally, stands for the set of boolean constraint formulae formed from inequalities between arithmetic expressions, inequalities between time variables, set membership (x belongs to the set of times denoted by E), logical connectives, and quantification over arithmetic, time and set variables.

$$true \equiv 0 \leq 1$$
$$false \equiv 1 \leq 0$$
$$c \vee d \equiv \neg(\neg c \wedge \neg d)$$
$$c \Rightarrow d \equiv \neg c \vee d$$
$$c \Leftrightarrow d \equiv (c \Rightarrow d) \wedge (d \Rightarrow c)$$
$$e = f \equiv e \leq f \wedge f \leq e$$
$$e \neq f \equiv \neg(e = f)$$
$$e < f \equiv e \leq f \wedge e \neq f$$

$$\exists v : c \equiv \neg(\forall v : \neg c)$$
$$\exists x : c \equiv \neg(\forall x : \neg c)$$
$$\exists X : c \equiv \neg(\forall X : \neg c)$$

$$\forall x \in E : c \equiv \forall x : x \in E \Rightarrow c$$
$$\exists x \in E : c \equiv \exists x : x \in E \wedge c$$
$$\exists X = E : c \equiv \exists X : X = E \wedge c$$
$$\{x \in E : c\} \equiv \{x : x \in E \wedge c\}$$

$$E \subseteq F \equiv \forall x : x \in E \Rightarrow x \in F$$
$$E = F \equiv E \subseteq F \wedge F \subseteq E$$
$$E \neq F \equiv \neg(E = F)$$
$$E \subset F \equiv E \subseteq F \wedge E \neq F$$
$$x \notin E \equiv \neg(x \in E)$$

$$E \cup F \equiv \{x : x \in E \vee x \in F\}$$
$$E \cap F \equiv \{x : x \in E \wedge x \in F\}$$
$$E^{\complement} \equiv \{x : x \notin E\}$$
$$E \backslash F \equiv \{x : x \in E \wedge x \notin F\}$$

Fig. 2. Standard syntactic abbreviations

The syntax of TiCL is thus entirely standard, and should—with the possible exception of the **Tvar/Avar** distinction—suggest an absolutely straightforward first-order logic semantics. The reason why time variables are kept distinct from their arithmetic counterparts is that absolute time values are never interesting in their own right; only their relative distances are. By making it impossible to form arithmetic expressions directly from time variables, the TiCL constraints become independent of the arbitrary point in time a user chooses to refer to as time "zero". This contrasts sharply to the arithmetic variables, which typically stand for aspects such as minimum interval length, maximum number of occurrences, etc—i.e., aspects whose absolute values are of prime interest in the definition of timing constraints.

As an example TiCL formula, here follows a constraint that demands the occurrences of event X to be no more than, and to occur no later than, the occurrences of event Y.[1]

$$|X| \leq |Y| \wedge \forall x : \forall y : \neg(x \in X \wedge y \in Y \wedge \neg(x \leq y))$$

---

[1] We use a concrete syntax where quantifiers scope as far to the right as possible, and standard operator precedences apply.

4   Abbreviations

For added convenience, we complement the basic syntax of TiCL with a series of syntactic abbreviations, the first of which is defined in Fig. 2. By taking advantage of these notational short-hands, we may choose to express the example constraint of the previous section as follows:

$$|X| \leq |Y| \wedge \forall x \in X : \forall y \in Y : x \leq y$$

Sets of time values do not only represent the generally sparse points in time where different events occur, but also the notion of dense intervals – i.e., sets that contain *all* time values above or below chosen endpoints. Fig. 3 defines some useful interval constructors, that take either single time values, or sets of such values, as starting points.

$$[x \leq] \equiv \{y : x \leq y\} \qquad\qquad [E \leq] \equiv \{y : \exists x \in E : x \leq y\}$$
$$[x <] \equiv \{y : x < y\} \qquad\qquad [E <] \equiv \{y : \forall x \in E : x < y\}$$
$$[\leq x] \equiv [x <]^{\mathsf{C}} \qquad\qquad [\leq E] \equiv [E <]^{\mathsf{C}}$$
$$[< x] \equiv [x \leq]^{\mathsf{C}} \qquad\qquad [< E] \equiv [E \leq]^{\mathsf{C}}$$
$$[x..y] \equiv [x \leq] \cap [< y] \qquad\qquad [E] \equiv [E \leq] \cap [\leq E]$$

Fig. 3. Interval constructors

Intervals are important for separating legal and illegal occurrences of events. The following operations filter out occurrences of an event that are either above or below a certain point in time.

$$E_{x<} \equiv E \cap [x <]$$
$$E_{<x} \equiv E \cap [< x]$$

The first of these filters, in combination with the previous interval constructors, allows us to express the range of time values starting at some point x and ending right before the *next* occurrence of an event E.

$$[x..E] \equiv [x \leq] \cap [< (E_{x<})]$$

Generalizing the previous notation to two events E and F, we end up with an operator that captures a set of ranges, where E contains the possible starting points, and F the possible end-points.

$$[E..F] \equiv \{x : \exists y \in E : x \in [y..F]\}$$

Fig. 4 shows the intuition behind this range operator in graphical form.

As an inverse of the range operator, we may also define two operations that extract the set of starting points and end-points, respectively, from a set of disjoint intervals.

$$E_{\uparrow} \equiv \{x \in E : \exists y < x : y \notin E \wedge \forall y' : y \leq y' < x \Rightarrow y' \notin E\}$$
$$E_{\downarrow} \equiv (E^{\mathsf{C}})_{\uparrow}$$

Fig. 4. Scenario illustrating the active ranges between two events

Since the length of an interval is captured by the measure operator, we may introduce the relative distance between two time values as an arithmetic expression.

$$x - y \equiv \lambda([y..x]) - \lambda([x..y])$$

Note how the use of two swapped intervals makes the distance operator capable of returning both positive and negative results, depending on which of the times x and y that is greater.

The distance operator allows time translation of sets to be expressed, and the range notation to be generalized accordingly.

$$E \gg e \equiv \{x : \exists y \in E : y - x = e\}$$
$$E \ll e \equiv E \gg 0 - e$$
$$[x+e..y+f] \equiv ([x \leq] \gg e) \cap ([< y] \gg f)$$

We also provide an option for indexing a set of time values from zero and up. Since indexing must fail if the set in question contains too few elements, or if an index falls inside a continuous interval of elements, the indexing operator is integrated into a constraint form that simply becomes false under those circumstances.

$$x = E(e) \equiv x \in E \wedge |E_{<x}| = e$$

Another useful constraint form that is definable in terms of intervals is the subrange relation:

$$E \trianglelefteq F \equiv \exists x : \exists y : E = F \cap [x..y]$$

As a generic mechanism for open-ended extension, TiCL allows user-defined constraints to be named and placed in the available abbreviation environment alongside the notational short-hands introduced above. Each such constraint definition is of the form

$$C(\overline{x}, \overline{X}, \overline{v}) \equiv c$$

where C is a name drawn from some set of constraint identifiers, c is a constraint expression, and $\overline{x}$, $\overline{X}$, and $\overline{v}$ are zero or more distinct time, event, and arithmetic variables, respectively. A named constraint can be referred to by writing

$$C(\overline{y}, \overline{E}, \overline{e})$$

where the number of terms in $\overline{y}$, $\overline{E}$, and $\overline{e}$ must match the corresponding parameter lists in the definition of C.

To constitute a valid constraint definition, $C(\overline{x}, \overline{X}, \overline{v}) \equiv c$ must fulfill two conditions:

1. c must not contain any other free variables than those in $\overline{x}$, $\overline{X}$, and $\overline{v}$.
2. c must not refer to C, or any other constraint definition that directly or indirectly refers to C.

These conditions ensure that in any context, named constraints can be removed by simply macro-expanding their respective definitions.

5   Expressing TADL Constraints

In this section we demonstrate the expressive power of TiCL by showing how the various timing constraints defined by both TIMMO and AUTOSAR can be captured formally. The intention is neither to explain the intuition behind these constraints here, nor to motivate any particular design choices in the definitions. In fact, some constraints are actually given multiple definitions, reflecting the alternatives that have appeared in different TIMMO or AUTOSAR versions. The focus in this section is primarily on the semantic details that distinguish such alternatives from each other.

The basic TADL *delay* constraint requires that for each occurrence of a stimulus event X, there must exist *some* occurrence of response event Y at a relative distance determined by a lower and an upper bound (v_l and v_u).

$$delay(X, Y, v_l, v_u) \equiv \forall x \in X : \exists y \in Y : v_l \leq y - x \leq v_u$$

Two *delay* constraints in a symmetric fashion form a *bidelay*. Such a constraint is not actually part of TADL, but we give it a name here nevertheless because it will prove useful in the specification of other TADL constraints.

$$bidelay(X, Y, v_l, v_u) \equiv delay(X, Y, v_l, v_u) \wedge delay(Y, X, -v_u, -v_l)$$

An alternative form of delay that will also be subsequently needed requires that each response occurrence is unique within the specified time window.

$$unidelay(X, Y, v_l, v_u) \equiv \forall x \in X : |Y \cap [x + v_l .. x + v_u]| = 1$$

Yet another useful form is the *strong* delay, which demands that the stimulus and response events are related for each indexed occurrence.

$$strongdelay(X, Y, v_l, v_u) \equiv \forall i : \forall x = X(i) : \exists y = Y(i) : v_l \leq y - x \leq v_u$$

The differences between these delay forms are subtle but important. The basic *delay* allows multiple responses to a single stimuli, as well as responses that are shared by multiple stimuli. *bidelay* does the same, but disallows orphan responses. The *unidelay* constraint rules out multiple possible responses, but still allows the mapping of many stimuli onto a single response. *strongdelay* requires the stimulus and response occurrences to appear in lock-step.

TADL further defines a *repetition* constraint, which can be conveniently captured in two stages. First we introduce the basic notion of a repetition, which says that any stretch of v_s periods (i.e., any subrange of $v_s + 1$ event occurrences) must have a distance between the first and last occurrence that is bounded by v_l and v_u.

$$repeat(X, v_l, v_u, v_s) \equiv \forall Y \trianglelefteq X : |Y| = v_s + 1 \Rightarrow v_l \leq \lambda([Y]) \leq v_u$$

Then we add the jitter component by means of a local event and *strongdelay*:

$$repetition(X, v_l, v_u, v_j, v_s) \equiv \exists Y : repeat(Y, v_l, v_u, v_s) \wedge strongdelay(Y, X, 0, v_j)$$

Notice how Y here takes the role of a set of ideal points in time, from which the actual event X may deviate by at most the jitter distance v_j.

The third pillar of TADL is the *synchronization* constraint, which in its weak form can be expressed as follows:

$$sync(X_1, \ldots, X_n, v_j) \equiv \exists Y : bidelay(Y, X_1, 0, v_j) \wedge \cdots \wedge bidelay(Y, X_n, 0, v_j)$$

That is, synchronization implies that each occurrence of each event X_i is sufficiently close to a "cluster" point of some set Y, and each such point in turn is sufficiently close to occurrences of all the X_i. Note that by choosing *bidelay* over the other delay forms in this definition, TADL deliberately accepts both overlapping synchronization clusters, and clusters containing more than one occurrence of some events. A strong synchronization variant, which requires all synchronized events to appear in a lock-step fashion akin to the *strongdelay* constraint, can easily be defined in terms of the latter (not shown here).

TADL has recently been extended with a constraint capturing the notion of bounded execution times, which is a bit challenging to formalize purely in terms of events. However, if one assumes the existence of events indicating not only the start and termination of the function of interest, but also preemption and resumption of that function, an *exectime* constraint can be defined quite succinctly in TiCL.

$$exectime(X, Y, X', Y', v_l, v_u) \equiv \forall x \in X : v_l \leq \lambda([x..Y] \setminus [X'..Y']) \leq v_u$$

This definition assumes that X and Y capture the points in time when the function of interest is started and terminated, and that preemption and resumption points for that function are given by events X' and Y', respectively. The set $[X'..Y']$ thus indicates the intervals during which the measured function is preempted, and those points in time should be excluded from each invocation interval in order to obtain an accurate execution time. The value to be constrained is the sum of the interval fragments that remain, which is equivalently expressed as the measure of the corresponding set. Fig. 5 shows a graphical illustration of an *exectime* scenario, where x_1 and x_2 denote the starting points of two separate invocations of the constrained function.

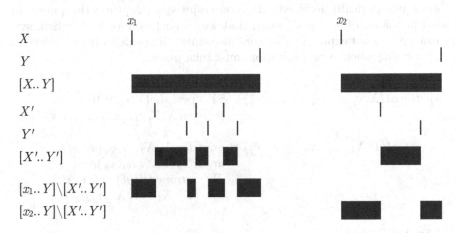

Fig. 5. Event scenario illustrating the *exectime* constraint

$$sporadic(X, v_l, v_u, v_j, v_m) \equiv repetition(X, v_l, v_u, v_j, 1) \wedge$$
$$minimum(X, v_m)$$
$$periodic(X, v_p, v_j, v_m) \equiv sporadic(X, v_p, v_p, v_j, v_m)$$
$$pattern(X, Y, v_1, \ldots, v_n, v_j, v_m) \equiv delay(Y, X, v_1, v_1 + v_j) \wedge \cdots \wedge$$
$$delay(Y, X, v_n, v_n + v_j) \wedge$$
$$minimum(X, v_m)$$
$$arbitrary(X, v_1, \ldots, v_n, v'_1, \ldots, v'_n) \equiv repeat(X, v_1, v'_1, 1) \wedge \cdots \wedge$$
$$repeat(X, v_n, v'_n, n)$$
$$burst(X, v_l, v_n, v_m) \equiv repeat(X, v_l, \infty, v_n + 1) \wedge$$
$$minimum(X, v_m)$$

Fig. 6. Derived TADL constraint definitions

Further TADL constraints are definable entirely in terms of the building blocks introduced so far. Fig. 6 shows the definitions that apply to TADL v2.[2] The *minimum* constraint referenced in several places is just a jitter-free repetition spanning subsequent occurrences, with infinity as its upper bound.

$$minimum(X, v) \equiv repeat(X, v, \infty, 1)$$

To further exemplify the precision that is possible to express using TiCL, we give a few alternative definitions of the *pattern* and *sync* constraints above. The *pattern1* variant represents one reasonable interpretation of the corresponding

---

[2] TADL v2 also includes a group of delay and synchronization constraints that use an externally provided *causality relation* to filter out the event occurences that that a particular delay or synchronization window should contain. TiCL can easily be complemented with the machinery necessary to express this extension, but we do not show it here in the interest of notational brevity.

AUTOSAR constraint, which assumes that the underlying periodic cycle of the pattern is automatically detected. Also, constraint *sync1* captures the quite complicated definition of synchronization that was a part of TADL v1, where synchronization was not expressible without also embedding a delay from a reference event governing when synchronization must take place.

$$pattern1\,(X, v_p, v_j, v_m, v_1, \ldots, v_n) \equiv \exists Y : periodic(Y, v_p, 0, 0) \wedge$$
$$pattern(X, Y, v_1, \ldots, v_n, v_j, v_m)$$

$$sync1\,(Y, X_1, \ldots, X_n, v_l, v_u, v_j) \equiv unidelay(Y, X_1, v_l, v_u) \wedge \cdots \wedge$$
$$unidelay(Y, X_n, v_l, v_u) \wedge$$
$$\exists Y' : strongdelay(Y, Y', v_l, v_u) \wedge$$
$$sync(Y', X_1, \ldots, X_n, v_j)$$

6   Modes

Mode dependency is a design pattern that is used frequently in many AUTOSAR and EAST-ADL models, and which naturally also has an impact on the notion of timing correctness of such models. Simply put, a mode is an abstraction over the state of a system, such that at each point in time, the mode is either *active* or *inactive*. Modes are typically used to guard different functional behaviors, emphasizing orderly distributed mode transitions over distributed behavior in general. A mode-dependent timing constraint is then understood as a constraint that only has to hold while the referenced mode is active; outside those active intervals, the constraint should count as being vacuously true.

However, while the basic intuition behind modes is relatively simple, its application to timing correctness presents some interesting design problems. The fundamental challenge is that timing constraints express properties that generally involve multiple points in time, and a mode change that occurs in the middle of such an interval may very well render a mode-dependent constraint ambiguous. A *delay* constraint serves as a simple illustration. Should an absent response be tolerated if a mode deactivation intervenes? Should a stray response be accepted if it *could* have been caused by a stimulus outside the current mode interval?

Examination of real world scenarios has led us to believe that the generic answer should be yes to all such questions. A mode-dependent constraint should be considered satisfied if it holds for the event occurrences within each active interval, *plus* some hypothetic and optimally chosen occurrence pattern outside each interval. If this idea is formalized correctly, it should be possible to put a mode-restriction on an arbitrary constraint and obtain a meaningful semantics, even if the constraint has not been defined with the specific challenges of mode-switching in mind.

The approach we have taken is to model modes as sets of time values, just like we do for events and arbitrary intervals. To make the mode intuition clear, however, we introduce a distinct class of variables to range over modes:

$$M \in \mathbf{Svar} \text{ (mode identifiers)}$$

Semantically, a mode identifier M stands for some set of time values, just like an X or a Y. In particular, if X and Y are events indicating the activation and deactivation of some mode M, a natural way to express this formally is to introduce M in some scope c as follows:

$$\exists M = [X..Y] : c$$

Alternatively, a mode M can be defined as some combination of other modes using union, disjunction, or any other defined operator on general sets.

We now introduce a syntax for mode-restricted constraints, by means of a decoration to the application of a named constraint macro.

$$C(\overline{y}, E_1, \ldots, E_n, \overline{e}) \% M$$

The core of our mode-restriction mechanism is the semantics given to this constraint form. As before, we proceed in terms of a translation of the syntax form, that results in a constraint term where the new syntax is absent. We begin with the simple case where C takes only one event argument.

$$C(\overline{y}, E, \overline{e}) \% M \equiv \forall x \in M_\uparrow : \exists Y = [x..M_\downarrow] : \exists X \subseteq Y^{\complement} : C(\overline{y}, (E \cap Y) \cup X, \overline{e})$$

The definition should be read as follows. For the given mode M, its activation and deactivation points ($M_\uparrow$ and $M_\downarrow$) are identified. Then, for each activation point x in $M_\uparrow$, a freely chosen X, subset of the possible time values *outside* the current activation interval Y, is added to the subrange of event parameter E that falls within Y. That is, the translated, mode-independent application of C takes $E \cap Y \cup X$ as an argument in place of E, which captures the intuition that a mode both ignores and assumes the best about occurrences that fall outside its active intervals. Generalized to n event arguments, the translation becomes

$$C(\overline{y}, E_1, \ldots, E_n, \overline{e}) \% M \equiv \forall x \in M_\uparrow : \exists Y = [x..M_\downarrow] :$$
$$\exists X_1 \subseteq Y^{\complement} : \ldots : \exists X_n \subseteq Y^{\complement} :$$
$$C(\overline{y}, (E_1 \cap Y) \cup X_1, \ldots, (E_n \cap Y) \cup X_n, \overline{e})$$

To illustrate the power of this interpretation of mode-dependencies, we define a somewhat contrived, but still perfectly sound, variant of a repetition constraint:

$$cyclic(X, v) \equiv delay(X, X, v, v)$$

This constraint is special because it only holds for infinitely repeating events.

The top of Fig. 7 shows the initial trace of an event E that certainly does not satisfy $cyclic(E, v)$ for any v. However, the intent is now that the constraint

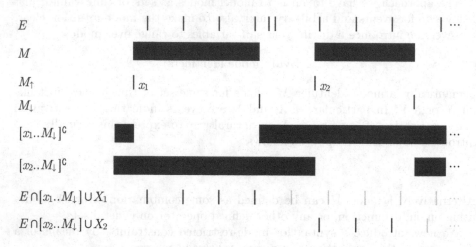

Fig. 7. Event scenario involving a mode-restricted constraint $cyclic(E, v)\%M$

only has to hold while mode M is active; i.e., $cyclic(E, v)\%M$ must be true. While it is clear that E is repetitive during the activity intervals, just limiting E to those intervals would not work—all such E subsets would be finite. But by interpreting mode-restriction as a constraint on mode-limited event subsets *extended with arbitrarily chosen points outside the mode interval*, even infinitely demanding constraints like *cyclic* become possible to apply in finite contexts.

What Fig. 7 depicts below the trace of E is the assumed activity intervals of mode M, its activation and deactivation points, the complements of the first and second activity intervals of M (i.e., the sets from which suitable subsets X may be drawn), and the resulting, purely cyclic patterns that result when the relevant subsets of E are suitably extended.

7   Related Work

TiCL shares its main objective with the various real-time (timed/temporal) logics that have been proposed in the context of model-checking and verification of timed automata: to offer a comprehensive formalism for specifying the timing behavior of a system in a logically robust way [3,7,13,12,1,9]. This line of research is uniformly dealing with *modal* logics; i.e., logics whose semantics is based on sequences of system states and atomic predicates on these. Such generality allows the integration of timing aspects into arbitrary specifications of functional behavior, as would be expected by the model-checking approach. TiCL exhibits a much weaker connection between timing properties and their underlying systems, by only allowing relations on the occurrences of abstract events as its atomic formulas. This makes TiCL unsuitable as a general model-checking specification language, although it also makes for a very clean identification of the properties that are purely concerned with timing.

At the same time, TiCL is fundamentally more expressive than the modal approaches in being a first-order logic. The additional power stems primarily from the universally (and existentially) quantified variables of TiCL, which may range over both points in time as well as sets of such values. Temporal logics allow only a limited form of quantification through temporal operators, whose closest counterparts in TiCL would be quantifiers introducing variables used just as event indices. A mode-dependency operator like ours, which critically depends on the ability to quantify over sets, appears very difficult to express in a temporal logic style, if at all possible. It should also be noted that the core TiCL operators and quantifiers are entirely standard in the logic field, whereas the various temporal and real-time logics are to a large extent identified by the custom operators they provide. Of course, TiCL pays a price for this generality by being undecidable, but its intended role as a disambiguation tool for humans is more dependent on a standard semantics and a carefully delimited syntax than on decidability issues. Moreover, there are reasons to believe that practically significant fragments of TiCL are indeed decidable, analogous to the case for first-order logics in general.

Amon et al. [4] define a specification language for capturing the logic of timing diagrams in a form that resembles our constraint language minus the event variables and with restricted integer arithmetic (no division operator, multiplication by literals only). This sublanguage corresponds to Presburger formulas, for which automatic and efficient verification procedures exist. It remains to be seen to what extent the approach allows extension towards the full TiCL syntax (one particular sub-case that appears particularly benign is top-level quantification over real-valued sets, which should imply little more than just iterated verification).

CCSL [5] is a language for specifying timing constraints in the UML profile MARTE [14] for modeling and analysis of real-time systems. CCSL can specify clocks, which correspond to events, and relations between them. Relations include various sub- and precedence constraints. It seems that TiCL quite readily could express counterparts to CCSL clock constraints on events.

Timed automata [2] are automata extended with various clock variables, which can be used to model real-time systems. Model checking can be performed over timed automata to verify that the models have certain properties. The properties, which typically are reachability properties, are then specified in some temporal logic. UPPAAL [11] is a well-known tool for modeling and verification using timed automata.

Transitions in timed automata can be guarded by constraints on the clocks: thus, timed automata can to some extent include timing constraints in the models. However, the style is state-oriented rather than event-oriented and thus quite different from TiCL. Also, timed automata and their temporal logics are usually designed to be decidable, allowing efficient procedures for model checking whereas TiCL favours expressiveness. An interesting question, of course, is whether some nontrivial fragment of TiCL can be translated into timed automata as it would allow automatic verification of that fragment.

8   Conclusions and Further Research

We have presented TiCL, a simple logic for expressing timing constraints on events. TiCL came out of the work with TADL, a language for specifying timing requirements and -properties that is intended to be used with AUTOSAR and EAST-ADL in the automotive domain. TiCL offers a rich syntax, on top of a simple kernel language, for defining constraints on events defined as sets of times. We showed how to express TADL's timing constraints in TiCL, as well as some other timing constraints that seem natural and useful. We also introduced mode-dependent TiCL constraints, with a special mode restriction operator, and gave the operator a semantics by translation into TiCL without this operator.

Expressing timing constraints by translation into a logic like TiCL has several advantages. One advantage is that the semantics of timing constraints becomes well-defined and unambiguous, since TiCL itself has a very clear, standard semantics. In particular this is true for mode-dependent constraints, since they have hitherto never been given a stringent semantics although they are present in both AUTOSAR, EAST-ADL, and TADL. We believe that we have found the "right" definition of mode dependency, and the semantics of this definition can be used to give a well-defined semantics for mode dependency in, say, TADL as well.

Another advantage is that tools for validating or verifying timing constraints can work by translation into TiCL. Tools that check the validity of event traces vis-a-vis some timing constraints, or that simulate systems based on timing properties expressed in, say, TADL, can work on TiCL rather than TADL. Since TiCL is simple, with a clear semantics, such tools will be easier to implement for TiCL. This is similar to compilers, where programs are first translated into some intermediate format that is easier to work on.

TiCL also offers a way to express timing constraints in situations where the fixed format constraints of languages like TADL turn out not to be applicable. A "power user" can easily define new timing constraints in TiCL that are tailored to special needs. Similarly, if later versions of AUTOSAR or TADL will have a modified set of timing constraints, then these will most likely be expressible in TiCL as well. Once a translation to TiCL is established the new constraints will have a well-defined semantics, and tools that are based on TiCL will work immediately.

Finally, TiCL opens a possible route for formal verification of timing constraints. Although TiCL itself is not a decidable logic, it does not seem unlikely that there are nontrivial fragments that are decidable. Timing constraints that can be expressed within such fragments will then be possible to verify formally by an automated decision procedure.

References

1. Abadi, M., Lamport, L., Taylor, R.W.: An old-fashioned recipe for real time. In: ACM Transactions on Programming Languages and Systems, pp. 1–27. Springer (1992)
2. Alur, R., Courcoubetis, C., Dill, D.: Model-checking for real-time systems. In: Proc. Logic in Computer Science, pp. 414–425. IEEE (June 1990)
3. Alur, R., Henzinger, T.A.: A really temporal logic. J. ACM 41(1), 181–203 (1994)
4. Amon, T., Borriello, G., Hu, T., Liu, J.: Symbolic timing verification of timing diagrams using Presburger formulas. In: Proc. 34th Annual Design Automation Conference, pp. 226–231. ACM, New York (1997)
5. André, C., Mallet, F.: Clock constraints in UML/MARTE CCSL. Research report, INRIA (May 2008)
6. Homepage of the AUTOSAR project (2009), http://www.autosar.org
7. Chaochen, Z., Hoare, C.A.R., Ravn, A.P.: A calculus of durations. Inf. Process. Lett. 40(5), 269–276 (1991)
8. Cuenot, P., Frey, P., Johansson, R., Lönn, H., Papadopoulos, Y., Reiser, M.-O., Sandberg, A., Servat, D., Tavakoli Kolagari, R., Törngren, M., Weber, M.: 11 The EAST-ADL Architecture Description Language for Automotive Embedded Software. In: Giese, H., Karsai, G., Lee, E., Rumpe, B., Schätz, B. (eds.) MBEERTS. LNCS, vol. 6100, pp. 297–307. Springer, Heidelberg (2010)
9. Grüninger, M., Menzel, C.: The process specification language (PSL) theory and applications. AI Mag. 24(3), 63–74 (2003)
10. Johansson, R., Frey, P., Jonsson, J., Nordlander, J., Pathan, R.M., Feiertag, N., Schlager, M., Espinoza, H., Richter, K., Kuntz, S., Lönn, H., Kolagari, R.T., Blom, H.: TADL: Timing augmented description language, version 2. Technical report (October 2009)
11. Larsen, K.G., Pettersson, P., Yi, W.: UPPAAL in a nutshell. Int. Journal on Software Tools for Technology Transfer 1, 134–152 (1997)
12. Mattolini, R., Nesi, P.: An interval logic for real-time system specification. IEEE Trans. Softw. Eng. 27(3), 208–227 (2001)
13. Moszkowski, B.: A temporal logic for multilevel reasoning about hardware. Computer 18, 10–19 (1985)
14. UML profile for MARTE: Modeling and analysis of real-time embedded systems. Tech. rep., OMG (November 2009), http://www.omg.org/spec/MARTE/1.0
15. Homepage of the TIMMO-2-USE project (2012), http://www.timmo-2-use.org

Generalized Weakly-Hard Constraints

Sophie Quinton* and Rolf Ernst

Institute of Computer Network and Engineering / TU Braunschweig

Abstract. Real-time systems must meet, in addition to their functional requirements, requirements regarding their timing behavior. In the case of hard real-time systems, such requirements include the absence of deadline misses. In contrast, for soft real-time systems, a "reasonable" number of deadline misses may happen without leading to a system failure. The usual definition of what a "reasonable" number of deadline misses formally means is based on probability distributions. Another option is to use weakly-hard constraints, which describe bounds on the number of allowed deadline misses in a given time window.

In this paper we show the interest of using weakly-hard constraints for other purposes than describing deadline misses, e.g. to describe execution times or jitter. We discuss in depth the semantics of weakly-hard constraints with an emphasis on how they can be inferred from other weakly-hard constraints and compared to probabilistic constraints.

1 Introduction

Real-time systems must meet, in addition to their functional requirements, requirements regarding their timing behavior. In the case of hard real-time systems, such requirements include the absence of deadline misses. In contrast, for soft real-time systems, a "reasonable" number of deadline misses may happen without leading to a system failure. The usual definition of what a "reasonable" number of deadline misses formally means is based on probability distributions. Another option is to use weakly-hard constraints, which describe bounds on the number of allowed deadline misses in a given time window.

In this paper, we make a proposal for an extension of the Timing Augmented Description Language [10] (TADL) to soft constraints, weakly-hard and probabilistic. TADL was first defined in the TIMMO project [12] and then integrated into EAST-ADL by the ATESST2 project [1]. An improved and extended version of TADL, called TADL2, is now being developed in the context of the TIMMO-2-USE project [13]. In particular, we show the interest of using weakly-hard constraints for other purposes than describing deadline misses, e.g. to describe execution times or jitter. We also discuss in depth the semantics of weakly-hard constraints with an emphasis on how they can be compared to probabilistic constraints.

* This work was funded by the ITEA2 project TIMMO-2-USE (EUREKA cluster N° 3674) through the German Ministry of Education and Research (BMBF) under the funding ID 01IS10034.

T. Margaria and B. Steffen (Eds.): ISoLA 2012, Part II, LNCS 7610, pp. 96–110, 2012.

This paper is organized as follows: in Section 2 we first present the key aspects of TADL and a new basic constraint needed for representing constraints on execution times in TADL2. In Section 3 we show how to extend the DELAY constraint from TADL in order to allow the expression of the weakly-hard constraints introduced in [2]. We then demonstrate the interest of providing similar extensions for the other constraints of TADL and provide a result for deriving new weakly-hard constraints from a given one. In Section 4, we first focus on probabilistic execution times as they are usually formalized, e.g. in [7]. Then we show how probabilistic constraints are represented in TADL2, in particular because histogram distributions must be permitted. Finally we relate weakly-hard constraints and probabilistic constraints.

2   Strongly-Hard Timing Constraints

The systems for which we want to express constraints consist of software components performing for example a computation or some storage or communication, which we call *tasks*. These components are mapped onto hardware components (e.g. processors, memories, buses) called *resources*, on which they execute. When a resource is shared by several tasks, a scheduling policy decides in which order tasks are executed.

The execution of a task is triggered by an input *event* received by the task, called *activation*. The end of the execution is indicated by the output of another event, called *termination*. As is the case in all event-based approaches, we abstract from the data often associated with events (e.g. the result of a computation associated with a termination event) and identify the behavior of the system with how events occur during execution. This makes the size of our system abstraction manageable. An *event trace* describes the set of instants at which a given event takes place. Note that we only use traces focusing on one specific type of event, which is for example the activation or the termination of a given task τ, as well as preemptions and resumptions if the scheduling policy is preemptive. The behavior of the system is then defined as a set of traces.

In this paper we assume that time is discrete ($Time = \mathbb{N}$), time windows can be of infinite size ($TimeWindow = \mathbb{N} \cup \{\infty\}$) and we consider infinite traces starting at an instant 0.

Definition 1. *A trace of an event e is an increasing function $\sigma_e : \mathbb{N}^+ \longrightarrow Time$ where $\sigma_e(n)$ is the point in time when e occurs for the n-th time.*

We use the notation $\mathfrak{S}_e$ for denoting the set of traces of e. By extension to a set of events E, $\mathfrak{S}_E$ denotes the set of trace sets containing exactly one trace per event in E. For example, if $E = \{s, t\}$ then an element of $\mathfrak{S}_E$ would contain one trace of s and one trace of t.

Definition 2. *The timing behavior of a system with respect to a set of events E_{sys} is represented by an element of $\mathfrak{S}_{E_{sys}}$, that is, one trace per event in E.*

Definition 3. *A constraint c on a vector of events $< \mathbf{e_1}, \ldots, \mathbf{e_n} >$ (for $n \in \mathbb{N}^+$) is a predicate on $\mathfrak{S}_{\{\mathbf{e_1},\ldots,\mathbf{e_n}\}}$, i.e., a function which takes one trace $\sigma_{\mathbf{e_i}}$ per event $\mathbf{e_i}$ and returns true if the set of traces $\{\sigma_{\mathbf{e_1}}, \ldots, \sigma_{\mathbf{e_n}}\}$ satisfies the constraint, and false otherwise.*

We now present the basic constraints of the Timing Augmented Description Language (TADL) defined in the TIMMO project [12] and developed now as TADL2 in TIMMO-2-USE [13]. TADL is based on three constraints from which all other constraints are derived:

- DELAY constrains the time window between the occurrence of a source event and that of some corresponding target event.
- REPETITION constrains the distance between occurrences of the same event.
- SYNCHRONIZATION constrains the maximum distance between events which are expected to occur at the same time.

We choose to focus on the first two constraints as the SYNCHRONIZATION constraint does not yield any specific problem. Note that the DELAY constraint presented here corresponds to the STONG-DELAY variant introduced in TADL2 for describing response times.

2.1   DELAY Constraints

Definition 4. *A DELAY constraint on two events $\mathbf{s}$ (source) and $\mathbf{t}$ (target) is a constraint parameterized by a pair of time windows:*

- *$(lower, upper) \in TimeWindow \times TimeWindow$*

A timing behavior $\{\sigma_{\mathbf{s}}, \sigma_{\mathbf{t}}\}$ satisfies $\mathrm{DELAY}_{\mathbf{s},\mathbf{t}}(lower, upper)$ if and only if

$$\forall n \in \mathbb{N}^+ : \sigma_{\mathbf{s}}(n) + lower \leq \sigma_{\mathbf{t}}(n) \leq \sigma_{\mathbf{s}}(n) + upper$$

In other words, a behavior satisfies such a DELAY-constraint iff the time window between an occurrence of $\mathbf{s}$ and the corresponding occurrence of $\mathbf{t}$ is bounded by *lower* and *upper*.

Example 1. If **act** and **end** are the events describing respectively the activation and the termination of an execution of a task τ with a deadline D, then the fact that τ should not miss any deadline is expressed by the constraint

$$\mathrm{DELAY}_{\mathbf{act},\mathbf{end}}(0, D)$$

which states that the response time of τ should always be between 0 and D.

2.2   REPETITION Constraints

Definition 5. *A REPETITION constraint on an event* **e** *is parameterized by:*

- $(lower, upper) \in TimeWindow \times TimeWindow$
- $\mathcal{J} \in TimeWindow$
- $span \in \mathbb{N}^+$

A timing behavior $\sigma_\mathbf{e}$ *satisfies* $\mathrm{REPETITION}_\mathbf{e}(lower, upper, \mathcal{J}, span)$ *if and only if one can build a trace* $\sigma'_\mathbf{e}$ *such that*

$$\forall n \in \mathbb{N}^+ : \sigma'_\mathbf{e}(n) + lower \leq \sigma'_\mathbf{e}(n + span) \leq \sigma'_\mathbf{e}(n) + upper$$

and

$$\forall n \in \mathbb{N}^+ : \sigma'_\mathbf{e}(n) \leq \sigma_\mathbf{e}(n) \leq \sigma'_\mathbf{e}(n) + \mathcal{J}$$

Such a REPETITION constraint relates for all $n \in \mathbb{N}^+$ the n-th occurrence of event **e** and its $(n + span)$-th occurrence. Note that because there may be some jitter, one cannot directly constrain the distance (in time) between $\sigma_\mathbf{e}(n)$ and $\sigma_\mathbf{e}(n + span)$. This phenomenon appears clearly in the PERIODIC constraint which can be derived from REPETITION as follows.

2.3   PERIODIC Constraints

Definition 6. *A PERIODIC constraint on an event* **e** *is parameterized by:*

- $P \in TimeWindow$
- $\mathcal{J} \in TimeWindow$

Its semantics is defined by

$$\mathrm{PERIODIC}_\mathbf{e}(P, \mathcal{J}) = \mathrm{REPETITION}_\mathbf{e}(P, P, \mathcal{J}, 1)$$

In the periodic case, the distance between two consecutive events is not necessarily P, however there exists a theoretical trace of reference which is fully periodic (i.e., without any jitter) and such that the distance between occurrences in $\sigma_\mathbf{e}$ and their counterparts of reference is bounded by $\mathcal{J}$.

2.4   REPEAT Constraints

The following derived constraint is not directly part of TADL. We present it here as the absence of jitter makes this constraint simpler to analyze than even the PERIODIC constraint, as we will see later. We furthermore explicit through two theorems its relation to the REPETITION constraint.

Definition 7. *A REPEAT constraint on an event* **e** *is parameterized by:*

- $(lower, upper) \in TimeWindow \times TimeWindow$
- $span \in \mathbb{N}^+$

A timing behavior $\sigma_{\mathbf{e}}$ satisfies a constraint $\text{REPEAT}_{\mathbf{e}}(lower, upper, span, m, k)$ *if and only if*

$$\forall n \in \mathbb{N}^+ : \sigma_{\mathbf{e}}(n) + lower \leq \sigma_{\mathbf{e}}(n + span) \leq \sigma_{\mathbf{e}}(n) + upper$$

Example 2. In the context of Compositional Performance Analysis [4] or Real-Time Calculus [11], $\text{REPEAT}_{\mathbf{e}}(lower, upper, k)$ bounds the distance between the first and the last occurrence of a sequence of k consecutive occurrences of $\mathbf{e}$ and can therefore be used to build a finite prefix of an arrival curve.

Theorem 1. *A REPEAT constraint can always be represented as an equivalent REPETITION constraint.*

$$\text{REPEAT}_{\mathbf{e}}(lower, upper, span) = \text{REPETITION}_{\mathbf{e}}(lower, upper, 0, span)$$

Proof. By definition of REPETITION, a timing behavior $\sigma_{\mathbf{e}}$ satisfies a given constraint $\text{REPETITION}_{\mathbf{e}}(lower, upper, 0, span)$ if and only if one can build a trace $\sigma'_{\mathbf{e}}$ such that

$$\forall n \in \mathbb{N}^+ : \sigma'_{\mathbf{e}}(n) + lower \leq \sigma'_{\mathbf{e}}(n + span) \leq \sigma'_{\mathbf{e}}(n) + upper$$

and

$$\forall n \in \mathbb{N}^+ : \sigma'_{\mathbf{e}}(n) \leq \sigma_{\mathbf{e}}(n) \leq \sigma'_{\mathbf{e}}(n) + 0$$

This is clearly equivalent to finding a trace $\sigma'_{\mathbf{e}}$ which satisfies the constraint $\text{REPEAT}_{\mathbf{e}}(lower, upper, span)$ and such that $\sigma_{\mathbf{e}} = \sigma'_{\mathbf{e}}$. Hence the result.

Theorem 2. *A behavior $\sigma_{\mathbf{e}}$ satisfies* $\text{REPETITION}_{\mathbf{e}}(lower, upper, \mathcal{J}, span)$ *if and only if one can build a trace $\sigma'_{\mathbf{e}}$ such that*

$$\sigma'_{\mathbf{e}} \text{ satisfies } \text{REPEAT}_{\mathbf{e}}(lower, upper, span)$$

and

$$\{\sigma'_{\mathbf{e}}, \sigma_{\mathbf{e}}\} \text{ satisfies } \text{DELAY}_{\mathbf{e}', \mathbf{e}}(0, \mathcal{J})$$

Proof. This is a direct consequence of the definitions of REPEAT and DELAY.

2.5   EXECUTION-TIME Constraints

Finally, the last strongly-hard constraint which we want to present in this section is a constraint which is not in TADL but has been added to TADL2 to express constraints on execution times. In contrast to response times, the execution time of a task represents the time during which the task is actually used by a resource. Describing such a time window requires to take into account preemptions, which is not possible with the existing DELAY constraint.

Definition 8. *Given a behavior $\omega = \{\sigma_{\mathbf{start}}, \sigma_{\mathbf{end}}, \sigma_{\mathbf{pre}}, \sigma_{\mathbf{res}}\}$ where* **start** *represents the start of the executions of a given task τ,* **end** *the termination of the executions of τ,* **pre** *its preemption times and* **res** *its resumption times, we define the* execution time *of the n-th execution of τ (for $n \in \mathbb{N}^+$), denoted $ET_\omega(n)$, as follows. Denote $\{\sigma_{\mathbf{pre}}(k), \ldots, \sigma_{\mathbf{pre}}(k+i)\}$ (with $k \in \mathbb{N}^+$ and $i \in \mathbb{N}$) the preemption times occurring during the n-th execution of τ. Then $\{\sigma_{\mathbf{res}}(k), \ldots, \sigma_{\mathbf{res}}(k+i)\}$ (with $k \in \mathbb{N}^+$ and $i \in \mathbb{N}$) should also correspond to the resumptions occurring during this execution, otherwise the behavior is not well formed. We define*

$$ET_\omega(n) = \sigma_{\mathbf{end}}(n) - \sigma_{\mathbf{start}}(n) - \sum_{j=0}^{i}(\sigma_{\mathbf{res}}(k+j) - \sigma_{\mathbf{pre}}(k+j))$$

Definition 9. *An* EXECUTION-TIME *constraint on four events* **start**, **end**, **pre** *and* **res** *is a constraint parameterized by:*

- *(lower, upper) $\in$ TimeWindow $\times$ TimeWindow*

A timing behavior $\omega = \{\sigma_{\mathbf{start}}, \sigma_{\mathbf{end}}, \sigma_{\mathbf{pre}}, \sigma_{\mathbf{res}}\}$ is said to satisfy a constraint EXECUTION-TIME$_{\mathbf{start}, \mathbf{end}, \mathbf{pre}, \mathbf{res}}$(lower, upper) *if and only if*

$$\forall n \in \mathbb{N}^+ : lower \leq ET_\omega(n) \leq upper$$

Example 3. If **start**, **end**, **pre** and **res** are the events describing respectively the activation, termination, preemption and resumption of a task τ, then the fact that the execution time of τ is bounded by *WCET* is expressed by the constraint

$$\text{EXECUTION-TIME}_{\mathbf{start}, \mathbf{end}, \mathbf{pre}, \mathbf{res}}(0, WCET)$$

3 Weakly-Hard Timing Constraints

In this section, we first recall the principle of weakly-hard constraints as they were introduced in [2]. We provide an extension of TADL that allows us to specify such constraints as DELAY constraints. We then explore the meaning of similar extensions for the other constraints of TADL. Finally, we discuss how new weakly-hard constraints can be inferred from a given one.

3.1 Weakly-Hard DELAY Constraints

Weakly-hard constraints were introduced for expressing the fact that a bounded number of deadline misses may be allowed in a sequence of consecutive executions. More precisely, the behavior of a task τ satisfies a weakly-hard constraint with parameters $m \in \mathbb{N}$ and $k \in \mathbb{N}^+$ if and only if for any sequence of k consecutive executions of τ *at least* m executions meet their deadline. In the context of TADL, such a constraint can be represented as an extension of the strongly-hard delay with two parameters.

Definition 10. *A weakly-hard DELAY constraint on two events* s *and* t, *which we denote* WH-DELAY$_{s,t}$, *is a constraint with four parameters:*

- *(lower, upper)* $\in$ *TimeWindow* $\times$ *TimeWindow*
- *(m, k)* $\in \mathbb{N} \times \mathbb{N}^+$

A timing behavior $\{\sigma_s, \sigma_t\}$ *satisfies* WH-DELAY$_{s,t}$*(lower, upper, m, k) if and only if*

$$\forall n \in \mathbb{N}^+ : \#\{l \in \mathbb{N}^+ \mid n \leq l < n + k \land \sigma_t(l) - \sigma_s(l) \in [lower; upper]\} \geq m$$

where $\#S$ *denotes the number of elements of a set* S.

This definition states that for any sequence $\{n, \ldots, n + k - 1\}$ of k consecutive natural numbers, the number of l in this sequence satisfying $pred(l)$ must be larger than m, where $pred(l)$ is the predicate asserting that the response time of the l-th execution is within the specified bounds [*lower, upper*].

Example 4. For a task with deadline D, the definition of weakly-hard constraint of [3] corresponds to a constraint WH-DELAY$(0, D, m, k)$.

The following well-known theorem relates the definition of weakly-hard delay to its strongly-hard version.

Theorem 3. *For all events* s *and* t *and all lower, upper* $\in$ *TimeWindow:*

$$\text{DELAY}_{s,t}(lower, upper) = \text{WH-DELAY}_{s,t}(lower, upper, 1, 1)$$

Proof. We have to show that

$$\forall n \in \mathbb{N}^+ : \sigma_s(n) + lower \leq \sigma_t(n) \leq \sigma_s(n) + upper$$

if and only if for $n = m = 1$

$$\forall n \in \mathbb{N}^+ : \#\{l \in \mathbb{N}^+ \mid n \leq l < n + k \land \sigma_t(l) - \sigma_s(l) \in [lower; upper]\} \geq m$$

The latter is equivalent to

$$\forall n \in \mathbb{N}^+ : \#\{l \in \mathbb{N}^+ \mid l = n \land \sigma_t(l) - \sigma_s(l) \in [lower; upper]\} \geq 1$$

which holds if and only if

$$\forall n \in \mathbb{N}^+ : \sigma_t(n) - \sigma_s(n) \in [lower; upper]$$

This last statement is trivially equivalent to DELAY$_{s,t}$(*lower, upper*), hence the result.

Note also that if the trace of s is constrained (using a REPETITION constraint) then the values of l in Definition 10 which do not satisfy $pred(l)$ are still implicitly constrained by the occurrences which do satisfy it. To keep the proof simple we show this only for REPETITION constraints with no jitter and a span of 1, but the same would be possible for any type of REPETITION.

Theorem 4. *Consider a timing behavior* $\{\sigma_s, \sigma_t\}$ *which satisfies two constraints* WH-DELAY$_{s,t}(lower_d, upper_d, m, k)$ *and* REPETITION$_s(lower_r, upper_r,$ $0, 1)$. *If* $m > 0$ *then:*

$$\forall n \in \mathbb{N}^+ : \sigma_t(n) - \sigma_s(n) \leq upper_d + k \times upper_r$$

Proof. Consider $n \in \mathbb{N}^+$. If $pred(n)$ holds then the result is obviously satisfied, so let us suppose that

$$\sigma_t(n) - \sigma_s(n) \notin [lower_d; upper_d]$$

Because of the WH-DELAY constraint, we know there exists $l \leq k$ such that

$$\sigma_t(n + l) - \sigma_s(n + l) \in [lower_d; upper_d]$$

Furthermore, because of the REPETITION constraint, we also know that

$$\sigma_s(n + l) - \sigma_s(n) \leq l \times upper_r$$

Finally, from the definition of a trace, we also know that

$$\sigma_t(n) \leq \sigma_t(n + l)$$

From all this we can conclude that

$$\sigma_t(n) - \sigma_s(n) \leq \sigma_t(n + l) - \sigma_s(n + l) + l \times upper_r \leq upper_d + l \times upper_r$$

This concludes our proof that the delay for the n-th occurrences of events in the trace is also bounded.

3.2   Towards Generalized Weakly-Hard Constraints

What we have done so far is generalizing the weakly-hard constraints of [3] to any type of DELAY constraint. A natural question now is how this generalization can extend to the other basic constraints of TADL, and whether this is of interest. This question was triggered by the development of Typical-Case Analysis [9,8] (TCA), which a new approach for timing analysis inspired by the analysis of weakly-hard systems. One major novelty is that weakly-hard constraints are used also for the description of the system and not only for bounding the number of deadline misses. Furthermore, because TCA is always coupled with the usual worst-case analysis, its result is slightly different from a standard weakly-hard constraint, namely it is a conjunction two DELAY constraints, one strongly-hard and the other weakly-hard.

As we have seen, the REPETITION constraint can be derived from the DELAY and REPEAT constraints, therefore we now focus on REPEAT before considering the fully general case.

Definition 11. *A weakly-hard REPEAT constraint on an event* **e** *is a constraint parameterized by:*

- $(lower, upper) \in TimeWindow \times TimeWindow$
- $span \in \mathbb{N}^+$
- $(m, k) \in \mathbb{N} \times \mathbb{N}^+$

A *timing behavior* $\{\sigma_e, \sigma_e\}$ *satisfies* $\text{WH-REPEAT}_e(lower, upper, span, m, k)$ *if and only if*

$$\forall n \in \mathbb{N}^+ : \# \left\{ \begin{array}{l} l \in \mathbb{N}^+ \mid n \leq l < n + k \\ \wedge\ \sigma_e(l + span) - \sigma_e(l) \in [lower, upper] \end{array} \right\} \geq m$$

Such a constraint can be used, for example, to express that a bounded number of shifts may be observed in a trace. It can then be used in complement of a strongly-hard REPEAT constraint to describe how often the shifts may occur, as in the following example.

Example 5. A behavior satisfying two constraints $\text{REPEAT}_e(P, P + shift, 1)$ and $\text{WH-REPEAT}_e(P, P, 1, 9, 10)$ is mostly periodic with at most one shift out of 10 consecutive events, where the shift is bounded by *shift*.

One point deserves to be clarified, namely the relation between the *span* parameter of the REPEAT constraint (and thus the REPETITION constraint) and the weakly-hard version of this constraint. Indeed, both the *span* and the weakly-hard parameters allow us to define a constraint on a sequence of consecutive occurrences in a trace ($span + 1$ occurrences and k occurrences, respectively). However the former constrains the distance (in time) between the first and the last occurrence in the sequence, which is also the sum of the distances between any two consecutive occurrences in the sequence, while the latter constrains how many of these distances may be above a given threshold.

Now let us consider another specific case of the REPETITION constraint, namely PERIODIC constraints. It should be clear by now that coming up with a weakly-hard variant of a constraint c requires that c be decomposable into a set of "local" predicates $pred(l)$ such that

$$\forall n \in \mathbb{N}^+ : \#\{l \in \mathbb{N}^+ \mid n \leq l < n + k \wedge\ pred(l)\} \geq m$$

The obvious candidate here is

$$\forall l \in \mathbb{N}^+ : pred(l) \triangleq [\sigma'_e(l + 1) = \sigma'_e(l) + P \wedge\ \sigma_e(l) - \sigma'_e(l) \leq \mathcal{J}]$$

However, unlike the REPEAT constraint, it is here unclear how useful a weakly-hard PERIODIC constraint as defined above could be. Indeed, a temporary violation of the constraint might result from a shift in the trace as well as from an overjitter. In practice these two types of unexpected behaviors are of a very different nature. This suggests that a PERIODIC constraint, and thus a REPETITION constraint, should have two distinct weakly-hard variants, one corresponding to a bounded number of shifts allowed in a trace (as for the WH-REPEAT constraint), and another one corresponding to a bounded number of occurrences allowed to happen outside the specified jitter. In the latter case for example, the expected global predicate would be the following: a timing behavior $\{\sigma_{\mathbf{e}}, \sigma_{\mathbf{e}}\}$ satisfies a constraint WH-PERIODIC$_{\mathbf{e}}(P, \mathcal{J}, m, k)$ if and only if one can build a trace $\sigma'_{\mathbf{e}}$ such that

$$\forall n \in \mathbb{N}^+ : \sigma'_{\mathbf{e}}(n+1) = \sigma'_{\mathbf{e}}(n) + P \wedge \# \left\{ \begin{array}{l} l \in \mathbb{N}^+ \mid n \leq l < n + k \\ \wedge \ \sigma_{\mathbf{e}}(l) - \sigma'_{\mathbf{e}}(l) \leq \mathcal{J} \end{array} \right\} \geq m$$

Hence the following definition for the general case .

Definition 12. *A* weakly-hard REPETITION *constraint on an event* **e** *is a constraint parameterized by:*

- $(lower, upper) \in TimeWindow \times TimeWindow$
- $\mathcal{J} \in TimeWindow$
- $span \in \mathbb{N}^+$
- $(m_r, k_r) \in \mathbb{N} \times \mathbb{N}^+$
- $(m_j, k_j) \in \mathbb{N} \times \mathbb{N}^+$

A timing behavior $\sigma_{\mathbf{e}}$ *satisfies* WH-REPETITION$_{\mathbf{e}}(lower, upper, \mathcal{J}, span, m, k)$ *if and only if one can build a trace* $\sigma'_{\mathbf{e}}$ *such that*

$$\sigma'_{\mathbf{e}} \text{ satisfies WH-REPEAT}_{\mathbf{e}}(lower, upper, span, m_r, k_r)$$

and

$$\{\sigma'_{\mathbf{e}}, \sigma_{\mathbf{e}}\} \text{ satisfies WH-DELAY}_{\mathbf{e}', \mathbf{e}}(0, \mathcal{J}, m_j, k_j)$$

3.3 Weakly-Hard EXECUTION-TIME Constraints

Finally, let us focus on the EXECUTION-TIME constraint, for which the weakly-hard version is obvious: the execution time of a task should be within the bounds defined by *lower* and *upper* at least m times out of k consecutive executions of the tasks. Such a constraint can be used for compositional performance analysis in [6], as this approach is based on a busy window which typically contains a sequence of executions.

Definition 13. *A* weakly-hard EXECUTION-TIME *constraint on four events* **start, end, pre** *and* **res** *is a constraint parameterized by:*

- $(lower, upper) \in TimeWindow \times TimeWindow$
- $(m, k) \in \mathbb{N} \times \mathbb{N}^+$

A timing behavior $\omega = \{\sigma_{\mathbf{start}}, \sigma_{\mathbf{end}}, \sigma_{\mathbf{pre}}, \sigma_{\mathbf{res}}\}$ *is said to satisfy the constraint* WH-EXECUTION-TIME$_{\mathbf{start,end,pre,res}}(lower, upper, m, k)$ *if and only if*

$$\forall n \in \mathbb{N}^+ : \#\{l \in \mathbb{N}^+ \mid n \leq l < n + k \wedge ET_{\omega}(l) \in [lower; upper]\} \geq m$$

3.4 Inference of Weakly-Hard Constraints

Properties of weakly-hard constraints have been studied for example in [3], however to the best of our knowledge the focus has always been on determining whether one constraint is stronger than another one. We present here a result about how to infer new constraints from existing ones. As this question is independent of which specific weakly-hard constraint is mentioned and only the values of the parameters m and k are relevant, we simply assume that we are given an (m, k)-weakly-hard constraint, meaning that a predicate $pred$ must be satisfied by at least m elements of a sequence $\{n, \ldots, n+k-1\}$, for any $n \in \mathbb{N}^+$.

Theorem 5. *If a behavior ω satisfies an (m, k)-weakly-hard constraint then for all $k' \in \mathbb{N}^+$:*

1. *if $k' \leq k-m$: ω also satisfies the corresponding $(0, k')$-weakly-hard constraint.*
2. *if $k - m < k' \leq k$: ω also satisfies the corresponding (m', k')-weakly-hard constraint where $m' = k' - k + m$.*
3. *if $k < k'$: ω also satisfies the corresponding (m', k')-weakly-hard constraint where $m' = m \times q + \max(0, r - k + m)$ for q and r denoted respectively the quotient and the remainder in the division of k' by k, that is $k' = k \times q + r$ and $0 \leq r < k$.*

Proof. We prove this theorem case by case.

1. Any behavior trivially satisfies an $(0, k)$-weakly-hard constraint.
2. We make a proof by contradiction: consider a behavior which does not satisfy the (m', k')-weakly-hard constraint. This means that there exists $n \in \mathbb{N}^+$ such that the predicate $pred(l)$ is violated more than $k' - m' = k - m$ times for $n \leq l < n+k'$. This implies that even if $pred(l)$ holds for $n+k' \leq l < n+k$ there will be more than $k - m$ violations of $pred(l)$ for $n \leq l < n + k'$, that is, ω does not satisfy the m, k-weakly-hard constraint either.
3. Let $k' = k \times q + r$ (where $q \geq 0$ and $0 \leq r < k$). Consider then a sequence of k' consecutive events and partition it into q subsequences of length k and 1 subsequence of length r. Each of the q subsequences contains at most m occurrences satisfying $pred$ and the subsequence of length r contains at least $\max(0, r - k + m)$ (this is obtained directly from 1. and 2.). Hence the result.

Note that these bounds are the best safe bounds possible. This theorem has a strong practical relevance, as one may not be able to choose the length of the sequence of executions to be observed.

4 Probabilistic Timing Constraints

In this section we propose a representation of probabilistic timing in TADL2 and then show how weakly-hard constraints relate to probabilistic constraints.

4.1 Generalities about Probabilities

Let us recall first some definitions and properties related to probabilities. A probability is defined on a *sample space* Ω which is a (possibly infinite and uncountable) set defining all existing values for this space. In other words, the sample space defines where the uncertainty comes from. Let us suppose that such an Ω is given.

Definition 14. *A probability[1] on Ω is a function $\mathbb{P} : \mathcal{P}(\Omega) \longrightarrow [0,1]$ such that:*

1. *$\mathbb{P}(\Omega) = 1$*
2. *for any indexed family $\{A_i\}_{i \in \mathbb{N}}$ of pairwise disjoint subsets of Ω:*

$$\mathbb{P}(\bigcup_{i \in \mathbb{N}} A_i) = \sum_{i \in \mathbb{N}} \mathbb{P}(A_i)$$

Here $\mathcal{P}(\Omega)$ denotes the set of subsets of Ω.

Definition 15. *A random variable is a function $X : \Omega \longrightarrow E$ for some set E. The* probability distribution[2] *of X is a probability on E denoted $\mathbb{P}_X$ and defined as*

$$\forall B \subseteq E : \mathbb{P}_X(B) = \mathbb{P}(X^{-1}(B))$$

where $X^{-1}(B) = \{\omega \in \Omega \mid X(\omega) \in B\}$.

For readability, $\mathbb{P}_X(B)$ is usually denoted $\mathbb{P}(X \in B)$, or even $\mathbb{P}(X = x)$ if B is a singleton $\{x\}$.

4.2 Probabilistic Execution Times

In the context of timing analysis of real-time systems, probabilities are mostly used for describing the execution time of tasks and then computing the response time of particular executions of tasks.

The sample space used for defining the probability is usually kept implicit. We choose here to mention it explicitly because it formalizes where the randomness comes from. As a first definition, we use $\Omega = \mathfrak{S}_{E_{sys}}$, meaning that the outcome of the random experiment is a timing behavior as formalized in Definition 2. Note that our sample space is not countable as Ω and $\mathcal{P}(\mathbb{N})$ are equinumerous.

Definition 16. *For each task τ, the execution time ET^n_τ of the n-th execution of τ is then a random variable, as it is a function ranging over Ω.*

Probabilistic methods for timing analysis are based on the assumption that for a given task τ, ET^n_τ has the same distribution for all values of $n \in \mathbb{N}^+$. Otherwise, one would have to provide a distribution for each ET^n_τ. Based on this and furthermore assuming that all ET^n_τ are independent (for all τ and all n), [7]

---

[1] This definition is not the most general since it is limited to the σ-algebra $\mathcal{P}(\Omega)$.
[2] *Also called probability law.*

computes the distribution of each response time RT^n_τ. Note that even if all execution times in $\{ET^n_\tau \mid n \in \mathbb{N}^+\}$ have the same distribution, the response times in $\{RT^n_\tau \mid n \in \mathbb{N}^+\}$ may still have different distributions, as shown in the following example.

Example 6. Consider a system consisting of one resource and two tasks activated periodically as in Figure 1. Suppose that the execution times are constant and the scheduling policy is static priority preemptive, τ_1 having higher priority than τ_2. The response time of τ_2 is not constant, although all execution times are.

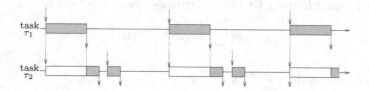

Fig. 1. A behavior scheduled according to a static priority preemptive policy

However, even though the distributions of the response times in $\{RT^n_\tau \mid n \in \mathbb{N}^+\}$ may be different, the result of a probabilistic timing analysis is usually given as a single distribution. This is achieved by assuming that the choice of n is also random and therefore the sample space Ω is in that case defined as $\mathfrak{S}_{E_{sys}} \times \mathbb{N}^+$ rather than $\mathfrak{S}_{E_{sys}}$ as before.

4.3   Representing Probabilistic Constraints in TADL2

We now focus on the representation of probabilistic timing in TADL2. It is beyond the scope of such a language to allow the expression of mathematical functions, therefore two options are proposed: the use of predefined distribution functions (namely: uniform, Gaussian, Fréchet, Gumbel and Weibull) or the approximation of distribution functions using histograms, as we explain now.

Definition 17. *Consider a partition $\{\alpha_1, \ldots, \alpha_q\}$ of an interval $[lower, upper]$. A histogram distribution $\mathbb{P}_h$ in $[lower, upper]$ is a function $\{\alpha_1, \ldots, \alpha_q\} \longrightarrow [0, 1]$ which associates a probability with each interval α_i (for $1 \leq i \leq q$) such that*

$$\sum_{i=1}^{q} \mathbb{P}_h(\alpha_i) = 1$$

Given a probability distribution $\mathbb{P}_d$ in $[lower, upper]$ and a partition $\{\alpha_1, \ldots, \alpha_q\}$ of $[lower, upper]$, it is possible to approximate $\mathbb{P}_d$ with a histogram distribution $\mathbb{P}_h$ defined by $\mathbb{P}_h(\alpha_i) = \mathbb{P}_d(\alpha_i)$ for $1 \leq i \leq q$.

We also allow in TADL2 the definition of pessimistic histogram distributions, that is, histogram distributions for which the sum of all probabilities is larger than 1. $\mathbb{P}_h(\alpha_i)$ must then be interpreted as an *upper bound* of the probability of α_i. Interestingly, this does not limit the expressivity of the original definition, as shown in the following theorem.

Theorem 6. *If* $\mathbb{P}_h$ *is a pessimistic distribution histogram upper bounding a probability distribution* $\mathbb{P}_d$ *in* $[lower, upper]$ *and* $\sum_{i=1}^{q} \mathbb{P}_h(\alpha_i) = 1$ *then*

$$\forall 1 \leq i \leq n : \mathbb{P}_d(\alpha_i) = \mathbb{P}_h(\alpha_i)$$

Proof. Suppose that $\sum_{i=1}^{q} \mathbb{P}_h(\alpha_i) = 1$. We know that

- $\sum_{i=1}^{q} \mathbb{P}_d(\alpha_i) = 1$ by definition of probability, and
- $\forall 1 \leq i \leq q : \mathbb{P}_d(\alpha_i) \leq \mathbb{P}_h(\alpha_i)$ because $\mathbb{P}_h$ is an upper bound.

By a simple arithmetic reasoning we obtain the result.

5   Probabilistic Interpretation of Weakly-Hard Constraints

Let us begin this section with a comment about the impact of dependencies between random variables on the expressivity of the model presented in the previous subsection. As a weakly-hard EXECUTION-TIME constraint describes a property over a sequence of consecutive executions of a task, it is of interest to discuss how much can be inferred about such a sequence from a probabilistic constraint represented as a distribution of the execution time of a task. We illustrate how this works on an example.

Example 7. Consider a task τ whose execution time is either equal to 1, with probability $\frac{1}{3}$, or equal to 2, with probability $\frac{1}{3}$. We focus on the execution time of two consecutive executions of τ, denoted respectively ET_τ^n and ET_τ^{n+1}. By definition, we have

$$\mathbb{P}(ET_\tau^n = 1, ET_\tau^{n+1} = 1) = \mathbb{P}(ET_\tau^{n+1} = 1 \mid ET_\tau^n = 1) \times \mathbb{P}(ET_\tau^n = 1)$$

where $\mathbb{P}(A|B)$ is the probability of A, given B. However, because we do not know the dependencies between ET_τ^n and ET_τ^{n+1}, we have to consider all possibilities. In this case $\mathbb{P}(ET_\tau^{n+1} = 1 \mid ET_\tau^n = 1)$ might be equal to anything between 0 and 1. As a result, we only know that $\mathbb{P}(ET_\tau^n = 1, ET_\tau^{n+1} = 1)$ is between 0 and $\frac{1}{3}$.

In the general case, the bounds on the probability of a sequence of executions to be in of a given value are obtained by using Fréchet bounds [5]. This example shows that weakly-hard constraints may be more adequate for systems in which there are dependencies between consecutive executions of a task.

Symmetrically, consider now a behavior satisfying an (m, k)-weakly-hard constraint where the property being monitored is denoted *pred*. What does this mean in terms of probabilities?

First, this implies that the probability of *pred*(n) to be violated for a value of $n \in \mathbb{N}^+$ chosen randomly is smaller than $\frac{k-m}{k}$. In addition, and more precisely, this means that for all $n \in \mathbb{N}^+$, if one chooses randomly $n \leq l < n+k$, then the probability that *pred*(l) be violated is smaller that $\frac{k-m}{k}$.

6 Conclusion

We have presented an extension of the Timing Augmented Description Language [10] (TADL) to weakly-hard and probabilistic constraints. In particular, we have shown the interest of using weakly-hard constraints for other purposes than describing deadline misses. The variety of formalisms which can be represented using our generic soft constraint emphasizes its practical relevance. A natural and exciting continuation of this work is the study of analysis methods based on these generic constraints.

References

1. ATESST2 project, http://www.atesst.org
2. Bernat, G.: Specification and Analysis of Weakly Hard Real-Time Systems. PhD thesis, Universitat de les Illes Balears (1998)
3. Bernat, G., Burns, A., Llamosí, A.: Weakly hard real-time systems. IEEE Trans. Computers 50(4), 308–321 (2001)
4. Henia, R., Hamann, A., Jersak, M., Racu, R., Richter, K., Ernst, R.: System level performance analysis - the SymTA/S approach. In: IEE Proceedings Computers and Digital Techniques (2005)
5. Ivers, M., Ernst, R.: Probabilistic Network Loads with Dependencies and the Effect on Queue Sojourn Times. In: Bartolini, N., Nikoletseas, S., Sinha, P., Cardellini, V., Mahanti, A. (eds.) QShine 2009. LNICST, vol. 22, pp. 280–296. Springer, Heidelberg (2009)
6. Jersak, M., Henia, R., Ernst, R.: Context-aware performance analysis for efficient embedded system design. In: Proceedings of DATE 2004, pp. 1046–1051. IEEE Computer Society (2004)
7. López, J.M., Díaz, J.L., Entrialgo, J., García, D.F.: Stochastic analysis of real-time systems under preemptive priority-driven scheduling. Real-Time Systems 40(2), 180–207 (2008)
8. Quinton, S., Ernst, R., Bertrand, D., Yomsi, P.M.: Challenges and new trends in probabilistic timing analysis. In: Proceedings of DATE 2012 (2012); Hot Topic Special Session
9. Quinton, S., Hanke, M., Ernst, R.: Formal analysis of sporadic overload in real-time systems. In: Proceedings of DATE 2012 (2012)
10. TADL: Timing Augmented Description Language – TIMMO public deliverable D6, http://timmo-2-use.org/timmo/pdf/D6_TIMMO_TADL_Version_2_v12.pdf
11. Thiele, L., Chakraborty, S., Naedele, M.: Real-time calculus for scheduling hard real-time systems. In: Proceedings of ISCAS 2000, vol. 4, pp. 101–104. IEEE Computer Society (2000)
12. TIMMO project, http://timmo-2-use.org/timmo/index.htm
13. TIMMO-2-USE project, http://timmo-2-use.org

Modeling a BSG-E Automotive System
with the Timing Augmented Description Language

Marie-Agnès Peraldi-Frati[1], Arda Goknil[1], Morayo Adedjouma[2],
and Pierre Yves Gueguen[2]

[1] AOSTE Project - UNS-I3S-INRIA - Sophia Antipolis, France
[2] Delphi - 22 Avenue des Nations - BP 65059 Villepinte, France
`map@unice.fr, arda.goknil@inria.fr,`
`{morayo.adedjouma,pierre.yves.gueguen}@delphi.com`

Abstract. Modeling and analysis of time is a key issue for the correct development of an automotive distributed embedded system. The paper presents new
extensions of the Time Augmented Description Language (TADL), applicable
at different abstraction levels of an EAST-ADL/AUTOSAR design. The new
extensions enable a precise modeling of multi clock characteristics of distributed systems together with parameterized timing expressions. In this paper, we
highlight some critical issues for the high–level time modeling of a Box Servitude Generic-External (BSG-E) provided by Delphi. This industrial example illustrates timing constraints coming from both hardware and software parts of
the system.

Keywords: Timing constraint language, Automotive case studies, Non-
functional requirements, EAST-ADL, AUTOSAR.

1   Introduction

The engineering of software in automotive becomes more and more complex today
due to the amount of new functionalities, constraints applied to these functions (timing, cost reduction, weight, energy saving, etc.) and the diversity of hardware supporting software execution and communication (current vehicles may have up to 70 ECUs
connected with each other by more than five different bus systems). From an engineering point of view, there is a need for a safe development process based on different abstraction levels providing capabilities for a clear separation of concerns between
hardware and software parts. For real-time critical systems the integration of timing
requirements at these different levels becomes mandatory for a high level analysis of
timing behavior early in the design.

The AUTOSAR standard [3] and EAST-ADL [5] provide supports for the development of such embedded systems. Both the new releases of AUTOSAR (V4) [3]
and EAST-ADL (V2) [5] have adopted the timing model proposed in the Timing
Architecture Description Language (TADL) [1]. TADL is a timing language compliant with AUTOSAR and EAST_ADL models for defining timing characteristics of

T. Margaria and B. Steffen (Eds.): ISoLA 2012, Part II, LNCS 7610, pp. 111–125, 2012.

systems (duration, period, synchronization, etc.). However, TADL still lacks the ability to express important timing aspects such as:

- The modeling of symbolic timing expressions with unset parameters,
- The integration of variations in timing values by using intervals,
- The integration of complex concepts of distributed systems such as multi rate and multi clock systems (car software being distributed on different ECUs).

In this paper we mainly focus on the modeling of symbolic timing expressions, the integration of variations in timing values and the definition of a single-rate time base. The new extension of TADL2 for defining multi rate and multi clock systems is out of scope of the example we are using in this paper.

We take as example an industrial application provided by Delphi: a Box Servitude Generic-External (BSG-E). This industrial use case illustrates timing constraints coming from both hardware and software parts of the system. The timing specification of the BSG-E system with TADL2 is built on top of EAST-ADL models that describe functional and hardware design architectures.

The paper is organized as follows. Section 2 is dedicated to TADL2 and its new extensions. Section 3 presents the industrial use case, the functional architecture and the timing requirements applied on it with a timing model in TADL2. A conclusion ends the paper.

2   TADL2 Language

In this section we introduce the TADL2 language and show how a TADL2 specification allows a high-level modeling of complex timing requirements that mix time bases and Symbolic Timing Expressions (STE) with unset parameters.

One main improvement with TADL2 is the ability to define explicit time bases in a system. We first introduce the associated modeling elements: the *TimeBase*, *Dimension* and *Unit*. In addition, TADL2 provides the *TimeBaseRelation* in order to relate time bases to each other. Since our focus in this paper is not multi clock systems, we do not illustrate the *TimeBaseRelation*. A recent paper [7] gives a detailed description of the *TimeBaseRelation*.

The second improvement concerns timing expressions in TADL2 with the *SymbolicTimingExpression*, *VariableTimingExpression* and *ValueTimingExpression*. Timing expressions are used conjointly with EAST-ADL2 to express duration such as *maximum/minimum delay*, *period*, *jitter* and *tolerance duration*. These concepts are represented in the metamodel in Figure 1.

2.1   TimeBase, Dimension and Unit in TADL2

The TADL2 metamodel shows that the *TimingSpecification* refers to the *TimeBase* which represents a discrete and totally ordered set of instants. An instant can be seen as an event occurrence called a "tick". It may represent any repetitive event in the system. Events may refer even to the "classical" time dimension or to some evolution of a hardware part (rotation of crankshaft, distance, etc.). The type of the *TimeBase* is the *Dimension*. The *Dimension* has a kind that represents the nature of the *TimeBase* (see the *DimensionKind* in Figure 1). The *Time*, *Angle* and *Distance* which are often

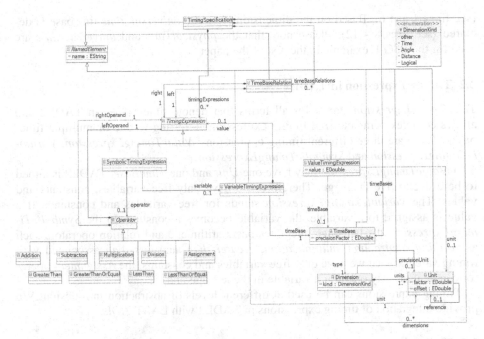

Fig. 1. TADL2 Metamodel for Timing Specification

used in the automotive domain are proposed as a dimension kind. Additionally, the *Logical* can be used to define a logical time reference. Finally, the *other* can be used for specific applications.

The *Dimension* defines a set of units that can be used to express duration measured on a given *TimeBase*. Each *Unit* is related to another *Unit* in order to enable conversions. The *factor*, *offset* and *reference* attributes in the *Unit* are used for conversions. Only linear conversions between units of the same dimension are allowed. Because a *Timebase* is a discrete set of instants, a discretization step is specified with the *precisionFactor* attribute which relies on the *precisionUnit*. Listing 1 gives a TADL2 specification where one Dimension and one TimeBase are declared.

```
1   Dimension physicalTime {
2      Units { micros{factor 1.0 offset 0.0},
3              ms{factor 1000.0 offset 0.0 reference micros}
4              second{factor 1000000.0 offset 0.0 reference micros}
5      }
6   }
7
8   TimeBase universal_time {
9      dimension physicalTime
10     precisionFactor 0.1
11     precisionUnit micros
12  }
```

Listing 1. Example of the Dimension and TimeBase

The *physicalTime* dimension has three units named *micros*, *ms* and *second* where 1 *second* unit is equal to 1000000 *micros* unit and 1 *ms* unit is equal to 1000 *micros* unit (see lines 1 and 6). Based on the dimension type, the *universal_time* timebase is declared (see lines 8 - 12). Please note that the *physicalTime* and *universal_time* are used for the BSG-E example in the rest of the paper.

2.2 Timing Expression in TADL2

The *TimingExpression* stands for all terms that denote time values in TADL2 and allows complex parameterized timing expressions referring to one or multiple timebases. There are three different timing expressions: *ValueTimingExpression, VariableTimingExpression* and *SymbolicTimingExpression*.

A *ValueTimingExpression* may have one *Unit* and one *TimeBase*. TADL2 is aimed to be a declarative language. Therefore, we have only free variables, constants and values. The *VariableTimingExpression* stands for free variables and constants. If a value is assigned to a variable, the variable becomes a constant. In the *SymbolicTimingExpression*, the language integrates basic arithmetic and relation operators such as *addition, subtraction, multiplication, greater than,* and *less than* associated with timing values. Since we have only free variables and constants, the *Assignment* operator can be used only once for a variable in the left operand.

Timing expressions can be used at different levels of abstraction in a design. We provide integration of timing expressions in TADL2 with EAST-ADL.

2.3 Timing Constraints in TADL2

TADL2 supports a number of timing constraints attached to EAST-ADL models. Figure 2 gives the metamodel for the basic timing constraints.

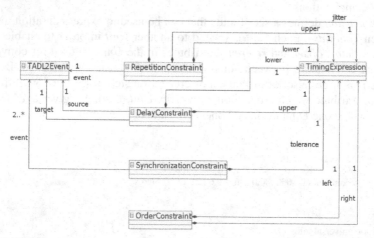

Fig. 2. The Basic Timing Constraints in TADL2 with TimingExpression

The complete description of the constraints can be found in [5]. A *Repetition* constraint describes the distribution of the occurrences of a single event. A *Delay* constraint describes how occurrences of an event called *target* are placed relative to each occurrence of an event called *source*. A *Synchronization* constraint describes how tightly the occurrences of a group of events follow each other. An *Order* constraint forces two timing expressions (presumably containing variables) to be ordered. Each constraint has one or more properties. In TADL2 we replace the initial integer type associated with these properties by the TimingExpression.

Listing 2 shows the textual concrete syntax for an EAST-ADL timing constraint extended with a TADL2 TimingExpression.

```
1    Event firstWheelBrakeActuation { }
2    Event secondWheelBrakeActuation { }
3    Event thirdWheelBrakeActuation { }
4    Event fourthWheelBrakeActuation { }
5
6    var X ms on universal_time
7
8    SynchronizationConstraint syc1 {
9        events firstWheelBrakeActuation,
10            secondWheelBrakeActuation,
11            thirdWheelBrakeActuation,
12            fourthWheelBrakeActuation
13
14       tolerance = X
15   }
```

Listing 2. Example Synchronization Constraint in TADL2

The constraint is about the maximum tolerated time difference – in a Brake By Wire system – between the first and last wheel brake actuations. The brake actuation is defined for each wheel as an event (see lines 1-4). The *var* keyword is used for defining both free variables and constants. The variable X is defined as a free variable in an instance of the *VariableTimingExpression* (see line 6). For the brake actuation events, the synchronization constraint *sc1* has the attribute *tolerance* which is equal to X (see line 14).

3   Use Case Description: The Box Servitude Generic External (BSG-E)

We take as example an industrial application provided by Delphi: a Box Servitude Generic-External (BSG-E). This industrial use case illustrates timing constraints coming from both hardware and software parts of the system. BSG-E means in French "Boîtier de Servitude Externe" (Box Servitude Generic - External). One of the main functions of the product is the management of vehicle front fog lights which is a critical functionality. These lights are also used as cornering lights. Moreover, the BSG-E covers the following main functions:

- *Function 1.* Ensure the dialogue with the main car ECU BSI (Box Servitude Internal) by using a CAN low speed communication network
- *Function 2.* Ensure the internal and output diagnostic
- *Function 3.* Management and storage of local defects
- *Function 4.* The electrical protection of downstream wires (not loads).

These functions require handling of real-time performance and some timing characteristics of the system.

3.1 Functional /Hardware Architecture of the BSG-E

The first step in the system development is to perform the requirement analysis phase. The requirement analysis phase allows classifying functional and non-functional requirements, identifying operational scenarios, and understanding the behavior of the system. This phase is suitable for handling timing constraints like duration and response time of functions.

One output of the requirements analysis phase is the functional architecture as a preliminary idea of the main functions involved in the design, boundaries, blocks of system and relations between them. In the EAST-ADL development cycle, such models correspond to the high level architecture at the analysis level.

The second step is perform the design phase where the Functional Design Architecture (see Figure 3) is detailed and a Hardware Design Architecture gives the execution platform and the sensors/actuators (see Figure 4).

The Functional Design Architecture focuses on the Software (SW) part of the system. It shows components and their interfaces (input and output ports).

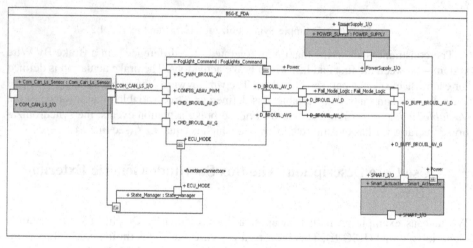

Fig. 3. Functional Design Architecture of the BSG-E System

The BSG-E receives orders from the BSI (Box Servitude Internal) which is the main ECU that communicates with the BSG-E through a CAN bus. Communication with the BSI is handled, at the software level, by the *Com_Can_Ls_Sensor* component (see Function 1). The *POWER_SUPPLY* component in Figure 3 ensures the acquisition of the alimentation. The *FogLights_Command* component is the main software component. It receives all messages from the main ECU (BSI) through the CAN frames and manages them for executing the functionalities of the system. Starting from it, the *Fail_Mode_Logic* component can manage the protection and diagnostic functions (see Function 2) and the *Smart_Actuator* component receives orders for activating the front fog lights. The *State_Manager* component handles the internal mode changes of the system.

The Hardware Design Architecture in Figure 4 represents the physical architecture of the system. Each element in the functional design architecture is allocated to one element in the hardware design architecture. Each Hardware (HW) component realizes one or many SW components.

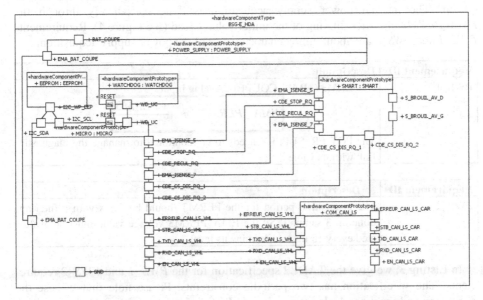

Fig. 4. Hardware Design Architecture of the BSG-E System

The *MICRO* component realizes the *FogLights_Command*, *State_Manager* and the *Fail_Mode_Logic* functions which appear in Figure 3. The *SMART*, *POWER_SUPPLY* and *Com_Can_Ls* are hardware components. The *SMART* is a driver to complete output command control and the *POWER-SUPPLY* ensures the alimentation distribution. The *Com_Can_Ls* is a bus used for the network management and control. Thus, these components manage the first two functions of the BSG-E (see Function 1 and Function 2). Another two functions are specifically managed at the HW level by the *EEPROM* and *WATCHDOG* components. The *EEPROM*, a memory component, is used to manage the SMART defect counter memorization and also to store the configuration data of the BSG-E (see Function 3). The *WATCHDOG* is an ASIC that triggers the system reset if the *MICRO* quits the "normal" mode operation (see Function 4).

Connectors between components are also refined regarding the system architecture. Output and input lines in the Functional and Hardware Design Architectures are submitted to timing requirements.

3.2 BSG-E Requirements Including Timing Characteristics

Some hardware components (together with the software functions they realized) are submitted to timing constraints. The BSG-E system contains timing constraints of different nature such as delay, synchronization and arbitrary constraints. In this section, we present the textual timing requirements for the BSG-E system obtained during the requirements analysis phase and the formalization of these requirements in TADL2. We use the TADL2 textual concrete syntax.

Timing Requirements for the POWER_SUPPLY

When the vehicle is under tension, all the components including the BSG-E are switched on. The internal power supply acquisition is done periodically through the *EMA_PERM3* line after filtering of the initial voltage read (see Figure 4). Requirements *PWS_1* and *PWS_2* are about timing characteristics of the power supply acquisition.

Requirement ID	Description
PWS_1	PERM3 (+BAT_COUPE) - Analog Input $$EMA\_PERM3 \approx \frac{+PERM3}{5}$$ The POWER_SUPPLY needs to be monitored to manage the diagnostic link with its value.

Requirement ID	Description
PWS_2	The acquisition period for the PERM3 should be 5 ms with a filtering done on 3 samples. So the EMA_PERM3 voltage value must be evaluated every 15 ms to determine its level.

In Listing 3, we give the TADL2 specification for the *PWS_1* and *PWS_2* requirements. The specification has two periodic constraints. Please note that we use the *dimension* and *timebase* declarations given in Listing 1.

```
1    var AcqPerm  ms on universal_time :=5.0
2
3    Event HAD_PowerSupply_PERM3 { }
4    Event HAD_PowerSupply_EMA_PERM3 { }
5
6    PeriodicConstraint pc1{
7        event HAD_PowerSupply_PERM3
8        period = AcqPerm
9        minimum = 0.0
10       jitter = 0.0
11   }
12
13   PeriodicConstraint pc2{
14       event HAD_PowerSupply_EMA_PERM3
15       period = (3*AcqPerm)
16       minimum = 0.0
17       jitter = 0.0
18   }
```

Listing 3. TADL2 Specification for the PWS_1 and PWS_2 Requirements

We have two periodic constraints (the *pc1* for the *PWS_1* and the *pc2* for the *PWS_2*). A periodic constraint describes periodic occurrence of an event. The events *HAD_PowerSupply_PERM3* and *HAD_PowerSupply_EMA_PERM3* are declared for power supply monitoring and acquisition (see lines 3 and 4). These events are attached to the corresponding input and/or output ports of the FDA/HDA.

The period value for the events is declared as a constant (see line 1). The *pc1* and *pc2* periodic constraints describe periodic occurrence of the events for power supply monitoring and acquisition with periods *AcqPerm* and *3*AcqPerm*. The variable *AcqPerm* is used twice in two different constraints.

Timing Requirements for the MICRO

The *MICRO* is the component which realizes the *State_Manager* whose role is to handle internal mode changes of the system. After power is switched ON, the BSG-E is initialized and it gets into the transitory mode *INIT*. When the system gets into a stable mode, it carries out its associated functions. It can also get into the *DEGRADED* or *RESET* mode if an abnormal operation is detected. The following *MICRO_1* requirement is the timing requirement for the mode transitions.

Requirement ID	Description
MICRO_1	- When the BSGE enters into the **INIT** mode, its initialization must be performed.
	- BSG_E must stay in the **INIT** mode for a maximum time of **T_init**.
	- **T_init** represents the time for the following transitions:
	OFF=>INIT=>NORMAL or RESET=>INIT=>NORMAL.
	- The BSG_E initialization time **T_init** corresponds to the time between the detection of the rising edge of the power supply in the EMA_PERM3 (EMA_BAT_COUPE) and the consumption of the first frame CAR_CDE_BSE.
	- This must be lower than **40 ms.**
	- In case of reset, **T_init** is the duration calculated between the reset activation and the consumption of the first frame CAR_CDE_BSE.

Listing 4 gives the TADL2 specification for the *MICRO_1* timing requirement.

```
1    Event EMA_PERM3 { }
2    Event CAR_CDE_BSE { }
3    Event RESET { }
4
5    var T_init ms on universal_time := 40.0
6
7    DelayConstraint dc1_a {
8        source EMA_PERM3
9        target CAR_CDE_BSE
10       lower = 0.0
11       upper = T_init
12   }
13
14   DelayConstraint dc1_b {
15       source RESET
16       target CAR_CDE_BSE
17       lower = 0.0
18       upper = T_init
19   }
```

Listing 4. TADL2 Specification for the MICRO_1 Requirement

The specification has two delay constraints with three events. The minimum and maximum duration between the occurrences of target and source events are given by the attributes *lower* and *upper*. The *dc1_a* delay constraint states that the duration between the detection of the rising edge of the power supply in the *EMA_PERM3* and the consumption of the first frame *CAR_CDE_BSE* should be less than 40 ms. The *dc1_b* delay constraint states the same timing constraint between the *RESET* activation and the consumption of the first frame *CAR_CDE_BSE*.

Timing Requirements for the SMART

The *SMART* driver is the component that completes the output control commands *S_BROUIL_AV_D and S_BROUIL_AV_G* (see Figure 4). In case of normal operation, i.e. the system is in the *NORMAL* mode, the fog lights are activated with the outputs *S_BROUIL_AV_D and S_BROUIL_AV_G*.

Requirement ID	Description
SMART_1	The BSG_E outputs (*S_BROUIL_AV_D* and *S_BROUIL_AV_G*) have to be activated or deactivated in less than **10 ms** for the CAR_CDE_BSE frame reception. This time is calculated between the end of the reception of the frame and the real output commutation.

In Listing 5, we give the TADL2 specification for the *SMART_1* timing requirement. The specification has two delay constraints with three events.

```
1    var BSG_E_O_Delay  ms on universal_time := 10.0
2
3    Event CAR_CDE_BSE { }
4    Event S_BROUIL_AV_D { }
5    Event S_BROUIL_AV_G { }
6
7    DelayConstraint dc2_a{
8       source CAR_CDE_BSE
9       target S_BROUIL_AV_D
10      lower = 0.0
11      upper = BSG_E_O_Delay
12   }
13
14   DelayConstraint dc2_b{
15      source CAR_CDE_BSE
16      target S_BROUIL_AV_G
17      lower = 0.0
18      upper = BSG_E_O_Delay
19   }
```

Listing 5. Example TADL2 Specification for the SMART_1 Requirement

The *dc2_a* delay constraint is for the activation of the *S_BROUIL_AV_D*. After the consumption of the first frame *CAR_CDE_BSE* (see lines 3 and 8 for the event *CAR_CDE_BSE*), the *S_BROUIL_AV_D* should be activated in less than 10 ms. The *dc2_b* is a similar delay constraint for the activation of the *S_BROUIL_AV_G*.

The two outputs *S_BROUIL_AV_D* and *S_BROUIL_AV_G* correspond to the left and right fog lights respectively. When they are commuted, the driver must see them simultaneously activated. The minimum dephasing time between the two signals should be very low (see the *SMART_2* requirement).

Requirement ID	Description
SMART_2	For the S_BROUIL_AV ("Brouillards AV allumés"), the dephasing time between right and left outputs must be lower than **25 ms**

Listing 6 gives the TADL2 specification for the *SMART_2* timing requirement with a synchronization constraint.

```
1    var dephasing_GD ms on  universal_time  := 25.0
2
3    SynchronizationConstraint sc1 {
4        events S_BROUIL_AV_G, S_BROUIL_AV_D
5        tolerance = dephasing_GD
6    }
```

Listing 6. TADL2 Specification for the SMART_2 Requirement

The *sc1* constraint is about the maximum tolerated time difference between the activation of left and right fog lights (the *S_BROUIL_AV_G* and the *S_BROUIL_AV_D*). The activation of left and right fog lights is defined by two events (see line 4). For these events, the synchronization constraint *sc1* has the attribute *tolerance* with the constant *dephasing_GD* which is 25 ms (see line 5).

Another function realized by the BSG-E is the internal and output diagnostic. It is useful to detect short circuit in the outputs. This functionality is performed at the *SMART* level through the *CDE_CS_DIS_RQ_1* and the *CDE_CS_DIS_RQ_2* lines in Figure 4.

Requirement ID	Description
SMART_3	The CDE_CS_DIS_RQ_2 must be reset to 0 (enable state) before reading the value of the CDE_STOP_RQ (BROUIL_AV_G) pin to perform diagnostic function. - This behaviour has to be done only if a diagnostic reading is performed. - The diagnostic reading has to be performed at least 600μs after the reset of the CDE_CS_DIS_RQ_2. - The CDE_CS_DIS_RQ_2 signal is set to 1 (inactive), when the diagnostic acquisition is terminated. Note: This behaviour is the same when PWM command @ 100% or when the output is not commanded.

Listing 7 gives the TADL2 specification for the *SMART_3* timing requirement with synchronization and delay constraints.

```
1    Event BROUIL_AV_G { }
2    Event CDE_CS_DIS_RQ_2 { }
3    Event DiagStart { }
4
5    SynchronizationConstraint sc2 {
6        events BROUIL_AV_G, CDE_CS_DIS_RQ_2
7        tolerance = (0.0 ms on universal_time)
8    }
9
10   var MinDelayForDiag micros on universal_time := 600.0
11   var PWM ms on universal_time := 5.0
12
13   DelayConstraint dc3 {
14       source CDE_CS_DIS_RQ_2
15       target DiagStart
16       lower = MinDelayForDiag
17       upper = PWM
18   }
```

Listing 7. TADL2 Specification for the SMART_3 Requirement

If the diagnostic detects abnormal operating conditions, the system gets into the *RESET* mode and the *WATCHDOG* ensures some operations.

Timing Requirements for the WATCHDOG

The *WATCHDOG* drives the following operations:

- Drive to specific value of the buffer outputs in order to drive some specific BSG outputs using the *WD_UC* line (see Figure 4).
- The WATCHDOG safe mode: reset the BSG μC through the input line *RESET*.

The *WD_UC* line is being triggered periodically. It is falling edge sensitive, i.e. the signal on the line is read only at the low state. Furthermore, this signal must be present for a minimum time. Otherwise, it is too short to be handled correctly by the *WATCHDOG*.

Requirement ID	Description
WD_1	The WD_UC line is falling edge sensitive.

Requirement ID	Description
WD_2	The WD_UC signal must be present at low state for at least 6μs to be taken into account by the WATCHDOG.

In Listing 8, we give the TADL2 specification for the *WD_1* and *WD_2* requirements with a delay constraint.

```
1    var WD_UC_Hold micros on universal_time := 6.0
2    var infinity ms on universal_time := 10000000000000.0
3    Event WD_UC_fallingEdge { }
4    Event WD_UC_risingEdge { }
5
6    DelayConstraint dc4 {
7        source WD_UC_fallingEdge
8        target WD_UC_risingEdge
9        lower = WD_UC_Hold
10       upper = infinity
11   }
```

Listing 8. TADL2 Specification for the WD_1 and WD_2 Requirements

The *dc4* delay constraint states that the *WD_UC* line should be maintained at a lower state for at least 6 microsecond (see lines 6 -11).

If the signal is not read in some fixed window area (for example it is not present long enough to be handled), the component resets the micro to return to the "normal" mode. It gets into the "fail" mode if the normal operation is not returned back after three attempts of reset (see the *WD_3* requirement).

Requirement ID	Description
WD_3	The WATCHDOG is monitoring its WD_UC line. If this line is not activated correctly, then WATCHDOG resets the MICRO. If the MICRO does not return to the normal operation after the 3rd reset pulse, then the WATCDOG enters into the fail mode after 180ms (130,7 to 256,9ms).

The TADL2 specification in Listing 9 states that it takes at least 180 ms for the *WATCHDOG* to get into the "fail" mode from the falling edge.

```
1    var delayBeforeFailMode ms on universal_time := 180.0
2    var infinity ms on universal_time := 10000000000000.0
3
4    Event WD_UC_failMode { }
5
6    DelayConstraint dc5 {
7        source WD_UC_fallingEdge
8        target WD_UC_failMode
9        lower = delayBeforeFailMode
10       upper = infinity
11   }
```

Listing 9. TADL2 Specification for the WD_3 Requirement

We specify 'infinity' as a special constant not to limit the upper bound of the delay for the 'fail' mode (see lines 2 and 10). The lower bound is specified by a constant with a value of 180 ms (see lines 1 and 9).

The *WATCHDOG* activates the reset of the *MICRO* in a time interval.

Requirement ID	Description
WD_4	Outside a window area of [150ms - 250ms] +/-10%, the WATCHDOG activates the material reset.

Listing 10 gives the TADL2 specification for the *WD_4* timing requirement with a delay constraint.

```
1    Event Micro_Reset { }
2
3    var delayBeforeFailMode2 ms on universal_time
4    { (delayBeforeFailMode2 ≤ 250.0) }
5    { (delayBeforeFailMode2 ≥ 150.0) }
6
7    DelayConstraint dc6 {
8        source WD_UC_fallingEdge
9        target Micro_Reset
10       lower = delayBeforeFailMode2
11       upper = infinity
12   }
```

Listing 10. TADL2 Specification for the WD_4 Requirement

The lower bound is specified by the variable *delayBeforeFailMode2* (see line 3) with a value interval which comprises between 150 ms and 250 ms on universal time (see lines 4 and 5). The final value of the variable is left unspecified in TADL2. It is a free variable and the final value can be determined later.

If the signal is correctly read, the reset is not set. To be sure of the right reading of the signal, the watchdog triggering must be submitted to a worst case time.

Requirement ID	Description
WD_5	To be sure that the reset will not occur, the time between two watchdog triggers on the WD_UC should be less than 50.85 ms in Worst Case.

In Listing 11, we give the TADL2 specification for the *WD_5* requirement with a repetition constraint.

```
1    var InterWD_UC ms on universal_time := 50.85
2
3    RepetitionConstraint rc1 {
4        event WD_UC_risingEdge
5        span = 1
6        lower = 0.0
7        upper = InterWD_UC
8        jitter = 0.0
9    }
```

Listing 11. TADL2 Specification for the WD_5 Requirement

The *rc1* arbitrary constraint states that every sequence of span occurrences of the the *WD_UC_risingEdge* event must have a length of at least the *lower* and at most the *upper* time units. The two watchdog triggers on the *WD_UC* (the *WD_UC_risingEdge* event) occur in a time interval less than 50.85 ms.

4   Conclusion

In this paper we presented the TADL2 language for the modeling of multiple timing referential (TimeBase) in a system and the integration of complex timing constraints. We illustrate the new features with the industrial application example of a Box Servitude Generic-External (BSG-E) provided by Delphi. We highlighted the formalization - with TADL2 - of timing constraints applied on both hardware and software parts of the system. The integration of the new features with EAST-ADL is presented with the textual concrete syntax of TADL2. The illustration of multi-time bases and their relations is out of scope of the paper.

With TADL2 we progress henceforth on the way of modeling and analyzing timing constraints early in the design phase. Analysis of TADL2 specifications can be obtained by using model transformation techniques to go towards simulation and analysis tools. One candidate for the simulation is the TimeSquare environment [4] and the associated language CCSL [6] which allow multi clock system specifications. In a second step and for a formal analysis of TADL2 specifications, a synchronous language environment such as SCADE [2] could be envisaged.

Acknowledgments. This paper is based on the TIMMO-2-USE project in the framework of the ITEA2, EUREKA cluster N°3674. The work has been funded by The French Ministry for Industry and Finances, the German Ministry for Education and Research (BMBF) under the funding ID 01IS10034, and the Swedish governmental agency for innovation systems (VINNOVA). The responsibility for the content rests with the authors.

References

1. The ITEA TIMMO-2-USE Project, http://timmo-2-use.org/
2. Abdulla, P.A., Deneux, J., Stålmarck, G., Ågren, H., Åkerlund, O.: Designing Safe, Reliable Systems Using Scade. In: Margaria, T., Steffen, B. (eds.) ISoLA 2004. LNCS, vol. 4313, pp. 115–129. Springer, Heidelberg (2006)
3. AUTOSAR AUTomotive Open System Architecture, http://www.autosar.org
4. DeAntoni, J., Mallet, F., André, C.: TimeSquare: on the formal execution of UML and DSL models. Tool Session of the 4th Model Driven Development for Distributed Real Time Systems (2008)
5. EAST-ADL Language Specification,
   http://www.atesst.org/home/liblocal/docs/
   ATESST2_D4.1.1 EAST-ADL2-Specification 2010-06-02.pdf
6. Mallet, F., André, C., de Simone, R.: CCSL: Specifying Clock Constraints with UML/Marte. ISSE 4(3), 309–314 (2008)
7. Peraldi-Frati, M.-A., Goknil, A., Deantoni, J., Nordlander, J.: A Timing Language for Specifying Multi Clock Automotive Systems: The Timing Augmented Description Language. In: ICECCS 2012, Paris, France (2012)

Formal Analysis of TESLA Protocol in the Timed OTS/CafeOBJ Method

Iakovos Ouranos[1,2], Kazuhiro Ogata[3], and Petros Stefaneas[4]

[1] Hellenic Civil Aviation Authority, Heraklion Airport
[2] Technological Educational Institute of Crete, Computer Science Department
[3] School of Info. Sci., Japan Adv. Inst. of Sci. and Tech. (JAIST)
[4] School of Appl. Math. and Phys. Sci., National Tech. Univ. of Athens (NTUA)
iouranos@gmail.com, ogata@jaist.ac.jp, petros@math.ntua.gr

Abstract. The Timed Observational Transition System (TOTS)/CafeOBJ method is a version of the OTS/CafeOBJ method for modeling, specification and verification of distributed systems and protocols with real time constraints. In this paper we report on a case study from the field of source authentication protocols, TESLA protocol, to show the application of the method to such complex systems. We prove that our model of the protocol satisfies that the receiver does not accept as authentic any message unless it was actually sent by the sender. To verify the property we have used several other invariants which include timing information. To our knowledge, this is the first time that the method has been applied to the formal analysis of such a complex protocol.

Keywords: Algebraic Specification, Source Authentication, TESLA, CafeOBJ, Timed Observational Transition Systems, Formal Verification.

1 Introduction

The Timed OTS/CafeOBJ method [1], is a version of the OTS/CafeOBJ [2] method for modeling real-time systems. The main advantage of these methods is that system's specification and verification is written in terms of equations, which are the most fundamental logical formulas, easier to learn and use than other formal methods.

Although the OTS/CafeOBJ method has been used in several complex, real life case studies [3-5], the real time version of it has been used only for simple systems [1]. The aim of this paper is to demonstrate the TOTS/CafeOBJ method by applying it to the modeling and verification of basic TESLA protocol [6-7], the simpler but yet very sophisticated version of TESLA protocol. TESLA, which stands for Time Efficient Source Loss-Tolerant Authentication Protocol, is a source authentication protocol used in multicast settings. It achieves properties of asymmetric cryptography by using symmetric primitives and time synchronization. Authentication of a data packet is based on information of the next and previous packets. The protocol finds application to the continuous authentication of radio and TV Internet broadcasts, authenticated data distribution by satellite, and has been published as an IETF standard [8].

T. Margaria and B. Steffen (Eds.): ISoLA 2012, Part II, LNCS 7610, pp. 126–142, 2012.
© Springer-Verlag Berlin Heidelberg 2012

In the OTS/CafeOBJ method, a protocol, algorithm, or software system is modeled as an Observational Transition System (OTS), which is a kind of transition system that can be written straightforwardly in terms of equations. Next, the OTS is described in CafeOBJ algebraic specification language [9]. Properties to verify are then expressed as CafeOBJ terms, and proof scores showing that the specified OTS model has desired properties are also written in CafeOBJ. Finally, proof scores are executed with the CafeOBJ system.

When dealing with real time systems, the system specification is extended with special data types called *clock observers* that model timing issues and a special time *advancing transition*, and OTSs are evolved to Timed OTSs. This approach can be seen as an application of the old-fashioned recipe of Abadi and Lamport [10].

The rest of the paper is organized as follows: Section 2 introduces the Timed OTS/CafeOBJ method, while in section 3, after the description of the protocol, we present the formal modeling and verification of it. Section 4 discusses some lessons learned and section 5 presents related works and closes the paper.

2   The Timed OTS/CafeOBJ Method

2.1   Timed Observational Transition Systems

U is the universal state space (the set of all possible states) and R^+ is the set of non-negative real numbers. Sets and types may be interchangeably used. *Bool* is the type for truth values.

Definition 1 (TOTS). A *TOTS* S consists of $< O, \mathcal{I}, \mathcal{T} \cup \{tick\}>$ where

- O: A set of observers. Each observer is a function $o : U D_{o1} \dots D_{om} \rightarrow D_o$. If D_o is a subset of $R^+ \cup \{\infty\}$, o is called a clock (observer). Otherwise, o is called a discrete observer. The equivalence between two states u_1, u_2 (denoted as $v_1 =_S v_2$) is defined w.r.t. values returned by the observers. Among clocks is $now : U \rightarrow R^+$ that plays a master clock and initially returns 0.

- $\mathcal{I}$: The set of initial states such that $\mathcal{I} \subseteq U$.

- $\mathcal{T} \cup \{tick\}$: A set of transitions. Each transition is a function $t : U D_{t1} \dots D_{tn} \rightarrow U$. Each transition t, together with any other parameters $y_1, \dots, y_n$, preserves the equivalence between two states. Each t has the effective condition that consists of the non-timing part c-t and the timing part tc-t whose types are $U D_{t1} \dots D_{tn} \rightarrow Bool$. If c-$t(u,y_1,\dots,y_n) \wedge tc$-$t(u,y_1,\dots,y_n)$ does not hold, then $t(u,y_1,\dots,y_n) =_S u$. *tick* is a time advancing transition whose type is $U R^+ \rightarrow U$. If c-$tick(u, r)$ holds, $now(tick(u,r))$ is $now(u)+r$, namely advancing the master clock by r. Any application of *tick* does not affect the values returned by any observers except for *now*, and the value returned by *now* is only affected by applications of *tick*.

For each $t \in \mathcal{T}$, there are two clocks $l_t : U D_{t1} \dots D_{tn} \rightarrow R^+$ and $u_t : U D_{t1} \dots D_{tn} \rightarrow (R^+ - \{0\}) \cup \{\infty\}$. The two clocks return the lower and upper bounds of t, and are used to force t to be applied during the interval. tc-$t(u,y_1,\dots,y_n)$ is $l_t(u,y_1,\dots,y_n) \leq now(u)$.

For each $t \in \mathcal{T}$, there are two functions d_t^{min} and d_t^{max} whose types are the same as l_t and u_t. d_t^{min} and d_t^{max} give the minimum and maximum delays of t, which are used to calculate the values returned by l_t and u_t as follows:

- Let *init* be an arbitrary initial state.

$$l_t(init, y_1, \ldots y_n) = \begin{cases} d_t^{min}(init, y_1, \ldots y_n) & c - t(init, y_1, \ldots y_n) = true \\ 0 & otherwise \end{cases}$$

$$u_t(init, y_1, \ldots y_n) = \begin{cases} d_t^{max}(init, y_1, \ldots y_n) & c - t(init, y_1, \ldots y_n) = true \\ \infty & otherwise \end{cases}$$

$c - t'(u, z_1, \ldots, z_n') \wedge lt'(u, z_1, \ldots, z_n') \leq now(u)$. Let u' be $t'(u, z_1, \ldots, z_n')$ and t be any other transition than t'.

$$l_{t'}(u', y_1, \ldots, y_{n'}) = \begin{cases} d_t^{min}(u, y_1, \ldots, y_{n'}) & c - t'(u', y_1, \ldots, y_{n'}) = true \\ 0 & otherwise \end{cases}$$

$$u_{t'}(u', y_1, \ldots, y_{n'}) = \begin{cases} d_t^{max}(u, y_1, \ldots, y_{n'}) & c - t'(u', y_1, \ldots, y_{n'}) = true \\ \infty & otherwise \end{cases}$$

$$l_t(u', y_1, \ldots, y_n) = \begin{cases} now(u) + d_{t'}^{min}(u, y_1, \ldots, y_{n'}) & c - t(u, y_1, \ldots y_n) = false \wedge c - t(u', y_1, \ldots y_n) = true \\ 0 & c - t(u, y_1, \ldots y_n) = true \wedge c - t(u', y_1, \ldots y_n) = false \\ l_t(u, y_1, \ldots y_n) & otherwise \end{cases}$$

$$u_t(u', y_1, \ldots, y_n) = \begin{cases} now(u) + d_{t'}^{max}(u, y_1, \ldots, y_{n'}) & c - t(u, y_1, \ldots y_n) = false \wedge c - t(u', y_1, \ldots y_n) = true \\ 0 & c - t(u, y_1, \ldots y_n) = true \wedge c - t(u', y_1, \ldots y_n) = false \\ u_t(u, y_1, \ldots y_n) & otherwise \end{cases}$$

Definition 2 (Execution). An execution of S is an infinite sequence $u_0, u_1, \ldots, u_i, \ldots$ of states satisfying,

- Initiation: $u_0 \in \mathcal{I}$,

- Consecution: For each natural number i, there exists $t \in \mathcal{T}$ such that $v_{i+1} =_S t(u_i, y_1, \ldots, y_n)$ for some parameters $y_1, \ldots, y_n$ or $v_{i+1} =_S tick(u_i, r)$ for some r.
- Time Divergence: As i increases, $now(u_i)$ increases without bound.
Let E_S be the set of all executions obtained from S.

Definition 3 (Reachable State). A state u is called reachable wrt S iff there exists an execution $e \in E_S$ such that $u \in e$. Let R_S be the set of all reachable states wrt S.

Definition 4 (Invariant). A predicate $p: U \to Bool$ is called invariant wrt S iff p holds in all reachable states, namely $(\forall u : R_S) p(u)$.

2.2   Specifying and Verifying TOTS in CafeOBJ

A TOTS is specified in CafeOBJ as an OTS. For specifying TOTSs in CafeOBJ, however, we prepare one module called TIMEVAL where extended non-negative real numbers are specified. TIMEVAL is declared with mod*. The signature of the module is as follows:

```
[Zero NzReal+ < Real+]
[NzReal+ Inf < NzTimeval]
[Real+ NzTimeval < Timeval]
  op 0 : -> Zero
  op oo : -> Inf
  op _<_  : Timeval Timeval -> Bool
  op _<=_ : Timeval Timeval -> Bool
  op _+_  : Timeval Timeval -> Timeval {assoc comm}
  op _+_  : Real+ Real+ -> Real+ {assoc comm}
  op _=_  : Timeval Timeval -> Bool {comm}
```

Zero, NzReal, Real+, Inf, NzTimeval and Timeval are visible sorts denoting $\{0\}$, $R^+ - \{0\}$, R^+, $\{\infty\}$, $(R^+ - \{0\}) \cup \{\infty\}$ and $R^+ \cup \{\infty\}$. Constants 0 and oo denote 0 and ∞. The operator _+_ adds two extended non-negative real numbers, the operator _<_ checks if one extended non-negative real number is greater than the other, the operator _<=_ checks if one extended non-negative real number is greater than or equal to the other and the operator _=_ checks if two extended non-negative real numbers are equal. The properties of the operators are specified in equations. Among equations are:

```
eq X < 0 = false . eq X < oo = true .
ceq X + T1 < X + T2 = true if T1 < T2 .
ceq T < T1 + T2 = true if T < T2 .
```

The same techniques used to verify that an OTS enjoys invariant properties, namely writing proof scores in CafeOBJ, can be used to verify that a TOTS enjoys invariant properties.

3   Analysis of TESLA Protocol

3.1   Description of the Protocol

Timed Efficient Stream Loss Tolerant Authentication (TESLA) protocol is a protocol used in broadcast settings for source authentication. It achieves properties of asymmetric cryptography by using symmetric primitives (except for the first digitally signed packet) and time synchronization. Authentication of a packet is based on information of the next and previous packets.

Basic TESLA, which is the simpler but sophisticated version of the protocol and applies the basic ideas in a one-to-one setting, informally works as follows: An initial authentication is achieved using a public key signature. The subsequent messages are authenticated using Message Authentication Codes (MACs) linked back to the initial signature.

In message $n\text{-}1$, the sender S generates a key k_n and transmits $f(k_n)$ to the receiver R, as a commitment to that key, where f is a suitable cryptographic hash function.

In message n, S sends a data packet m_n, authenticated using a MAC with key k_n. The key itself is revealed in message $n+1$.

Each receiver checks that the received key k_n corresponds to the commitment received in message $n-1$, verifies the MAC in message n, and then accepts the data packet m_n as authentic. Message n also contains a commitment to the next key k_{n+1}, authenticated by the MAC, thus allowing a chain of authentications. The messages exchanged in Basic TESLA are as follows:

> Init Message: $R \rightarrow S$: n_R
> Reply Message: $S \rightarrow R$: $f(k_1)$, n_R, $\{f(k_1), n_R\}_{PK(S)}$
> Msg_1: $S \rightarrow R$: d_1, $f(k_2)$, $MAC(k_1, d_1, f(k_2))$
> Msg_n: $S \rightarrow R$: d_n, $f(k_{n+1})$, k_{n-1}, $MAC(k_n, d_n, f(k_{n+1}), k_{n-1})$, $n > 1$.

where n_R is a nonce generated by the receiver to ensure freshness and d_1, d_n the data transmitted.

The protocol requires an important time synchronization assumption, the security condition: the receiver will not accept message n if it arrives after the sender might have sent message $n+1$, otherwise an intruder can capture message $n+1$, and use the key k_n from within it to fake a message n.

3.2   Timed OTS Modeling and Specification

We suppose that there exist untrustable nodes as well as trustable ones. Trustable nodes exactly follow the protocol, but untrustable ones may do something against the protocol as well, namely eavesdropping and/or faking of messages. The combination and cooperation of untrustable nodes is modelled as the most general intruder [11]. The cryptosystem used is perfect and so, the intruder can do the following:

• Eavesdrop any message flowing in the network.
• Glean any nonces, data, commitments, keys, message authentication codes (MACs) and signatures from the message; however the intruder can decrypt an encrypted text only if he knows the corresponding key to decrypt.
• Fake and send messages based on the gleaned information; however the intruder cannot guess unknown data.

We first formalize data types that constitute messages in terms of order-sorted algebras. We declare the following visible sorts and the corresponding data constructors for those data types:

• Sender denotes the set of agents that participate in the protocol as server. Two special sender nodes are *enemy* denoting a malicious intruder, and server modeling the legitimate server.
• Receiver denotes the set of receivers of the protocol. In our case we assume one legitimate receiver which is modelled by constant client.
• Data denotes data to be sent by the sender. For sender a and index i, d(a,i) models the data. Projection operator p1 returns the data creator and i the index of the data.
• Sort Key denotes the symmetric key used for the formation of commitments and MACs (we assume that is used the same key). The key used in an interval i, for sender a and receiver b is k(a,b,i). Projections p1, p2, and i return the three arguments.

- Sort PKey models the private key used in the signature of the Reply message. Given a sender a, its private key is given by pk(a), while projection p returns the agent.
- The pseudorandom function for the formation of the commitments is denoted by Prf. Given a key k, f(k) returns the commitment to that key. Projection k returns the argument.
- Rand denotes random numbers which makes nonces unguessable and unique.
- Nonce denotes nonces. Given sender a, receiver b and a random number r, n(a,b,r) returns the nonce created by a for b. Projections creator, forwhom and rand return the first, second and third arguments.
- Sign denotes the digital signature used in the Reply message. Given a private key pk, nonce n and prf p, enc(pk,n,p) returns the signature. Projections pk, n and p return the arguments.
- Mac1 denotes MACs of the first message (*m1*). Given key k, data d and prf p, mac1(k,p,d) is the data constructor and k, p, d the projectors.
- Mac2 denotes MAC used in message *mn*. Given keys k, k', data d and prf p, mac1(k,p,d,k') is the data constructor and k, k', p, and d the projectors.
- Msg models the four types of messages exchanged in a protocol session.
- Network models network as a multiset of messages exchanged.
- Timeval is a special sort modeling the time values.

In addition to the above visible sorts, we use the built-in visible sort Bool that denotes truth values, declared in the built-in module BOOL.

Formalization of Messages. There are four different kind of messages exchanged in the protocol:

- The initial message (im) that a receiver sends to the sender (server) to initiate a session, containing a nonce to ensure freshness, in clear. This is the only message sent by the receiver agent. The constructor of the message is

```
op im : Receiver Receiver Sender Nonce -> Msg
```

The first argument is meta-information that is only available to the outside observer and the node that has sent the corresponding message, and cannot be forged by the intruder, while the remaining arguments may be forged by the intruder. So, if the first argument is the enemy and second one is not, then the message has been faked by the intruder. Second and third arguments are the seeming sender and receiver, while the last argument is the nonce created by the sender of the message (i.e. the Receiver) for the server (i.e. the Sender), using a fresh random number. Projections crt-im, src im, dst-im return the first (actual creator), second (seeming sender), and third (receiver) arguments of each message. A predicate im?, checks if the given message is of the type im. Finally, j returns the identification number of the message, which is zero (0) for message im.

- The reply message (rm) sent by the server in response to the im. It contains the digital signature which encrypts with its private key, the nonce received, and the application of a pseudorandom function to the first key k1 (the so-called key commitment).

The constructor is: op rm : Sender Sender Receiver Nonce Prf Sign while the projections in CafeOBJ notation:

```
op rm? : Msg -> Bool      -- returns whether is an rm.
op crt : Msg -> Sender    -- creator
op src : Msg -> Sender    -- source
op dst : Msg -> Receiver  -- destination
op n : Msg -> Nonce       -- nonce
op p : Msg -> Prf         -- commitment
op c : Msg -> Sign        -- signature
op j : Msg -> Int         -- returns the id of the message.
                          -- We assume it is zero (0) for im and rm
```

- The first message that sends some data (m1). We model it separately because it does not reveal a key and as a consequence has different body. It contains the data, the commitment to the key used in the next message (k2), and both of them encrypted with the k1 in a message authentication code.

```
                op m1 : Sender Sender Receiver Data Prf Mac1 -> Msg
```
Projections:
```
  op m1? : Msg -> Bool      -- returns whether is an m1.
  op crt : Msg -> Sender    -- creator
  op src : Msg -> Sender    -- source
  op dst : Msg -> Receiver  -- destination
  op d : Msg -> Data        -- data
  op p : Msg -> Prf         -- commitment
  op mc1 : Msg -> Mac1      -- mac
  op j : Msg -> Int         -- returns the id of the message which
                            -- is 1 for m1
```

- The nth message (mn). It contains the data, the commitment to the key used in the next message (k_n+1), the key used in the previous message (k_n-1) and all of them encrypted with the kn in a message authentication code. We also add the index of the message, n.

```
  op mn : Sender Sender Receiver Data Prf Key Mac2 Int -> Msg
```
Projections:
```
  op mn? : Msg -> Bool      -- returns whether is an mn.
  op crt : Msg -> Sender    -- creator
  op src : Msg -> Sender    -- source
  op dst : Msg -> Receiver  -- destination
  op d : Msg -> Data        -- data
  op p : Msg -> Prf         -- commitment
  op k : Msg -> Key         -- key
  op mc2 : Msg -> Mac1      -- mac
  op j : Msg -> Int         -- index of the message n
```

Formalization of the Network. The network is modeled as a multiset of messages, which is used as the storage that the intruder can use. Any message that has been sent or put into the network is supposed to be never deleted from the network. As a consequence, the emptiness of the network means that no messages have been sent.

The intruder tries to glean seven kinds of quantities from the network. These are the nonces, data, commitments, the keys, two kinds of the message authentication codes and the signatures. The collections of these quantities are denoted by the following operators:

```
op nonces : Network -> ColNonces .
op keys : Network -> ColKeys . op macs2 : Network -> ColMacs2 .
op data : Network -> ColData. op signs : Network -> ColSigns .
op prfs : Network -> ColPrfs . op macs1 : Network -> ColMacs1 .
```

`Network` is the visible sort denoting networks. `ColX` is the visible sort denoting collections of quantities denoting by visible sort `X` (`X = Nonce`, `Sign`, `Data`, `Prf`, `Mac1`, `Mac2`, `Key`). For example, given a snapshot `nw` of the network, `nonces(nw)` and `macs1(nw)` denote the collection of nonces and message authentication codes appeared in the `m1` message available to the intruder.

Those operators are defined with equations. For the case of `nonces` the equations are as follows:

```
eq N \in nonces(void) = (creator(N) = enemy) .
ceq N \in nonces(M,NW) = true if im?(M) and n(M) = N .
ceq N \in nonces(M,NW) = true if rm?(M) and n(c(M)) = N and
                                   p(pk(c(M))) = enemy .
ceq N \in nonces(M,NW) = true if rm?(M) and n(M) = N .
ceq N \in nonces(M,NW) = N \in nonces(NW) if       not (im?(M) and
                n(M) = N) and not (rm?(M) and n(c(M)) = N and
          p(pk(c(M))) = enemy) and not(rm?(M) and n(M) = N) .
```

Constant `void` denotes the empty bag, while `N`, `M`, `NW` are CafeOBJ variables for `Nonce`, `Msg` and `Network`, respectively. Operator `_\in_` is the membership predicate of collection, while `_,_` is the data constructor of bags. So, `M,NW` denotes the network obtained by adding message `M` to the network `NW`. The first equation says that initially, the intruder's nonce is the only available to him. The second equation says that if there exists a message `M` of the type `im` in the network, then the nonce `N` of the message is available to the intruder. In the case of an `rm` message, we have two subcases: The nonce sent in clear is available to the intruder (equation 4), while the nonce encrypted with sender's private key in the signature is available to the intruder only if the key belongs to the intruder(equation 4). These are the only nonces available to the intruder.

The equations defining `data` are:

```
eq D \in data(void) = (p1(D) = enemy) .
ceq D \in data(M, NW) = true if m1?(M) and D = d(M) .
ceq D \in data(M, NW) = true if m1?(M) and D = d(mc1(M)) and
                                   p1(k(mc1(M))) = enemy .
ceq D \in data(M, NW) = true if mn?(M) and D = d(M) .
ceq D \in data(M, NW) = true if mn?(M) and D = d(mc2(M)) and
                                   p1(k(mc2(M))) = enemy .
ceq D \in data(M, NW) = D \in data(NW) if
        not (mn?(M) and D = d(M)) and
        not (m1?(M) and D = d(M)) and
not (m1?(M) and D = d(mc1(M)) and p1(k(mc1(M))) = enemy) and
not (mn?(M) and D = d(mc2(M)) and p1(k(mc2(M))) = enemy) .
```

The first equation says that the data initially available to the intruder are those constructed by him. The rest equations describe how intruder can glean data by messages m1 and mn.

Equations defining the remaining operators are written likewise.

TOTS Model of TESLA Protocol. Having specified the data part of the specification, we proceed to the specification of the behavior of the protocol in the module TESLA, as an Observational Transition System with real time extensions. The assumptions made for modeling reasons are as follows:

1. Time constraints for sending and receiving messages m1 and mn.
2. Ordering of packets using an integer packet id. We assume that messages im and rm have id = 0, m1 has id = 1, and mn, n > 1, id = n.
3. One sender - one receiver (basic scheme).
4. Intruder is modeled following Dolev Yao general intruder model [11].
5. A Boolean flag-s is set to true if the sender has received the im message.
6. A Boolean flag-r is set to true if the receiver has sent the im message.
7. A Boolean received? is used to check the receipt of a message by the receiver. Since the message is not deleted from the network, when received, the Boolean is set to true, in order not to be received again by the same receiver.
8. The observation next returns the id of the packet to be received by the client.

Real Time Issues and Model. The protocol requires an important synchronization assumption, the security condition: The receiver will not accept message n if it arrives after the sender might have sent message $n+1$, otherwise an intruder can capture message $n+1$, and use the key k_n to fake a message n. This is the reason for using timing constraints to some transitions and the Timed OTS model.

When the sender sends message rm, then receiver can receive it, while also sender can send message $m1$, since he does not know whether the receiver has already received it (the Boolean received? is not shared between sender and receiver). If the sender sends the $m1$ before receiver gets the rm, then there exist in the network rm and m_1 with received? values set to false. But in that case there is no problem, since m_1 does not reveal a key, while also rm contains a digital signature. So in that case there is no need for timing constraints other than 0 and oo.

But, if the sender sends message m_2 (m_{n+1}) before receiver received m₁ (and in general m_n), then the intruder can capture the key that is revealed in the m₂ (k_1), and fake the data part of m₁. This can be avoided if some time constraints are used. So, after sender sends the m_1 message, m2 (mn) should be sent between l-$sdm2$ (l-$sdmn$) and oo, m1 should be received between 0 and u-$rcvm1$, with u-$rcvm1$ < l-$sdm2$. Similarly, the next mn message should be sent after the previous has been received (i.e. u-$sdmn$ < l-$sdmn$). We assume that the delays are constant.

So, we have the following clock observers: now(t) returns the time at state t, 1-sdm2(t)(1-sdmn(t)) the lower bound of sending message m2 (mn), u-rcvmn(t) the upper bound of receiving message mn, and u-rcvm1(t) the upper bound of receiving message m1, at a state t.

The constants are: init denotes the initial state, d1 is the lower bound of sending an mn message, d2 is the upper bound of receiving m1 message and d3 is the upper bound of receiving mn message. The relation between time delays is declared in the OTS module as follows:

```
-- delays
op d1 : -> Real+
op d2 : -> Timeval+
op d3 : -> Timeval+
eq d2 < d1 = true .   eq d3 < d1 = true .
eq 0 < d1 = true .    eq 0 < d2 = true . eq 0 < d3 = true .
```

Finally the time advancing transition is denoted by `tick(t,r)`.

Formalization of Trustable Nodes. The non clock values observable from the outside of the protocol are `nw(t)` that returns the set of messages in the network at a state t, `ur(t)` which returns the set of random numbers used until state t, `flag-r(t)` that returns whether the receiver has sent im message, `flag-s(t)` that returns whether the sender has received im message, `received?(t,m)` that returns whether message m has been received or not at state t, while `next(t)` returns the id of the next packet to be received.

The behavior of the trustable principals is modeled with the corresponding sending and receiving transitions. Each action has an effective condition which is divided into the timing and the non-timing part. There are four transitions modeling receiver and five transitions modeling the behavior of sender. The transitions that have timing part are sdm1, sdm2 and sdmn.

For example, `sdmn(t,m,J)` corresponds to that if a message m of the type mn with id = J, J > 2, that has been sent by server to client exists in the network, agent server makes the data d(a,J+1), f(k(server,client, J+2), the key k(server,client, J) and the message authentication code mac(k(server,client,J+1),d(server,J+1),f(k(server,client, J+2),k(server,client,J)) and sends it in the message mn with the id J+1 of the message, providing that 1-sdmn(t) <= now(t).

The above are specified with equations in CafeOBJ as follows:

```
-- for action sdmn
op c-sdmn : Tesla Msg Int -> Bool
eq c-sdmn(T, M, I) = (M \in nw(T) and mn?(M) and j(M) = I and
crt(M) = server and src(M) = server and dst(M) = client and d(M) =
d(server, I) and p(M) = f(k(server, client, s I))
and k(M) = k(server, client, I - 1) and mc2(M) =
mac2(k(server,client,I), d(server,I), f(k(server, client, s I)),
k(server,client, I - 1)) and  I > 1 and 1-sdmn(T) <= now(T)) .
ceq nw(sdmn(T, M, I)) = (mn(server, server, client, d(server,s
I), f(k(server,client, (I + 2))), k(server, client, I),
mac2(k(server,client, s I), d(server, s I), f(k(server,client, (I +
2))), k(server,client, I)), s I), nw(T))  if c-sdmn(T, M,  I) .
eq ur(sdmn(T, M, I)) = ur(T) . eq now(sdmn(T, M, I)) = now(T) .
eq flag-s(sdmn(T, M, I)) = flag-s(T) .
eq flag-r(sdmn(T, M, I)) = flag-r(T) .
eq next(sdmn(T, M, I)) = next(T) .
eq received?(sdmn(T, M, I),M') = received?(T,M') .
eq u-rcvm1(sdmn(T, M, I)) = u-rcvm1(T) .
eq 1-sdm1(sdmn(T, M, I)) = 1-sdm1(T) .
```

```
eq l-sdm2(sdmn(T, M, I)) = l-sdm2(T) .
ceq l-sdmn(sdmn(T, M, I)) = now(T) + d1 if c-sdmn(T, M, I) .
ceq u-rcvmn(sdmn(T, M, I)) = now(T) + d3 if c-sdmn(T, M, I) .
bceq sdmn(T, M, I) = T if not c-sdmn(T, M, I) .
```

As is shown in the above CafeOBJ code, the observations nw, l-sdmn and u-rcvmn change their value after the application of sdmn in a state T, provided that the effective condition, which is defined by the first equation, holds. The rest observation value does not change. The delays d1 and d3 are declared in the OTS module with relation d3 < d1 and define the time order of sending and receiving a message *mn*.

Formalization of the Intruder. The intruder tries to glean information from the messages flowing in the network, create and send fake messages based on it. The gleaned quantities are nonces, data, commitments, keys, macs1, macs2, and signatures. The intruder's fake messages follow the format of the messages of the protocol, in order to be accepted by the receiver.

For example, if the intruder has some data D, D' commitments P, P' and a key K, then, if he/she create a message of type m1: D, P, mac1(K, D', P'), then it will be rejected by the receiver since when he/she will decrypt mac, D =/= D' and P =/= P'. So we assume that the format of such a fake message will be: m1: D, P, mac1(K,D,P). There are 18 transitions modeling the behavior of the intruder. For a fake message of the type mn, the application of transition fkmn7(t,k,k',k'',i) corresponds to that the enemy fakes mn(enemy,server,client,d(enemy,i),f(k),k', mac2(k'',d(enemy,i),f(k),k'),i) and put it into the network.

The CafeOBJ equations are:

```
-- for action fkmn7
op c-fkmn7 : Tesla Key Key Key Int -> Bool
eq c-fkmn7(T,K,K',K'',I) = (K \in keys(nw(T)) and K' \in keys(nw(T)) and
K'' \in keys(nw(T)) and I > 1) .
ceq nw(fkmn7(T,K,K',K'',I)) =
mn(enemy,server,client,d(enemy,I),f(K),K',mac2(K'',d(enemy,I),f(K),K'),I
),nw(T) if c-fkmn7(T,K,K',K'',I) .
eq ur(fkmn7(T,K,K',K'',I)) = ur(T) .
eq now(fkmn7(T,K,K',K'',I))= now(T) .
eq flag-s(fkmn7(T,K,K',K'',I)) = flag-s(T) .
eq flag-r(fkmn7(T,K,K',K'',I)) = flag-r(T) .
eq next(fkmn7(T,K,K',K'',I)) = next(T) .
eq received?(fkmn7(T,K,K',K'',I),M) = received?(T,M) .
eq u-rcvm1(fkmn7(T,K,K',K'',I)) = u-rcvm1(T) .
eq l-sdm1(fkmn7(T,K,K',K'',I)) = l-sdm1(T) .
eq l-sdm2(fkmn7(T,K,K',K'',I)) = l-sdm2(T) .
eq l-sdmn(fkmn7(T,K,K',K'',I)) = l-sdmn(T) .
eq u-rcvmn(fkmn7(T,K,K',K'',I)) = u-rcvmn(T) .
ceq fkmn7(T,K,K',K'',I) = T if not c-fkmn7(T,K,K',K'',I) .
```

3.3   Verification

The protocol satisfies the following invariant property (definition taken from the original paper): *The receiver does not accept as authentic any message mi unless mi was actually sent by the sender.*

We have expressed the above property based on our specification as three different invariants:

Invariant 1. Whenever you receive the three messages *rm, m1, m2,* i.e. *f(k1), n_R, {f(k1), n_R}_PK(S)* and *d1, f(k2), MAC(K1, d1,f(K2))* and *d2, f(k3), k1, MAC(...),*
then *m1* originates from the claimed source *S.*

Invariant 2. Whenever you receive the three messages *m1, m2, m3* i.e., *d1, f(k2), MAC(K1, d1,f(K2))* and *d2, f(k3), k1, MAC(...),* and *d3, f(k4), k2, MAC(...),*
then *m2* originates from the claimed source *S.*

Invariant 3. Whenever you receive the three messages *m_n-1, m_n, m_n+1, n > 2* i.e., *d_n-1, f(k_n), k_n-2, MAC(...),* and *d_n, f(k_n+1), k_n-1, MAC(...),* and
    d_n+1, f(k_n+2), k_n, MAC(...),
then *mn* originates from the claimed source *S.*

The above invariants are expressed in CafeOBJ notation in a module called *inv.mod* as operators *inv1, inv2* and *inv3* respectively. The most important property, *inv3* is declared as follows:

```
eq inv3(T, X, Y, Z, N) = (N > 2) and
mn(X, server, client, d(server, N - 1), f(k(server,client, N)),
k(server, client,N - 2), mac2(k(server,client,N - 1), d(server,N - 1),
f(k(server,client, N)), k(server, client, N - 2)), N - 1) \in nw(T)
and received?(T,mn(X, server, client, d(server, N - 1),
f(k(server,client, N)), k(server, client,N - 2), mac2(k(server,client,N
- 1), d(server,N - 1), f(k(server,client, N)), k(server, client, N -
2)), N - 1)) and
mn(Y, server, client, d(server,N), f(k(server,client, s N)),
k(server,client, N - 1), mac2(k(server,client,N),d(server,N),
f(k(server,client, s N)), k(server,client, N - 1)), N) \in nw(T)
and received?(T,mn(Y, server, client, d(server,N), f(k(server,client, s
N)), k(server,client, N - 1), mac2(k(server,client,N),d(server,N),
f(k(server,client, s N)), k(server,client, N - 1)), N)) and
mn(Z, server, client, d(server,s N), f(k(server,client, s s N)),
k(server,client, N), mac2(k(server,client,s N), d(server,s N),
f(k(server,client, s s N)), k(server,client, N)), s N) \in nw(T) and
received?(T,mn(Z, server, client, d(server,s N), f(k(server,client, s s
N)), k(server,client, N), mac2(k(server,client,s N), d(server,s N),
f(k(server,client, s s N)), k(server,client, N)), s N))and next(T)>N + 1
implies
```

```
mn(server, server, client, d(server,N), f(k(server,client, s N)),
k(server,client, N - 1), mac2(k(server,client,N),d(server,N),
f(k(server,client, s N)), k(server,client, N - 1)), N) \in nw(T)
and received?(T,mn(server, server, client, d(server,N),
f(k(server,client, s N)), k(server,client, N - 1),
mac2(k(server,client,N),d(server,N), f(k(server,client, s N)),
k(server,client, N - 1)), N)) .
```

To prove the above invariant, we used five more invariants as lemmas that we had then to prove. In general, to prove the three invariants that constitute the basic property of TESLA protocol, we used 29 invariants. Most of them were state invariants, while there were also lemmas on data types, such as Network.

Two invariants that were used as lemmas and include timing information are *inv8* and *inv12* and are defined as follows:

For any reachable state T and any message index N,

```
eq inv8(T,N) = N > 1 and l-sdmn(T) <= now(T) and
mn(server,server,client,d(server,N),f(k(server,client,(1 +
N))),k(server,client,(N + -
1)),mac2(k(server,client,N),d(server,N),f(k(server,client,(1 +
N))),k(server,client,(N + -1))),N) \in nw(T) implies
received?(T,mn(server,server,client,d(server,N),f(k(server,client,(1 +
N))),k(server,client,(N + -
1)),mac2(k(server,client,N),d(server,N),f(k(server,client,(1 +
N))),k(server,client,(N + -1))),N)) .
```

```
eq inv12(T,N) = N > 1 and
mn(server,server,client,d(server,N),f(k(server,client,(N +
1))),k(server,client,(N + -
1)),mac2(k(server,client,N),d(server,N),f(k(server,client,(N +
1))),k(server,client,(N + -1))),N)\in nw(T) and
not received?(T,mn(server,server,client,d(server,N),f(k(server,client,
(N + 1))),k(server,client,(N + -
1)),mac2(k(server,client,N),d(server,N),f(k(server,client,(N +
1))),k(server,client,(N + -1))),N)) implies u-rcvmn(T)<l-sdmn(T) .
```

The former says that if an original message mn exists in the network in a state T with n >1 and l-sdmn(T) <= now(T) then the message has been already received by the client. The latter says that if an original message mn exists in the network in a state T with n>1 and it has not yet been received by the client, then u-rcvmn(T)<l-sdmn(T). Apart from the lemmas, the proof scores written include exhaustive case analysis. In general the verification of Timed OTS specifications follow the same principles and methodology as the Standard OTS [2].

4   Lessons Learned and Proposals

Writing algebraic specifications and verifying them with CafeOBJ system has the advantage of a simple underlying theory, since it is based on equations, but can be very difficult and time consuming for an inexperienced user.

The two basic tasks that a specification engineer has to perform to specify and verify a system is the system and property description. Both suppose a deep understanding of the system/protocol.   In many cases, an incorrect system's specification may lead to unsuccessful verifications, which implies specification revisions/updates and verification retries. In an interactive theorem proving system and proof score verification style this can be very time consuming.

In the case of TESLA protocol specification and verification, many verification retries and specification revisions were performed. The reason was basically protocol functions misunderstanding, that lead to wrong descriptions. For instance, at the initial steps of our work on TESLA, we made two fundamental errors. The first was that we tried to model the protocol without timing constraints, only by adding some index to each packet. But when we tried to express the security condition, we found out that a counterexample was obvious: An intruder could steal a message and put into the network with altered data. Then the receiver could not identify the faked from the original message.

The second error was related to the expression of the property. We expressed it as:

$m_{n-1}(x, server, client, ...data_{n-1}...) \setminus in\ nw(t) \wedge m_n(y, server, client, ...data_n...) \setminus in\ nw(t) \wedge$
$m_{n+1}(z, server, client, ...data_{n+1}...) \setminus in\ nw(t) => m_n(server, server, client, ...data_n...) \setminus in\ nw(t)$
instead of $m_{n-1}(x, server, client, ...data_{n-1}...) \setminus in\ nw(t) \wedge$
$received?(t, m_{n-1}(x, server, client, ...data_{n-1}...)) \wedge m_n(y, server, client, ...data_n...) \setminus in\ nw(t) \wedge$
$m_{n+1}(z, server, client, ...data_{n+1}...) \setminus in\ nw(t) \wedge received?(t, m_{n+1}(z, server, client, ...data_{n+1}...)) =>$
$m_n(server, server, client, ...data_n...) \setminus in\ nw(t) \wedge received?(t, m_n(server, server, client, ...data_n...))$

During the process of verifying/writing proof scores, we realized that without the boolean observation *received?* in our property expression, a message could exist in the network without having been received by the receiver, which was not representative for the protocol's behavior.

Some less important, but necessary modifications that we had to do are:

• Initially we did not use an observation *next* to model the id of the next packet to be received by the client. As a result the client could accept a faked message that existed in the network with smaller id than the last received.

• Without a special transition *sdm2* for the sending of the second message *m2*, it was not possible to model the effective condition *c-sdmn, n=2*, since *sdmn, n=2* depends on the existence of message *m1* in the network which has different format from *mn, n>1*.

Some level of automation for Timed OTS method can be possible. This include proof score reusability and case analyses with tool support similar to that of Standard OTSs [12-13]. Additionally, editors such as Emacs and Eclipse make specification and verification writing easier, and can be more useful with CafeOBJ oriented extensions.

Using CafeOBJ for complex real life systems and protocols is still difficult for non-experts. To overcome this, some library support for reusable similar modules used to real time, security protocols, etc. can be useful. Additionally, combination of model checking and theorem proving techniques is necessary [14].

5   Related Work

TESLA protocol has been formally specified and verified in three different works [15-17]. In [15], the protocol is analysed using TAME [18], an interface to PVS [19] specialized for proving properties of automata. In this approach the system is first modelled as an LV timed automaton, [20] next any desired system property is expressed as a state invariant and finally, the validity of the state invariant is established by developing auxiliary invariants that supports its proof. Both our approach and this approach belong to the theorem proving family, but the main difference between them is that in the case of timed automata you should identify all the states involved in the real time system in advance, which may be difficult. On the contrary, you have not to explicitly identify states involved in a real time system in advance to model the system as an TOTS.

In [16], a CSP [21] finite model of TESLA is model checked using the FDR [22] model checker. The authors' challenge was to apply model checking to such an infinite system. A number of reduction strategies were developed and incorporated into the model to keep state space within a feasible range. They have also extended their model to capture the Scheme II of the protocol that involve modelling of unbounded hash-chains. Synchronization between sender and receiver processes in this approach is captured by introducing a special event *tock* that represents the passage of one time unit. This synchronization allows the receiver to tell whether it has received message n before sender might have sent message $n+1$.

Finally, in [17], the authors present the application of an extension of a model checker for multi agent systems called MCMAS-X to the verification of TESLA. The model of the protocol is written in an SMV-like programming language called ISPL which is based on TDL [23] temporal epistemic logic.

All approaches, including ours, take the simple case of one sender – one receiver, but it is straightforward to extend the model to capture the most complex cases, with an increase to verification complexity.

Generally, formal verification of real time systems has been studied by many researchers. Another OBJ language that has a real time extension is Maude [24], with Real-time Maude[25]. The main difference between our approach and that of Maude, is that the system to be analyzed with Maude should have finite state space.

Some of the reasons for selecting algebraic specifications and CafeOBJ to model and verify the protocols are as follows:

- CafeOBJ is not an interactive theorem prover, but an algebraic specification language and system with interactive theorem proving facilities. Hence, documents described in CafeOBJ can be used not only for verification, but also as specifications with which human beings can communicate with each other.
- Since it is straightforward to describe complex data structures such as multisets in CafeOBJ, security protocols and their properties can be naturally described.
- It is the first time that such a complex system is modeled with Timed OTSs, which was a challenge with successful results.

Acknowledgements. This research has been co-financed by the European Union (European Social Fund – ESF) and Greek national funds through the Operational Program "Education and Lifelong Learning" of the National Strategic Reference Framework (NSRF) - Research Funding Program: THALIS.

References

1. Ogata, K., Futatsugi, K.: Modeling and Verification of real-time systems based on equations. In: Science of Computer Programming. Elsevier (2007)
2. Ogata, K., Futatsugi, K.: Some Tips on Writing Proof Scores in the OTS/CafeOBJ Method. In: Futatsugi, K., Jouannaud, J.-P., Meseguer, J. (eds.) Goguen Festschrift. LNCS, vol. 4060, pp. 596–615. Springer, Heidelberg (2006)
3. Ogata, K., Futatsugi, K.: Flaw and modification of the iKP electronic payment protocols. IPL 86(2), 57–62 (2003)
4. Ogata, K., Futatsugi, K.: Equational approach to formal analysis of TLS. In: Proc. 25th ICDCS, pp. 795–804 (2005)
5. Ogata, K., Futatsugi, K.: Proof score approach to analysis of electronic commerce protocols. IJSEKE 20(2), 253–287 (2010)
6. Perrig, A., Canetti, R., Tygar, J.D., Song, D.: Efficient Authentication and Signing of Multicast Streams over Lossy Channels. In: Proc. IEEE Symposium on Security and Privacy, pp. 56–73 (2000)
7. Perrig, A., Tygar, J.D.: Secure Broadcast Authentication. In: Wired and Wireless Networks. Springer (2002)
8. Perrig, A., Canetti, R., Tygar, J.D., Briscoe, B., Song, D.: TESLA: Multicast Source Authentication Transform. IETF RFC 4082 (2005)
9. Diaconescu, R., Futatsugi, K.: CafeOBJ Report. World Scientific, Singapore (1998)
10. Abadi, M., Lamport, L.: An old fashioned recipe for real time. ACM Transactions on Programming Languages and Systems 16(5), 1543–1571 (1994)
11. Dolev, D., Yao, A.C.: On the Security of Public Key Protocols. IEEE Trans. on Inf. Theory 29, 198–208 (1983)
12. Seino, T., Ogata, K., Futatsugi, K.: A toolkit for generating and displaying proof scores in the OTS/CafeOBJ method. In: Proc. of the 6th RULE. ENTCS. Elsevier (2005)
13. Nakano, M., Ogata, K., Nakamura, M., Futatsugi, K.: Crème: An automatic invariant prover of behavioural specifications. IJSEKE 17(6), 783–804 (2007)
14. Ogata, K., Nakano, M., Kong, W., Futatsugi, K.: Induction-Guided Falsification. In: Liu, Z., Kleinberg, R.D. (eds.) ICFEM 2006. LNCS, vol. 4260, pp. 114–131. Springer, Heidelberg (2006)
15. Archer, M.: Proving correctness of the basic TESLA multicast stream authentication protocol with TAME. In: Proc. of WITS 2002, Portland (2002)
16. Broadfoot, P., Lowe, G.: Analysing a Stream Authentication Protocol Using Model Checking. In: Gollmann, D., Karjoth, G., Waidner, M. (eds.) ESORICS 2002. LNCS, vol. 2502, pp. 146–161. Springer, Heidelberg (2002)
17. Lomuscio, A., Raimondi, F., Wozna, B.: Verification of the TESLA protocol in MCMAS-X. Fundamenta Informaticae 79(1-2), 473–486 (2007)

18. Archer, M.: TAME: Using PVS strategies for special-purpose theorem proving. Annals of Mathematics and Artificial Intelligence 29(1-4) (2000)
19. Shankar, N., Owre, S., Rushby, J.M., Stringer-Calvert, D.W.J.: The PVS prover guide. Technical Report, Computer Science Lab., SRI Intl. Menlo Park, CA (1998)
20. Lynch, N., Vaandrager, F.: Forward and backward simulations – Part II: Timing based systems. Information and Computation 128(1), 1–25 (1996)
21. Hoare, C.A.R.: Communicating Sequential Processes. Prentice Hall (1985)
22. Formal Systems Europe Ltd. Failures – Divergence Refinement – FDR2 User Manual (2000)
23. Lomuscio, A., Wozna, B.: A complete and decidable security-specialised logic and its application to the tesla protocol. In: Stone, P., Weiss, G. (eds.) Proc. of the Fifth International Joint Conference on Autonomous Agents and Multiagent Systems (AAMAS 2006), pp. 145–152 (2006)
24. Clavel, M., et al.: Maude: Specification and Programming in Rewriting Logic. TCS 285(2), 187–243 (2002)
25. Ölveczky, P.C., Meseguer, J.: Real-Time Maude: A tool for simulating and analyzing real time and hybrid systems. In: 4th WRLA. ENTCS, vol. 36 (2000)

Formal Specification and Verification of Task Time Constraints for Real-Time Systems*

Ning Ge, Marc Pantel, and Xavier Crégut

University of Toulouse, IRIT/INPT
2 rue Charles Camichel, BP 7122, 31071 Toulouse cedex 7, France
{Ning.Ge,Marc.Pantel,Xavier.Cregut}@enseeiht.fr

Abstract. Safety critical real-time systems (RTS) have stringent requirements related to the formal specification and verification of system's task-level time constraints. The most common methods used to assess properties in design models rely on the translation from user models to formal verification languages like Time Petri Net (TPN), and on the expression of required properties using Timed Linear Temporal Logic (LTL), Computation Tree Logic (CTL) and μ-calculus. However, these logics are mainly used to assess safety and liveness properties. Their capability for expressing timing properties is more limited and can lead to combinatorial state space explosion problems during model checking. In addition, the existing methods are mainly concerned with logical relations between the events without the consideration of time tolerance.

This paper introduces a formal specification and verification method for assessing system's task-level time constraints, including synchronization, coincidence, exclusion, precedence, sub-occurrence and causality, in both finite and infinite time scope. We propose a translation method to formally specify task-level time constraints, and decompose time constraints by a set of event-level time property patterns. These time property patterns are quantitative and independent from both the design modeling language and the verification language. The observer-based model checking method relying on TPN is used to verify these time property patterns. This contribution analyses the method's computational complexity and performance for the various patterns. This task-level time constraints specification and verification method has been integrated in a time properties verification framework for UML-MARTE safety critical RTS.

Keywords: MDE, RTS, Task, Time Constraint, Formal Specification, Verification, Time Property Patterns, Time Petri Net, Observer-Based Model Checking.

1 Introduction

Model-Driven Engineering (MDE) enables to verify system model's properties since the early phases of its lifecycle and to iteratively improve the models according to the verification results. Safety critical real-time systems (RTS) have

---

* This work was funded by the French ministries of Industry and Research and the Midi-Pyrénées regional authorities through the ITEA2 OPEES and FUI Projet P projects.

stringent requirements related to the specification and verification of system's task-level time constraints. As the commonly used modeling languages in the industry, for example UML [6], are only semi-formal, they cannot be directly verified by the formal methods. The common approaches used to assess the properties in design models rely on translating semi-formal models into fully formal and verifiable languages and on expressing the properties in a formal way. To assess the task-level time constraints, two main issues should be solved in the state-of-the-art methods.

First, the common verifiable formal assertions used to express time properties are Timed Linear Temporal Logic (LTL), Computation Tree Logic (CTL) and μ-calculus. These logics are mainly used to assess safety and liveness properties. Their capability for expressing timing properties is more limited and can lead to combinatorial state space explosion problems during model checking.

Second, the common methods are mainly concerned with the logical relations between events, for example the partial orders, whereas RTS requirements usually focus on task-level time constraints with the consideration of time tolerance, for example *Whether Task$_A$ and Task$_B$ are coincident within the time tolerance 10ms, in each of their occurrences*. The concept of *time tolerance* should be introduced, because two simultaneous events cannot be measured without errors in real world.

To solve the above two problems, this paper presents a formal specification and verification method for system's task-level time constraints, in both finite and infinite time scope. Clock Constraints Specification Language (CCSL) [8] standardizes clock constraints semantics in UML. However, it only covers the event-level constraints. In order to follow OMG MARTE modeling language [7], we extend the basic semantic elements of CCSL to cover the requirements of task-level time constraints with time tolerance, including coincidence, synchronization, exclusion, sub-occurrence, precedence and causality. We translate non verifiable task-level time constraints into verifiable specifications composed by a set of time property patterns. These time property patterns are quantitative and independent from both the design modeling language and the verification language. To assess these time property patterns, we use an observer-based model checking method relying on Time Petri Nets (TPN) [5]. The computational complexity of this proposal is then analysed. To provide a concrete illustration and to validate our approach, we have integrated it in a time properties verification framework for UML-MARTE safety critical RTS [3].

The paper is organized as follows: Section 2 compares our work with related works; Section 3 introduces a case study; Section 4 introduces the methodology; Section 5 presents the formal specification method for task-level time constraints; Section 6 gives the specifications of time property patterns, illustrates time property patterns verification using observer-based model checking, and discusses the computational complexity and performance to demonstrate the method's applicability; Section 7 gives some concluding remarks and discusses the future works.

2   Related Works

Several works aim to specify event-level time constraints. CCSL standardizes clock constraint semantics within UML in MARTE profile to formally express causal and temporal constraints between previously defined symbolic discrete clocks and proposes a process to model time specification. It defines a complete set of clock constraints, which are driven by instantaneous events. However, as it focuses on event-level concept, some adaptations are required to specify task-level time constraints. Meanwhile, although it can express the concept of time tolerance in event-level constraints, to our knowledge, no efficient verification method is available yet.

Concerning the verification method, [1] transforms UML model to SyncCharts, and uses Esterel assertions to express clock constraints. Esterel has a well-defined notion of instant, and at each reaction, any signal has a unique status. This is not the case with non-strictly synchronous languages. It is thus less applicable at detailed design and implementation phases, as the time tolerance must be taken into account. [9] describes component patterns in ProCom, a language for component-based design of embedded systems. Further, the patterns are formally verified to satisfy relevant timing properties. This is done by translating the pattern specifications in ProCom, into corresponding timed automata models, and model-check the resulting models using UPPAAL [4]. This related work focuses on component based patterns, and it validates the patterns by UPPAAL model checker. It does not mention the verification performance of the proposal, while we think the performance is an important issue in the complex systems.

3   Case Study

A classical asynchronous RTS model is specified in Fig. 1. According to the general asynchronous message-driven pattern, in the system model Fig. 6(a), the *Sender* will regularly distribute data to the two receivers *Calculator A* and *Calculator B* through the *Router*. The receivers provide redundant control service. They will do some computation after receiving the data, as shown in the behavior model Fig. 1(b). The redundant controller requires that the computation of two calculators starts at the same time and the output of the two calculators must be available at the same time in each working cycle; otherwise, the servo of the corresponding actuator cannot correctly unify the redundant command. In this case, the designer need to verify the coincidence between computation tasks of calculators A and B. As it is impossible to respect a strict simultaneous timing with an explicit local synchronisation, a time tolerance is defined. Once the two time instants fall into the same time window (size of window equals to tolerance), they are considered as coincident.

4   Methodology

The proposed method is illustrated by Fig. 2. The *Transformation of Design Model* activity transforms the *Design Model* into *TPN* models. Meanwhile,

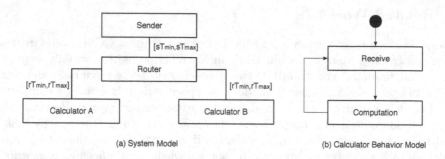

(a) System Model   (b) Calculator Behavior Model

Fig. 1. Case Study Model

the *Transformation of Task Time Constraints* activity first translates the *Task Time Constraint* into *Time Constraint Formal Specification*, then decomposes the specification into *Time Property Patterns*. The time property patterns are quantitative. Each of them can be assessed using observer-based model checking relying on TPN, which means each time property pattern corresponds to one TPN observer structure added in the original TPN models and a set of marking assertions. The integrated TPN models are model checked by TINA toolset [2] with the marking assertions. The formal specification method is independent from the design modeling language, making it reusable in other verification frameworks.

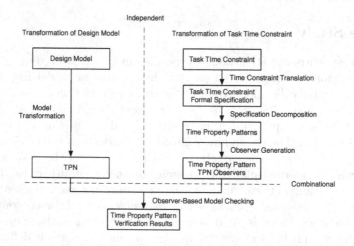

Fig. 2. Independence of the Formal Specification

When designing the formal specification and verification method for task-level time constraints, three temporal aspects are taken into account. *First, both logical and physical time concepts.* Logical symbolic time can be seen as instantaneous physical time, i.e. physical time with tolerance being zero. *Second, both discrete and dense time domains.* Dense time does not introduce any issue in the specification. Problems can occur during the verification phase. This proposal's model checking relies on TINA toolset, which supports TPN in dense time domain. *Last, both finite and infinite time scopes.* Time constraint must be assessed for each task occurrence. Finite scope means that the tasks will occur finite times in a finite time range, for example aperiodic tasks, while infinite scope concerns the tasks that occur infinite times like periodic tasks.

As the formal verification relies on observer-based model checking, it is mandatory to check whether the specification approach allows feasible and efficient model checking or not. According to our study so far, the specification and verification methods are different for finite and infinite time scopes. For example, in finite time scope, we know the maximum occurrence number for a pair of tasks, and we can compare the corresponding occurrence of the two. However, in infinite time scope, the maximum occurrence number is uncountable. The solution is to assess the difference of two tasks' occurrence number. If the difference is inferior to 2, the two tasks are possible coincident in this working cycle.

Another important issue is that, although the notion of synchronization should enforce things to occur simultaneously, in the real world, the strict simultaneous character cannot be achieved. This requirement is thus usually associated with a time tolerance. In order to take into account this more realistic fact, this time tolerance is introduced for all the time constraints specification, and it is denoted by δ ($\delta \in \mathbb{R}^+$).

5 Formal Specification of Task-Level Time Constraints

5.1 Preliminary Definitions

Definition 1 (Event). *An event is the happening of the start of task and the end of task, noted as E_s and E_e.*

Definition 2 (Task). *In the system, a task is considered as the smallest computable unit, which consumes time and modifies resources (consumes and produces). It contains two inner events, E_s and E_e. A task could be executed infinitely or finitely according to the design.*

Definition 3 (Occurrence). *Occurrence is used to represent the appearance of a task and its associated inner events E_s and E_e.*

To simplify the presentation, some symbols are defined in Table 1.

5.2 Coincidence Time Constraint

Definition 4 (Coincidence). *Tasks X and Y are coincident iff the nth occurrence of X occurs simultaneously with the nth occurrence of Y while $n \in \mathbb{N}$. It is equivalent saying the nth occurrence of X_s occurs simultaneously with the nth*

Table 1. Symbols for Formal Specification

Symbol	Definition
X	Task X
X^i	The ith occurrence of task X
X_a	The inner event a of task X (E_s and E_e)
X_a^i	The ith occurrence of X_a
X_a^t	The ith occurrence of X_a, where i is the nearest occurrence number to the time instant t (forward or backward)
$T(X_a^i)$	The occurring time instant of X_a^i
$T(X_a^t)$	The occurring time instant of X_a^t
$O(X)$	The maximum possible occurrence number of task X
$O(X_a)$	The maximum possible occurrence number of event X_a
$O(X_a^t)$	The maximum possible occurrence number of event X_a before time instant t

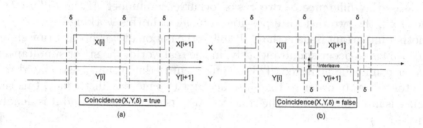

Fig. 3. Coincidence

occurrence of Y_s, and the nth occurrence of X_e occurs simultaneously with the nth occurrence of Y_e. In Fig. 3(a), X and Y are coincident.

Specification 1 (Coincidence - Infinite Time Scope). $C_{ift}(X, Y, \delta) \equiv$

$$\forall t \in \mathbb{R}_+ : (|O(X_s^t) - O(Y_s^t)| < 2) \wedge (|O(X_e^t) - O(Y_e^t)| < 2) \tag{1}$$

$$\forall t \in \mathbb{R}_+ : (|T(X_s^t) - T(Y_s^t)| < \delta) \wedge (|T(X_e^t) - T(Y_e^t)| < \delta) \tag{2}$$

$$\forall i \in \mathbb{N}^* : (T(X_e^i) + \delta < T(Y_s^{i+1})) \wedge (T(Y_e^i) + \delta < T(X_s^{i+1})) \tag{3}$$

Specification 2 (Coincidence - Finite Time Scope). $C_{ft}(X, Y, \delta) \equiv$

$$(O(X_s) = O(Y_s)) \wedge (O(X_e) = O(Y_e)) \tag{4}$$

$$\forall i \in [1, O(X_s)] : (|T(X_s^i) - T(Y_s^i)| < \delta) \wedge (|T(X_e^i) - T(Y_e^i)| < \delta) \tag{5}$$

$$\forall i \in [1, O(X_e) - 1] : (T(X_e^i) + \delta < T(Y_s^{i+1})) \wedge (T(Y_e^i) + \delta < T(X_s^{i+1})) \tag{6}$$

We illustrate coincidence time constraint used in the case study. Due to page limits, the formal specifications of other time constraints are given without detailed explanations. In formula (1) of infinite time scope, at time t, the difference of occurrence number between X_s and Y_s (X_e and Y_e) should be inferior to 2. If this occurrence difference is equal or superior to 2, it means one task is too fast to be coincident with the other. In formula (4) of finite time scope, the occurrence number is countable, thus we can compare the two numbers and ensure they are the same. According to the definition, in formulas (2) and (5), the ith occurrence of X_s (X_e) occurs simultaneously with the jth occurrence of Y_s (Y_e), within time tolerance δ. $i = X_s^t, j = Y_s^t$, as defined in Table 1. In formula (3) and (6), with the time tolerance introduced, it is possible that an interleave exists between i^{th} occurrence of X and $(i + 1)^{th}$ occurrence of Y, which violates the coincidence definition. So constraints for consequent occurrences must be added. In Fig. 3(b), the model satisfies formulas (1) (4) and (2) (5), but violates the formulas (3) (6). The two tasks are not coincident.

5.3   Synchronization Time Constraint

Definition 5 (Synchronization). *Logical synchronization is a reduced coincidence relation without restricting a simultaneously execution. The only concern is that the execution order must persist. In Fig. 4(a), X and Y are coincident.*

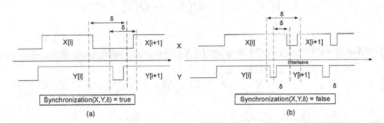

Fig. 4. Synchronization

Specification 3 (Synchronization - Finite Time Scope). $Syn_{ft}(X, Y, \delta) \equiv$
$(O(X_s) = O(Y_s)) \land (O(X_e) = O(Y_e))$
$\forall i \in [1, O(X_e) - 1] : (T(X_e^i) + \delta < T(Y_s^{i+1})) \land (T(Y_e^i) + \delta < T(X_s^{i+1}))$

Specification 4 (Synchronization - Infinite Time Scope). $Syn_{ift}(X, Y, \delta) \equiv$
$\forall t \in \mathbb{R}_+ : (|O(X_s^t) - O(Y_s^t)| < 2) \land (|O(X_e^t) - O(Y_e^t)| < 2)$
$\forall i \in \mathbb{N}^* : (T(X_e^i) + \delta < T(Y_s^{i+1})) \land (T(Y_e^i) + \delta < T(X_s^{i+1}))$

5.4   Exclusion Time Constraint

Definition 6 (Exclusion). *As shown in Fig. 5, task X and Y are excluded, iff not any presence of X occurs simultaneously with any presence of Y. It could be considered as another form of coincidence with some time offset.*

Specification 5 (Exclusion - Finite Time Scope). $E_{ft}(X, Y, \delta) \equiv$
$\forall i \in [1, O(X_s)], \forall j \in [1, O(Y_s)] :$
$T(X_s^i) + \delta < T(Y_s^j) \Rightarrow (T(X_e^i) + \delta < T(Y_s^j)) \land (T(Y_e^j) + \delta < T(X_s^{i+1}))$

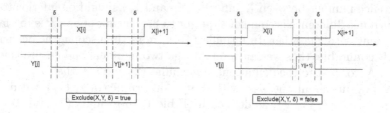

Fig. 5. Exclusion

$$T(X_e^i) + \delta < T(Y_s^j) \Rightarrow T(Y_e^j) + \delta < T(X_s^{i+1})$$
$$T(X_s^i) + \delta < T(Y_e^j) \Rightarrow T(X_e^i) + \delta < T(Y_s^j)$$
$$T(X_e^i) + \delta < T(Y_e^j) \Rightarrow (T(X_e^i) + \delta < T(Y_s^j)) \wedge (T(Y_e^j) + \delta < T(X_s^{i+1}))$$

As the finite time semantics are not computable in infinite time scope. Some constraints are required to ensure that between two continuous occurrences of task X, it exists and only exists one occurrence of task Y, and vice versa.

Specification 6 (Exclusion - Infinite Time Scope). $E_{ift}(X, Y, \delta) \equiv$
$\quad \forall t \in \mathbb{R}_+ : (|O(X_s^t) - O(Y_s^t)| < 2) \wedge (|O(X_e^t) - O(Y_e^t)| < 2)$
$\quad \forall i \in \mathbb{N}^* :$
$\quad T(X_s^i) + \delta < T(Y_s^i) \Rightarrow (T(X_e^i) + \delta < T(Y_s^i)) \wedge (T(Y_e^i) + \delta < T(X_s^{i+1}))$
$\quad T(X_e^i) + \delta < T(Y_s^i) \Rightarrow T(Y_e^i) + \delta < T(X_s^{i+1})$
$\quad T(X_s^i) + \delta < T(Y_e^i) \Rightarrow T(X_e^i) + \delta < T(Y_s^i)$
$\quad T(X_e^i) + \delta < T(Y_e^i) \Rightarrow (T(X_e^i) + \delta < T(Y_s^i)) \wedge (T(Y_e^i) + \delta < T(X_s^{i+1}))$

5.5 Sub-occurrence Time Constraint

Definition 7 (Sub-occurrence). *Task Y is a sub-occurrence of task X, iff the ith occurrence of X and the jth occurrence of Y occur simultaneously, where always $j \leqslant i$. The schema of sub-occurrence is shown in Fig. 6.*

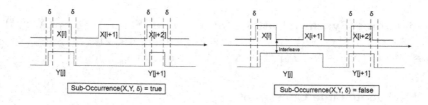

Fig. 6. Suboccurrence

Specification 7 (Sub-occurrence - Finite Time Scope). $S_{ft}(X, Y, \delta) \equiv$
$\quad (O(X_s) \geqslant O(Y_s)) \wedge (O(X_e) \geqslant O(Y_e))$
$\quad \forall j \in [1, O(Y_s)], \exists i \in [j, O(X_s)] : (|T(X_s^i) - T(Y_s^j)| < \delta) \wedge (|T(X_e^i) - T(Y_e^j)| <$
$\delta) \wedge (T(X_e^{i-1}) + \delta < T(Y_s^j)) \wedge (T(Y_e^j) + \delta < T(X_s^{i+1}))$

As the finite time semantics are not computable in infinite time scope, a compromise should be made, which means that the faster one's occurrence is always $k (k \in \mathbb{N}^*)$ times multiple of the slower one's.

Specification 8 (Sub-occurrence - Infinite Time Scope). $S_{ift}(X, Y, \delta, k) \equiv$
$\forall t \in \mathbb{R}_+ : (|O(X_s^t)/k - O(Y_s^t)| < 2) \wedge (|O(X_e^t)/k - O(Y_e^t)| < 2)$
$\forall i \in \mathbb{N}^* : (|T(X_s^{i \cdot k}) - T(Y_s^i)| < \delta) \wedge (|T(X_e^{i \cdot k}) - T(Y_e^i)| < \delta) \wedge (T(X_e^{i \cdot k}) + \delta <$
$T(Y_s^{i+1})) \wedge (T(Y_e^i) + \delta < T(X_s^{i \cdot k + 1}))$

5.6   Precedence Time Constraint

Definition 8 (Precedence). *Task X precedes task Y iff at any time, the occurrence of X is more than or equal to the occurrence of Y. This implies X_s^i must precede Y_s^i, however it is not necessary to also have X_e^i precedes Y_s^i in all context. There strict levels are defined, $\mathcal{L}_1$ (less strict), $\mathcal{L}_2$ (strict), $\mathcal{L}_3$ (very strict).*

Specification 9 (Precedence - Finite Time Scope).
$P_{ft}(X, Y, \delta, \mathcal{L}_1) \equiv \forall i \in [1, O(X_s)] : T(X_s^i) + \delta < T(Y_s^i)$
$P_{ft}(X, Y, \delta, \mathcal{L}_2) \equiv \forall i \in [1, O(X_s)] : (T(X_s^i) + \delta < T(Y_s^i)) \wedge (T(X_e^i) + \delta < T(Y_e^i))$
$P_{ft}(X, Y, \delta, \mathcal{L}_3) \equiv \forall i \in [1, O(X_s)] : T(X_e^i) + \delta < T(Y_s^i)$

The computable specification for infinite time scope is the same as the causalities' in infinite time scope.

5.7   Causality Time Constraint

Definition 9 (Causality). *Causality is similar to Precedence, except that it requires the maximum possible occurrence of X equals to that of Y, because each occurrence of X causes the corresponding occurrence of Y.*

Specification 10 (Causality - Finite Time Scope).
$C_{ft}(X, Y, \delta, \mathcal{L}_1) \equiv O(X) = O(Y), P_{ft}(X, Y, \delta, \mathcal{L}_1)$
$C_{ft}(X, Y, \delta, \mathcal{L}_2) \equiv O(X) = O(Y), P_{ft}(X, Y, \delta, \mathcal{L}_2)$
$C_{ft}(X, Y, \delta, \mathcal{L}_3) \equiv O(X) = O(Y), P_{ft}(X, Y, \delta, \mathcal{L}_3)$

Specification 11 (Causality - Infinite Time Scope).
$C_{ift}(X, Y, \delta, \mathcal{L}_1) \equiv$
    $\forall t \in \mathbb{R}_+ : (|O(X_s^t) - O(Y_s^t)| < 2) \wedge (|O(X_e^t) - O(Y_e^t)| < 2)$
    $\forall i \in \mathbb{N}^* : T(X_s^i) + \delta < T(Y_s^i)$
$C_{ift}(X, Y, \delta, \mathcal{L}_2) \equiv$
    $\forall t \in \mathbb{R}_+ : (|O(X_s^t) - O(Y_s^t)| < 2) \wedge (|O(X_e^t) - O(Y_e^t)| < 2)$
    $\forall i \in \mathbb{N}^* : (T(X_s^i) + \delta < T(Y_s^i)) \wedge (T(X_e^i) + \delta < T(Y_e^i))$
$C_{ift}(X, Y, \delta, \mathcal{L}_3) \equiv$
    $\forall t \in \mathbb{R}_+ : (|O(X_s^t) - O(Y_s^t)| < 2) \wedge (|O(X_e^t) - O(Y_e^t)| < 2)$
    $\forall i \in \mathbb{N}^* : T(X_e^i) + \delta < T(Y_s^i)$

6   Verification of Time Property Patterns

6.1   Time Property Patterns

All the above specifications are composed by a set of time property patterns. For example, in section 5.2, formula (2) contains the time property pattern *Max interval between two events*. All the time property patterns used in the formal specifications are listed in Table 2.

Table 2. Time Property Patterns

Time Property Pattern (Finite)	Formal Specification
Max Occurrence Count	$\forall i \in \mathbb{N}^* : O(X_s^i) < constant$
Min time interval between the ith occurrence of E$_1$ and the jth occurrence of E$_2$	$\forall i,j \in \mathbb{N}^* : T(E_1^i) - T(E_2^j) > \delta$
Max time interval between the ith occurrence of E$_1$ and the jth occurrence of E$_2$	$\forall i,j \in \mathbb{N}^* : T(E_1^i) - T(E_2^j) < \delta$

Time Property Patterns (Infinite)	Formal Specification
The next kth occurrence of event E^i	E^{i+k}
The (i/k)th occurrence of event E^i	$E^{i/k}$
Occurrence difference	$\forall t \in \mathbb{R}_+, k \in \mathbb{N}^* :$ $|O(X_s^t)/k - O(Y_s^t)| < \delta$
Min time interval between the ith occurrence of E$_1$ and the jth occurrence of E$_2$	$\forall i \in \mathbb{N}^*, k \in \mathbb{N}^*, b \in \mathbb{N}, j = i \cdot k + b :$ $|T(E_1^i) - T(E_2^j)| > \delta$
Max time interval between the ith occurrence of E$_1$ and the jth occurrence of E$_2$	$\forall i \in \mathbb{N}^*, k \in \mathbb{N}^*, b \in \mathbb{N}, j = i \cdot k + b :$ $|T(E_1^i) - T(E_2^j)| < \delta$

In the case study, the specification of coincidence time constraint in infinite time scope is composed by 4 time property patterns (Table 3). To assess the coincidence time constraint, the method will compute the values of these 4 quantitative property patterns. The verification method will be introduced in the next section.

Table 3. Time Property Patterns in Coincidence Constraint (Infinite Time Scope)

Formal Specification	Time Property Pattern
X_s^{i+1}	Representation of the next occurrence of event X_s^i
$|O(X_a^t) - O(Y_a^t)| < \delta$	Occurrence number difference between events X_a^t and Y_a^t
$|T(X_a^t) - T(Y_a^t)| < \delta$	Max time interval between events X_a^t and Y_a^t
$T(X_e^i) + \delta < T(Y_s^{i+1})$	Min time interval between events X_a^t and Y_b^t

6.2   Observer-Based Model Checking on TPN

To assess the time property patterns by model checking, the commonly used formal methods rely on a translation of the user models into a formal verifiable language and express the required properties using verifiable formal expressions.

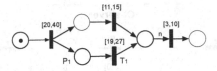

Fig. 7. Time Petri Net Example

TPN is selected as the verification model in this work, because it allows expressing and verifying time properties within both logical and chronometric time models. Fig. 7 is a TPN example. Compared to Petri Nets, the transitions in TPN are extended with a time constraint that controls the firing time. For example, transition T_1 is attached with time constraint [19,27]. When the token arrives at place P_1, the local timer of T_1 starts. Between 19 and 27 time units, T_1 can be fired.

To verify one time property pattern, the user model is translated into TPN model, then an observer TPN structure is added into it, and TINA is used to verify the observer-dedicated LTL/CTL/Marking assertions on the combined TPN. As model checking significantly consumes time and memory resource, we use 2 approaches to ensure verification performance. First, when model checking, TPN shall perform the highest possible abstraction to unfold the reachability graph. This high abstraction model should preserve the desired time property. The model-checking is on-the-fly. Second, each formula's verification is independent in terms of reachability graph generation, so a parallel computation is possible.

6.3   Verification of Time Property Pattern $|T(a^t) - T(b^t)| < \delta$

One of the property patterns, $|T(a^t) - T(b^t)| < \delta$, is used to illustrate the verification method. For the page limits, the other observers will be presented in another paper or technical report. The principle for deciding whether two events are always occurring in a given bound is to find out whether one could advance the other by time δ.

An observer pattern (Fig. 8) is added to the original TPN. The middle transition will always instantly neutralize the tokens from the places *Occ A* and *Occ B* except when one token waits for a time longer than δ that leads to the firing of the *Pass* transition. To guarantee the termination of model checking, the pattern is extended by adding a large overflow number on the tester's incoming arc. Places *tester A* and *tester B* are used to detect this exception. In the generated reachability graph, it only requires to verify if *tester A* or *tester B* has marking. The formula is: $\Diamond(testerA = 1) \vee \Diamond(testerB = 1)$.

Once it is known how to verify $|T(a^t) - T(b^t)| < \delta$, it is possible to change δ to compute a near optimal tolerance. If $|T(a^t) - T(b^t)| < \delta + 1$ is verified as true, but false for $|T(a^t) - T(b^t)| < \delta$, then the near optimal tolerance is $\delta + 1$. In order to improve the computation efficiency, a dichotomy search is used to reduce the complexity from $O(N)$ to $O(\log N)$ using divide and multiply by two instead of add or subtract one.

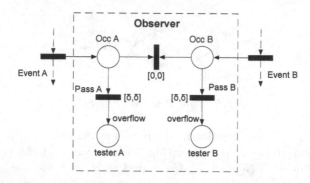

Fig. 8. $|T(A^t) - T(b^t)| < \delta$ Pattern TPN Observer

6.4 Computational Complexity Analysis

Coincidence time constraint is taken as example to analyse the computational complexity. As the observers for infinite and finite time scope are different, the two cases are respectively analyzed. To simplify the presentation, one Kripke Transition Systems (KTZ) generation time is taken as the unit of time (ut).

In the infinite time scope, according to Table 3 and *Specification 1*, its formal specification contains 4 time property patterns: Representation of the next occurrence of event, Occurrence difference between events X_a^t and Y_a^t, Maximum time interval between events X_a^t and Y_a^t, and Minimum time interval between events X_a^t and Y_b^t. For formula (1), it will respectively calculate the value for $|O(X_s^t) - O(Y_s^t)| < 2$ and $|O(X_e^t) - O(Y_e^t)| < 2$. Each of them corresponds to one KTZ generation for the TPN with observer. Thus, the computational complexity for formula (1) is 2(ut). Likewise, the computational complexity for formulas (2) and (3) are both 2(ut). The computational complexity of coincidence in infinite time scope is 6(ut). Thus, in the infinite time scope, the computational complexity is a constant, which means it is independent of the system's design.

In the finite time scope, according to *Specification 2*, it also contains 3 property patterns. In formula (4) $(O(X_s) = O(Y_s)) \wedge (O(X_e) = O(Y_e))$, it will calculate the occurrence's upper bound of start event and end event. The upper bound of event's occurrence is denoted A. As a dichotomy search is used to reduce the complexity, the computational complexity of $O(X_s$ or $O(X_e)$ is $A \cdot \log_2 A$, denoted as B. Thus, the computational complexity of formula (4) is 2B(ut). In formula (5), to calculate $|T(X_s^i) - T(Y_s^i)| < \delta$, is in fact to calculate respectively $T(X_s^i) - T(Y_s^i) < \delta$ and $T(Y_s^i) - T(X_s^i) < \delta$. For each of them the complexity is A(ut), because it should calculate the times of the upper bound of the event's occurrence. Thus, the complexity of formula (5) is 4A(ut), and of formula (6) is 2A(ut). The whole computational complexity of coincidence in finite time scope is 6A+2B. Thus, in the finite time scope, the computational complexity depends on the complexity of system's design.

Table 4. Computational Complexity of Task Time Constraints

Task Time Constraint	Finite Time	Infinite Time
Coincidence	$6A + 2B$	6
Synchronization	$2A + 4B$	4
Exclusion	$6A^2$	8
Sub-occurrence	$7A^2 + 2B$	6
Precedence (less strict)	A	3
Precedence (strict)	$2A$	4
Precedence (very strict)	A	3
Causality (less strict)	$A + 2B$	3
Causality (strict)	$2A + 2B$	4
Causality (very strict)	$A + 2B$	3

The computational complexity of all the mentioned time constraints are listed in Table 4, for both finite and infinite time scope. These numbers allow to conclude that the verification method guarantees a low computational complexity.

6.5   Performance Analysis

In TPN model checking, the computational performance depends on both the cost of generating the KTZ and the cost of assessing the formulas for the KTZ. The former produces the major cost, while the later produces the minor cost once the decidability has been proved. The computational performance is analyzed for the time property patterns, then the computational performance of the task time constraints can be deduced using the complexity table, Table 4.

As the performance depends on the system's scale, it is important to measure the performance influence produced by the observer TPN added into the original TPN. Both the performance of the original TPN and of the observer-added TPN are evaluated. This influence is computed by comparing the KTZ generation cost of the original TPN and that of the observer-added TPN. In order to make this performance result demonstrate that the method is applicable for pragmatic systems, the systems are randomly generated scaling from 2 to 10 parallel threads, where each thread disposes of 10 to 100 periodic tasks. As shown in Fig. 9, the influence for pattern *Occurrence Difference* is controlled in 15%; for pattern *Maximum Time Interval*, it is controlled in 40%; and for pattern *Minimum Time Interval* is also controlled in 40%. The influence test result demonstrates that the over-cost of the observer is very slight, thus, the observer-based model checking method's performance is very stable. If the original TPN can terminate its KTZ generation in an acceptable time range, the cost of time constraint's verification is also acceptable. This demonstration is for the infinite time scope property patterns.

The same approach allows to demonstrate the performance for the property patterns in finite time scope, the results are given in Fig. 10. For the page limits, the analysis is not detailed.

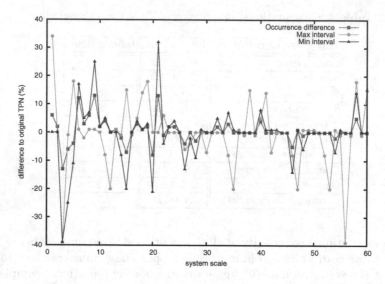

Fig. 9. Performance Influence of the Observer-Based Model Checking Method

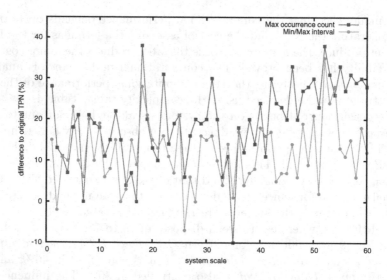

Fig. 10. Performance Influence of the Observer-Based Model Checking Method

7   Conclusion

The common specification and verification methods of system's time constraint focus on event-level constraints without the consideration of quantitative time tolerance. This paper presents a formal specification and verification method for system's task-level time constraints, including synchronization, coincidence, exclusion, precedence, sub-occurrence, causality in both finite and infinite time scope. We translate non verifiable task-level time constraints into verifiable specifications composed by a set of time property patterns. These time property patterns are quantitative and independent from both the design modeling language and the verification language. To assess these time property patterns, we use an observer-based model checking method relying on TPN. The computational complexity and the method's performance are analyzed. This task-level time constraints specification and verification method has been integrated in a time properties verification framework for UML-MARTE safety critical RTS.

In the future, on the technical side, we will optimize TPN models by finding some reducible structural patterns non-influencing the system's behavior to improve the performance of verification. On the application side, we will apply this approach in the industrial applications, and integrate this reusable approach into other time properties verification dedicated frameworks.

References

1. André, C.: Verification of clock constraints: CCSL Observers in Esterel. Rapport de recherche RR-7211, INRIA (February 2010)
2. Berthomieu, B., Ribet, P.O., Vernadat, F.: The tool tina - construction of abstract state spaces for petri nets and time petri nets. International Journal of Production Research 42(14), 2741–2756 (2004)
3. Ge, N., Pantel, M.: Time Properties Verification Framework for UML-MARTE Safety Critical Real-Time Systems. In: Vallecillo, A., Tolvanen, J.-P., Kindler, E., Störrle, H., Kolovos, D. (eds.) ECMFA 2012. LNCS, vol. 7349, pp. 352–367. Springer, Heidelberg (2012)
4. Larsen, K.G., Pettersson, P., Yi, W.: Uppaal in a nutshell. International Journal on Software Tools for Technology Transfer (STTT) 1, 134–152 (1997)
5. Merlin, P., Farber, D.: Recoverability of communication protocols–implications of a theoretical study. IEEE Transactions on Communications 24(9), 1036–1043 (1976)
6. Object Management Group, Inc.: OMG Unified Modeling Language™, Superstructure (February 2009)
7. Object Management Group, Inc.: UML profile for MARTE: modeling and analysis of real-time embedded systems version 1.0 (2009)
8. Peraldi-Frati, M., DeAntoni, J.: Scheduling multi clock real time systems: From requirements to implementation. In: 14th IEEE International Symposium on Object/Component/Service-Oriented Real-Time Distributed Comptuing (ISORC), pp. 50–57. IEEE (March 2011)
9. Suryadevara, J., Seceleanu, C., Pettersson, P.: Pattern-driven support for designing component-based architectural models. In: 18th IEEE International Conference on Engineering of Computer-Based Systems (ECBS). IEEE CS (April 2011)

The WCET Analysis Tool CalcWcet167

Raimund Kirner

University of Hertfordshire, United Kingdom
r.kirner@herts.ac.uk

Abstract. Determining upper bounds for the worst-case execution time (WCET) is mandatory to ensure timeliness of hard real-time systems. To be of practical use, such WCET estimates also have to be precise.

In this paper we present the WCET analysis tool CalcWcet167, which supports the Infineon C167 processor as its main target. CalcWcet167 was designed with the goal to enable research on WCET analysis. This is achieved by interfacing to a modified version of the GCC compiler. Besides describing the tool by itself, we show what kind of useful research has been enabled by this approach.

1 Introduction

The knowledge of the worst-case execution time (WCET) [1] is a vital input for proving the temporal correctness of real-time systems. While two decades of research on WCET analysis have created significant progress, there are still hurdles towards widespread use of WCET analysis in practice [2].

It would push the industrial practice if vendors of commercial development tools find their niche to support WCET analysis, especially compiler vendors [3]. Also from the academic side it is highly beneficial to have WCET support by development tools, in order to bring together and link the different research activities of WCET analysis [4].

In this paper we present the WCET analysis tool CALCWCET167 and its tool chain. Central to this tool chain is that the compiler is a modified GCC version that supports WCET analysis. The contribution of this paper is on one side the technical aspect of how to model the jump cache of the Infineon C167CR within the establish IPET method to calculate the WCET estimate. On the other side, the contribution is to summarise several research activities around CALCWCET167, providing evidence that support of WCET analysis by development tools like a compiler, would provide an effective leverage to widen the industrial use of WCET analysis methods. CALCWCET167 has been also applied to industrial case studies within the FP5 project *SETTA*. In one industrial case study from the automotive domain is has been possible with that to explain the reasion behind some rarely occuring timing variations of significant magnitude.

Section 2 motivates and explains the tool chain of CALCWCET167. In Section 3 we describe WCETC, the annotation language of CALCWCET167. CAL-CWCET167 supports as main processor backend the Infineon C167CR, which

T. Margaria and B. Steffen (Eds.): ISoLA 2012, Part II, LNCS 7610, pp. 158–172, 2012.
© Springer-Verlag Berlin Heidelberg 2012

is described in Section 4. In Section 5 we discuss how the architecture of CAL-CWCET167 has inspired and enabled research on WCET analysis beyond WCET analysis tools themselves. There is no explicit section of related work, as this paper focuses on telling the story around the tool CALCWCET167. However, individual sections cite relevant articles, which contain the related work for further reading. Section 6 concludes this paper.

2 Overview of CalcWcet167

The development of the WCET analysis tool CALCWCET167 wasn't started in the classical way, i.e., choosing a target platform where the program to be analysed will be running on and a compiler that produces the code to be analysed. CALCWCET167 was started as a research activity with the primary goal of providing WCET bounds for simulation models programmed in MATLAB/Simulink. The choice of the target hardware was merely driven by interest of research partners and the choice of compiler was driven by the requirement of being open source and of providing code generation for the chosen target hardware. As target hardware, the Infineon C167CR has been chosen, as it was a common processor in the automotive domain. This left as the only compiler choice the GCC 2.7.2 ported by the German company *HighTec EDV-Systeme GmbH* to the C167. This section summarises the overall tool chain of the WCET analysis framework. Further details on the input language and the hardware backend are described in Section 3 and Section 4.

The result of this initial research requirements resulted in a WCET analysis tool chain as shown in Figure 1. What is important, is the fact that the compiler has become part of the WCET analysis tool chain. This was needed, as we did also research on the MATLAB/Simulink code generator in order to generate automatically flow information like loop bounds [5]. To support this, we designed a variant of the ANSI C language, which we called WCETC, and extended the GCC compiler to parse the additional keywords and maintain the flow information during the compilation. In the following we call this modified compiler *wcet-GCC*. The annotation concepts of WCETC are detailed in Section 3. Furthermore, we restricted the programming language compared to ANSI C in order to allow for better WCET analysability [6]: No use of function pointers, recursive function calls, `goto`, `setjmp()`, `longjmp()`, `signal()`, and `exit()`.

Inherited from GCC, *wcet-GCC* processes during compilation each subroutine separately. Thus we generate for each subroutine `func()` of the source program a machine code file `wcet_func.s` that includes the flow information transformed to the machine code, as shown in the centre of Figure 1.

The WCET analysis tool CALCWCET167 takes as main input 1) the annotated machine code files of each subroutine of the source program, 2) an optional list of WCET bounds for library functions, and 3) an optional description of the target hardware configuration.

The output of the WCET analysis is the calculated WCET bound. But since this analysis framework includes the complete development tool chain, we also

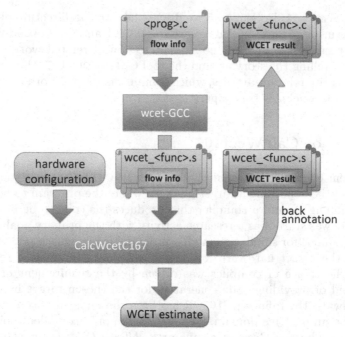

Fig. 1. WCET Analysis with Compiler-support

provide back-annotation of the WCET results to the machine code and the source code. The WCET results at machine code level are given per machine instruction, and for the source code per source line, using the debug information generated by the compiler in order to map the instruction timings. Here we have to state that the back-annotation to the source code is only as good as it can be with the compiler's debug information: With full optimisation during compilation, the distribution of the individual WCET contributions to the source code can be counter-intuitive to the users. For example, in order to further manually optimise the code, the developer might need to have a look at the WCET results at machine-code level as well.

Implementation details of the presented WCET analysis tool chain can be found in [6]. Further features of the tool CALCWCET167 are briefly described in it's user's manual [7], available at the tool homepage[1].

3   The Annotation Language WCETC

Flow information to guide the WCET analysis can be annotated manually, or, with the help of an appropriate static program analysis, calculated automatically. The preferred code level to annotate with properties of flow information in our tool chain is the source code. Annotations at source code allow to write compiler/hardware-independent automatic calculations of flow information. Also

---

[1] CALCWCET167: http://www.vmars.tuwien.ac.at/~raimund/calc_wcet/

manual annotations are more convenient at the source level, since the user has typically more knowledge about program behaviour at source level than on machine-code level, and the machine code would have to be re-done or checked whenever the compiler switches are changed.

The mapping between flow information and source code could be done in several ways. On one side it could be done by separate annotation files that have hooks to link to the source code. On the other hand, it could be done inside the code, either by compiler-specific pragma statements or by extending the source language by additional keywords. We have chosen for the language WCETC the latter option, as this provides to most robust mapping between annotations and source code in the case the code gets modified.

```
 1   /* Constants for LANG_WCET to select the right keywords. */
 2
 3   #define OTHER    0x00   /* no annotations */
 4   #define WCETC    0x01   /* wcetC          */
 5   #define WCETCC   0x02   /* wcetCc         */
 6
 7   #ifndef LANG_WCET
 8   #define LANG_WCET WCETC
 9   #endif
10
11   /* Definitions of wrappers for the wcetC grammar */
12
13   #if defined(LANG_WCET) && ((LANG_WCET)==WCETC || (LANG_WCET)==WCETCC)
14   #if (LANG_WCET) == WCETC  /* WCETC */
15   #define WCET_LOOP_BOUND(x)    maximum (x) iterations
16   #define WCET_SCOPE(x)         scope x
17   #define WCET_MARKER(x)        marker x
18   #define WCET_RESTRICTION(x)   restriction x
19   #define WCET_ADD_CYCLES(x)    addcycles(x)
20   #else   /* WCETCC */
21   #define WCET_LOOP_BOUND(x)    wcet_maximum (x) wcet_iterations
22   #define WCET_SCOPE(x)         wcet_scope x
23   #define WCET_MARKER(x)        wcet_marker x
24   #define WCET_RESTRICTION(x)   wcet_restriction x
25   #define WCET_ADD_CYCLES(x)    wcet_addcycles(x)
26   #endif
27   #define WCET_BLOCK_BEGIN(x,y) wcet_blockbegin(x,y)
28   #define WCET_BLOCK_END(x)     wcet_blockend(x)
29   #define WCET_BUILD_INFO(x)    wcet_buildinfo(x)
30   #else   /* ANSI C */
31   #define WCET_LOOP_BOUND(x)
32   #define WCET_SCOPE(x)
33   #define WCET_MARKER(x)
34   #define WCET_RESTRICTION(x)
35   #define WCET_ADD_CYCLES(x)
36   #define WCET_BLOCK_BEGIN(x,y)
37   #define WCET_BLOCK_END(x)
38   #define WCET_BUILD_INFO(x)
39   #endif
```

Fig. 2. Excerpt of `wcet.h` - The language dialect selection mechanism

Even though WCETC extends the ANSI C language by additional keywords, the annotated programs can still be compiled by any non-WCET-aware C compiler. This is achieved by using macro definitions for all the keywords, as shown in Figure 2. As detailed in [8] there are two versions of the annotation language: the original definition (chosen by defining macro WCETC) proposes short names for the added keywords, quite likely resulting in name conflicts with an existing program code. Thus we later proposed another version (chosen by defining macro WCETCC), which has added the prefix wcet_ to each keyword in order to make name conflicts less likely. In the following we briefly discuss these language extensions based on the macro names given in Figure 2:

WCET_LOOP_BOUND(x) is added to loops in order specify with the expression X the loop bound, i.e., the maximum loop iteration count. X is an integer expression, allowing operands like pow, min, max, log, log2, and log10. Using macro definitions helps to hold code behaviour and flow annotations in sync.

WCET_MARKER(x)/WCET_RESTRICTION(x)/WCET_SCOPE(x) allows to express linear constraints between the total program execution count at different code locations. The different code locations are given symbolic names by WCET_MARKER(X), which labels the place where it is written with the name X. The WCET_RESTRICTION(X) statement allows to specify as argument X a linear flow constraint of the total program execution count between an arbitrary number of code locations, labelled by WCET_MARKER. To enforce a more regular placement of flow restrictions, we added WCET_SCOPE(x) as a scope boundary, were flow restrictions described by WCET_RESTRICTION can be only placed at the end of such a scope.

WCET_ADD_CYCLES(x) can be added at a code location in order to tell the WCET analysis to add to the execution cost of the local block further execution time of X cycles. This statement can be used to specify the WCET of library calls for which the code is not available for analysis, or to describe timing that depends on the underlying platform, e.g., flash update times.

WCET_BLOCK_BEGIN(x)/WCET_BLOCK_END(x) are used to partition the program source code into named regions, with the name specified in X. The purpose of this mechanism can be manifold, but originally we developed it in order to mark code borders of different MATLAB/Simulink block sets at source code level, which is mapped by the compiler *wcet-GCC* down to machine code, where the WCET analysis is done. Finally, this provides a back-propagation mechanism of WCET results beyond the level of source code.

WCET_BUILD_INFO(x) is a simple version control support for the WCET analysis framework, as it allows to pass a character string X to all the different output files produced by the WCET analysis.

To give an impression of how the use of the language WCETC looks like, an annotated version of the commonly known search algorithm BubbleSort is given in Figure 3. The constant N_EL, defined in line 6, serves for both, the implementation of the algorithm, as well as the flow information given by the annotations. In line 20 and 25 the loop bounds for the nested loops is given. The linear flow constraint given in line 36 together with the auxiliary annotations in line 15 and 27 expresses the fact that the execution count of the inner loop is significantly lower than the execution count of the entry of the outer loop multiplied

```
1   #ifndef LANG_WCET
2   #define LANG_WCET WCETCC
3   #endif
4   #include "wcet.h"
5
6   #define N_EL 10
7
8   /* Sort an array of 10 elements with bubble-sort */
9   void bubble (int arr [])
10  {
11          /* Definition of local variables */
12          int i, j, temp;
13
14          /* Main body */
15          WCET_SCOPE(BS)
16          {
17                  for (i=N_EL-1;
18                       i > 0;
19                       i--)
20                  WCET_LOOP_BOUND (N_EL - 1)
21                  {
22                       for (j = 0;
23                            j < i;
24                            j++)
25                       WCET_LOOP_BOUND (N_EL - 1)
26                       {
27                            WCET_MARKER (M);
28                            if (arr[j] > arr[j+1])
29                            {
30                                 temp = arr[j];
31                                 arr[j] = arr[j+1];
32                                 arr[j+1] = temp;
33                            }
34                       }
35                  }
36                  WCET_RESTRICTION (M <= (N_EL*(N_EL-1)/2));
37          }
38  }
```

Fig. 3. WCETC source code of BubbleSort, annotated with flow information

by both loop bounds. This additional information allows to eliminate a WCET overestimation of about 100%.

4   Processor Modelling

In this section the processor backend for the Infineon C167CR of the tool CAL-CWCET167 is presented.

4.1   The Infineon C167CR

The Infineon C167CR processor is a relatively simple architecture compared to many newer processors of the embedded domain, like the Infineon TriCore 1796, which includes three microcontrollers in one chip. However, the challenge with modelling the temporal behaviour of the C167CR was that there is no accurate timing documentation of the processor available. When deriving the timed processor model from the available documentation, we used systematic measurements in order to calibrate the timing behaviour against the observed timing deviations compared to the processor documentation [9]. We were also working in close collaboration with Infineon in order to explain our measured timing behaviour. The results of the obtained timing model are documented in detail in [10].

```
 1  #
 2  # info: memory location can be a combination of ROM | RAM | EXT
 3  #
 4  EXEC_LOCATION    =        EXT
 5  READ_LOCATION    =        EXT
 6  WRITE_LOCATION   =        EXT
 7  #
 8  # info: ACT = 2 + (BTYP & 1) + (15 - MCTC) + (1 - MTTC) + ALECTL
 9  #
10  # BTYP    (2 bit), External Bus Configuration
11  #       00 ...  8 bit demultiplexed bus
12  #       01 ...  8 bit    multiplexed bus
13  #       10 ... 16 bit demultiplexed bus
14  #       11 ... 16 bit    multiplexed bus
15  # MCTC   (4 bit), Memory Cycle Time Control: 15-MCTC
16  # MTTC   (1 bit), Memory Tristate Time Control
17  # ALECTL (1 bit), ALE Lengthening Control
18  #
19  BTYP    =        b_11
20  MCTC    =        b_0000
21  MTTC    =        b_1
22  ALECTL  =        b_1
23  MODEL_JUMP_CACHE        =        true
```

Fig. 4. Hardware configuration options for the C167CR backend

To give an impression of hardware configuration parameters that influence the instruction timing of the Infineon C167CR, Figure 4 shows a documented example of a CALCWCET167 hardware configuration file for the C167CR backend. As shown in lines 4 to 6, one can specify the memory type for different memory access categories (instruction fetching, data read operations, and data write operations). The current version does not allow to specify multiple memory types for a memory access category. The lines 19 to 22 specify the access time to the external memory, following the formula given as a comment in line 8. The meaning of the different hardware register names can be found in the hardware documentation given by the manufacturer [11]. The flag in line 23 specifies whether CALCWCET167 should model the jump cache of the C167CR processor. More details on the jump cache and how it is modelled is given in Section 4.3.

4.2 The IPET Method

The *implicit path enumeration method* (IPET) is the standard method in static WCET analysis to calculate the WCET estimate [12,13]. The IPET method operates on the control-flow graph (CFG) of the program to be analysed. The CFG is a tuple $\langle N, E, s, t \rangle$, where N is the set of program nodes (e.g., basic blocks or single instructions), $E \subseteq N \times N$ is the set of control-flow edges between the program nodes, and s is a unique start node and t a unique termination node of the program. The requirement of s and t to be unique is for simplicity reasons only.

The IPET method can be applied to the CFG in different ways, by either modelling the nodes, the edges, or the combination of them. Modelling only the nodes would have the serious disadvantage that flow information about CFG edges cannot be expressed in the model. This would be dissatisfactory, as the general benefit of the IPET method is, compared to other methods, that it can directly take into account arbitrary linear flow constraints [14]. Thus we chose to model the edges of the CFG, while modelling both, nodes and edges, would not add any expressiveness, but just adds convenience in writing some of the flow information at the price of a longer constraint system with more constraints.

We map the instructions of a CFG node n_i to all of its outgoing edges $e_j = \langle n_i, \_ \rangle$. In case that a node has more than one outgoing edge, then the different edges represent program instructions with a conditional branch at the end, each edge representing a different branch decision (taken or not taken). For each edge $e_i \in E$ we assume an execution cost c_i, given as a constant value. Using variables f_i for each edge e_i that denotes the total execution count of edge e_i during program execution, we can formulate the following goal function for the IPET method:

$$WCET_c = \max \sum_{i=j, e_j \in E} f_i * c_i \tag{1}$$

To complete the IPET constraint system, additional constraints have to be added to make the resulting WCET estimate bounded and precise:

1. All the execution frequency variables must no be assigned negative values:

$$\forall e_i \in E. \ f_i \geq 0 \tag{2}$$

2. The structure of the CFG has to be expressed as flow equations over the execution frequency variables:

$$\forall n_i \in N \backslash \{s, t\}. \sum_{k=j, e_j = \langle \_, n_i \rangle} f_k = \sum_{k=j, e_j = \langle n_i, \_ \rangle} f_k \tag{3}$$

$$\forall e_j = \langle n_i, t \rangle \in E. \ f_j = 1 \tag{4}$$

$$\forall e_j = \langle s, n_i \rangle \in E. \ f_j = 1 \tag{5}$$

Equation 3 expresses the fact the flow going into a node has to be the same as the flow leaving the node. Equation 4 and Equation 5 state that the entry edge and exit edge of the program has to executed exactly once.

3. Flow information that restricts the count and form of traces the CFG is able to describe. Such flow information can be of any form of flow constraints. For example, assuming there is loop in the program with loop-entry edge e_i

and loop-body edge e_j and the upper bound of the loop iteration count is LB. Then the following constraint describes this loop bound:

$$f_i * LB \leq f_j \tag{6}$$

Maximising Equation 1 in combination with the additional constraints will result in a WCET estimate by IPET. Besides that, the valuation of the different flow variables gives a rather abstract hint of what has been considered the worst-case execution path.

4.3 Extended IPET to Model Processor Behaviour

With the IPET model presented in Section 4.2 we are already able to model processor behaviour with different execution times of a conditional branch if being taken or not. What is missing, is the ability to express different execution costs of an edge $e_i \in E$ depending on the execution history, as, for example, would be necessary to model caches. Steven Li et al. have shown in an impressive way that behaviour of direct-mapped and even set-associative caches can be modelled directly inside the IPET constraint system [12,15]. However, this original work already revealed that IPET does not really scale to that level of complexity, as the resulting constraint systems are much bigger than the purely CFG-based systems.

However, the jump cache of the C167CR is rather simple to model, as it contains only a small state, one jump target instruction, and is only relevant in rather local code areas, the innermost loops of programs. Basically, the jump cache stores the jump target of the latest previously executed and taken conditional jump. In the C167CR, only the instructions JB, JBC, JNBS, JMPA, and JMPR can influence the content of this single-entry jump cache. A jump cache has a similar effect to a dynamic branch predictor, but instead of pre-fetching it caches the target instruction.

To model the jump cache we have to identify those CFG edges whose last instruction can potentially benefit from the jump cache. We denote this set of edges as JCC (jump-cache candidates), which is a strict subset of the edges: $JCC \subset E$. In our implementation JCC contains only those edges $e_i \in E$ that fulfil all of the following properties:

1. The last instruction of e_i is one of the conditional jump instructions JB, JBC, JNBS, JMPA, or JMPR.
2. The edge e_i represents the jump-taken outcome of the conditional jump instruction.
3. The edge e_i is the back-edge of an innermost loop.

This is the most common pattern to be observed in practical code, where the jump cache may have an effect. Another case would be, for example, where a callee is called multiple times in sequence from within the caller. However, for simplicity, we focused only on what we considered the most effective code pattern to be supported.

Furthermore, we have to identify all the other CFG edges that can destroy the jump cache content of each edge $e_i \in JCC$. We denote this set as $CCC(e_i)$ (cache-conflict candidates). For an edge $e_i \in JCC$ the set $CCC(e_i)$ includes all the edges e_j that fulfil all of the following properties:

1. The last instruction of e_j is one of the conditional jump instructions JB, JBC, JNBS, JMPA, or JMPR.
2. The edge e_j represents the jump-taken outcome of the conditional jump instruction.
3. The edge e_j is placed within the innermost loop of which e_i is the back edge.
4. There is no other edge e_k with a taken conditional branch inside the innermost loop of which e_i is the back edge, such that e_k dominates e_j. If such an e_k would exist, than there would be no need to include e_j as well, since e_k already causes the eviction of e_i's target from the jump cache.

To model the jump cache in IPET we assign for each edge $e_i \in JCC$ the basic execution cost c_i for the case of a cache hit. The extra fetch penalty that has to be paid in case of a cache miss is denoted as cp_i. Actually, in reality the status of the jump caches influences the execution time of the jump-target instruction, as fetching the instruction is part of it, and not the execution time of the conditional jump. However, it can be more easily modelled if we assign this jump penalty to the edge with the jump instruction.

By using p_i as the execution-frequency variable that represents all cache-miss branch-taken of an edge $e_i \in JCC$ we extend the original IPET goal function of Equation 1 to the goal function that includes the jump-cache miss penalties, as given in Equation 7.

$$WCET_c = \max \left(\sum_{i=j, e_j \in E} f_i * c_i + \sum_{i=j, e_j \in JCC} p_i * cp_i \right) \tag{7}$$

All these additional constraints listed in Section 4.2 still have to be applied. But besides that, we have to add additional constraints to limit the number of miss-penalties of the jump cache. For this we define p_i^j as the execution-frequency variable of how often an edge $e_j \in CCC(e_i)$ destroys the jump-cache content of edge e_i. Further, we denote $e_{entry,i}$ the loop-entry edge and $e_{body,i}$ the loop-body edge of the surrounding loop of any edge $e_i \in JCC$. Based on these definitions, the following constraints have to be added:

1. The number of miss-penalties caused by all the interfering edges of $CCC(e_i)$ cannot be at most the execution count of the body-edge of the surrounding loop:

$$\forall e_i \in JCC. \left(\sum_{e_j \in CCC(e_i)} p_i^j \right) \le f_{body,i} \tag{8}$$

2. An interfering edge $e_j \in CCC(e_i)$ cannot cause more miss penalties than e_j is executed:

$$\forall e_i \in JCC \; \forall e_j \in CCC(e_i). \; p_i^j \leq f_j \tag{9}$$

3. There can be no more miss penalties than the number of executed interring edges $e_j \in CCC(e_i)$ and number of entries into the surrounding loop of e_i:

$$\forall e_i \in JCC. \; p_i \leq \left(\sum_{e_j \in CCC(e_i)} p_i^j \right) + f_{entry,i} \tag{10}$$

4. The surrounding loops of any $e_i \in JCC$ can only be of do-while form, since the cached jump needs to be a taken jump. Thus, the last iteration of the surrounding loop cannot cause any miss penalty:

$$\forall e_i \in JCC. \; p_i \leq (f_{body,i} - f_{entry,i}) \tag{11}$$

```
1    #define UPPERLIMIT 20
2    typedef int vec_t [UPPERLIMIT];
3    vec_t ArrayA, ArrayB;
4
5    void ArrCopy(vec_t ArrayA, vec_t ArrayB)
6    {
7       int Index=0;
8
9       do WCET_LOOP_BOUND (UPPERLIMIT)
10      {
11         ArrayB[Index] = ArrayA[Index];
12         Index++;
13      }
14      while (Index < UPPERLIMIT);
15   }
```

Fig. 5. Example program that potentially facilitates the C167's jump cache

Discussion. The jump cache modelling within IPET is safe in the sense that it will not underestimate the penalties resulting from jump cache misses. But overestimation is possible. For example, assuming two or more conditional jumps are inside the loop body and these jumps are executed at the same loop iterations, then this behaviour cannot be expressed by the flow information and modelled in the IPET method. However, loops often do not have such complex control, resulting in a precise modelling of the jump cache.

To give an example of the effect of the jump cache modelling, consider the sample program given in Figure 5. Without modelling the jump cache, the WCET would be 3198 cycles, while enabing the jump cache analysis reduces the WCET to 3090 (3.4% reduction).

5   Enabling Research WCET-Related Research

After describing the unconventional initial requirements for developing the tool
CALCWCET167 and the WCET analysis tool chain it belongs to, we give in
the following examples, of how this approach was helpful to facilitate further
research on WCET analysis.

5.1   Annotation Languages at Source Code-Level

The WCET analysis framework based on CALCWCET167 allowed to work on
flow information annotation languages at source-code level. While the WCET
analysis has to be done at machine-code level to get utmost accuracy, it is more
convenient to provide code annotations at source-code level [16,17]. Even though
first contributions to source-level languages for WCET analysis started at least
as early as 1986 [18], the design of WCETC for source-level code annotations
with flow information (see Section 3) provided one of the first contributions
of source-based annotation languages that provide information to be used for
WCET analysis at machine-code level.

The topic of source-level annotation languages for WCET analysis is still a
demanding one, as much more work has to be spent towards a common WCET
annotation language, for which a design challenge has been raised in 2007 [19].
As a contribution in that direction we made a discussion and comparison of
different existing annotation languages of WCET tools [20].

5.2   Transformation of Flow Information

The compiler as a tool that knows the relation between program representation
at different levels, can provide very helpful support for the WCET analysis.
Especially the update of code annotations and ensuring of code properties are
domains where the compiler could help [16,3].

After an early attempt of transforming flow information during optimising
compilation that solved the problem only partially [21,22], the research around
the WCET analysis tool chain of CALCWCET167 finally provided a solution
that has been proven powerful enough to transform and update arbitrary flow
constraints during code optimisation [5,17].

Besides our own tool chain, this approach has also been implemented [23]
within another research compiler [24,25].

5.3   WCET Analysis for Case Tools Like Matlab/Simulink

Modelling tools like MATLAB/Simulink provide automatic code generation from
the model. Research on WCET analysis for such case tools is naturally supported by the presented WCET analysis tool chain that provides a WCET-aware
compiler. It was actually the original motivation to perform WCET analysis
of MATLAB/Simulink models, which led to the design of the WCET analysis

framework facilitating CALCWCET167. We extended the code generator of MAT-LAB/Simulink to generate code annotations at C level, in order to speed up and simplify WCET analysis [26].

5.4   TU-Bound

The tool CALCWCET167 does not provide any automatic extraction of flow information from the program code and relies on code instrumentations instead. However, its ability to accept annotations at C-code level, made it easy to combine it with source-level-based program analysis tools in order to generate flow information automatically. This resulted in the WCET analysis framework TuBound [27]. TuBound is driven by CALCWCET167 and the *wcet-GCC* compiler to perform the WCET analysis, while research on TuBound focuses on automatic calculations of flow information [28,29].

6   Summary and Conclusion

In this paper we have presented the tool chain behind the WCET analysis tool CALCWCET167. While one contribution of the paper is the description of how a jump cache, as it exists in the Infineon C167CR processor, can be modelled within the popular IPET method, the second message of the paper is to demonstrate how development tools geared towards supporting WCET analysis have provided fruitful inspiration to the WCET analysis community to make WCET analysis easier to use and more precise. We have shown this on the activities of designing source-level WCET annotation languages, automatic transformation of flow information during optimising compilation, WCET analysis for case tools like modelling environments with code generation, and on automatic calculation of flow information.

The next step for the benefit of the WCET community as a whole, could be the establishment of a common WCET analysis tool chain, where researchers can bring in their specialised expertise. Furthermore, it would be interesting to see when tool support for WCET analysis finds a niche in the commercial domain of real-time computing, bringing the obtained research results into industrial practice.

Acknowledgements. The research leading to these results has received funding from the IST FP7 research project "Asynchronous and Dynamic Virtualization through performance ANalysis to support Concurrency Engineering (ADVANCE)" under contract no IST-2010-248828, the European Community's Seventh Framework Programme [FP7,2008-2011] under grant agreement no 214373 (ArtistDesign, http://www.artist-embedded.org/http://www.artist-embedded.org/), the Austrian Science Fund (Fonds zur Förderung der wissenschaftlichen Forschung) within the research project "Formal Timing Analysis Suite of Real-Time Systems" (FORTAS-RT) under contract P19230-N13, the Austrian Science Fund (Fonds zur Förderung der wissenschaftlichen Forschung) within the research project "Compiler-Support for Timing Analysis" (COSTA) under contract P18925-N13, and the IST FP5 research project "Systems Engineering for Time-Triggered Architectures (SETTA)" under contract IST-10043. The author would also like to thank Pavel Atanassov for his time-intensive effort of deriving the instruction timing for the Infineon C167CR processor.

References

1. Wilhelm, R., Engblom, J., Ermedahl, A., Holsti, N., Thesing, S., Whalley, D., Bernat, G., Ferdinand, C., Heckman, R., Mitra, T., Mueller, F., Puaut, I., Puschner, P., Staschulat, J., Stenstrom, P.: The worst-case execution time problem - overview of methods and survey of tools. ACM Transactions on Embedded Computing Systems (TECS) 7(3) (April 2008)
2. Kirner, R., Puschner, P.: Obstacles in worst-cases execution time analysis. In: Proc. 11th IEEE International Symposium on Object-oriented Real-time Distributed Computing, Orlando, Florida, pp. 333–339 (May 2008)
3. Kirner, R.: Development and Analysis of Time-Predictable Real-Time Systems. Habilitation treatise, Technische Universität Wien, Vienna, Austria (February 2010)
4. Huber, B., Puffitsch, W., Puschner, P.: Towards an open timing analysis platform. In: Proc. 11th International Workshop on Worst-Case Execution Time Analysis, Porto, Portugal, OCG (July 2011)
5. Kirner, R., Puschner, P.: Transformation of path information for WCET analysis during compilation. In: Proc. 13th IEEE Euromicro Conference on Real-Time Systems, Delft, The Netherlands, Technical University of Delft, pp. 29–36 (June 2001)
6. Kirner, R.: Integration of static runtime analysis and program compilation. Master's thesis, Technische Universität Wien, Vienna, Austria (May 2000)
7. Kirner, R.: User's Manual - WCET-Analysis Framework based on WCETC. Vienna University of Technology, Vienna, Austria. 0.0.3 edn. (July 2001),
   http://www.vmars.tuwien.ac.at/~raimund/calc_wcet/
8. Kirner, R.: The programming language WCETC. Technical Report 02/2002, Technische Universität Wien, Institut für Technische Informatik, Treitlstr. 1-3/182-1, 1040 Vienna, Austria (2002)
9. Atanassov, P., Kirner, R., Puschner, P.: Using real hardware to create an accurate timing model for execution-time analysis. In: International Workshop on Real-Time Embedded Systems RTES (in Conjunction with 22nd IEEE RTSS 2001), London, UK (December 2001)
10. Atanassov, P.: Experimental Assessment of Worst-Case Program Execution Times. PhD thesis, Technische Universität Wien, Vienna (May 2003)
11. INFINEON: C167CR Derivatives. 16-Bit Single-Chip Microcontroller. User's Manual. Version 3.0. Infineon Technologies AG (February 2000)
12. Li, Y.T.S., Malik, S., Wolfe, A.: Cache modeling for real-time software: Beyond direct mapped instruction caches. In: Proc. 17th Real-Time Systems Symposium, pp. 254–263. IEEE (December 1996)
13. Puschner, P., Schedl, A.V.: Computing maximum task execution times – a graph-based approach. Journal of Real-Time Systems 13, 67–91 (1997)
14. Kirner, R., Puschner, P.: Classification of WCET analysis techniques. In: Proc. 8th IEEE International Symposium on Object-oriented Real-time distributed Computing, Seattle, WA, pp. 190–199 (May 2005)

15. Li, Y.T.S., Malik, S., Wolfe, A.: Efficient microarchitecture modeling and path analysis for real-time software. In: Proc. IEEE Real-Time Systems Symposium, pp. 298–307 (December 1995)
16. Kirner, R., Puschner, P.: Classification of code annotations and discussion of compiler-support for worst-case execution time analysis. In: Proc. 5th International Workshop on Worst-Case Execution Time Analysis, Palma, Spain (July 2005)
17. Kirner, R., Puschner, P., Prantl, A.: Transforming flow information during code optimization for timing analysis. Real-Time Systems 45(1), 72–105 (2010)
18. Klingerman, E., Stoyenko, A.D.: Real-time euclid: A language for reliable real-time systems. IEEE Transactions on Software Engineering 12(9), 941–989 (1986)
19. Kirner, R., Knoop, J., Prantl, A., Schordan, M., Wenzel, I.: WCET analysis: The annotation language challenge. In: Proc. 7th International Workshop on Worst-Case Execution Time Analysis, Pisa, Italy, pp. 83–99 (July 2007)
20. Kirner, R., Knoop, J., Prantl, A., Schordan, M., Kadlec, A.: Beyond loop bounds: Comparing annotation languages for worst-case execution time analysis. Software and Systems Modeling 10(3), 411–437 (2011)
21. Engblom, J.: Worst-case execution time analysis for optimized code. Master's thesis, Uppsala University, Uppsala, Sweden (September 1997)
22. Engblom, J., Ermedahl, A., Altenbernd, P.: Facilitating worst-case execution time analysis for optimized code. In: Proc. 10th Euromicro Real-Time Workshop, Berlin, Germany (June 1998)
23. Schulte, D.: Flow Facts für WCET-optimierende Compiler: Modellierung und Transformation. VDM Verlag, Germany (2007) ISBN: 978-3836448130
24. Lokuciejewski, P.: A WCET-Aware Compiler. Design, Concepts and Realization. Vdm Verlag Dr. Müller (August 2007) ISBN: 978-3836418485
25. Lokuciejewski, P., Falk, H., Marwedel, P., Theiling, H.: WCET-driven, code-size critical procedure cloning. In: Proc. 11th International Workshop on Software and Compilers for Embedded Systems, Munich, Germany, pp. 21–30 (March 2008)
26. Kirner, R., Lang, R., Freiberger, G., Puschner, P.: Fully automatic worst-case execution time analysis for Matlab/Simulink models. In: Proc. 14th Euromicro Conference on Real-Time Systems, Vienna, Austria, Vienna University of Technology, pp. 31–40. IEEE (June 2002)
27. Prantl, A., Schordan, M., Knoop, J.: Tubound - a conceptually new tool for worst-case execution time analysis. In: Proc. 8th International Workshop on Worst-Case Execution Time Analysis, Prague, Czech Republic (July 2008)
28. Knoop, J., Kovács, L., Zwirchmayr, J.: Symbolic loop bound computation for wcet analysis. In: Proc. 8th Ershov Informatics Conference. PSI Conference Series (2011)
29. Knoop, J., Kovács, L., Zwirchmayr, J.: r-TuBound: Loop Bounds for WCET Analysis (Tool Paper). In: Bjørner, N., Voronkov, A. (eds.) LPAR-18 2012. LNCS, vol. 7180, pp. 435–444. Springer, Heidelberg (2012)

Abstract Execution for Event-Driven Systems – An Application from Automotive/Infotainment Development

Klaus Birken

Harman/Becker Automotive Systems, Raiffeisenstr. 34,
70794 Filderstadt, Germany
klaus.birken@harman.com

Abstract. Event-driven systems are ubiquitous – in technical as well as non-technical domains. Often these systems are safety-critical, and static analysis methods are applied in order to reduce risks and increase quality. The Abstract Execution analysis method provides valuable results for imperative programs, which are used for WCET analysis. In this paper, an enhancement for Abstract Execution is presented, which allows handling the concurrent program flow of event-driven systems. An abstract event queue is defined which is able to represent multiple concrete event queues. This queue handling is embedded into the Abstract Execution engine without further changes to the original algorithm. A elaborated real-world example will be shown, which applies the new analysis method to the model-based development of on-board diagnostics software in the Automotive/Infotainment domain.

Keywords: Abstract execution, static analysis, event-driven, concurrency, on-board diagnostics, automotive, infotainment.

1 Introduction

Event-driven systems play an important role in many technical as well as non-technical domains. This ranges from embedded systems like medical devices, automotive systems and production control to personal computers and tablets which are used by humans, e.g., graphical user interfaces and web-based systems. In order to increase the quality of these systems, static analysis methods can be applied to their software, especially if these systems have safety-critical parts.

In terms of their execution model, these event-driven systems typically have two aspects: The actual event-based, asynchronous command/control layer, which is using events for communication between subsystems and components, and some imperative detail code inside the event handlers of those components. The static analysis method has to take into account the different properties of these two layers.

Abstract Execution (AE) is an analysis method for imperative programs, which executes the code based on variables which are defined in an abstract domain [1, 2]. During this execution, information about variable values, executed program scopes etc. is collected and stored for later analysis. This is used primarily for computing

T. Margaria and B. Steffen (Eds.): ISoLA 2012, Part II, LNCS 7610, pp. 173–186, 2012.

worst-case execution times (WCET) in the context of runtime analysis for imperative programs.

In this paper, we will show how the Abstract Execution method can be extended in order to additionally support the command/control layer of event-driven systems. This allows handling not only parallel concurrent execution flows, but also their timing behavior. Moreover, we will provide a detailed example from the Automotive domain, which shows how the AE method with concurrency extensions can be used for validating On-Board Diagnostics (OBD) software against abstract test cases already during development.

The paper has the following structure: In section 2, we present related work and how this paper combines and enhances existing approaches. Section 3 briefly describes event-driven systems. In Section 4, we outline the Abstract Execution method and how it can be extended in order to handle concurrency and event timings. Section 5 applies this extended method to the development of On-Board Diagnostics software from the Automotive/Infotainment domain. Finally, the paper gives a short conclusion and planned future steps.

2   Related Work

Event-driven systems are commonly being modeled using finite state machines (FSMs). For static analysis of the FSM-formalism, *model checking* is a well-established technique [3]. Model checking will prove that temporal-logic formulas hold for a given FSM system or provide a counter-example. However, if the finite state machine uses an elaborated detail code action language (e.g., for entry/exit actions of states or transition actions), model checking will be hard, if not impossible. Thus, either the expressivity of the detail language has to be limited in order to still allow model checking to produce results, or the static analysis will not be possible anymore.

Static analysis for sequential imperative programs, on the other hand, can be done with a variety of techniques, e.g. Abstract Interpretation [4], Symbolic Execution and Abstract Execution [1, 2]. The common idea behind these techniques is to approximate the program semantics by an abstract semantics. The abstraction is done by lifting the values of variables and the corresponding operations to an abstract domain. Those methods offer full support for many general-purpose programming languages (e.g., C, Ada, C++, Java), but are limited with regard to concurrency and parallel asynchronous execution. If the goal of the static analysis is the computation of WCET bounds, the results of the analysis (i.e., *flow facts*) are combined with a low-level timing model in order to do the WCET calculation. Recently, it has been shown that the WCET calculation can be merged into the actual AE, leading to an algorithm which is capable of computing WCET bounds more efficiently than conventional methods [2].

Based on the advent of tools for easy creation of domain-specific languages (DSLs) during the past years, a plethora of special-purpose executable languages with restricted expressivity has been and still is being invented. For those languages, formal methods for static analysis can be applied in a pragmatic way [5]. The key to success for this combination of DSLs and formal methods is that the DSL is as expressive as necessary, but still limited in order to allow the formal methods to be applied. Depending on the complexity resulting from the static analysis of the DSL models, the analysis can be executed while the models are being changed by the developer/designer. This allows immediate feedback and thus improves the quality of the resulting software.

In this paper, we propose an enhancement of the Abstract Execution method in order to support a combination of imperative and event-driven paradigms. This method will be applied to DSL models which describe the combined system. If some restrictions on the size and expressivity of models can be ensured, the static analysis can be done interactively providing immediate feedback to the developer. Our enhancement to the AE method is focused on handling concurrent executions well instead of computing exact WCET bounds for linear programs as shown in [2].

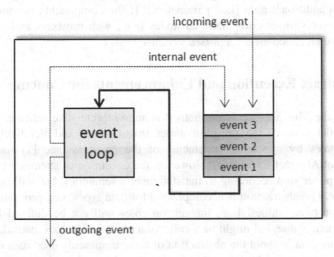

Fig. 1. Schematic event-driven system with event queue, event loop and internal vs. external (incoming) events. The event loop may generate internal and outgoing events during its execution.

3   Event-Driven Systems

A variety of technical and non-technical systems are using messages or events for the top-level communication of subsystems and components. Some examples of event-driven systems are:

- graphical user interfaces (e.g. for desktop PCs, tablets and smartphones)
- web-based clients and servers
- communication protocols (e.g., TCP/IP, D-Bus, HTTP)
- automation / production control systems
- Automotive systems, including In-Vehicle Infotainment (IVI)

The typical design of an event-driven system consists of subsystems or components. Each component has an event queue and an event handler (see Fig. 1). The *event queue* will collect internal and external events. The *event loop* will block until an event is available in the queue. As soon as the queue contains at least one event, the event loop will unblock and an event handler for the specific event will be executed.

The handler's execution semantics is either run-to-completion (on a small embedded system without operating system scheduler), or handled by one single thread of execution (if an operating system scheduler is present). During its execution the event handler might generate and send new events. *Internal* events will be put into the component's own queue; other events will be sent to other components and put into their queue as *incoming* or *external* events.

The event loop can be implemented in different ways, for example as a mapping of events to handlers or as finite state machine. In the latter case, transitions of the state machine will be selected according to the current state and the incoming event. Events may contain additional data (i.e., parameters). If the components or subsystems are distributed over various computational nodes (e.g., web browsers and servers), this structure is often called *message-based* systems.

4   Abstract Execution and Enhancements for Concurrency

The core of the Abstract Execution method is an interpreter-like scheme, which starts with an initial state of the program under investigation and iteratively computes successor states by executing statements of the program (see [1] for a detailed description of Abstract Execution). However, the execution of statements is not just a simple interpreter step according to the statement's semantics, but will be done in an abstract way. The abstraction is accomplished for data types, i.e., program values and operations on those values. E.g., integer variables will not be defined by a single, specific numeric value, but might be a collection of several values instead. Section 4.1 will give more details about the abstraction of some commonly used data types.

A program state in Abstract Execution is a 4-tupel containing (among other information) the current program state, which itself includes the instruction pointer, the stack and all memory contents (i.e., variable values). As the evaluation of Boolean conditions might lead to several possible results depending on the abstract values of the contained variables, the Abstract Execution engine has to handle multiple possible execution flows simultaneously. For example, this might occur for the branches of if/else-statements and for varying loop iterations due to abstract iteration limits. In order to manage the computational complexity of the analysis, branched execution paths might be joined at *merge points*. The selection of merge points and the order of their application is a means for trading the performance of the static analysis algorithm against the accuracy of its results.

During the Abstract Execution run, results will be collected based on *program scopes*. As it is not relevant for the extension we are describing in this paper, we will skip this part of AE (see [1] for more details of collecting results and how this is used to compute WCET data). The Abstract Execution of the program under investigation ends as soon as all execution paths end by reaching a *final state*.

4.1   Abstractions Used for Data Types

The Abstract Execution method operates on abstractions of the data types being used in the program under investigation. Therefore, both its analysis performance and its accuracy depend on the abstractions chosen for the values and operations of those data types. Nevertheless, design decisions regarding this abstracted type system can be chosen quite locally without impacts on the overall Abstract Execution algorithm.

For our current implementation used in the real-world example which is described in the next chapter, we are using the following, pragmatic abstractions:

- Abstract integers are represented as sets of integer intervals. This offers improved accuracy compared to the usual abstraction method using just one interval. In order to still ensure affordable (i.e., linear) complexity, the maximum number of intervals for an abstract integer has to be limited by adding a heuristics for merging intervals (e.g., based on the minimum distance of neighbored intervals).
- Abstract Boolean values might have one of the values *{F}*, *{T}* or *{F, T}*. Thus, the Boolean condition *{2, 5, 11}* < *{7}* comparing two abstract integers can be represented by the resulting value *{F, T}*.
- Abstract strings are represented as a set of concrete strings up to a certain number of elements. If this number of concrete strings exceeds a configurable limit, the string representation switches to a mere abstract integer, representing the length of the abstract string. This nicely satisfies the requirements of a typical application, where strings will be either well-known and therefore concrete, or a limited number of strings (e.g., from a test case specification), or rather abstract with limited size.
- Abstract arrays are represented by a head part and a tail part. The head part consists of a real array of abstract element values. The tail part is an abstract integer defining an abstract number of additional elements. Thus, this representation can handle arrays with a specific number of abstract elements, as well as arrays with a number of elements which is not fixed.

Operations with mixed-type signatures will often have to rely on implementation details of all participating types, e.g., *length(abstract string)* will return an abstract integer.

While extending Abstract Execution in order to properly handle concurrency and timed events, the additional data type *abstract time period* will be needed. Abstract time periods will usually not be available in the target language for the analysis, but will be used for the specification and Abstract Execution of concurrent events. The additional data type is defined as follows:

- Abstract time periods are represented by a single interval of concrete time periods. Example: *[2sec...4sec]* is any time period with duration between 2 sec and 4 sec. We will choose *[t_0...t_1]* as the general notation for the set of time periods with durations between t_0 and t_1. An abstract time period with $t_0=t_1=t$ represents a concrete time period with duration t.

Depending on the expressivity of the target language more data types will have to be supported. The abstractions above have been chosen pragmatically and oriented at the use-cases expected for the application domain. Their correctness has not been formally proven yet, but has been validated by test cases.

4.2   Abstract Execution of Event-Driven Systems

For the discussion of Abstract Execution of event-driven systems we will first assume that the system is built of just one event queue and one event loop (as depicted in Figure 1). At the end of this section we will generalize this assumption to a system of multiple event-driven components.

In the original Abstract Execution algorithm as described in [1] the execution engine repeatedly uses a interpreter step which executes a single statement in a given program state and provides the set of successor states. The handling of concurrency can be introduced by applying the following local extensions without changing the core Abstract Execution algorithm:

- The program state is extended by an *abstract event queue*, representing all events which might be handled in the future and their possible orderings. The abstract event queue of a program state also holds the current time, which will progress in discrete steps as the execution goes on. See section 4.3 on details about the abstract event queue concept.
- Some statements of the programming language under analysis will create events, e.g., starting of timers and timeouts, sending of requests across interfaces, raising signals, or forking new execution threads. The interpreter has to be extended to provide the proper behavior depending on the semantics of these primitives.
- In sequential Abstract Execution, the interpreter computes successor states based on the program's sequential control flow. The execution ends if all remaining program states do not have any successor states (i.e., reached a *final* state). In the extended Abstract Execution presented here, we will in this situation check the abstract event queue for waiting events and create new program states from these. Thus, the imperative program parts will be executed with priority and the asynchronous part will only be activated if all sequential execution flows have been finished (run-to-completion semantics).
- In general, multiple execution paths will have to be handled because several events might be ready for execution in the same period of time. This can be tackled very similar to the handling of multiple execution paths in the sequential Abstract Execution method: The computation of *merge points* has to take into account also the abstract event queue's current state.

Although the extensions described in this paper enable the Abstract Execution scheme to compute the timing behavior of event-driven systems, it is important to mention that it is not a detailed real-time simulation. There are no assumptions about the runtimes of sequential parts of the system (e.g., event handler code). Thus, we can compute the order of events, but will approximate the detail code's runtime.

This approach allows extending the scheme to systems with multiple event queues and event loops. The abstraction of the system will still contain just one abstract event queue, which serves multiple event loops.

4.3   Abstract Event Queue

The central ingredient of the concurrency extension for the Abstract Execution method is the *abstract event queue*. An abstract event queue Q_{abs} is defined as

$$Q_{abs} := \{ t, C \},$$

where t is the current time and C is a set of *continuations*. A continuation $c \in C$ is defined as pair

$$c := \{ [t_0...t_1], \Delta s \},$$

with $[t_0...t_1]$ specifying the time when the event will be triggered relative to the queue's current time t. This time period is specified as *abstract* time period (see section 4.1), which allows approximations to concrete orders of events. The delta program state Δs provides all information needed for Abstract Execution after the event loop removes the event from the queue and executes it. Typically, Δs will contain a reference to the event handler which should be executed, an event id and the (abstract) parameters of the event (if any).

In a *concrete* event-driven system, the time between creation of an event and the arrival in the receiver's event queue is determined by the underlying communication system. For the execution of an *abstract* event-driven system we specify the expected event arrival time as abstract time period $[t_0...t_1]$ relative to the creation time of the event and store it in the receiver's abstract event queue immediately. This can be used for the approximation of communication channel timings, the response time of a server component, but also for timers which provide exact timing intervals. In the latter case $t_0=t_1=t$, where t is the actual duration after which the timer should fire.

An event queue in a concrete event-driven system has concrete arrival times for each continuation (i.e., incoming event). Thus, the queue has a deterministic order of events. With an abstract event queue, the abstract time periods of its continuations may overlap; this requires a more complex handling of the order of events: the *candidate computation*. Basically, the algorithm for candidate computation consists of the following steps:

1. First, it computes the next point in time $t' \geq t$ where some continuation $c \in C$ begins or ends.
2. Afterwards, it selects two subsets from the set of continuations C based on t':
   - *must*-continuations C_{must} will definitely be triggered before time t', i.e., $t_1 \leq t'$ for $c \in C_{must}$.
   - *may*-continuations C_{may} may be triggered after time t', i.e., $t_0 \leq t'$, $t' < t_1$ for $c \in C_{may}$.
3. The continuations $c \in C_{must}$ could be triggered in any order during the time interval $t...t'$. Thus, the enhanced Abstract Execution must handle the execution paths for all continuations in C_{must} in parallel (similar to *if/else*-statements where the condition has the abstract Boolean value $\{F, T\}$). The candidate computation

algorithm ends here and the resulting execution paths are interpreted by sequential Abstract Execution according to run-to-completion semantics.

4. If $C_{must}=\emptyset$, the execution paths for all $c \in C_{may}$ are started and time progresses by setting $t':= t$. This is repeated until either $C_{must}\neq\emptyset$ holds, or both $C_{must}=\emptyset$ and $C_{may}=\emptyset$. In the former case, new *must*-continuations have been detected by progressing in time and processing must be continued with step 3. In the latter case, neither *must*- nor *may*-continuations are available, which indicates an empty abstract queue.

If a continuation c is going to be taken from the queue and executed, it has to be removed from the queue's continuation set C and the initial program state for the event handler has to be computed based on Δs.

4.4   Example of Abstract Execution with Abstract Event Queue Handling

In order to illustrate the algorithm defined in the previous sections, a small example will be presented here. For the example, we assume that the component under analysis has sent a request to a remote server and starts a timeout of 1 sec in order to remain reactive in case the server doesn't respond. From an environment model we deduce that the server's response might take between 0.1 seconds and 1.3 seconds. After those two events have been initiated, the component's abstract event queue is defined as (times are given in seconds):

$$Q_{abs} := \{ t=0, C \}, \text{ with } C = \{ c_R, c_T \} \text{ and}$$
$$c_R = \{ [0.1...1.3], \Delta s_{response} \}, c_T = \{ [1...1], \Delta s_{timeout} \}$$

The continuation c_R represents the server response event, the continuation c_T represents the timeout event. The first candidate computation based on Q_{abs} will provide the following results:

$$t = 0, t' = 0.1, C_{must} = \emptyset, C_{may} = \{ c_R \}$$

According to step 4 in the algorithm described in section 4.3, a new program state will be created from continuation c_R and prepared for Abstract Execution. In this new program state, we will have an updated abstract event queue with $t=0.1$ and $C=\{ c_T \}$. During the Abstract Execution of this program state the client might react to the server response by stopping the current timeout.

After creating this new program state, the candidate computation progresses in time and repeats step 2. This results in:

$$t = 0.1, t' = 1, C_{must} = \emptyset, C_{may} = \{ c_R \}$$

A similar reaction as before will occur; we skip the details here for sake of simplicity. As there are still *may*-continuations, but no *must*-continuations, we again progress in time and repeat step 2, resulting in:

$$t = 1, t' = 1, C_{must} = \{ c_T \}, C_{may} = \{ c_R \}$$

According to step 3 in the algorithm of section 4.3, continuation c_T will be removed from the queue and another new program state will be prepared for sequential Abstract Execution. As specified in step 3, the candidate computation ends and the sequential Abstract Execution algorithm proceeds by interpreting the two resulting program states. In the program state resulting from continuation c_T, the timeout handler will be called.

Depending on the implementation of the timeout handler, the server request might be canceled. If the server request is not canceled, Q_{abs} in that program state will still contain continuation c_R, which will be classified as *must*-candidate for time $t'=1.3$. Thus, it will be abstractly executed and the static analysis ends. From the resulting execution paths it can be seen that the server's response has been accepted, although the timeout handler has been called. This should be classified as a program error.

From the execution paths resulting from the extended Abstract Execution analysis, it can be concluded that the timeout value of 1 second will lead to a non-deterministic behavior, depending on the server's concrete reaction time to the client request.

5 Application to On-board Diagnostics Development

Electronic control-units in automobiles (ECUs) have to support diagnostics functionality, which is used both during production at the manufacturer as well as when the car is at the dealer's service shop. Therefore, the On-Board Diagnostics (OBD) functionality is critical for the vehicle's production process, but also important for customer satisfaction after the car has been delivered.

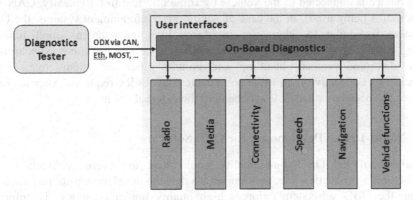

Fig. 2. Architecture of On-Board Diagnostics software as part of an Automotive/Infotainment System. An external tester is connected with the OBD subsystem via some external interface. The OBD subsystem will communicate asynchronously with the various application subsystems.

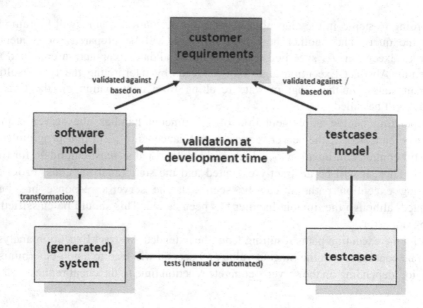

Fig. 3. Validation of implementation against test cases on model level and on target system level. Both software model and test cases model are tightly linked to customer requirements. The actual code for system and concrete test cases is being generated from the models.

5.1   Typical Architecture of OBD for Infotainment Systems

The overall architecture of OBD is depicted in Figure 2. An external diagnostics testing device is connected to the vehicle by some physical link (typically, CAN-Bus or Ethernet is being used). In the case of Automotive/Infotainment systems, the OBD subsystem is similar to other user interfaces like touch-screens, multi-function steering wheels or speech dialog systems. It has to handle incoming asynchronous events, do some protocol handling and contact other subsystems (e.g., tuner, navigation or connectivity) in order to execute diagnostics requests. After a proper response has been compiled, it is sent back to the external tester.

5.2   Model-Driven Development for OBD Software

As failures of the OBD functionality could lead to severe problems at the manufacturer's production site, it is important that the development tooling used for creating the OBD subsystem enforces high quality implementations. Therefore, a proprietary development tool based on Eclipse technologies [6] had been created at Harman which offers a domain-specific language (*DSL*) for OBD development. This language has a procedural semantics with a static type system (similar to C/C++), and additionally supports asynchronous primitives. These primitives reflect the event-driven aspects of the OBD architecture, e.g., the asynchronous communication with the external tester and the interaction with the application subsystems.

Programs using the OBD development DSL basically consist of a set of service-implementations. Each service can be called from the external testing device and is required to reply with a positive or negative response message. The implementation of each service-section consists of the following parts:

- Exactly one action-block, which will be executed if the service is called. The block consists of a sequence of statements, which will be executed in a run-to-completion way. Statements include assignments, if/else, for-loops (restricted to iterators over array-type variables), positive/negative responses, and commands for triggering asynchronous events (starting timers, sending requests via the internal APIs).
- Zero or more on-handlers, each consisting of a set of event ids and a command block. The command block may consist of the same statements as the action-block. It will be executed as soon as *all* events from the event id set have been triggered. If an incoming event triggers more than one handler (because its id is a member of their event id sets), then the handlers will be executed in increasing order of their set sizes.

The OBD development tool offers a state-of-the-art editor (created with the Xtext framework [8]), which is used to develop software for OBD subsystems. From the service implementations (formulated using the DSL) the source code for the target system is generated automatically.

As the car manufacturer is providing the specification of the diagnostics services as machine-readable XML format, an important part of the implementation can be derived directly from the specification. The APIs of the application subsystems which are used by the OBD service implementations are formally modeled as well. Thus, the developer is guided by specification and APIs, which leads to a development speed-up and quality increase. Additionally, the DSL for OBD implementation by design doesn't offer error-prone concepts like pointers or dynamic memory allocation. These expressivity restrictions help to increase the software quality even more, while only removing language features which are not needed for this domain.

5.3   Application of Abstract Execution for Event-Driven OBD Software

In order to push productivity and software quality even further, a model-based test concept has been added to the OBD development tool. The model-based testing approach uses test cases on a model level and generates actual test scripts from these models [7]. This approach is applied to test cases for OBD service implementations. The test scripts generated from those test cases will be validated against the real target system, running the generated source code. Figure 3 shows the overall relationships of specification, test cases, models and code.

It turned out that a huge number of test cases are necessary to achieve a reasonable coverage. This situation could be improved significantly by the following measures:

- Allow the specification of test cases based on abstract values for parameters and expected results. Thus, one abstract test case may represent a large set of concrete test cases.

- For the test script generation, create concrete test cases from abstract ones. This is not a topic for this paper.
- Apply the abstract test cases to the OBD implementation already on the model level. In this step, Abstract Execution and the extensions for event-driven systems are applied as described in previous chapters. All asynchronous primitives from the implementation DSL will be transformed into events, which can be interpreted by the extended Abstract Execution scheme.
- Represent the results of the abstract execution as direct feedback for the implementer, either on the implementation side or on the test case side.

The complexity of the Abstract Execution procedure is limited due to quite small portions of code which have to be analyzed and due to an aggressive strategy of merging execution paths at merge points during the Abstract Execution. Nevertheless, the accuracy of the analysis results is sufficient for increasing the overall quality. By carefully choosing the merge strategy, the triggers for starting the Abstract Execution and the implementation of the abstract data types (see section 4.1), the trade-off between reactivity of the static analysis and its accuracy can be adjusted in a wide range. In any case, we didn't suffer from performance bottlenecks so far.

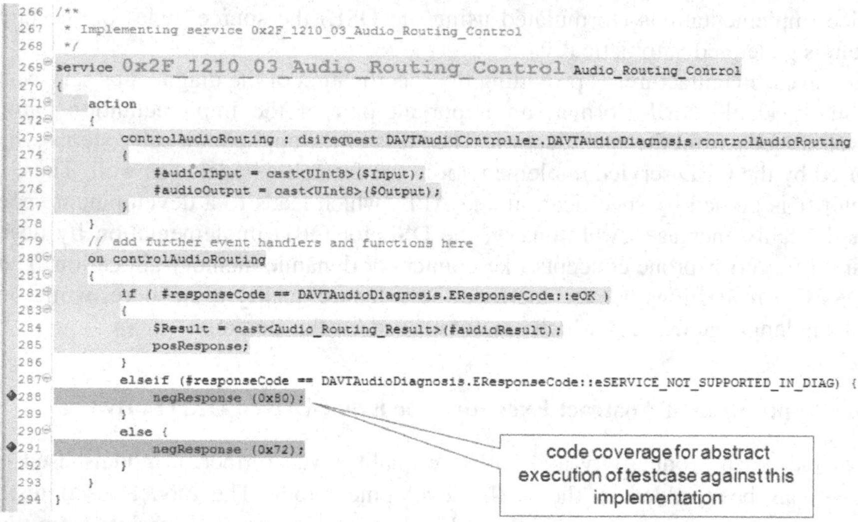

```
266  /**
267   * Implementing service 0x2F_1210_03_Audio_Routing_Control
268   */
269  service 0x2F_1210_03_Audio_Routing_Control Audio_Routing_Control
270  {
271      action
272      {
273          controlAudioRouting : dsirequest DAVTAudioController.DAVTAudioDiagnosis.controlAudioRouting
274          {
275              #audioInput = cast<UInt8>($Input);
276              #audioOutput = cast<UInt8>($Output);
277          }
278      }
279      // add further event handlers and functions here
280      on controlAudioRouting
281      {
282          if ( #responseCode == DAVTAudioDiagnosis.EResponseCode::eOK )
283          {
284              $Result = cast<Audio_Routing_Result>(#audioResult);
285              posResponse;
286          }
287          elseif (#responseCode == DAVTAudioDiagnosis.EResponseCode::eSERVICE_NOT_SUPPORTED_IN_DIAG) {
288              negResponse (0x80);
289          }
290          else {
291              negResponse (0x72);
292          }
293      }
294  }
```

code coverage for abstract execution of testcase against this implementation

Fig. 4. Screenshot of DSL editor in OBD development tool with activated code coverage. The code coverage is being computed while editing as a result from the extended Abstract Execution scheme.

The Abstract Execution analysis produces a lot of detailed data, which has to be post-processed and displayed to the developer properly in order to be useful. There is a variety of possibilities to represent the results, among them:

- Direct feedback in the implementation's code (source model) and the test case model by showing *error markers* and corresponding messages. Sometimes it is useful to additionally offer *quick fixes* which provide automatic proposals of how to improve or resolve the issue.

- A *test result view* which shows detailed execution traces for all test cases in a hierarchical tree-view structure. This includes abstract values of variables as well as return values and results. The execution traces are folded onto the *program scope* structure described in [1].
- *Test case coverage* information can be added optionally to the service implementations. Figure 4 shows an example, where some parts of the implementation are not yet covered by abstract test cases. Coverage can be displayed regarding all test cases available for a section of the implementation, which provides the overall coverage status. It can also be displayed for a small selection of test cases, which provides feedback on how these test cases impact the implementation under test.

All this information does not require that actual code and test code is being generated, built and executed; instead, it is resulting from the extended Abstract Execution analysis which is running in the background while the developer is editing his code.

6   Conclusions and Future Work

In this paper, we have presented an extension to the sequential Abstract Execution method which allows the proper handling of event-driven systems. The extensions are non-invasive, as it is not required to change the execution engine of the sequential scheme. The algorithm is based on the concept of an abstract event queue and the computation of continuation candidates.

The algorithm has been illustrated by a small example and a real-world application in the domain of Automotive On-Board Diagnostics development. In the latter, a model-based development tool for OBD software has been extended to provide a facility for online validation of implementations against abstract test cases. It has been shown that the immediate feedback given to the developer from the Abstract Execution leads to software with high quality and speeds up the development process.

As a next step, we will generalize the current implementation of the extended Abstract Execution and extract it from the OBD development tool as a separate component. This component will be used in other environments, e.g., an open-source, model-based development tool offering a hierarchical component model and hierarchical state machines.

References

1. Gustafsson, J., et al.: Automatic derivation of loop bounds and infeasible paths for WCET analysis using Abstract Execution. In: Proceedings of the 27th IEEE Real-Time Systems Symposium (RTSS 2006). IEEE Computer Society, Rio de Janeiro (2006)
2. Ermedahl, A., Gustafsson, J., Lisper, B.: Deriving WCET Bounds by Abstract Execution. In: Proceedings of the 11th International Workshop on Worst-Case Execution Time Analysis (WCET 2011), Porto, Portugal (2011)

3. Clarke, E.M., Heinle, W.: Modular translation of Statecharts to SMV. Technical report, Carnegie Mellon University (2000)
4. Cousot, P., Cousot, R.: Abstract interpretation: a unified lattice model for static analysis of programs by construction or approximation of fixpoints. In: Conference Record of the Sixth Annual ACM SIGPLAN-SIGACT Symposium on Principles of Programming Languages, Los Angeles, California, pp. 238–252 (1977)
5. Ratiu, D., Völter, M., Schätz, B., Kolb, B.: Language Engineering as an Enabler for Incremental Formal Analysis. In: Proceedings of FORMSERA 2012 Workshop (2012)
6. Eclipse platform, http://www.eclipse.org
7. El-Far, I.K., Whittaker, J.A.: Model-based Software Testing. In: Encyclopedia on Software Engineering. Wiley (2001)
8. Xtext framework, http://www.eclipse.org/Xtext

Formal Methods
for Intelligent Transportation Systems

Alessandro Fantechi[1,3], Francesco Flammini[2], and Stefania Gnesi[3]

[1] Universit degli Studi di Firenze DSI
Via S. Marta 3, Florence, Italy
fantechi@dsi.unifi.it
[2] Ansaldo STS I&C
Via Argine 425, Naples, Italy
francesco.flammini@ansaldo-sts.com
[3] Istituto di Scienza e Tecnologie dell'Informazione "A. Faedo", CNR, Pisa, Italy
Via Moruzzi 1, Pisa, Italy
stefania.gnesi@isti.cnr.it

1 Motivation

The term Intelligent Transportation Systems (ITS), [4,5], refers to information
and communication technology (applied to transport infrastructure and vehicles) that improve transport outcomes such as transport safety, transport productivity, travel reliability, informed travel choices, social equity, environmental
performance and network operation resilience [2,3]. Safety-critical ITS include
the so called X-by-wire (where 'X' can stand for 'fly', 'brake', 'accelerate', 'steer',
etc.) systems used in domains like aerospace, automotive and railways. The
importance of ITS is increasing as novel driverless/pilotless applications are
emerging.

2 Goals

This track, inspired by discussions held inside the ERCIM Working Group on
Formal Methods for Industrial Critical Systems (FMICS), addresses the application of formal methods to model and analyze complex systems in the context
of ITS. In fact, modeling and analysis activities are very important to optimize
system life-cycle in the design, development, verification and operational stages,
and they are essential whenever assessment and certification is required by international standards. On this regard, several approaches suggest a specification
methodology based on the Unified Modeling Language (UML), together with its
extensions/profiles, to generate analyzable formal models. Methodologies integrating the requirements of incremental and modular development are especially
challenging [1]. Both qualitative and quantitative evaluations can be performed
on formal models, including model-checking and stochastic simulations. Finally,
on-line model-checking (e.g. for adaptive route planning) issues are also very
important in the context of ITS, when objects exchange information about their

T. Margaria and B. Steffen (Eds.): ISoLA 2012, Part II, LNCS 7610, pp. 187–189, 2012.
© Springer-Verlag Berlin Heidelberg 2012

states to reach consistency among their decisions. In particular, this track addresses applications and case studies with a conceptual message, surveys on the state of the art on the application of formal methods on specific domains within ITS, and experience papers with a clear link to tool construction.

3   Contributions

The contributions to the track "Formal Methods for Intelligent Transportation Systems" address three distinct aspects. The first two papers address from a general perspective the introduction of formal methods in the development process of safety critical systems: F. Flammini et al. [6] discuss model-driven verification techniques, both for functional and non-functional system properties, with reference to a complex railway signalling equipment. G. Gigante et al.[7] introduce a novel software development guideline for safety-critical systems (namely, the avionic DO178-C standard), that for the first time specifically includes formal methods as one of the means to produce software at the highest Assurance Levels.

The other contributions are related to two category of systems in the railway domain, that for their complexity pose several challenges to current software and system development technology. The first category addresses driverless metros, that integrate in a complex architecture several subsystems which are geographically distributed, featuring strict dependability requirements: while A. Ferrari et al. [8] propose to cope with the architectural complexity and variety of Communication-Based driverless metro control systems by means of the discipline of product lines, S. Marrone et al. [9] address the complexity of verification of such kind of system by means of a common verification Reference Technology Platform exploiting a set of advanced model-based verification tools.

The second category is the one of railway interlocking systems: here the complexity lies in the geographical layout of the tracks, points and signals that can be found in a station or in a railway yard: verifying that the designed interlocking logics actually satisfies safety properties (that guarantee for example that two trains do not collide) for medium to large size interlockings is actually a challenge for current model-checking technology. On this regard, K. Winter [10] investigates possible optimisations for symbolic model checking, by means of specific reorderings of BDD variables which are strictly related to the topology of the controlled layout. A. E. Haxthausen [11] focuses on the formal definition of safety properties to be checked on models of legacy relay-based interlocking systems. A. Fantechi [12] proposes to adopt a distributed, geographical modelling in order to better attack the state space explosion typical of model checking when dealing with large size interlocking systems.

It is our opinion that the contributions to the track, even in the limited space available, succeed to give a good overview of the state-of-the-art and of the hard-to-solve open issues, as well as to give significant directions for the future research in this field.

References

1. Bonnefoi, F., Hillah, L.M., Kordon, F., Renault, X.: Design, modeling and analysis of ITS using UML and Petri Nets. In: IEEE Intelligent Transportation Systems Conference (ITSC 2007), pp. 314–319 (2007)
2. Cascetta, E.: Transportation Systems Engineering: Theory and Methods. Kluwer Academic Publishers (2001)
3. Flammini, F.: Railway Safety, Reliability, and Security: Technologies and Systems Engineering. IGI Global (2012)
4. IEEE Intelligent Transportation Systems Society home-page, http://sites.ieee.org/itss/ (last access June 2012)
5. International Journal of Intelligent Transportation Systems Research, http://www.springer.com/engineering/electronics/journal/13177
6. Flammini, F., Marrone, S., Mazzocca, N., Nardone, R., Vittorini, V.: Model-Driven V&V Processes for Computer Based Control Systems: A Unifying Perspective. In: Margaria, T., Steffen, B. (eds.) ISoLA 2012, Part II. LNCS, pp. 190–204. Springer, Heidelberg (2012)
7. Gigante, G., Pascarella, D.: Formal Methods in Avionic Software Certification: The DO-178C Perspective. In: Margaria, T., Steffen, B. (eds.) ISoLA 2012, Part II. LNCS, pp. 205–215. Springer, Heidelberg (2012)
8. Ferrari, A., Spagnolo, G.O., Martelli, G., Menabeni, S.: Product Line Engineering Applied to CBTC Systems Development. In: Margaria, T., Steffen, B. (eds.) ISoLA 2012, Part II. LNCS, pp. 216–230. Springer, Heidelberg (2012)
9. Marrone, S., Nardone, R., Orazzo, A., Petrone, I., Velardi, L.: Improving Verification Process in Driverless Metro Systems: The MBAT Project. In: Margaria, T., Steffen, B. (eds.) ISoLA 2012, Part II. LNCS, pp. 231–245. Springer, Heidelberg (2012)
10. Winter, K.: Optimising Ordering Strategies for Symbolic Model Checking of Railway Interlockings. In: Margaria, T., Steffen, B. (eds.) ISoLA 2012, Part II. LNCS, pp. 246–261. Springer, Heidelberg (2012)
11. Haxthausen, A.E.: Automated Generation of Safety Requirements from Railway Interlocking Tables. In: Margaria, T., Steffen, B. (eds.) ISoLA 2012, Part II. LNCS, pp. 262–276. Springer, Heidelberg (2012)
12. Fantechi, A.: Distributing the Challenge of Model Checking Interlocking Control Tables. In: Margaria, T., Steffen, B. (eds.) ISoLA 2012, Part II. LNCS, pp. 277–290. Springer, Heidelberg (2012)

Model-Driven V&V Processes for Computer Based Control Systems: A Unifying Perspective

Francesco Flammini[1], Stefano Marrone[2], Nicola Mazzocca[3],
Roberto Nardone[3], and Valeria Vittorini[3]

[1] AnsaldoSTS, Innovation and Competitiveness Unit (Italy),
via Nuova delle Brecce 260, 80147 - Napoli, Italy
francesco.flammini@ansaldo-sts.com
[2] Seconda Università di Napoli, Dipartimento di Matematica,
viale Lincoln, 5, 81100 - Caserta, Italy
stefano.marrone@unina2.it
[3] Università di Napoli "Federico II", Dipartimento di Informatica e Sistemistica,
Via Claudio 21, 80125 Napoli, Italy
{nicola.mazzocca,roberto.nardone,valeria.vittorini}@unina.it

Abstract. A recent trend in software engineering is to support the development process by providing flexible tool chains allowing for effective Model-Driven approaches. These solutions are very appealing in industrial settings since they enable the creation of development and verification processes, enhancing abstraction and reuse, and hence improving productivity. This paper addresses advantages and challenges in extending Model-Driven approaches to system engineering and specifically to verification and validation (V&V) of critical computer-based systems. Specifically, the paper highlights the needs for real-world industrial contexts and proposes the definition of a unifying Model-Driven process for V&V of functional and non-functional system properties. Some enabling techniques which aim at improving the reuse of Model-Driven artifacts are addressed to deal with process scalability and effectiveness. Two sample applications are described for ERTMS/ETCS signalling system in order to show the advantages of the approach: formal modeling for performance evaluation of message delivery between train and track controllers and test case generation for the verification of functional requirements of trains outdistancing.

Keywords: Model-Driven Engineering, Verification & Validation, Critical Systems, Domain Specific Languages, Railway Systems.

1 Introduction

Verification & Validation (V&V) processes within critical control systems development must guarantee the fulfillment of both functional and RAMS (Reliability Availability Maintainability Safety) requirements [11]. Two main approaches are employed in order to predict/evaluate the dependability attributes of those systems: the first relies on simulation based techniques, e.g. fault-injection [14] at

T. Margaria and B. Steffen (Eds.): ISoLA 2012, Part II, LNCS 7610, pp. 190–204, 2012.
© Springer-Verlag Berlin Heidelberg 2012

the hardware level (either physical or simulated) or software testing [8] at the various abstraction and integration levels; the second is based on formal methods, which can be used at any abstraction level (both hardware and software) and at any stage of system development and validation. Both simulative and formal approaches are used in real world applications, for different or same purposes, and can be classified as model-based techniques, as they require designers to generate an accurate model of the system under analysis and of the external environment (i.e. interacting entities). They may be used in combination with formal models possibly interacting with simulative ones (an example of this is the class of approaches known as model-based testing). Formal methods are employed in a variety of industrial applications, from microprocessor design to software engineering and verification (see [9] for a survey of widespread methods and applications). Despite of such a variety of methods, tools and applications, V&V activities are still critical in costs and results. The optimization of V&V processes is the focus of several ongoing national and international projects carried out in industrial settings [2]. A recent trend is to define and develop tool chains to support the developer in the V&V process. They are based on the Model Driven Engineering (MDE) paradigm and rely on the usage of models as the primary artifact in the development cycle. The idea to derive dependability models (e.g. Stochastic Petri Nets models) from high-level specifications of the system to be developed (e.g. expressed by UML) is not new ([5,6,24,22,7]). The cutting edge between those approaches and MDE may be summarized by the following words: integration, automation and traceability. That means a complete suite of integrated tools covering and linking all the stages of the V&V process has to be available, featuring automated generation of artifacts (models, test cases, log files, etc.) and requirements traceability. This paper describes how MDE may provide a unifying framework for V&V activities for critical systems, and specifically how this can be applied to railways control systems. Section 2 introduces some MDE concepts, starting from its primary nest: software development; Section 3 presents a brief state-of-the-art on a) Model-Driven analysis of non-functional properties of systems, according to its main fields of application, b) Model-Driven approach to functional testing. In Section 4 an overview of a Model-Driven approach to V&V is given; it is then applied to the railway domain in Section 5. Section 6 contains a brief discussion on some open issues and challenges.

2   The Model-Driven Approach

MDE approaches are very used in software development to support software production: they are the starting point from which source code, can be generated in an automatic or semi-automatic way. Models of software systems are usually constructed by using visual modeling languages like UML, SysML, Mat-Lab Simulink/Stateflow; successively, transformational approaches are applied to automate the overall process.

   In this context, the Object Management Group (OMG) has developed a set of standards providing an advanced meta-modeling architecture (Model Driven

Architecture, MDA [4]) whose primary goals are to cope with complexity and heterogeneity of different platforms and application domains and obtain automation and reuse. These goals are pursued by abstracting at three different levels: the *platform independent model (PIM)* is a model of the system structure and functions which must be independent by specific technical details related to its implementation, it is translated by proper Model to Model (M2M) transformations into one or more *platform specific models (PSMs)* and then to *system code.*

MDA relies on OMG standards including MOF (Meta-Object Facility, which is used to define modeling languages), UML (that is a MOF model), and QVT (Query/View/Transformation, a standard language for model transformation). MDA processes are supported by well established workbenches and tool chains, based on easily extensible plug-in systems such as Eclipse. Nevertheless, MDE is more general than MDA. Its strength is in using abstract representations of concepts and activities that characterize a specific application domain. Hence, it could be applied to several fields and to different purposes. In this paper we show how MDE may be used to define a V&V process for critical control systems according to a unifying perspective able to held together (semi) automatic generation of code, test cases, and dependability models. This may be done by exploiting the usage of proper languages to represent domain specific concepts and solutions at the conceptual level. This is a tricky aspect of the question that is briefly discussed here below.

2.1 Domain Specific Languages

UML is a general purpose modeling language, rich of modeling notations and semantic, which can be applied to a wide class of application domains. Despite of this great advantage, the effective usage of Model-Driven Development solutions in industrial settings asks for the availability of specialized modeling languages for several reasons: Domain Specific Modeling Languages (DSMLs) are small and well focused on domain scope, they simplifies the design process, tracing recurring design patterns in the application domain, and promote communication by standardizing the terminology and the best practices to be used in the specific application domain. Domain specific concepts are grouped into a domain meta-model, which defines the relationships among them and precisely specifies semantics and constraints associated with the domain concepts. The definition of a DSML is an activity performed by "language engineers" and it is still an emerging discipline with few established guidelines and patterns. Three main approaches to the definition of a DSML are reported in the literature [23]: (1) definition of a new modeling language from scratch; (2) extension of an existing modeling language by supplementing it with fresh domain specific constructs; and (3) refinement of an existing more general modeling language, as UML, by specializing some of its general constructs to represent domain specific concepts. Clearly the first one allows a precise characterization of domain specific concepts, but it requires the implementation of the model editors that involves an extra effort when put into practice. The second one suffers from the same problems but it can rely on the experience. The third one is more practical and presents minor development and maintenance costs: it bases on UML profiling techniques when UML is the general modeling language chosen.

The proposed approach is based on the third solution since inheriting UML syntax and semantics avoids the re-definition of existing concepts (e.g. state machines); moreover UML (and its good tool support) shortens the time to realization of languages that is of great interest for industries.

3   Model Driven V&V of Critical Systems

Model-driven approaches have been extended to support V&V activities, both for software and complex systems in general, in order to prove properties (Model-Driven Analysis) and to generate test cases (Model-Driven Testing). This is possible applying the two main principles, described previously, on which a Model-Driven process is based: the definition and usage of an high-level model for the system, and model transformation techniques. Model-Driven Analysis and Model-Driven Testing are separate techniques and are also supported by different tools but, since they rely on the same high-level model, some attempt to integrate them have been tried and are still under study: an ARTEMIS ongoing project MBAT [2] is an example of a European project that will provide a new leading-edge V&V technology in form of a Reference Technology Platform (MBAT RTP) for effective and cost-reducing validation and verification, primarily focusing on transportation domain combining Model-Driven Analysis and Testing techniques.

3.1   Model-Driven Analysis

The goal of Model-Driven Analysis is to construct formal models or artifacts, able to verify requirements, from input design models (high-level model) assuring the achievement of system quality, such as safety targets. Several projects addresses the analysis of dependability attributes of complex systems, based on MDE principles (e.g. the projects PRIDE [3], CHESS [1]), even if performance evaluation is perhaps the most addressed feature assessed in the literature by means of Model-Driven Analysis (see for example [18], [20] and [21]) The ArgoSPE tool [12] implements a performance3 evaluation process translating some performance annotated UML diagrams into Stochastic Petri nets models. MARTE [17] is a UML profile which intends to replace the UML profile for Schedulability, Performance and Time, adding capabilities to UML for Model-Driven development of Real Time and Embedded Systems. The MARTE profile is able to annotate, in an high-level model, system non functional properties (NFPs), according to a well-defined Value Specification Language (VSL) syntax. In a recent work [6] the "Dependability Analysis and Modeling" (DAM) profile has been proposed to extend MARTE with dependability concepts (e.g., annotating a UML State Machine transition as a failure step). Hence, DAM is useful to annotate dependability requirements and properties in UML specifications, in particular, reliability, availability, maintainability and safety. The DAM domain model represents the main dependability concepts according to a component-based view of the system under analysis. The system is defined as a set of components and delivers a set of services that can be detailed as a set of steps. Possible hw/sw redundancies are modeled through the redundant structure, made of fault tolerant components which can play different roles. The system can be affected by threats according to the fault, error, impairment (failure or hazard) chain. The maintenance actions are modeled through maintenance model, which includes the concepts necessary to represent components repair and service restore.

3.2 Model Driven Testing

Model-Driven Testing techniques deal with the efficient and automated generation of test cases from different kinds of models. Model-Driven Testing promises higher quality and conformance to the respective functional safety and quality standards at reduced costs through increased coverage, advanced test generation techniques, and increased automation of the process, including support for certification. As depicted in Fig. 1, Model-Driven Testing applies the same abstraction of platform independent model (PIM) and platform specific models (PSM) concepts into the test design model: it have been introduced the concepts of platform specific test design model (PST) that can be derived from platform independent test design model (PIT) ([10]). Both PIT and PST can be refined and enriched with test specific properties and it is possible to obtain from them executable test suites (and code) with the aim to verify the properties. To date transformations between the different abstraction levels (from platform independent to platform specific, and from models to executable test) have been made, but only few progress in the transformations between system models and test models are remarkable, in particular for non-software systems.

A recent OMG standard, the UML Testing Profile (UTP), defines a language for designing, visualizing, specifying, analyzing, constructing and documenting test cases [19]. This language can work with all major object and component technologies and can be applied in various application domains. UTP defines a MOF-based meta-model, enabling compliance between MOF-based tools and UTP standard. In4 of the profile, in which the behavioral aspects are left out because they are considered not relevant and require an inclusion of a significant portion of the UML 2.0 meta-model. For these reasons the UTP can be used standalone or in an integrated way with UML. This profile introduces four logical concept groups, that include test specific concepts, covering the following aspects: *test architecture, test behavior, test data* and *test time*. The *test architecture* contains the concepts able to describe the organization and the realization of test cases. One or more objects can be stereotyped as the *SUT* (system under

Fig. 1. Model Driven Testing reference schema

test), that refers to a system, subsystem, or component that is being tested. The features and behavior of the SUT is given entirely by the type of the property to which the stereotype is applied; the internal portion of the SUT is not known during the test execution due to its black-box nature. Different test cases can be groupend into a *TestContext*, the *TestContext* is realized by a set of *TestComponents* able to communicate with the SUT. The *TestContext* is also connected with an *Arbiter* able to determine the final outcome, the *Verdict*, of a test case. The concepts of *text behavior* specify the behavior of test cases: one *Behavior* is included into each *TestCase*. *TestCases* are connected with *TestLog* entities, able to log information. The concepts of *test data* group are able to specify data values. They include wildcards for a flexible data definition such as special characters for "any value" and "any or omitted value" definition. At last *test time* defines time concepts for a precise time specification using the primitives of *Time* and *Duration* to define respectively time values and duration. In [10] a set of transformations from UML model to UTP model is showed, proposing to generate test cases using three layers of transformations that are UML to PIT, PIT to PSM and PSM to testcase.

4   How It Could Be Used: A Unifying Approach

In this Section a unifying "industry-friendly" Model-Driven approach for V&V processes (for both formal analysis and testing) is presented. In Fig. 2 a reference schema for this approach is provided.

The first step is related to meta-modeling activities: proper languages, if not available, should be created by means of extension and/or merging of existing languages. These may be domain-independent (as MARTE-DAM and UTP) or domain-specific according to their focus on technical or business concepts. In our approach we need both kinds of languages since the first improves reusability while the second improves usability. In the proposed approach the Verification&Validation Profile (VVP) (an "horizontal" language) is created: it extends MARTE-DAM and UTP. Moreover it could be possible to specialize VVP concepts into a specific business domain (*Specific*).

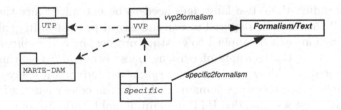

Fig. 2. Unifying Model-Driven V&V approach

Model transformations are defined generating a formal model according to a well specified formalism[1] from an high level model expressed into VVP or Specific. The definition of model transformations can be a modular task too, since it is possible to exploit composition and inheritance techniques [16]. Best results can be obtained if model transformations are defined on the basis of VVP since these transformations allow every specific derived language to inherit them improving reusability. Nevertheless some peculiarities of the Specific language may need to partially create further model transformations in order to best translate these features into the target formalism (*specific2formalism*).

4.1   Focus on the V&V Profile

In this subsection we define a V&V domain model to merge the concepts represented in the two cited UML profiles: MARTE-DAM and UTP. The first is used to model both performance and dependability aspects and the second allows the modeling of system and software testing. Fig. 3 depicts the V&V domain model we constructed to obtain the VVP.

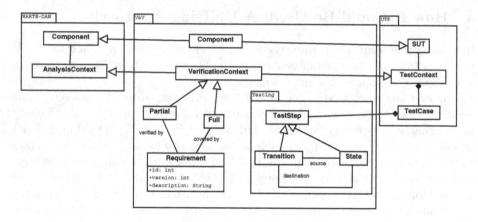

Fig. 3. Extract of V&V domain model

Notwithstanding these two languages need to be extended since they do not provide to all the features required in real industrial processes. In general three kinds of operations can be applied to existing profiles: *merge*: resulting domain model contains all the concepts of existing ones; *extension*: resulting domain model is refined by adding new concepts; *synthesis*: redundant concepts are reduced refactoring the resulting domain model. In the construction of the V&V domain model, first we extended UTP domain model by adding some important features in the modeling of the behaviour of system under test: under the hypothesis to model the behaviour of a component in terms of state machines (a

---

[1] If we think about performance analysis, suitable formalisms are: Queueing Networks, Petri Nets, etc.

very common practice in industry), the UTP's *TestCase* is refined by defining *TestStep*, a elementary unit of the *TestCase*, that can be a *State* or a *Transition* of the state machine. Other important added concepts are related to specification of requirements (the *Requirement* class) and the *VerificationContext* (that can be reported to a series of *TestSteps*). Testing specification and case can be modeled by specializing *VerificationContext* in *Partial* and *Full* according to the test detail level. Then some synthesis are made between some elements of MARTE-DAM and UTP (e.g. *Component* for both MARTE-DAM's *Component* and UTP's *SUT*). Finally the VVP is generated by the V&V domain model [15].

5   Application to Railway Signalling

The proposed V&V Model-Driven approach is here instantiated to the railway signalling domain. In particular it will be studied the European Railway Traffic Management System/European Train Control System (ERTMS/ETCS) [25] that is a standard for the interoperability of the European railway signalling systems in charge of providing the safe movement of trains and the optimal regulation of traffic flows.

5.1   The ERTMS/ETCS System

The mission of ERTMS/ETCS is to ensure railway interoperability. To this aim, it provides the specification of a traffic management and train control system that enables the transit of high speed trains through national borders. The ERTMS/ETCS standard ensures both technological compatibility among transeuropean railway networks and integration of the new signalling system with the existing national train interlocking systems. An ERTMS/ETCS system consists of heterogeneous, distributed components that are installed on the trains, along the tracks and in several control centers. A reference schema for ERTMS/ETCS systems is shown in Fig. 4. It consists of the Radio Block Centre (RBC), that is a central computer responsible of an entire track area, and the European Vital Computer (EVC), that is the on board controller. The communication between these two subsystems is provided by the GSM-R network. The control of the movement of the train is realized by means of a message that RBC sends to EVC: the authorization to safely move within a defined area that is called Movement Authority (MA)[2]. Attached to the MA, additional information describing a Temporary Speed Restriction (TSR) inside the length of the MA may be sent to the train.

In this paper we focus on V&V of both non-functional and functional properties of the delivery of the MA. We consider two representative requirements:

1. $U_{TX} < 1.6 * 10^{-5}$ where U_{TX} is the unavailability due to transmission error of communication networks [26];

---

[2] The MA is built according to the information about train position and speed each EVC periodically sends via GSM-R to RBC (Position Report).

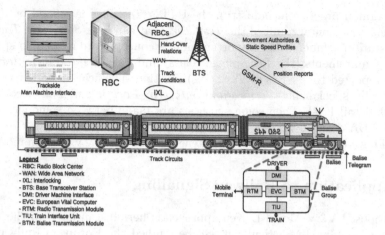

Fig. 4. ERTMS/ETCS reference schema

2. the message containing the TSR is sent periodically to EVC until EVC does not ack; if EVC does not send any ack message, RBC must send a braking command (Unconditionally Emergency Stop - UES) [25].

The first requirement can be verified by a performance evaluation of MA message delivery while the second by means of a functional test. The performance analysis is provided by automatic generation of Generalized Stochastic Petri Nets (GSPN) in Subsection 5.2; the functional test case is generated by model checking techniques in the Subsection 5.3 and is supported by the definition of a model transformation into Promela language [13]. Hence the general schema depicted in Fig. 2 is instantiated into the one depicted in Fig. 5.

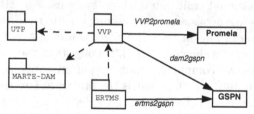

Fig. 5. ERTMS specific Model-Driven V&V

5.2   A DSML for GSM-R Unavailability Analysis

The MA is also used in some implementations as a channel monitoring message. If a train does not receive a new MA within a chosen number of seconds after the last received message, EVC tries to re-establish the connection within a specified timeout period and the following situations may happen: if EVC does not receive any valid message within a timeout, it brakes and passes in a degraded mode from which can exit after a reconnection procedure. VVP is specialized into ERTMS/ETCS domain specific language. A sample of this domain model is depicted in Fig. 6 where the three cited components are represented by three UML classes, each of them containing proper attributes. The meaning of the parameters of EVC and RBC classes are briefly described in the following:

- *numRetry*: number of reconnection attempts by the EVC;
- *timeToRestore*: mean time from a disconnection to the next balise group commanding a recall to the RBC;
- *timeToRetry*: time between reconnection attempts;
- *timeToBrake*: time-out after that a received message is no more valid;
- *messageCycle*: time between monitoring messages sent by RBC;

GSM-R networks does not need to be fully characterized by specific attributes since some quantitative parameters needed for a performance analysis are contained in some clases derived from MARTE and MARTE-DAM:

- *ssAvail* (from MARTE-DAM): unavailability of GSM-R connection;
- *packetTime* (from MARTE): mean message transmission time (in milliseconds) on the GSM-R network;
- *trasmissionError* (newly added): probability of a messages being corrupted during transmission.

According to this specific domain model (and the relative UML profile), we can describe the situation where a EVC and a RBC are connected by a redundant GSM-R network as in Fig. 7. The tagged value *ftLevel* is the level of fault tolerance of the *RedundantStructure*: if set to 1, it means that at least one operating GSM-R is needed to accomplish delivery service.

Dam2gspn and *ertms2gspn* are defined after the definition of a metamodel for GSPN language, omitted for brevity. These transformations are implemented in Atlas Transformation Language (ATL): for clarity the rules defining the transformations are described by means of the generated GSPN subnets. These rules translate: the redundancy of GSM-R networks, single GSM-R behaviour and RBC. The GSPNs are respectively depicted in Fig. 8 (*DaRedundantStructure* with *ftLevel* = 1), Fig. 9 (a) (*GSMR* stereotype) and Fig. 9 (b) (*RBC* stereotype).

The i-th "cloud" in the GSPN of Fig. 8 is filled with one of the GSPN of Fig. 9 (a) by means of the superposition of transition couples (*OK,Replicai_out*) and (*FROM_RBC,Replicai_in*), then the *in* transition of RedundantStructure

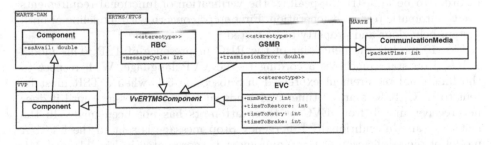

Fig. 6. ERTMS/ETCS domain model

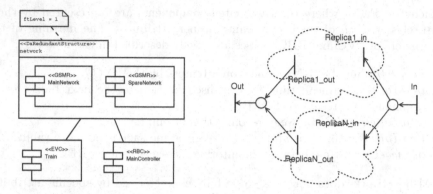

Fig. 7. ERTMS/ETCS Performance Model

Fig. 8. RedundantStructure GSPN pattern

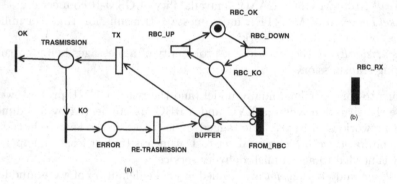

Fig. 9. GSPN patterns of GSM-R (a) and RBC (b)

net is superposed with *RBC_RX* of RBC GSPN model Fig. 9 (b) while the *out* transition is then linked to the EVC GSPN model. We can now apply the *dam2gspn* and *ertms2gspn* transformations to this model, generating a complete GSPN model not fully represented for sake of space.

5.3   Temporary Speed Restriction Behaviour Testing

In order to be industrial appealing, the verification of functional requirements needs automatic test case generation. First steps concern with modeling of both system behaviour and property to be tested.

Fig. 10 models the behaviour of the RBC in presence of TSR. This model is based on state machines according to the VVP language. With respect to the functional requirement expressed in Subsection 5.1, when a TSR must be sent to EVC, RBC starts a timer and sends such kind of message until it does not receive an ack from EVC or three attempts has not been made. In the last case, an Unconditionally Emergency Stop message is sent to the EVC. A model of the verification of the requirement is represented in Fig. 11: an UML activity diagram is stereotyped with *Partial VerificationContext* and contains

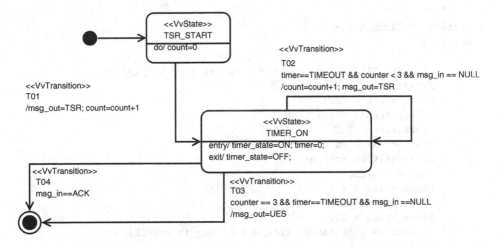

Fig. 10. Model of the RBC behaviour of TSR mechanism

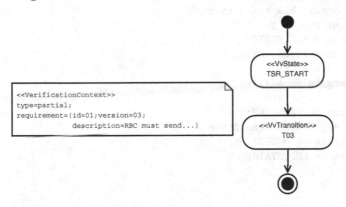

Fig. 11. Specification of TSR mechanism requirement

the necessary *TestStep*s to develop in a full specified *Full VerificationContext* (the object of the automatic generation).

In order to generate the related test case (full specification of input and output conditions), we use model checking technique. In particular we rely on SPIN model checker [13] and Promela language. After the definition of a metamodel for Promela language, both M2M and M2T tranformations can be defined starting from VVP. These transformations can be used to translate both the system behaviour and the requirement for which generate the test case; then the two parts are merged into a single Promela model and translated into Promela concrete syntax. Formal definition of the model transformations is out of the scope of the paper; notwithstanding we report a snippet of the Promela file generated by the TSR model.

```
...
:: (state == TIMER_ON) ->
  atomic {
    if
      :: (timer==TIME_OUT && count < 3 && msg_in == NULL) ->
         // exit - state
         timer_state = OFF;
         // applicable transition
         transition = TO2;
         state = TIMER_ON;
         // transition action
         msg_out = TSR;
         count = count + 1;
         // entry - state
         timer_state = ON;
      :: (count == 3 && timer==TIME_OUT && msg_in ==NULL) ->
         // exit - state
         timer_state = OFF;
         // applicable transition
         transition = TO3;
         state = END_STATE;
         // transition action
         msg_out = UES;
      :: (msg_in == ACK) ->
         // exit - state
         timer_state = OFF;
         // applicable transition
         transition = TO4;
         state = END_STATE;
    fi;
  }
...
```

The code snippet is the result of the translation of the *TIMER_ON* state: it's possibile to see the three transitions that start from this state with trigger conditions as specified in the high level. For each transition a "case" statement is generated containing all the actions that must be accomplished: *state exiting activities, transition activation, new state entering* tasks.

If a specified test is feasible, SPIN finds a counterexample and a full detailed trace containing all the changes in Promela variables can be generated. This trace can be used to extract the sequence of states-transitions on the state machines inducing the sequence of inputs to give to system during the test execution phase.

6   Conclusions and Open Issues

This papers has presented a novel approach in Verification&Validation of critical railway systems that exploits the benefits of formal analysis and sofwtware/system testing. An important point is related to the capability of defined process to be both theoretically unifiying and be appealing in real industrial contexts. The methodology has been applied to the railway domain specifically addressing the two different aspects: two applications of ERTMS/ETCS signalling control systems show complementary features and advantages of the proposed approach. Indeed the applications show how to develop novel techincal and business oriented specific languages and mode transformations both improving language usability and transformation reuse. It's important to remark that this is part of an ongoing work and the VVP is currently in development phase: future research efforts will investigate on extends VVP in particural in the interaction between the analysis and testing subparts of the approach.

References

1. ARTEMIS-2008-1-100022 CHESS - composition with guarantees for high-integrity embedded components software assembly, https://www.artemis-ju.eu/chess
2. MBAT: Combined Model-based Analysis and Testing of Embedded Systems, http://www.mbat-artemis.eu/
3. PRIDE - ambiente di progettazione integrato per sistemi dependable, transformations for dependability analysis, deliverable 2.1 (February 2003)
4. Model driven architecture guide, Version 1.0.1, OMG document (2003)
5. Bernardi, S., Flammini, F., Marrone, S., Merseguer, J., Papa, C., Vittorini, V.: Model-Driven Availability Evaluation of Railway Control Systems. In: Flammini, F., Bologna, S., Vittorini, V. (eds.) SAFECOMP 2011. LNCS, vol. 6894, pp. 15–28. Springer, Heidelberg (2011)
6. Bernardi, S., Merseguer, J., Petriu, D.C.: A dependability profile within MARTE. Journal of Software and Systems Modeling (2009)
7. Bondavalli, A., Dal Cin, M., Latella, D., Majzik, I., Pataricza, A., Savoia, G.: Dependability analysis in the early phases of UML-based system design. Comput. Syst. Sci. Eng. 16(5), 265–275 (2001)
8. Causevic, A., Sundmark, D., Punnekkat, S.: An industrial survey on contemporary aspects of software testing. In: 2010 Third International Conference on Software Testing, Verification and Validation (ICST), pp. 393–401 (April 2010)
9. Clarke, E.M., Wing, J.M.: Formal methods: state of the art and future directions. ACM Comput. Surv. 28(4), 626–643 (1996)
10. Dai, Z.: Model-driven testing with UML 2.0. In: Proceedings of the 2nd European Workshop on Model Driven Architecture (2004)
11. Flammini, F.: Railway safety, reliability, and security. Technologies and systems engineering. IGI Global (2012)
12. Gómez-Martínez, E., Merseguer, J.: ArgoSPE: Model-Based Software Performance Engineering. In: Donatelli, S., Thiagarajan, P.S. (eds.) ICATPN 2006. LNCS, vol. 4024, pp. 401–410. Springer, Heidelberg (2006)
13. Holzmann, G.J.: The SPIN model checker (September 2003)
14. Hsueh, M.C., Tsai, T.K., Iyer, R.K.: Fault injection techniques and tools. Computer 30(4), 75–82 (1997)
15. Lagarde, F., et al.: Improving UML profile design practices by leveraging conceptual domain models. In: 22nd Int.l Conf. on Automated Software Engineering, Atlanta, USA, pp. 445–448. ACM (November 2007)

16. Marrone, S., Papa, C., Vittorini, V.: Multiformalism and Transformation Inheritance for Dependability Analysis of Critical Systems. In: Méry, D., Merz, S. (eds.) IFM 2010. LNCS, vol. 6396, pp. 215–228. Springer, Heidelberg (2010)
17. UML profile for modeling and analysis of real-time and embedded systems (marte), Version 1.0, OMG document (2009)
18. Moreno, G.A., Merson, P.: Model-driven performance analysis. In: Proceedings of the 4th International Conference on the Quality of Software Architectures, QoSA (2008)
19. UML testing profile, Version 1.1, OMG document (2012)
20. Petriu, D.B., Woodside, M.: A metamodel for generating performance models from UML designs. In: Proceedings of the 7th Int. Conference on the Unified Modeling Language. Modelling Languages and Applications, pp. 41–53 (2004)
21. Petriu, D.B., Woodside, M.: An intermediate metamodel with scenarios and resources for generating performance models from UML designs. In: Software and Systems Modeling, Special Issue, SoSyM, pp. 163–184 (2007)
22. Rugina, A., Kanoun, K., Kaâniche, M.: A system dependability modeling framework using AADL and GSPNs, pp. 14–38. Springer, Heidelberg (2007)
23. Selic, B.: A systematic approach to domain-specific language design using UML. In: 10th IEEE Int.l Symposium on Object and Component-Oriented Real-Time Distributed Computing (ISORC 2007), pp. 2–9 (2007)
24. Tadano, K., Xiang, J., Kawato, M., Maeno, Y.: Automatic Synthesis of SRN Models from System Operation Templates for Availability Analysis. In: Flammini, F., Bologna, S., Vittorini, V. (eds.) SAFECOMP 2011. LNCS, vol. 6894, pp. 296–309. Springer, Heidelberg (2011)
25. UIC. ERTMS/ETCS class1 system requirements specification, ref. SUBSET-026, issue 2.2.2 (2002)
26. UNISIG. ERTMS/ETCS RAMS requirements specification, ref. 96s1266

Formal Methods in Avionic Software Certification: The DO-178C Perspective

Gabriella Gigante and Domenico Pascarella

CIRA (Italian Aerospace Research Centre), Via Maiorise,
81043 Capua, Italy
{g.gigante,d.pascarella}@cira.it
http://www.cira.it

Abstract. The ideal of correct software has always been the goal of research in the field of Information Technologies. For the next years scientific communities hope for a great challenge: a complete strategy in software programming and software engineering supported by a range of analysis tools to design, develop, integrate, verify and maintain software applications with mathematical rigor. In this challenge formal methods shall play a key role. The adoption of these methodologies should be placed in the proper software engineering framework according to the software domain. In the avionic domain safety-critical software has to accomplish Federal Aviation Regulations by DO-178C or DO-278A means of compliance giving evidence that software implements its intended functions and does not perform unintended functions. DO-178B and DO-278A allowed formal methods without addressing specific process requirements. DO-178C instead is accompanied by a new RTCA Guideline DO-333 "Formal methods supplement to DO-178C and DO-278A". The paper aims to provide an overview of the above mentioned standard. It highlights key concepts about the proper adoption of formal methods to accomplish the standard and the related certification objectives and provides different cases according to the different granted verification techniques.

1   Introduction

Correctness is a key issue in the design process of safety-critical software. Defects in such software may lead to catastrophic consequences. Software verification is the software engineering discipline whose goal is to assure that the product under consideration possesses the required functionalities and does not perform unintended functions.

The most used verification techniques are still reviewing and testing. For example, an average part between 30% and 50% of the software costs are dedicated to testing. Moreover testing and reviews are complementary means of verification because they are able to detect different types of errors. Thereby a typical design process uses testing, reviews and other best practices for software assurance.

This approach has three main pitfalls:

-    testing and reviewing are not exhaustive methods: they cannot analytically show the absence of defects, but they can only improve in some way the confidence about the good functioning of the product;

T. Margaria and B. Steffen (Eds.): ISoLA 2012, Part II, LNCS 7610, pp. 205–215, 2012.
© Springer-Verlag Berlin Heidelberg 2012

- testing and reviewing are mostly manual techniques: they are strongly related to the verifier experience and they cannot be completely automated;
- testing and reviewing are more effective in the latter stages of the development cycle: testing is not applicable in the earliest stages, while empirical studies indicate that reviews obtain better results if they are directed to specific errors.

These weaknesses are more significant for complex systems and safety-critical software, where more effort is spent on verification than in development. Besides an earlier detection of defects would considerably reduce the fixing costs. Formal methods and formal analysis could resolve these issues.

2   Depth and Issues of Application in Formal Methods

Formal methods are the use of mathematical techniques in the design and analysis of computer hardware and software. Mathematical rigor provides for the construction of specifications and their verification is less reliant on human intuition, thus could give evidence of correctness and robustness of software.

Formal specification and verification means creating a mathematical model of a system, using a language to specify desired properties of the system in a concise and unambiguous way, and using a method of proof to verify that the specified properties are satisfied by the model.

The literature provides numberless of case studies demonstrating that formal methods can be used for a wide variety of purposes:

- to derive premises or logical consequences of the specification, for user confirmation, through deductive theorem proving techniques [8];
- to generate counterexamples to claims about a declarative specification;
- to generate concrete scenarios illustrating desired or undesired features about the specification [9] or, conversely, to infer the specification inductively from such scenarios;
- to produce animations of the specification in order to check its adequacy [10];
- to check specific forms of specification consistency/completeness efficiently;
- to generate higher-level specifications such as invariants or conditions for liveness or for safety or for reachability and functional correctness [11];
- to generate test cases and oracles from the specification [12];
- to support formal reuse of components through specification matching [13].

According to the intended purposes formal methods can be applied to the specification and verification of products from each development lifecycle: requirements, high-level and low-level design, and implementation.

Early software lifecycle phases are currently less automated and less tightly coupled to specific languages and notations, and related work products are typically less effectively analyzed than those of later development stages. Formal methods could compensate for these limitations supporting the existing process by the provided systematic, repeatable analysis specification and proof.

Formal approaches used later in lifecycle phases, raises more technically challenging integration problems. For example, the languages adopted for formal specification and proof and those used for programming generally exhibit semantic differences making it difficult to synthesize a process that effectively uses both [16].

Formal methods seem to find their most effective application early in the lifecycle.

First of all the activity of modeling in itself has been widely experienced to raise many questions and detect serious problems in original informal formulations. Besides, the semantics of the formalism being used provides precise rules of interpretation allowing many of the problems with natural language to be overcome. These semantic rules can fix accuracy problems. Second, the formal language can guarantee a proper and uniform level of abstraction. In real development processes we experienced that is difficult "to standardize" the proper level of abstraction and at the same time is difficult for software engineers to describe thoroughly what the software has to do to implement the system requirements, abstracting from how the software will implement that behavior. Third, formal specifications can discovery incompleteness or ambiguity. Fourth, formal specifications are closely connected to automatic verification, they encourage atomicity. Fifth, formal specifications can be subjected to various forms of automatic analysis that are rather effective in detecting certain kinds of faults. Simple syntax analysis identifies many clerical errors, and type checking is a very potent debugging. Sixth, formal methods based on state exploration can automatically examine all the possible behaviors of simplified instances of many design problems, unlike rapid prototyping and simulation.

Generally speaking formal methods require discrete phases or steps clearly defined and documented with fixed work products. Whatever the lifecycle is, it should give evidence of compliance to applicable standards and guidelines. In the avionic domain the adoption of formal approaches is guided by DO-178B [1], DO-178C [2] and DO-333 [15].

3   Formal Methods in Support Certification

3.1   DO-178B and DO-178C

Software failures are usually systematic and not random. They arise from faults (defects) in requirements specification, design, coding or integration, so their occurrences are deterministic: they always come true if there is a certain combination of inputs and system state. However, this combination can be treated as a random process, therefore software failures can have a stochastic model and a probabilistic characterization, i.e. we may estimate a software failure rate.

As regards airborne software, its development needs an integral safety engineering approach to minimize failure rates. We can classify this kind of software as "ultra-dependable" as it typically requires failure rates of 10^{-7} to 10^{-12} per hour. For example, catastrophic failures in a civil aircraft must have a rate less than 10^{-9} [7]. Failure rates of ultra dependable systems are so low that we cannot generally provide an experimental validation of their fulfillment. We can't even decompose software into simply related components which can fail independently and can be easily modeled from a reliability point of view: software structures present complex relationships, they can influence each other and they can propagate their errors. For this reason, certification of airborne software can't be globally experimental or analytical, but it can only involve different aids, such as specific life-cycle processes, configuration management, fault-tolerant techniques, experience with similar software, qualifications of tools and developers, and so on. Assurance of ultra-dependable software can be guaranteed only by an intensive analysis of its design activities ("we cannot measure how well we've done, we instead look at how hard we tried", [4]). Anyway, testing is essential, but it cannot formally prove dependability properties: it can only support in verification of requirements coverage due to the infeasibility of experimental estimation of the real failure rates in the ultra-dependable region.

This is the core issue of DO-178B and DO-178C (but also of other standards for safety-critical software). They are both prescriptive standards for airborne software development: they point out requirements on the process by which software is developed and deployed.

DO-178C is a revision of DO-178B. Unlike DO-178B, it takes into account more mature software technologies, such as object-oriented programming, model-based design (automatic code generation), COTS tools (such as real-time operating systems). As regards verification, it goes beyond testing and reviewing and addresses formal analysis. It tries to remove ambiguities to minimize the possibility of subjective judgments by certification authorities.

DO-178C explicitly addresses "new" software technologies in supplements: in this way, the basic prescribed approach for software development process is practically the same of DO-178B, but it can be partially replaced or extended by some variants that include other means of compliance (for example, formal methods). These supplements are about tool qualification, model-based development, object-oriented design and formal methods.

3.2   DO-178C Overview

Certification is the legal recognition by a certification authority that a product, service, organization or person complies with some specific requirements. The applicant has to convince the relevant certification authority that all required steps have been taken to match the required requirements. DO-178C (Software Considerations in Airborne Systems and Equipment Certification) is the current reference for software certification in the aeronautical domain (even though it could be theoretically applied in other domains, too). It has been used by FAA and EASA to approve software for commercial aircrafts. Like DO-178B, it has been produced by RTCA "to establish software considerations for developers, installers, and users when the aircraft equipment design is implemented using microcomputer techniques" [3]. So DO-178C does not provide real certification requirements (which are based on other existing regulations), but it points out some fundamental guidelines. For example, it does not prescribe a particular development process, but identifies the main design activities and their objectives. It does not dictate approaches for hazard assessment (for example, fault tree analysis), specific programming languages or tools, requirements for personnel training or format for artifacts, too.

This is summarized in [2]: "the certification authority establishes the certification basis for the aircraft or engine in consultation with the applicant". Besides, "the applicant proposes a means of compliance that defines how the development of the airborne system or equipment will satisfy the certification basis. The Plan for Software Aspects of Certification defines the software aspects of the airborne system or equipment within the context of the proposed means of compliance".

From a qualitative point of view, DO-178C requires that each line of code must be directly traced to a requirement, that every requirement must be traced to some test cases and that no extraneous code is present in the delivery. Obviously the applicant has to provide some evidence to the authority in order to gain certification credits, i.e. to prove that all required objectives (requirements for certification) are satisfied. These objectives are not all mandatory, but their imposition is related to the software level.

Software level is "the designation that is assigned to a software component as determined by the system safety assessment process" and establishes the rigor necessary to demonstrate compliance with [2]. Therefore, the certification authority does not consider the software as a stand-alone product, but in its relationships to the total system (aircraft) which contains it. For this reason, the software level is related to the software contribution to system failure conditions. Software levels are identified from levels A to E according to the severity of their potential conditions: level A is software whose malfunction could contribute to catastrophic failure conditions; level E (not addressed in DO-178C) corresponds to software whose malfunction is always anomalous behavior, with no effects on aircraft operational capability and on pilot workload.

DO-178C organizes software design process into three processes: software planning process, software development process and integral processes.

The planning process addresses both development and integral processes. Its artifacts (Plan for Software Aspects of Certification, Software Development Plan, Software Verification Plan, Software Configuration Management Plan, Software Quality Assurance Plan, Software Standards and tool qualification plans) must conform to DO-178C. Then, the applicant has to provide evidence that the software lifecycle processes are compliant with the software plans.

Software development process is further composed of four sub-processes:

- software requirements process develops High Level Requirements (HLR, a description of the intended software functionalities, i.e. what the software shall do) from the outputs of the system process (system requirements);
- software design process develops Low Level Requirements (LLR, a description about how the software shall executes its delegated functionalities) and Software Architecture from the HLR;
- software coding process develops source code from the Software Architecture and the LLR;

- software integration process loads executable object code into the target hardware for hardware/software integration.

Integral processes ensure correctness, control and confidence of the software activities and their artifacts. Verification, configuration management, quality assurance and certification liaison are part of integral processes.

3.3   Formal Methods in DO-178C Processes

DO-178C makes some preliminary remarks in order to guide the applicant to a sound use of formal approach. It creates a common understanding on the words: formal methods, formal model, formal analysis. A formal method is constituted by a formal model combined with a formal analysis. It can be applied at various stages in software development, that is in different processes.

Formal models are produced by the development process, for example requirements process or detailed design or by formal analysis of a software artifact. Different formal models can be applied to different type of analysis, as well as not all the specifications need to be modeled in a formal way.

Formal analysis provides guarantees/proofs of software properties, in other words compliance with requirements. Subject to the formal model employed is correct, formal analysis provides assurance that the artifact at that stage does not contain certain kind of faults.

Compliance between artifacts can never be shown between a formal model and an informal model, using formal analysis. Besides tools adopted to execute formal analysis or formal modeling should follow guidelines related to tools.

Planning Process

Planning process should develop a thorough analysis about benefits of applying formal methods in the specific software lifecycle. Trade-off must be driven by skill, communications needs, software design assurance level, commercial tools availability and effectiveness of other verification techniques on the specific application.

Once decided on the adoption of formal methods, the purposes, the relative outputs and framework should be fixed.

The Plan for Software Aspects Certification (PSAC) should address such considerations in order to make certification authorities aware of the soundness of formal approach. In details formal methods purposes should be mapped to the specific process objectives, the use in software lifecycle should be clarified identifying the affected processes (development, verification, integration, assurance), the relative outputs should be defined together with their intended use within the software lifecycle.

The Software Development Plan should detail the integration of formal modeling within the development activities identifying the relative process data, in other words the relative outputs and the intended use within the process. The Software Verification Plan should detail the verification activities stating explicitly which properties are intended to be verified, which objectives must be accomplished and describing step by step the working procedure to exercise verification. Formal verification cases must be repeatable. The verification environment should be described in detail with particular attention to the assumptions that may invalidate the verification itself.

Software Standards also should be considered by the planning process. According to the stage at which the formal methods are applied, the standard of formal modeling should be provided. Standard should also guide developers and verifiers to the definition of properties to be satisfied by models.

Development Process
The objectives of the Development Process require the production of artifacts representing intermediate steps towards the executable object code. Such artifacts are the means of compliance to the objectives.

Artifacts are: High Level Requirements, Software Architecture, Low Level Requirements, source code, object code.

Each one can be developed by applying formal modeling. The intended purpose could be the need of defining high quality software artifacts eventually combined with the need of a rigorous verification technique. Each artifact could be independently modeled by means of a specific formal language, or an artifact could represent the model and the higher level artifact could represent the properties that the model should satisfy. Formal modeling of object code implies the semantics are managed in the same by formal analysis as they are by the target hardware.

Anyway each possible approach allows the applicant to comply with the recommended objectives of Annex A Table A-2 [2], but encompasses different verification objectives. Besides each approach implies a different planning of development standards. Duplication of artifacts expressed in different models should be avoided. The presence of different models of the same artifact could generate confusion during the verification activity, and the evidence of equivalence between the different models could raise some problems. This approach could minimize benefits in saving effort. Typically this approach is adopted when software developers do not have the skill needed to provide directly a formal model of the artifact, and an independent group executes the activity, or when there are binding constraints by customer. In this case the development process should clearly identify the process data and their utilization within the certification process, verification process should manage and resolve the intrinsic ambiguity.

An hybrid approach could be encouraged by the presence on the market of CASE tools. In this case, to enable formal analysis, the process should address the transformation the "semi-formal model" into a formal model, providing that a tool exists. In this case the planning process must pay great attentions in tools assurance: models should be equivalent.

Verification Process
According to DO-178C, the objectives of the Verification Process require:

- evidence of fully and exclusive compliance of each level of specification to the requirements of its superior specification;

- evidence of correctness of object code satisfying the system requirements, that is it implements the intended functions;
- confidence that the object code does not perform unintended functions.

Formal methods do not replace this process, but rather augment the already foreseen verification techniques analysis, review and testing. Different approaches can be adopted according to the different objectives that are intended to be accomplished formally.

High Level Requirements are required to meet system requirements, to be accurate, to be verifiable, to be consistent, to comply standards, to be traceable to system requirements, to define accurate algorithms.

Compliance to system requirements by formal analysis would require formal modeling of system requirements.

If a set of system requirements and a set of High Level Requirements are expressed as formal notations, formal analysis can provide evidence of compliance. The proof of evidence could be supplied in different ways according to the approach. High Level Requirements can be "logical consequences" of system requirements, or they can define the model, and system requirements identify the properties of the model. In the latter case reachability analysis could provide a counter-example of something not reachable and this could lead to identify unnecessary High Level Requirements that would probably originate dead code.

Derived High Level Requirements (HLR not traceable to system requirements) might not be assured by formal methods, therefore they should always be reviewed and reported to verify any conflict at system level.

Anyway in a typical process, the system project team is different from the software project team, and the activity, if not executed by the system team itself, could result heavy and the relative benefits of a sound verification could be minimized by the effort spent for the activity.

If a set of High Level Requirements is expressed as formal notation, relative accuracy and verifiability are intrinsically assured by the formalism itself, being precise and unambiguous and verifiable. The remaining set of High Level Requirements should be verified by different means.

A set of High Level Requirements in formal notations can be easily checked for conformance to standards by means of formal analysis. The verification process should clarify if all standards can be verified by means of formal analysis, otherwise it should identify clearly which standards are verified formally and which one by means of review.

Traceability should be verified by review, anyway it could be supported by the verification of compliance to system requirements.

Low Level Requirements are required to meet High Level Requirements, to be accurate, to be verifiable, to be consistent, to comply to standards, to be traceable to High Level Requirements, to define accurate algorithms and to be compatible with target computer.

For Low Level Requirements the same approach of that for High Level Requirements can be adopted to assure the same objectives (compliance, accuracy, consistency). Compatibility with software/hardware target environment means assuring that no conflict exists on aspects about bus loading, system response time, and input/output hardware. Verification by formal analysis would require formal modeling of hardware/software features of the target computer.

Software Architecture is required to be compatible with High Level Requirements, consistent, conform to standards, compatible with the target computer and coherent with respect the partitioning integrity identified at PSAC level.

Compatibility with High Level Requirements requires that architecture does not conflict with them. If both are expressed by formal notations, formal analysis can be applied. If only some parts of artifacts are formally modeled, the remaining parts should be verified by other means for example by review.

Consistency aims to assure the correct relationships between the software components concerning both the aspects of data flow and control flow, and to guarantee protection mechanism between every higher level component and the related low level components. Consistency could be guaranteed by formal analysis.

Compatibility with software/hardware target environment aims to assure that no conflict exists in initialization, asynchronous and synchronous operations and interrupts. It could be verified by formal analysis only if target environment is formally modeled.

Partitioning integrity could be expressed by appropriate formal properties satisfied by the architectural formal model.

Source code is required to be compliant with Low Level Requirements, with Software Architecture, to be conform to standards, verifiable, accurate and consistent.

Compliance, conformity to standards, accuracy, consistency and verifiability could be assured by formal analysis provided that both artifacts are formally modeled.

Accuracy means the verification of properties as stack usage, memory usage, fixed point arithmetic overflow, floating-point arithmetic, resource contention and limitations, worst case execution timing, exception handling, initializations run-time problems, cache management, unused variables, data corruption, compiler and the relative options, linker and the relative options.

Formal analysis could verify this properties if a semantic model of the code exists.

Objectives accomplished by source code could be considered accomplished by object code if the similarity between two artifacts can be demonstrated.

Verification of Verification Process
Verification of Verification Process aims at assure the "completeness" of Verification Process itself demonstrating that verification cases and results are correct and full coverage is achieved. Correctness of formal verification cases and relative results is a specific objective to accomplish when using formal methods. Coverage can be achieved by means of:

- requirement-based coverage analysis: that is a formal case for each formalized requirement (exhaustive verification provided by formal methods guarantees a complete coverage with a single formal case);
- completeness of the set of requirements: that is for all input conditions the required output has been specified and for all output the required input conditions have been specified.

If completeness cannot be achieved, structural coverage analysis by means of testing must be considered.

3.4   Additional Specific Objectives

In addition to the core objectives, the formal methods supplement of DO-178C prescribes some specific objectives concerning the application of formal methods. They are intuitively an extension of verification of verification objectives, applied to formal specification and analysis. These objectives are:

- Correctness of formal analysis cases and procedures: all assumptions included in the formal analysis must be justified and false assumptions must be identified and removed because they would invalidate the analysis.
- Correctness of formal analysis results: the applicant must provide evidence that formal analysis results are correct and discrepancies between actual and expected results are explained.
- Correctness of requirements formalization: if informal requirements (i.e., natural language or semi-formal expressions) are translated into formal specifications, the applicant must prove that the formalization is an equivalent representation of the starting requirement.
- Formal method soundness: the applicant must provide evidence about formal method soundness, i.e. notations have an unambiguous and mathematically defined syntax and semantics and the analysis method never asserts that a property is true even when it may be not true.

4   Conclusions and Future Works

Formal methods and their benefits within a project for the development of safety-critical airborne software must be evaluated for effectiveness and efficiency. Many specific objectives must be accomplished in order to be fully compliant to RTCA guideline. The planning process should choose a proper framework for formal development and formal verification. Framework encompasses objectives, activities for identification of specific aspects of system to be investigated, and tools. Objectives covered by formal analysis should be precisely identified avoiding duplicates in processes. Property and modeling languages should be appropriate to the specific system domain, and their scope should be precisely clarified. Notations should be clear and intuitive to the average user and reviewer. Additional activities should be defined to identify rigorously the "most critical aspects of the system" to investigate. Tools should guarantee confidence about their outputs.

Analysis should not be an isolated phase in the software verification process. Rather methods and tools for design, analysis and coding should be well integrated, and support similar approaches to system development. Defining for the first time a sound framework to gain certification credits requires effort, but building it "reusable", allows to gain in time more and more benefits.

Future works should investigate the open points: formal methods to detect unintended functions hidden in the software model, an integrated framework that can well map the recommended processes within the "formal method lifecycle".

References

1. RTCA/DO-178B, EUROCAE/ED-12B: Software Considerations in Airborne Systems and Equipment Certification (December 1, 1992)
2. RTCA/DO-178C: Software Considerations in Airborne Systems and Equipment Certification (December 13, 2011)
3. RTCA Inc., Document RTCA/DO-178B, Federal Aviation Administration (January 11, 1993), Advisory Circular 20-115B
4. Formal Methods and the Certification of Critical Systems, John Rushby, Technical Report CSL-93-7 (December 1993)
5. Heimdahl, M.P.E., Leveson, N.G.: Completeness and Consistency in Hierarchical State-Based Requirements. IEEE Transactions on Software Engineering 22(6) (June 1996)
6. van Lamsweerde, A.: Formal Specification: a Roadmap. In: ICSE - Future of SE Track, pp. 147–159. ACM (2000)
7. System Design and Analysis, Federal Aviation Administration (June 21, 1988), Advisory Circular 25.1309-1A
8. Manna, Z.: STeP: Deductive-Algorithmic Verification of Reactive and Real-Time Systems. In: Alur, R., Henzinger, T.A. (eds.) CAV 1996. LNCS, vol. 1102, pp. 415–418. Springer, Heidelberg (1996)
9. Hall, R.J.: Explanation-Based Scenario Generation for Reactive System Models. In: ASE 1998, Hawaii (October 1998)
10. Thompson, J.M., Heimdahl, M.P.E., Miller, S.P.: Specification-Based Prototyping for Embedded Systems. In: Wang, J., Lemoine, M. (eds.) ESEC 1999 and ESEC-FSE 1999. LNCS, vol. 1687, pp. 163–179. Springer, Heidelberg (1999)
11. Jeffords, R., Heitmeyer, C.: Automatic Generation of State Invariants from Requirements Specifications. In: Proc. FSE-6: 6th ACM SIGSOFT Intl Symposium on the Foundations of Software Engineering, Lake Buena Vista, pp. 56–69 (1998)
12. Roong-Ko, D., Frankl, P.G.: The ASTOOT approach to testing object-oriented programs. ACM Transactions on Software Engineering and Methodology 3(2), 101–130 (1994)
13. Zaremski, A.M., Wing, J.: Specification Matching of Software Components. ACM Transactions on Software Engineering and Methodology 6(4), 333–369 (1997)
14. Lutz, R.R.: Analyzing software requirements errors in safety-critical embedded systems. In. IEEE International Symposium on Requirements Engineering, San Diego, CA, pp. 126–133 (January 1993)
15. RTCA/DO-333: Formal Methods Supplement to DO-178C and DO-278A (December 13, 2011)
16. NASA-GB-002-95, Formal Methods Specification and Verification Guidebook for Software and Computer Systems – Volume I: Planning and Technology Insertion, Office of Safety and Mission Assurance (July 1995)

Product Line Engineering
Applied to CBTC Systems Development

Alessio Ferrari[1], Giorgio Oronzo Spagnolo[1],
Giacomo Martelli[2], and Simone Menabeni[2]

[1] ISTI-CNR, Via G. Moruzzi 1, Pisa, Italy
lastname@isti.cnr.it
http://www.isti.cnr.it/
[2] DSI, Università degli Studi di Firenze, Via di S.Marta 3, Firenze, Italy
lastname@dsi.unifi.it
http://www.dsi.unifi.it/

Abstract. Communications-based Train Control (CBTC) systems are
the new frontier of automated train control and operation. Currently
developed CBTC platforms are actually very complex systems including
several functionalities, and every installed system, developed by a different company, varies in extent, scope, number, and even names of the
implemented functionalities. International standards have emerged, but
they remain at a quite abstract level, mostly setting terminology.

This paper reports intermediate results in an effort aimed at defining
a global model of CBTC, by mixing semi-formal modelling and product line engineering. The effort has been based on an in-depth market
analysis, not limiting to particular aspects but considering as far as possible the whole picture. The adopted methodology is discussed and a
preliminary model is presented.

Introduction

Communications-based Train Control (CBTC) is the last technological frontier
for signalling and train control in the metro market [16,11]. CBTC systems offer
flexible degrees of automation, from enforcing control over dangerous operations
acted by the driver, to the complete replacement of the driver role with an
automatic pilot and an automatic on-board monitoring system.
Depending on the specific installation, different degrees of automation might
be required. Furthermore, companies shall be able to provide complete CBTC
systems, but also subsets of systems. The aim is to satisfy the needs of green-field
installations, and address the concerns of the operators who wish to renew only
a part of an already installed system. In this sense, the product line engineering
technology provides a natural tool to address the need for modularity required
by a market of this type [7,10].

Entering the CBTC market with a novel product requires such a product to
be compliant with the existing standards. Two international standards provide
general requirements for CBTC systems. The first is IEEE 1474.1-2004 [11], while

T. Margaria and B. Steffen (Eds.): ISoLA 2012, Part II, LNCS 7610, pp. 216–230, 2012.

the second is IEC 62290 [1,2]. The standards differ in terminology and structure. Therefore, a product satisfying the former is not ensured to accomplish also the requirements of the latter.

A novel CBTC product shall also take into account the existing similar products and installations to be competitive w.r.t. the other vendors. The CBTC market is currently governed by six main vendors, namely Bombardier [20], Alstom [19], Thales [21], Invensys Rail Group [12], Ansaldo STS [3], and Siemens [18]. Each vendor provides its own solution, and different technologies and architectures are employed.

In this paper an experience is presented, where domain analysis has been used to derive a global CBTC model, from which specific product requirements for novel CBTC systems can be derived. The global model is built upon the integration of the guidelines of the standards, and is driven by the architectural choices of the different vendors. The model is represented in the form of a *feature diagram* [14,4,8], following the principles of the product-line engineering technology. From the global feature diagram, we derive the actual product requirements. To this end, we draw graphical formal models of the product architecture, together with scenario models in the form of simplified sequence diagrams. Architecture and scenario models are finally used to define and enrich the natural language requirements of the actual product. Examples are presented throughout the paper to explain the approach, and to show the results of the current implementation of the proposed methodology.

The paper is structured as follows. In Sect. 1, the CBTC operational principles are presented. In Sect. 2, an overview of the approach is given. In Sect. 3, an analysis of the standards and of the architectures of the CBTC vendors is presented. In Sect. 4, the global CBTC model is described. In Sect. 5, the architecture and scenario models are derived, together with the requirements for the actual product. In Sect. 6, related works are discussed. Sect. 7 draws final conlusions and remarks.

1 Communications-Based Train Control Systems

CBTC systems [16,11] are novel signalling and control platforms tailored for metro. These systems provide a continuous automatic train protection as well as improved performance, system availability and operational flexibility of the train.

The conventional metro signalling/control systems that do not use a CBTC approach are exclusively based on track circuits and on wayside signals. Track circuits are used to detect the presence of trains. Wayside signals are used to ensure safe routes and to provide information to the trains. Therefore, the position of the train is based on the accuracy of the track circuit, and the information provided to the train is limited to the one provided by the wayside signals. These systems are normally referred as *fixed block* systems, since the distance between trains is computed based on fixed-length sections (i.e., the length of a track circuit - see upper part of Figure 1).

CBTC overcomes these problems through a continuous wayside-to-train and train-to-wayside data communication. In this way, train position detection is provided by the onboard equipment with a high precision. Furthermore, much more control and status information can be provided to the train. Currently, most of CBTC systems implement this communication using radio transmission [15].

The fundamental characteristic of CBTC is to ensure a reduction of the distance between two trains running in the same direction (this distance is normally called *headway*). This is possible thanks to the *moving block* principle: the minimum distance between successive trains is no longer calculated based on fixed sections, as occurs in presence of track circuits, but according to the rear of the preceding train with the addition of a safety distance as a margin. This distance is the limit distance (MA, Movement Authority) that cannot be shortened by a running train (see lower part of Figure 1).

The control system is aware at any time about the exact train position and speed. This knowledge allows the onboard ATP (Automatic Train Protection) system to compute a dynamic braking curve to ensure safe separation of trains, which guarantees that the speed limit is not exceeded. The ATP system ensures that the MA is not shortened by the train, in addition to the continuous protection of the train in every aspect.

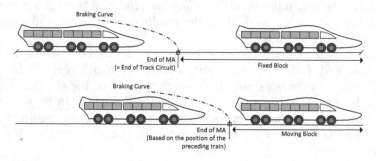

Fig. 1. Fixed block *vs* moving block

From the architectural point of view, CBTC systems are characterized by a division in two parts: onboard equipment and wayside equipment. The first is installed on the train and the latter is located at a station or along the line.

CBTC systems also allow automatic train control functions by implementing both the ATO (Automatic Train Operation) and the ATS (Automatic Train Supervision) systems. The ATO enables driverless operation, ensuring the fully automatic management of the train in combination with ATP. The ATS offers functions related to the supervision and management of the train traffic, such adjustment of schedules, determination of speed restrictions within certain areas and train routing.

A CBTC system might include also an interlocking (noted in the following as IXL). The IXL monitors the status of the objects in the railway yard (e.g., switches, track circuits) and, when routing is required by the ATS, allows or denies the routing of trains in accordance to the railway safety and operational regulations.

2   Method Overview

In this work an approach has been defined to identify a global model of CBTC and derive the product requirements for a novel CBTC system. The method starts from the available international requirements standard – IEEE 1474.1-2004 [11] and IEC 62290 [1,2] – and from the public documents provided by the current CBTC vendors. Three main phases have been identified to move from these heterogeneous natural language description of the expected CBTC features to the actual CBTC product requirements.

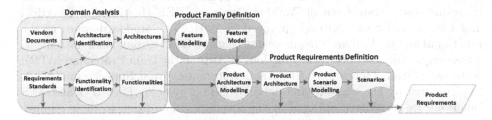

Fig. 2. Overview of the product requirements definition process adopted

Figure 2 summarizes the approach followed. Activities are depicted as circles and artifacts are depicted as rectangles with a wave on the bottom side.

First, domain analysis is performed (Sect. 3). During this phase, the requirements standards are analysed together with the documents of the different vendors. The former are used to identify the functionalities expected from a standard-compliant CBTC system (Functionality Identification), while the latter are used to identify the system architectures adopted by the competitors (Architecture Identification). Requirements standards are also employed in the Architecture Identification task to provide a common vocabulary to describe the architectures.

In the second phase, a product family for CBTC systems is defined (Sect. 4). The architectures identified in the previous phase are evaluated, and a feature model is derived to hierarchically capture all the different architectural options available in the market (Feature Modelling).

The last phase drives the definition of the actual product features (Sect. 5). From the feature model that represents the product family, a product instance is chosen. A detailed architecture is defined for such a product instance, taking into account the functionalities extracted from the standards (Product Architecture Modelling). Then, scenarios are derived to analyse the different behavioural aspects of the product (Product Scenario Modelling).

The final product requirements are the results of the adaptation of the standard CBTC requirements to the desired product. This adaptation is provided according to the (1) functionalities extracted from the standards, (2) the product architecture, and (3) the product scenarios.

3 Domain Analysis

3.1 Functionality Identification

In this phase, functionalities are identified for a generic CBTC system by evaluating the available international standards. Currently, the reference standards are IEEE 1474.1-2004 [11] and IEC 62290 [1,2], which are briefly summarized below.

IEEE 1474.1-2004. The IEEE 1474.1-2004 has been defined by the Communications-based Train Control Working Group of IEEE (Institute of Electrical and Electronic Engineers) and approved in 2004. Such standard concerns the functional and performance requirements that a CBTC system shall implement. These requirements concern the functions of Automatic Train Protection (ATP), Automatic Train Operation (ATO) and Automatic Train Supervision (ATS), implemented by the wayside and onboard CBTC system. The ATO and ATS functions are considered optional by the standard. In addition to these requirements, the standard also establishes the headway criteria, system safety criteria and system availability criteria applicable to different transit applications, including the Automated People Movers (APM).

IEC 62290. The IEC 62290 is a standard defined by the IEC (International Electrotechnical Commission) gone into effect in 2007. This standard brings the fundamental concepts, the general requirements and a description of the functional requirements that the command and control systems in the field of urban guided transport, like the CBTC, shall possess. In reference to the fundamental concepts, the standard establishes four levels or Grades of Automation (GoA-1 to 4). The increasing GoA corresponds to increasing responsibility of the command and control system w.r.t. the operational staff. For example, a GoA-1 system simply enforces brakes when the driver violates the braking curve. A GoA-4 system does not have a driver, nor yet an onboard human supervisor.

The standards have been evaluated to derive a complete set of CBTC functionalities. The approach adopted is as follows. First, the functionalities that the IEEE 1474.1-2004 standard specifies have been extracted. Such functionalities have been divided between ATP, ATO and ATS according to the anticipated classification provided by the same standard. Starting from this first group of functionalities, the activity continued with the analysis of the IEC 62290 standard, for identifying possible additional functionalities in comparison to those already extracted. Each functionality is traced to the paragraph of the corresponding standard from which it has been originally derived. Example functionalities, which are useful to understand the examples reported in the rest of the paper, are reported below together with the related subsystem and the reference to the standard documents.

Train Location Determination. (ATP onboard - IEEE 6.1.1) This functionality determines the position of the train;

Safe Train Separation. (ATP onboard - IEEE 6.1.2) This functionality uses the location information of the train to compute the braking curve and ensure safe separation of trains;

Movement Authority Determination. (ATP wayside - IEC 5.1.4.1) This functionality computes the MA message to be sent to the train based on the position of the other trains and on the railway status;

Route Interlocking Controller. (ATP wayside - IEEE 6.1.11) This functionality controls an external IXL and performs the route requests and locks. IXL systems are normally based on fixed block principles. This function is able to bypass the interlocking inputs concerning the position of the trains coming from the track circuits. In this way, the functionality is also able to ensure the increased performance guaranteed by the moving block principles;

Train Routing. (ATS - IEEE 6.3.4) This functionality allows setting the route for the train in accordance with the train service data, predefined routing rules and possible restrictions to the movement of the train;

Train Identification and Tracking. (ATS - IEEE 6.3.3) This functionality monitors the position and the identity of the trains.

3.2   Architecture Identification

In this phase, different possible architectures for a CBTC system are identified by evaluating the available information about the CBTC products on the market.

Several implementations of CBTC systems are offered by different vendors. In our work, we focus on the systems proposed by Bombardier, Alstom, Thales, Invensys Rail Group, Ansaldo STS, and Siemens.

The major subsystems identified in the evaluated CBTC systems are ATP, ATS, ATO and IXL. There are also other additional subsystems, which include, e.g., the fire emergency system, the passenger information system, and the closed-circuit television. The system architectures are identified by analyzing the relationships among all these subsystems.

As examples, we focus on the relationships among ATP, ATS and IXL. The most relevant configurations identified for these systems are summarized below.

Centralized Control. (Figure 3a) In this configuration, the ATS controls both the ATP and the IXL. The ATS is called `ATS Router` since it has a direct interface with the IXL to perform routing. The wayside ATP is called `Wayside ATP Simple` since it has no direct interface with the IXL, and the communication among these two subsystems is managed through the ATS. Furthermore, the wayside ATP communicates with the onboard ATP, as in all the other configurations.

Built-in IXL. (Figure 3b) In this configuration there is no external IXL, since the ATP encapsulates also the functions of the IXL (`ATP Wayside IXL`). We call the ATS of this configuration `ATS Simple` since it has no direct interface with an IXL.

Controllable IXL. (Figure 3c) The wayside ATP has a control interface (`ATP Wayside Controller`) with an external IXL, and acts as intermediary between the `ATS Simple` and the IXL. We call the IXL of this configuration

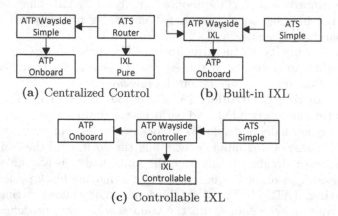

(a) Centralized Control   (b) Built-in IXL

(c) Controllable IXL

Fig. 3. Architectures extracted

`IXL Controllable` since, unlike the `IXL Pure` of the first configuration, allows the `ATP Wayside Controller` to bypass some of its controls to achieve improved performances. It is worth noting that this solution would not be possible with an ATS controlling the IXL. Indeed, the ATS is normally not meant as a safety-related system, while the ATP and the IXL are safety-critical platforms.

Configurations 3a and 3b are both used by Bombardier. The second architecture is described in the Bombardier documentation as CITYFLO 650 with built-in IXL. Though architecture 3a is not explicitly described, the Bombardier documentation states that, when available, the IXL works as a backup system in case of ATP failure. Therefore, we can argue that the IXL control resides in the ATS and not in the ATP.

Architecture 3c has been derived evaluating the Alstom system. The IXL employed by Alstom is provided by the same supplier of the Bombardier IXL, but Alstom does not use this IXL as a backup system. Therefore, we can argue that the ATP is in charge of controlling the IXL, as in architecture 3c.

4   Product Family Definition

The development of industrial software systems may often profit from the adoption of a development process based on the so-called *product families* or *product line* approach [10,7]. This development cycle aims at lowering the development costs by sharing an overall reference architecture for each product. Each product can employ a subset of the characteristics of the reference architecture in order to, e.g., serve different client or jurisdictions.

The production process in product lines is hence organized with the purpose of maximizing the commonalities of the product line and minimizing the cost of variations [17]. A description of a product family (PF) is usually composed of two parts. The first part, called *constant*, describes aspects common to all products of the family. The second part, called *variable*, represents those aspects, called variabilities, that will be used to differentiate a product from another. Variability modelling defines which features or components of a system are optional, alternative, or mandatory.

The product family engineering paradigm is composed of two processes: *domain engineering* and *application engineering*. *Domain engineering* is the process in which the commonality and the variability of the product family are identified and modelled. *Application engineering* is the process in which the applications of the product family are built by reusing domain artefact and exploiting the product family variability [17].

4.1 Feature Modelling

The modelling of variability has been extensively studied in the literature, with particular focus on *feature modelling* [14,4,8]. Feature modelling is an important technique for modelling the product family during the domain engineering.

The product family is represented in the form of a *feature model*. A feature model is as a hierarchical set of features, and relationships among features.

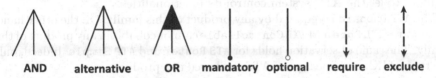

Fig. 4. Feature diagram notations

Relationships between a parent feature and its child features (or subfeatures) are categorized as: *AND* - all subfeatures must be selected; *alternative* - only one subfeature can be selected; *OR* - one or more can be selected; *mandatory* - features that required; *optional* - features that are optional; *a require b*, if a and b are present; *a exclude b*, if a is present and b is not present and vice-versa. A feature diagram is a graphical representation of a *feature model* [14]. It is a tree where primitive features are leaves and compound features are interior nodes. Common graphical notations are depicted in Figure 4.

4.2 A Global Feature Diagram for CBTC

At this stage of the research, we have been able to define a global feature model for CBTC at the GoA-1 level, according to the IEC 62290 terminology [1]. In other terms, our model assumes the presence of a driver on board. The model has been defined by integrating the different architectural choices identified during the architecture identification task (Sect. 3.2).

A simplified excerpt of the global feature diagram associated to our model is given in Figure 5. The diagram includes the architectural components (which in our diagram becomes *features*) already identified in Sect. 3.2.

The *require* constraint requires a product to include IXL Pure and ATS Router whenever the product includes ATP Simple. Indeed, the control interface with

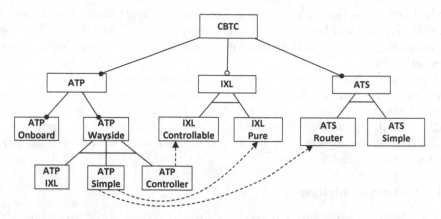

Fig. 5. Simplified excerpt of the CBTC global feature diagram

the IXL has to be implemented by the ATS if the ATP does not include it, as in the case of ATP Simple. Also IXL Controllable is required whenever ATP Controller is used. In this case, a proper controllable interface of the IXL is required to let the ATP system control its functionalities.

The ATP Onboard is required by any product of this family. On the other hand, the features IXL Pure and IXL Controllable cannot cohabit in any product of this family. The same observation holds for ATS Router and ATP Simple. Indeed, only one type of IXL and one type of ATS is allowed in a product.

It is worth noting that the feature diagram allows new configurations that were not identified in the domain analysis phase performed. These configurations represent new possible products. For example, an ATP IXL can - optionally - cohabit with an IXL of any type. In this case, the additional IXL works as a backup system.

5   Product Features Definition

The provided feature model represents a global model for CBTC at the GoA-1 level. From this global model we choose a product instance, which in our example case corresponds to the Controllable IXL architecture of Figure 3c. Then, we model the *detailed architecture* of the product according to the functionalities extracted from the standards in the domain analysis phase. The architecture represents a static view of our product in the form of a block diagram. In order to assess the architecture, we provide realistic scenarios using architecture-level sequence diagrams. This phase can be regarded as the application engineering process of the product family engineering paradigm. Architecture and scenarios are employed to derive requirements for the actual product.

5.1   Product Architecture Modelling

The graphical formalism adopted to model the product architecture is a block diagram with a limited number of operators. We have designed this simple language in agreement with our industrial partner, and according to our previous experiences in the railway industry. Companies tend to be skeptical about the benefit given by the adoption of complex and rigid languages during the early stages of the development. Instead, they are more keen to accept a lightweight formalism that allows them to represent architectures intuitively and with a limited effort.

The diagrams are composed of blocks and arrows. Blocks can be of two types: *system blocks*, which represent individual hardware/software systems, or *functionality blocks*, which represent hardware/software functionalities inside a system. Two types of arrows are also provided: *usage arrows*, allowed between any block, and *message arrows*, allowed solely between functionalities belonging to different systems. If a usage arrow is directed from a block to another, this implies that the former uses a service of the latter. If a message arrow is directed from a functionality to another, this implies that the former sends a message – the label of the arrow – to the latter.

We describe the usage of this formalism with an example. Given the global CBTC model, we first select the features that we wish to implement in our final product. For example, Figure 6 highlights in pink (grey if printed in B/W) the features that are selected for a CBTC system that uses a controllable interlocking (see Figure 3c).

An excerpt of the detailed architecture for the selected product is depicted in Figure 7. It is worth noting that the functionality blocks used are part of the functionalities identified during the domain analysis phase.

The `Train Location Determination` functionality belonging to the onboard ATP sends the train location information to the ATP wayside system. The `Movement Authority (MA) Determination` functionality forward this information to the ATS for train supervision, and uses this information to compute the MA. The `Train Routing` functionality of the ATS requires the routes to the wayside ATP, which controls the routing by means of the `Route Interlocking Controller` functionality connected to the IXL. We recall that the `Route Interlocking Controller` functionality is used to modify the interlocking inputs concerning the location of the trains – normally based on fixed block principles – to achieve the increased performance of the moving block paradigm.

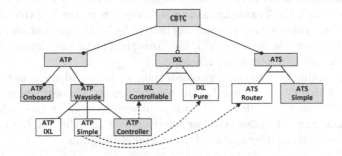

Fig. 6. Selection of features for our example product

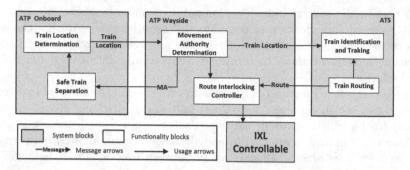

Fig. 7. Architecture example for a CBTC system

5.2   Product Scenario Modelling

The architecture provided during the previous activity has been defined according to the functionalities extracted from the standards. Nevertheless, some connections among functionalities, or some message exchange, might be missing from the model, since the architecture has not been evaluated against actual scenarios. In order to refine the architecture, and provide coherent requirements for the product, graphical scenarios are defined.

The graphical formalism adopted to model the scenarios at the architectural level is a simplified version of the UML sequence diagrams. Lifelines are associated to systems, while blocks along the lifelines are associated to the functionalities of the system. The arrows among different blocks are indicating message communication or service requests. In case of message communication, the arrow is dashed. In case of service requests the arrow is solid.

Figure 8 reports a scenario for a train that moves from a station to another according to a route defined by the ATS.

In the operational center, the ATS sends the `Route` information to the wayside ATP. The wayside ATP requests the IXL to move the switches in the proper position, and to lock the resources (the `setRoute` service request). Once the route has been locked by the IXL, the wayside ATP sends the `Movement Authority` to the onboard ATP. The onboard ATP allows the train departure, so the driver can start the train movement. While moving, the onboard system updates its position and sends the `Train Location` information to the wayside ATP. This system uses such information to compute new MAs for the current and preceding trains. Furthermore, the wayside ATP forwards the `Train Location` information to the ATS for identification and tracking.

It is worth noting that in this representation, we have added the `setroute` service request, which was not defined in the block diagram. This explicit request is an example of refinement enabled by the usage of scenarios: the relationship among the `Route Interlocking Controller` functionality and the `IXL Controllable` system has been clarified by means of the sequence diagram.

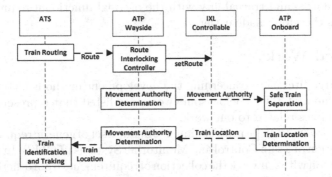

Fig. 8. Example sequence diagram: a train moves from one station to another

5.3 Requirements Definition

The information provided throughout the process are used to define the requirements of the final product. In particular, the requirements of one of the standard are used as a reference for the definition of the actual product requirements. In our case, we take the IEEE 1474.1-2004 standard as a reference.

The requirements are tailored according to the functionalities extracted from the standards, and evaluating the product architecture and the scenarios. For example, consider the following requirement referred to the ATP system:

6.1.11 – **Route Interlocking.** A CBTC system shall provide route interlocking functions equivalent to conventional interlocking practice to prevent train collisions and derailments. [...]

Where an auxiliary wayside system is specified by the authority having jurisdiction, interlocking functions *may* be provided by separate interlocking equipment [...].

In our example product, the interlocking is an auxiliary wayside system external from the ATP. Therefore the Derived (D) requirement for our product is:

6.1.11(D) – **Route Interlocking.** Interlocking functions *shall* be provided by separate interlocking equipment [...].

Additional requirements on the actual behaviour can be derived from the architecture and the example scenario, as in the following:

6.1.11(D − 1) – **Route Interlocking Controller.** When a route is requested from the ATS, The ATP system shall require route setting (setRoute) to the interlocking to lock the interlocking resources. [...]

The behaviour expected from this requirement is clarified by the scenario, which is also attached to the requirement in the final specification.

Consider now a vendor that wish to accomplish also the IEC 62290 standard with his product. The product is already defined according to IEEE 1474.1-2004 following the presented approach. In this case, we argue that the compliance with the IEC 62290 standard can be demonstrated by reasoning at functional level. Indeed, the functions identified in the domain analysis phase integrate the content of both standards, and traceability with the original functional requirements of IEC 62290 is therefore made easier.

6 Related Works

There is a large literature concerning the development methods of train control systems, including CBTC. Below some works are listed that represent the most relevant examples related to our work.

The MODCONTROL [5] project aimed to define a set of generic requirements for a new generation of Train Control and Monitoring Systems (TCMS). In particular, it has in common with our work the collection of requirements from different sources such as specifications of existing systems, standards or draft specifications from other EU projects. The second part of the MODCONTROL project differs from our work since it is more focused in finding linguistic defects in the requirements.

The work performed by LS Industrial Systems [23] concerns the software development of a CBTC system by means of a process based on model-driven development principles. In particular, the UML language is used to model the CBTC software, and source code for the model is derived through the IBM Rhapsody tool. Unlike our case, where requirements are represented in textual form and derived from the analysis of existing systems and standards, the authors use a UML notation (Use Cases) to represent the customer requirements, and do not give details concerning the domain analysis phase.

Wang and Liu [22] present an approach for developing a CBTC system based on a 3-levels hierarchical modelling of the system. The three levels are the functional model, the behavioural model of the train, and the model of all control actions. To illustrate this approach, authors use SCADE applied to a case study of a specific CBTC subsystem.

Essamé and Dollé [9] present the application of the B method in the METEOR project led by Siemens Transportation Systems. According to the authors, the use of the B method to realize the vital software system for the automatic control of the train, called METEOR, is economical if considered in relation with the entire development process of the CBTC system, which includes the validation of the specification and the product certification.

Yuan *et al.* [24] illustrate a modelling approach and verification of the System Requirement Specifications (SRS) of a train control system based on the Specification and Description Language (SDL). The application of this approach has allowed the authors to identify possible ambiguities and incompatible descriptions of SRS, useful for making changes on the SRS.

L. Jansen et al. [13] illustrate a modelling approach of the European Train Control System (ETCS) based on Coloured Petri Nets (CPN) and the Design / CPN tools. The proposed approach has been developed within a research project for Deutsche Bahn AG and aims to model the ETCS system according to an hierarchical multi-level decomposition. Specifically, are considered and integrated three aspects of ETCS: components, scenarios and functions. The computed models are then simulated by the Design/CPN tool and each simulation is performed on a sequence of scenarios with function calls.

The first two works mainly concern the usage of semi-formal methods or structured approaches, while the other four works are focused on formal methods. Our work does not strictly employ formal techniques, and can be therefore attached to the first group. Besides other process-related differences, the current paper mainly differs from all the other works for the emphasis given to the product line aspects of the CBTC development. The main novelty is indeed the domain analysis performed, and the process adopted to define requirements for a novel CBTC system. We argue that this approach enables the development of a modular, competitive, and standards-compliant CBTC system.

7 Conclusion

In this paper, preliminary results are presented concerning the definition of a global model for Communications-based Train Control (CBTC) systems. The model is derived from existing CBTC implementations and from the guidelines of international standards, and is represented in the form of a *feature model*. A methodology has been also outlined to derive product requirements from the global model.

The current model is limited to the functionalities of a CBTC system that requires a driver. However, the most relevant safety-critical components are already detailed in our representation.

The approach has been considered higly valuable by our industrial partner, who acted as external supervisors for the presented work. The most promising commercial aspect is the value given to (1) the consideration of the competitor's choices, and (2) to the adherence to the standards. Indeed, though a migration strategy from a standard to the other is not fully defined yet, we expect the transition to be simplified by the consideration of all the available standards during the functionality identification phase.

Another aspect that has been highly appreciated by our partner is the choice of the modelling languages. The feature model by itself provides an abstract view of the product family that is easily understood by the stakeholders [6]. On the other hand, the block digram notation and the sequence diagrams defined allows focusing on the essential concepts, even employing a limited number of operators. Other languages, such as SysML or Simulink/Stateflow, have been considered too complex to be useful in this analysis phase.

Given the promising results of the current approach, we are presently working on an enhanced version of the model that includes also capabilities for driverless and unattended operation. Integration of the approach with natural language requirements analysis methods is also foreseen.

References

1. IEC 62290-1: Railway applications: Urban guided transport management and command/control systems. Part 1: System principles and fundamental concepts (2007)
2. IEC 62290-2: Railway applications: Urban guided transport management and command/control systems. Part 2: Functional requirements specification (2011)

3. Ansaldo STS. CBTC Brochure (2011), http://goo.gl/3Kmb0
4. Batory, D.: Feature Models, Grammars, and Propositional Formulas. In: Obbink, H., Pohl, K. (eds.) SPLC 2005. LNCS, vol. 3714, pp. 7–20. Springer, Heidelberg (2005)
5. Bucchiarone, A., Fantechi, A., Gnesi, S., Trentanni, G.: An experience in using a tool for evaluating a large set of natural language requirements. In: Proc. of SAC, pp. 281–286 (2010)
6. Chastek, G., Donohoe, P., Kang, K.C., Thiel, S.: Product Line Analysis: A Practical Introduction. Technical Report CMU/SEI-2001-TR-001, Software Engineering Institute, Carnegie Mellon University (2001)
7. Clements, P.C., Northrop, L.: Software product lines: practices and patterns. Addison-Wesley Longman, Inc., Boston (2001)
8. Czarnecki, K., Eisenecker, U.: Generative programming: methods, tools, and applications. ACM Press/Addison-Wesley, New York, NY, USA (2000)
9. Essamé, D., Dollé, D.: B in Large-Scale Projects: The Canarsie Line CBTC Experience. In: Julliand, J., Kouchnarenko, O. (eds.) B 2007. LNCS, vol. 4355, pp. 252–254. Springer, Heidelberg (2006)
10. Fantechi, A., Gnesi, S.: Formal modeling for product families engineering. In: Proc. of SPLC, pp. 193–202 (2008)
11. Institute of Electrical and Electronics Engineers. IEEE Standard for Communications Based Train Control (CBTC) Performance and Functional Requirements. IEEE Std 1474.1-2004 (Revision of IEEE Std 1474.1-1999) (2004)
12. Invensys Rail. SIRIUS Brochure (2009), http://goo.gl/YFUiL
13. Jansen, L., Horste, M.M.Z., Schnieder, E.: Technical issues in modelling the European Train Control System (ETCS) using Coloured Petri Nets and the Design/CPN tools (1998)
14. Kang, K.C., Cohen, S.G., Hess, J.A., Novak, W.E., Peterson, A.S.: Feature-Oriented Domain Analysis (FODA) Feasibility Study. Technical report, Carnegie-Mellon University Software Engineering Institute (1990)
15. Kuun, E.: Open Standards for CBTC and CBTC Radio Based Communications. In: APTA Rail Rail Transit Conference Proceedings (2004)
16. Pascoe, R.D., Eichorn, T.N.: What is Communication-Based Train Control? IEEE Vehicular Technology Magazine (2009)
17. Pohl, K., Böckle, G., van der Linden, F.J.: Software Product Line Engineering: Foundations, Principles and Techniques. Springer-Verlag New York, Inc., Secaucus (2005)
18. Siemens Transportation Systems. Trainguard MT CBTC (2006), http://goo.gl/XiOhO; The Moving Block Communications Based Train Control Solution
19. Signalling Solutions Limited. URBALIS Communication Based Train Control (CBTC) Delivery Performance and Flexibility (2009), http://goo.gl/G3hEe
20. Stover, J.S.: CITYFLO 650 System Overview (2006), http://goo.gl/e26SZ
21. Thales Transportation. Seltrac Brochure (2009), http://goo.gl/OjhvK
22. Wang, H., Liu, S.: Modeling Communications Based Train Control system: A case study. In: Proc. of ICIMA, pp. 453–456 (2010)
23. Yang, C., Lim, J., Um, J., Han, J., Bang, Y., Kim, H., Yun, Y., Kim, C., Cho, G.Y.: Developing CBTC Software Using Model-Driven Development Approach. In: Proc. of WCRR (2008)
24. Yuan, L., Tang, T., Li, K.: Modelling and Verification of the System Requirement Specification of Train Control System Using SDL. In: Proc. of ISADS, pp. 81–85 (2011)

Improving Verification Process
in Driverless Metro Systems: The MBAT Project

Stefano Marrone[1], Roberto Nardone[2], Antonio Orazzo[3],
Ida Petrone[4], and Luigi Velardi[3]

[1] Dip. di Matematica, Seconda Università di Napoli,
Via Lincoln 5, 81100 Caserta, Italy
stefano.marrone@unina2.it
[2] Dip. di Informatica e Sistemistica, Università di Napoli "Federico II",
Via Claudio 21, 80125 Napoli, Italy
roberto.nardone@unina.it
[3] Ansaldo STS, via Argine 425, 80147 Napoli, Italy
{antonio.orazzo,luigi.velardi}@ansaldo-sts.com
[4] Intecs SpA, Via G. Porzio, 80023 Napoli NA, Italy
ida.petrone@intecs.it

Abstract. Complex systems are experiencing increasing needs to obtain a higher level of safety and to reduce time to market. This is in particular true for automotive, aerospace and railway domains, pushing the research community to define novel development and verification methods and techniques. The ARTEMIS EU-project MBAT (Combined Model-Based Analysis and Testing of Embedded Systems) represents one of the most important attempts in this direction since it aims to achieve such improvements in several application domains. Starting from the Ansaldo STS implementation of Communication-Based Train Control system (CBTC), which is the base of automatic driverless metro systems, we describe in this paper the improvement that MBAT would bring to the Verification process. To this aim an accurate description of existing Verification process in automatic metro systems and discussion about critical points are provided. Then we describe the expected results of MBAT project on such kind of processes. The proposed approach and developed tools will be part of a common reference platform and, also if related to the railway domain, for its generality, they can be used for different domains with similar needs. The basic agreement in the project will guarantee the cross use of the platform and will give quantitative measures of the obtained improvement.

Keywords: Model-based analysis, Model-based testing, Validation process, Safety Critical Embedded Systems, Automatic Metro Systems.

1 Introduction

Critical systems, in particular in transportation domains, are asking higher and higher quality but, at the same time, technology providers must face with global and competitive markets with strict requirements of development costs and time. Proper

T. Margaria and B. Steffen (Eds.): ISoLA 2012, Part II, LNCS 7610, pp. 231–245, 2012.
© Springer-Verlag Berlin Heidelberg 2012

development and verification methodologies and processes should be searched in order to guarantee at the same time both high quality artifacts in systems and software and fast and cheap testing and verification activities. The scientific community has always addressed formal methods as the main way to satisfy both the needs; since first experiments in application of formal methods in real industrial contexts, they show a great capability to allow high integrity systems building. But industry wants more from formal methods: industrial settings require (two above all) a great level of integration of formal methods in existing development processes and a lower entrance barrier in their adoption (i.e. higher level of usability and complexity hiding). Moreover industry heavily relies on simulation techniques (testing), due to its simplicity and great adaptability in existing and assessed processes, so formal methods are required to be integrated with testing activities, too.

Model-based design would be the connection point to facilitate the usage of formal methods in industrial settings and to integrate them with testing activities, increasing both productivity and quality of systems. In model-based approaches a system model would be at the center of the development process instead of code. This model is developed in a common design environment, aiming at facilitating communication between different development groups, spanning from requirements descriptions and management, model-based design, simulation and verification. The explicit existence of models allows the definition and use of complex and correct-by-design development steps. As well as shift from assembler to higher level programming languages increases the abstraction for control structures, similarly model-based design increases the abstraction level in terms of domain specific concepts and solutions already identified in the reference domain. Model-based design is not just the application of graphical languages for code production, but it is a paradigm for system development that improves the use of languages, including explicit operational descriptions of the relevant entities that occur during development in terms of both product and process. Applications of the model-based concepts in embedded system context are shown in [1] and in [2] where, also, brief overviews on general concepts as *abstraction and restriction, separation of concerns* and *model levels* are given. An approach to the development of discrete-continuous system is shown in [3] where modeling and description techniques, semantics, tool support and test case generation is shown with a high degree of abstraction. The application of model-based techniques in the automotive context is shown in [4] where a tool prototype, able to apply model-based design for the automotive control software, is depicted. Specifically for the adoption of model checking for safety analyses on a system model, a survey on current research trends is in [5], where a discussion on reasons that make the model checking not widely adopted in industries is addressed.

In the development of critical systems, the SCADE product family [6] is a complete design environment to design and model critical system and software, able to generate certified source code according to some international safety standards in the domains of aerospace&defence, heavy equipments, and railway. SCADE is also a tool suite for the flexible graphical design of embedded display systems, as well it is able to support the management of the entire development workflow, from requirements management to verification, through documentation generation.

To manage and formalize requirements, one of the languages that best fits into the double mission to be formal and usable is Boilerplate. Boilerplate [7] is a semi-formal language for stating and formulating requirements having the advantage of being close to the natural language, easy to write and to understand, in the future suitable to be used to directly write the requirements specification, bypassing the natural language. Boilerplate strongly improves the understandability and identification of requirements reducing ambiguity and spelling mistakes and is template-based: starting from a set of templates composed by fixed syntax and attributes, the requirements engineer is able to compile it with concepts and entities obtaining the boilerplate requirements. Concepts and entities are collected in a domain ontology [8], that is a domain vocabulary plus a set of rules for relationships between vocabulary items which adds additional information about system components used in the requirements.

The research community is currently searching for general frameworks in industrial applications of model-based process for critical systems. CESAR[1] is an European funded project that aims to constitute a common methodological and technological platform shared among several application domains (and companies) in the field of embedded systems. Through boilerplates and ontology, the tool developed in the CESAR project for entering and analyzing the requirements provides also a check for completeness, consistency and correctness on the entire set of boilerplate requirements [9].

Following CESAR directions, MBAT[2] is an ongoing funded ARTEMIS EU-project that wants to push further the results of CESAR. The main concrete objective of MBAT is to provide European industry with a new Verification & Validation (V&V) technology in form of a *Reference Technology Platform* (the MBAT RTP). This platform will unleash the power of model-based methodologies enabling the construction of high-quality dependable embedded systems reducing, at the same time, both costs and development times. This will be made possible by focusing on a tighter integration between (formal) analysis and testing. In addition, MBAT RTP will be connected to other ARTEMIS RTPs (as e.g. the CESAR RTP) to extend these platforms pursuing the ARTEMIS goal to provide an European RTP for the development of embedded systems.

This paper will show how MBAT project can affect the current development and Verification process in railway systems. To this aim, the paper proposes a new V&V activities workflow that is built upon the existing one that is currently adopted in Ansaldo STS (ASTS). The process accepts the vision and aims of the MBAT project, in which ASTS is an active partner: the state of the art on model-based methodologies and techniques is used in order to match these aims and to develop a demonstrator able to verify the improvements obtained by the project.

The paper is organized as follows: this Section 1 introduces the aim of the paper and provides a quick background in model-based design; Section 2 describes current

[1] http://cesarproject.eu/. The research leading to these results has received funding from the ARTEMIS Joint Undertaking within the European project CESAR under grant agreement n°100016 and from specific national programs and/or funding authorities.

[2] http://www.mbat-artemis.eu/. This research project is funding from the ARTEMIS Joint Undertaking under grant agreement n° 269335 and from ARTEMIS member states Austria, Denmark, Estonia, France, Germany, Italy, Sweden and U.K.

V&V process in ASTS whereas Section 3 defines a novel process inspired by MBAT project. Section 4 tries to instantiate such process on a portion of a real use case: the Communication-Based Train Control (CBTC) automatic metro system. Section 5 ends the paper and addresses some future issues.

2   Verification Processes for Railway and Metro Systems

During last 10 years, the efforts of ASTS allowed the definition of the methodology described in this paper in order to optimize and implement systematic approaches for verification and validation activities. Non-functional analysis processes, in particular for safety related issues, and functional testing have been improved.

The hazard analysis methodology defined and used in ASTS to assess safety requirements, and the results obtained by its application to the European Standard for signaling systems ERTMS/ETCS system have been shown in [10]. Starting from this analysis, several mitigations have been identified. Mitigations become new requirements for the systems: only by providing the evidence of their correct implementation the system can be certified to be safe.

On the other hand testing phases are fundamental steps of embedded systems development cycle in terms of time and cost efforts, therefore improve this step is crucial to optimize the whole process. Due to the large complexity of these systems, it is impossible to achieve the completeness of test set needed to verify and validate the final implementation. For these reasons in the course of time reduction techniques, avoiding test-case explosion, and well-formed activities, automating test phases, have been attempted. A detailed methodology to increase the test coverage, in terms of number of stressed aspects, keeping the number of test-cases below a reasonable threshold, has been described in [11] and in [12]. This grey-box testing methodology, combining black-box and white-box techniques, is based on the identification and reduction of influence variables and test cases. Due to the increasing complexity of railway systems not managed by traditional validation techniques, several issues to handle the complexity of heterogeneous distributed systems have been addressed. [13] presents the working principles of ERTMS/ETCS and the functional testing approach followed by ASTS in 2005 in order to thoroughly test this system. Furthermore, to meet the necessity to re-execute the test set in the regression test campaign that could provoke the testing time explosion, ASTS proposed the adoption of a classical Service Oriented Architecture (SOA) in order to address the building of such an environment for safety-critical control systems [14]. In [15] a methodology is presented to perform an "abstract testing" of such large control systems in an efficient way: an abstract test, configuration independent, is specified directly from system functional requirements and has to be instantiated in more test runs to cover the given configuration, comprising any number of control entities (sensors, actuators and logic processes).

The current development process in ASTS (Fig. 1) is already centered on the optimization of functional requirements verification. It starts from the high level system functional requirements specification (*FRS*) in natural language where all the functionalities and clients requirements are reported. This specification can suffer from ambiguity, incompleteness or inconsistency and, for these reasons, subsequently the refinement and formalization process is performed, where requirements are detailed manually, whose output are System Requirements Specification (*SRS*), System Architecture Specification (*SAS*), System Detailed Description (*SDD*) and Software Requirements Specification (*SwRS*).

At this point two models are developed: a *system descriptive model* for the static analysis and a *system high-level model* for the dynamic testing are here produced. Both models rarely represent two replicas of the same entire system, but commonly they represent it with respect to different points of view: the first kind of models, developed in SCADE, is used to describe the system components, their functionalities and their behavior; whereas the latter are used to give just a high-level overview on system structure with a specific focus on the expected functionalities.

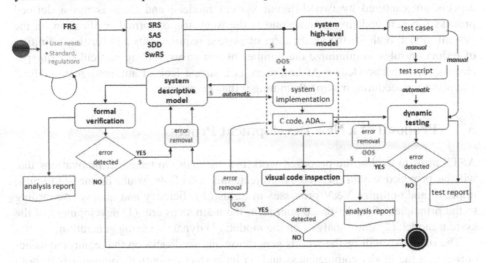

Fig. 1. Ansaldo STS current development process (S stands for "in SCADE", OOS stands for "out of SCADE")

Source code production starts here and it is done manually for the components that have not been modeled with a system descriptive model in the SCADE environment (out of SCADE – OOS), where present, whereas it is automatically generated for the portion represented in SCADE (with SCADE – S). The choice to develop or not system portions in SCADE depends on the necessity to perform static analysis on them; this activity is conducted through formal verification techniques, as model checking, symbolic execution or others, depending on the property and on the model under test. For the OOS portion, static analysis activities can be also required: here static analysis is needed to find deadlocks, infinite loops, un-required dead code in order to assure high quality levels in code. These activities are performed by experts through visual code inspection.

From the *system high-level model*, test case specifications are generated and then they can be manually implemented, or test scripts (written in ASTS proprietary language) for automatic execution can be written. The system under test runs on the real target platform or in a simulated ASTS environment. To reduce the number of tests some empirical reduction rules, based on specialists' domain knowledge, are applied.

Both for analysis (for OOS and S portion) and testing, the potential discovery of errors is obtained at the end of the implementation, so the corrections strongly impact on the overall costs due to expensive and time consuming loops in the process. A combined approach for the analysis and testing activities, although still rough, has been already implemented in the current process thanks to the high expertise of ASTS in the safety critical embedded systems development; as an example, when the specialists perform the visual code inspection, they are able to determine test cases with the aim of increasing the coverage level in terms of tested system/software parts.

The shortcomings noticed in current process are, mainly, three. The first resides in the lack of a common model of the system to perform analysis and testing: different aspects are captured by two different system models, and there is not a defined process for their updating. The second is the weak use of formal verification on the system model, both for the verification of system requirements and for the definition of reduction rules to minimize the number of test cases, relying particularly on specialists' domain knowledge. At last, there is a strong lack of automation in analysis and testing procedures, making them longer than necessary.

3   Proposal of a New Development Process

ASTS aims to exploit the proposed workflow through the technical innovations that will be provided within the MBAT project; this workflow would be the solution to improve and optimize V&V processes in terms of efficiency and quality. According to the principles of model-based approach, the main steps are: (1) development of the system model; (2) static analysis on the model; (3) dynamic testing generation.

The outcomes will be the reports generation and feedbacks on the requirements accuracy, on the model completeness and on its correct definition compared with both functional requirements, that is the one arising from customer needs, and nonfunctional ones imposed by international regulations and internal standards. Moreover the dynamic testing will trace the activated components of the system to better understand the coverage factor reached by test cases in terms of stressed system portion.

The proposed workflow is shown in Fig. 2, where the activities coming from the CESAR projects are also outlined. Starting from system requirements (*System FRS*), the *System Model* shall be defined in order to perform the verification of some characteristics and to execute test cases. The static analysis and the dynamic testing must be performed on the same *System Model*: the real system will be implemented at the end of the process through certified transformations, so the real system will be already compliant to safety standards and to properties formally verified.

The left side concerns with the dynamic functional testing steps. A technical demonstrator to obtain the automatic test generation starting from functional system requirements has been implemented by ASTS engaged in the CESAR project. These relevant results are integrated in this workflow as follows:

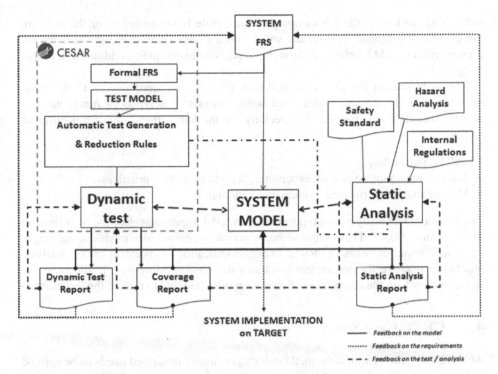

Fig. 2. Ansaldo STS process workflow

1. Refinement of system functional requirements (*System FRS*) and their translation from natural language at first to semi-formal language (Boilerplate) and then to formal language (Pattern) (leading to *Formal FRS*);
2. Definition of a *Test Model* highlighting inputs and outputs for each function-under-test;
3. Definition of some reduction rules, on the basis of domain assumptions and/or architectural high-level model, to avoid the tests number explosion;
4. Automatic generation of all possible combinations of input variables for the function-under-test, taking into account the reduction rules, after a preventive consistency check between *Test Model* and *Formal FRS*.

The output is a reasonably complete set of test cases which have to be converted in a proprietary data format in order to be executed on the system under test. These results must be optimized to avoid some applicability limits of existing tools, decreasing the possibility to use/apply these procedures in ASTS processes, and must be extended to the automatic drawing up of document report, not yet implemented in CESAR.

Another important step is to perform the test on the system model as defined in the central part of the schema, since the test definition phase is finalized to the execution of the abovementioned tests, that have been drawn up from the system requirements.

The result is fed back on the model (if it is compliant with the expected behavior), on the requirements (if they are complete, consistent, not ambiguous and not conflicting) and/or on the test campaign (if test suite is not complete or the tests are not correctly designed). Test results will be used to drive the analysis where the reduction rules should be checked through the analysis techniques, in addition to everything else.

The right side of the proposed workflow contains the steps related to the static analysis tasks. Properties, which need static analysis, concern both functional and non-functional requirements and, especially for the latter, they come from different sources:

- Safety Standards;
- Internal regulations based on experience, statistics and best practices;
- Hazard analysis performed to known notable risks.

The output of this analysis is a report that allows the improvement or the modification of the *System Model*. These improvements permit to remove any mistakes that might have been found or errors in FRS or to obtain indications to perform further analysis and better improve the consequent test cases description. Moreover, it allows to obtain a feedback on the correctness of reduction rules adopted to reduce the test cases.

4   CBTC Case Study

An ASTS system on which the methodology previously described needs to be applied is here shown. The ASTS Communication-Based Train Control (CBTC) system has been chosen as a case study, and the application of the methodology on a its single function is shown in this paragraph.

4.1   The CBTC System

The Rapid Transit Metro system is an electric passenger railway in an urban area with high capacity and frequency. The Communication-Based Train Control (CBTC) is an automatic innovative system for the management of railway traffic. It is particularly used for metropolitan projects with the aim to overcome the limitations of conventional fixed-block systems optimizing the transportation levels, ensuring safety and shortest headways. ASTS participated in developing the IEEE Standard 1474.1 [17] for CBTC performance and functions and it is also an active participant in European Union sponsored working groups, writing the standards for future Mass Transit systems in Europe. A Metro system is based on several sub-systems and principally on:

- *Signalling system*: combination of the Interlocking and communication system that transmits the information necessary to control the train movement to the on board sub-system;
- *Automation system*: trains scheduling and interface with the central Operator;
- *Power Supply system*: line electrification and supply of all civil loads in a metro system (e.g. station lighting and elevators);
- *Platform Screen Doors*: doors on the platform to screen it from the train;

- other auxiliary systems as *Intrusion Detection System, Passengers Information System*, etc.

A Metro system can operate at different basic grades of automation. The definition of suitable grades results from sharing responsibility for given basic functions of transport management between operations staff and system.

The key to automation is the Automatic Train Control (ATC) system. CBTC technology, used to implement the ATC system, ensures that the trains stop at the right place at the stations, open and close the doors, leave the stations, keep the correct speed and keep the secure distance between the trains, and so on, by means of systems integrated in the trains, on the tracks, on the stations and in the control room that have the capability to exchange real-time data in continuous way (the main system architecture is shown in Fig. 3).

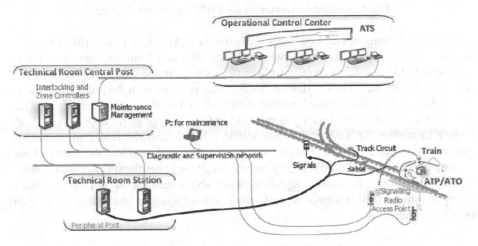

Fig. 3. Architecture overview of the CBTC system

The ATC consists of three subsystems each of them having its own functionalities: (1) Automatic Train Protection (ATP) constantly supervises the position and the speed of the trains ensuring the correct distance between themselves and is able to automatically intervene to adjust the speed or to stop the train for safety reasons; (2) Automatic Train Operation (ATO) ensures that the trains stop at the right position at the platform, open and close the doors and adjust the speed within the limits imposed by the ATP. An ATO system is capable to survey the entire operation and monitoring the status of each vehicle on the track; (3) Automatic Train Supervision (ATS) controls and coordinates all traffic and maintains a schematic review of the entire Metro for the operators in the control room. It controls the arrival and the departure of trains from all the stations and also includes automatic vehicle dispatching, automatic routing, schedule control and zone speed restriction.

In the CBTC technology these functionalities can be traced on several components, the main ones indicated in the Fig. 4.

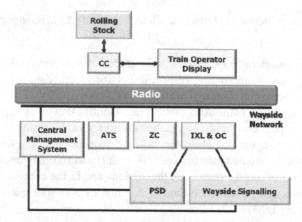

Fig. 4. Functional overview of the CBTC system architecture

The Zone Controller (ZC) manages the Movement Authority Limits (MALs) of all trains. Each ZC unit is integrated with adjacent ZCs and communicates with Interlockings (IXLs) and Carborne Controllers (CCs) to guarantee that specific headway requirements are met. The CC determines the train position with the highest accuracy. This information is then relayed back to the ZC. Based on the MAL received from the ZC, the CC calculates its braking curves and enforces speed restrictions. The IXL & Object Controller (OC) determines the traffic schedule and the minimum headway. The Platform Screen Doors (PSDs) have a controller that monitors the status of the doors and, interacting with the CC by means the ZC, enables them to open and close. In order to ensure the correct integration of the above subsystems and the necessary safety requirements it is needed to perform an intense analysis and testing activity on the CBTC functions.

4.2   The "Determine Doors Opening Side" Function

The case study presented in this paper is based on a particular function of the CBTC system: the "Determine Doors Opening Side" function. The role of this function is to determine which side of train doors (Train Doors, TDs) should open at first (or second) and which side of the Platform Screen Doors (PSDs) should open at first (or second) when the train is stopped at the platform (in the most general case of the presence of double platform at the two sides of the line). This function also provides a safety check on the correctness of the train side (and platform side) selected by the driver to be opened, when the doors are not in automatic opening mode.

The CBTC system splits the whole line into several virtual segments and associates an orientation to each one of them that can be concordant or contrasting to the one of the line (in the Fig. 5a, for the segment 'i' the polarity is '+', according to the conventional direction of the line whereas the polarity for the segment 'j' is '-'). The two platforms, where present, are named *Right* or *Left* according to the position with respect to the conventional direction of the line. Given the conventional direction of the train as in Fig. 5b, defined from Cab 2 to Cab 1 ends (conventional), the train polarity could get '+' or '-' with reference to the orientation of the crossed virtual segment of line, it is '+' if the train direction is concordant to the one of the crossed virtual segment, '-' otherwise.

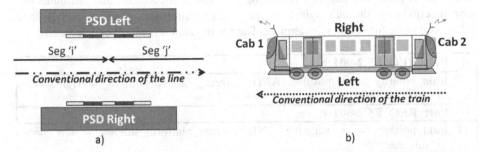

Fig. 5. Determination of the train doors and platform screen doors opening side

The realization of this function requires a computational block that takes as input the signals about the *current_platform_side*, *TP_train_polarity* and *platform_tp_line_direction*; this block is able to evaluate: (1) which is the right side of train doors to "move" (open and close) at first (*td_1st_side*) and, potentially, at second (*td_2nd_side*); (2) which is the right side of platform doors to move at first (*psd_1st_side*) and, potentially, at second (*psd_2nd_side*). Hence one functional requirement for this function describes how it determines the side train door to move in case of single platform (output: *td_1st_side*). In the following example, the requirement part related to the right side of the train doors is reported.

ID: **REQ_F5.2-001_R**
The first Train Doors to be moved shall be the right side of a train if one of the following conditions is true: • that train's polarity is positive and the right side of the related platform is configured as the first side to be opened. • that train's polarity is negative and the left side of the related platform is configured as the first side to be opened.

4.3   Dynamic Functional Testing

At first, the requirement has been refined and translated in two Boilerplate requirements.

ID: **BP_REQ_F5.2-001_R_a**
If <train polarity is positive> and <current platform side is right>, the <CBTC system> shall <open the right side of train doors>
ID: **BP_REQ_F5.2-001_R_b**
If <train polarity is negative> and <current platform side is left>, the <CBTC system> shall <open the right side of train doors>

The second step is the formalization of the requirements in a language (Pattern), in a semi-automatic way with the support of a specific tool, to allow the successive automatic generation of test cases, as implemented in the CESAR project and already described in [16]. The patterns, consisting of static text elements and attributes describing conditions through logical operators in a requirements specification language (RSL), are more formal then boilerplate. The formalization is reported here below.

ID: **Patt_REQ_F5.2-001_a**
TP_train_polarity = = positive AND current_platform_side = = right ==> td_1st_side = = right
ID: **Patt_REQ_F5.2-001_b**
TP_train_polarity = = negative AND current_platform_side = = left ==> td_1st_side = = right

The automatic test generator, on the basis of the pattern requirements and the reduction rules, defines the test set, including the expected output against the given combination of inputs, following the steps listed below.

1. For each requirement a positive test vector (PTV) and a negative test vector (NTV) are here generated: the positive test vector corresponds to the test in which all the variables involved into the requirement are set as indicated in the same requirement. The negative test vector corresponds to the same input sequence (as in the PTV) containing, as expected output, the opposite of the desired one, indicated into the requirement. So, with the NTV, we can get a test case that is expected to fail, if the system is correctly implemented with respect to the requirement, and this requirement is not violated.
2. The expert user can define some rules in order to limit the number of tests, without jeopardizing the completeness related to the whole set of functional requirements needed to test the system. The reduction rules (RRs) allow to discard some particular permutations of system variables. In detail, the RRs imply two assumptions: the independence among variables not involved into the output definition (*independence rules*) and combinations of variables defining a non-significant or not admissible condition for the system (*domain rules*).

An example of a typical reduction rule has been applied in this example, it concerns the assumption of input variables being independent of each other: analyzing the set of requirements that define the output *td_1st_side*, it appears that the only variables involved in its definition are *TP_train_polarity* and *current_platform_side*. On the basis of this hypothesis, the RR sets all the values of the not involved inputs to a default value, avoiding the generation of all the possible combinations of the other inputs of the system not involved in a specific output. In detail, the computational block takes as input also the signals *platform_tp_line_direction*: this value has been not taken into account in the test cases; this is due to the fact that this input, together with the *current_platform_side*, is not involved in determine the right side of train doors to move whereas it is necessary to determine the side of platform doors to move.

4.4   Static Functional and Non-functional Analysis

In the previous subsection a reduction rule about the independency between inputs of a computational block has been considered. This rule is able to restrict the number of generated test cases leaving out other inputs of the computational block, not involved in the evaluation of the specific output. This rule needs to be validated because, due to errors in the model implementation, unexpected interactions among variables could exist and cause unwanted behavior of the system. Due to the inclusion of that rule in the test generation phase to limit the number, these not foreseen interactions may not be discovered. For this reason it is necessary to validate them through static analysis techniques. As an example, these analysis techniques can be applied on the component diagram related to the computational block implementing the function: it is necessary to verify that the inputs leaved out in the test cases does not have an influence on the specific output evaluation.

Other kinds of analysis can be performed in order to validate non-functional properties: it is possible to prove system properties descending from the hazard analysis on the same high-level models. A hazard identified for the function under analysis is the incorrect doors opening side (the function sets the wrong side for TD and PSD). The consequences are several: passengers on the train or on the platform could fall in the track with serious injuries, passengers could fall in the track with electric shock due to the contact with power rail, or others.

Formal properties to be verified have to demonstrate that the system cannot fail in determining the correct side to be opened for the doors of the train. Referring to the requirement *Patt_REQ_F5.2-001_a*, an example of a property, that must be verified always false, is the following one:

```
td_1st_side = = right AND TP_train_polarity = = negative AND
current_platform_side = = right
```

Tools used for the static analysis shall allow the validation of the correctness of the system model implementation, because if these properties had been verified, it would mean that the model is not correct since the hazardous state defined has been reached.

Due to the high complexity of these systems, it can happen that the static analysis is not able to give the proof of a property, because it is not possible to investigate the whole space of reachable states. In this case, the result can be considered on a probabilistic base.

5   Conclusions and Future Development

The main motivation that pushed ASTS participating to MBAT project is the possibility to exploit the model-based analysis and testing and in a combined approach to obtain a reduction in overall V&V costs by already keeping high quality and safety standards. Therefore, the main objective is the achievement of an efficient and effective use of the MBAT results. The important result reached with CESAR is the automatic definition of the set of test cases reasonably complete, starting from functional system requirements.

The first aim will be the compatibility between the CESAR tool chain and the proposed workflow based on the MBAT technical innovation. The second aim is represented by the execution of analysis and testing on the system model when, nowadays, is executed on the real system. The possibility of anticipating this check to the design phase allows decreasing the development efforts of time and cost. Furthermore, the introduction of systematic activities of static analysis allows verifying properties that are not yet formally verified at the moment, filling a gap and strongly improving the quality of the work and decrease of V&V and certification costs compared to imposed standards.

Other benefits are the improvement of automation to minimize human error and the introduction of the traceability among the FRS, test cases, system model and report documents. The model allows strongly decreasing time/costs in case of correction of possible anomalies on the system, since a lot of checks are preliminary performed on the model and not on the real system and in case of, whereas needed, introduction of modifications on the system arising from new constraints identified in later steps of the project (new requirements added).

Further expected benefits might be the sharing and the comparison of best practices among different companies, the improvement of standardization degree of the V&V processes among different industrial domains (European standardization) and the reduction of the efforts for the certification of the overall system at the end of the processes.

References

1. Schätz, B., Pretschner, A., Huber, F., Philipps, J.: Model-based development. Technical Report TUM-I0204, Institut für Informatik, Technische Universitat Munchen (2002)
2. Schätz, B., Pretschner, A., Huber, F., Philipps, J.: Model-Based Development of Embedded Systems. In: Proceedings of Advances in Object-Oriented Information Systems, OOIS (2002)
3. Bender, K., Broy, M., Péter, I., Pretschner, A., Stauner, T.: Model Based Development of Hybrid Systems: Specification, Simulation, Test Case Generation. In: Modelling, Analysis, and Design of Hybrid Systems (2002)
4. Ziegenbein, D., Braun, P., Freund, U., Bauer, A., Romberg, J., Schatz, B.: AutoMoDe - model-based development of automotive software. In: Proceedings of Design, Automation and Test in Europe, pp. 171–176 (2005)
5. Fantechi, A., Gnesi, S.: On the Adoption of Model Checking in Safety-Related Software Industry. In: Flammini, F., Bologna, S., Vittorini, V. (eds.) SAFECOMP 2011. LNCS, vol. 6894, pp. 383–396. Springer, Heidelberg (2011)
6. http://www.esterel-technologies.com/products/
7. Stålhane, T., Omoronyia, I., Reichenbach, F.: Ontology-Guided Requirements and Safety Analysis. In: Proc. 6th International Conference on Safety of Industrial Automated Systems, SIAS (2010)

8. Omoronyia, I., Sindre, G., Stålhane, T., Biffl, S., Moser, T., Sunindyo, W.: A Domain Ontology Building Process for Guiding Requirements Elicitation. In: Wieringa, R., Persson, A. (eds.) REFSQ 2010. LNCS, vol. 6182, pp. 188–202. Springer, Heidelberg (2010)
9. Farfeleder, S., Moser, T., Krall, A., Stålhane, T., Zojer, H., Panis, C.: DODT: Increasing Requirements Formalism using Domain Ontologies for Improved Embedded System Development. In: 14th IEEE Symposium on Design and Diagnostics of Electronic Circuits and Systems, Germany (2011)
10. di Tommaso, P., Esposito, R., Marmo, P., Orazzo, A.: Hazard Analysis of Complex Distributed Railway Systems. In: Proc. of International Symposium on Reliable Distributed Systems, SRDS 2003, Florence, Italy, pp. 283–292 (2003)
11. De Nicola, G., di Tommaso, P., Esposito, R., Flammini, F., Orazzo, A.: A Hybrid Testing Methodology for Railway Control Systems. In: Heisel, M., Liggesmeyer, P., Wittmann, S. (eds.) SAFECOMP 2004. LNCS, vol. 3219, pp. 116–129. Springer, Heidelberg (2004)
12. De Nicola, G., di Tommaso, P., Rosaria, E., Francesco, F., Pietro, M., Antonio, O.: A Grey-Box Approach to the Functional Testing of Complex Automatic Train Protection Systems. In: Dal Cin, M., Kaâniche, M., Pataricza, A. (eds.) EDCC 2005. LNCS, vol. 3463, pp. 305–317. Springer, Heidelberg (2005)
13. De Nicola, G., di Tommaso, P., Esposito, R., Flammini, F., Marmo, P., Orazzo, A.: ERTMS/ETCS: Working Principles and Validation. In: Proceedings of the International Conference on Ship Propulsion and Railway Traction Systems, SPRTS 2005, Bologna, Italy, pp. 59–68 (2005)
14. Donini, R., Marrone, S., Mazzocca, N., Orazzo, A., Papa, D., Venticinque, S.: Testing complex safety-critical systems in SOA context. In Proc. of the 2008 International Conference on Complex, Intelligent and Software Intensive Systems (CISIS), Barcelona, Spain (2008)
15. Flammini, F., Mazzocca, N., Orazzo, A.: Automatic instantiation of abstract tests on specific configurations for large critical control systems. Journal of Software Testing, Verification & Reliability (STVR) 19(2), 91–110 (2009)
16. Bonifacio, G., Marmo, P., Orazzo, A., Petrone, I., Velardi, L., Venticinque, A.: Improvement of Processes and Methods in Testing Activities for Safety-Critical Embedded Systems. In: Flammini, F., Bologna, S., Vittorini, V. (eds.) SAFECOMP 2011. LNCS, vol. 6894, pp. 369–382. Springer, Heidelberg (2011)
17. Institute of Electrical and Electronics Engineers. IEEE Standard for Communication Based Train Control (CBTC) Performance and Functional Requirements. IEEE Std 1474.1-2004 (Revision of IEEE Std 1474.1-1999) (2004)

Optimising Ordering Strategies
for Symbolic Model Checking of Railway Interlockings

Kirsten Winter

School of Information Technology and Electrical Engineering, The University of Queensland,
St.Lucia, QLD 4072, Australia

Abstract. Interlockings implement Railway Signalling Principles which ensure
the safe movements of trains along a track system. They are safety critical systems
which require a thorough analysis. We are aiming at supporting the safety analysis
by automated tools, namely model checkers.

Model checking provides a full state space exploration and is thus intrinsically
limited in the problem's state space. Current research focuses on extending these
limits and pushing the boundaries. In our work we investigate possible optimisations for symbolic model checking. Symbolic model checkers exploit a compact
representation of the model using Binary Decision Diagram. These structures
provide a canonical representation which allows for reductions. The compactness
of this data structure and possible reductions are dependent on two orderings: the
ordering of variables and the ordering in which sub-structures are manipulated.
This paper reports on findings of how a near to optimal ordering can be generated
for the domain of interlocking verification.

1 Introduction

Railway signalling interlockings are safety critical systems. Therefore special attention
has to be given to the correctness of the design and the implementation of an interlocking system. The development of such systems is very labour intensive and prone to
error. It requires specialised skills. Moreover, possible errors in the design are detected
very late in the design process. To mitigate these problems Queensland Rail (QR), the
major railway operator and owner in Queensland, Australia, intended to support its design process by a specialised tool set called the Signalling Design Toolset (SDT) [1].
Parts of this toolset were intended for supporting the verification task.

In this paper we summarise our findings on how to formally model a functional
specification of an interlocking system, the control table, and how to optimise symbolic
model checking of these interlocking models. Our results render the approach feasible
for industrial practise.

Others have applied model checking to analyse railway interlocking systems: Gnesi
et al. [2], Bernadeschi et al. [3], and Cleaveland et al. [4], for instance, have analysed
fault tolerance of interlocking systems. The main focus in their work were communication aspects between components rather than the control logic as in our work.

The first approaches on applying model checking to verify railway interlocking systems represented as control tables or equations were reported by Groote et al. [5], using
μCRL and its tools, and Eisner [6,7] using SMV. Also Simpson et al. [8], and Huber

T. Margaria and B. Steffen (Eds.): ISoLA 2012, Part II, LNCS 7610, pp. 246–260, 2012.

et al. [9] are focusing on the control logic similar to our approach. In particular, the approach by Eisner and Huber et al. is very close to ours as they also use a symbolic model checker. The interlocking systems, however, are modelled on a lower level of abstraction. This leads to significantly different models and in particular a more complex model of the requirements which in our case can be simply expressed as train collision and train derailment.

In [10] Ferrari et al. attempt a comparison of different model checkers when applied to interlocking control tables. Although the work is very interesting it is lacking to take into account the potential of optimising symbolic model checking as it has been proposed in this work.

While most existing work on signalling design verification targets the later interlocking design phase, the focus of our approach was to enable verification of the interlocking design at an early stage, when specified as control tables. The results presented here consolidate work published in [11,12] and [13,14].

2   The Context

The research this paper reports on has been conducted in the context of the Signalling Design Tools projects (SigTools), a collaboration of Queensland Rail (QR), the Software Verification Research Centre (SVRC), and later the University of Queensland. Aim of these projects was to design tool support for the creation and verification of control tables[1,15].

Control Tables provide the functional specification for railway signalling interlockings and contain the key safety requirements. They act as (1) an agreement between the railway administration and the train operators on when moves will be permitted on a track layout, (2) a specification for designing the interlocking itself, and (3) a test specification for use by testers.

A control table is a structured, tabular presentation of the rules governing route setting on a railway track layout. An example of a QR (signal) control table is shown in Figure 1. A *route*, a sequence of tracks from an entry signal to an exit signal, is a key concept in the table. One row of the table indicates the conditions needed to "set" a single route (i.e., reserve it for a train to safely use it).

Signal	Route Number	Route to	Route Indication	Points Locked		Routes		Route Holding	or Until		Tracks		Replaced by Tracks Occ
				Normal	Reverse	Normal	Reverse	Maintained by Tracks occ	Tracks occ	for Time secs	Clear	Occ	
he2	1m	ng8	-	p500							HE1BT HE1AT HE2AT HE2BT		HE1BT
						he3(1s)		HE1BT			HE2CT NG7BT NG7AT NG8AT		
						he1(1M) he1(2M)		HE1BT HE1AT					

Fig. 1. Control Table for a small verification area (as shown in Figure 2); depicted is the row for the route from signal HE2 to NG8

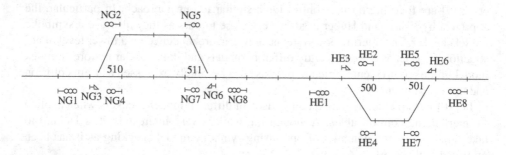

Fig. 2. Track Layout of a small verification area

The control table is specific to a *track layout* which represents the local arrangement of the railway equipment on a selected part of the railway network while abstracting from the actual length of the tracks and distances between the signalling equipment. In our context we refer to the area covered by the track layout as the *verification area*. Figure 2 shows the track layout for the above control table. It contains the signals HE2, NG8, etc., the points 500, 501, etc., and tracks which are not named in the figure but indicated as sections on the railway.

2.1 The Signalling Design Tools Project

Intention of the SigTools project was to design a tool suite to enable generation of (parts of) signalling control tables, the editing of generated control tables, and the verification of control tables against safety principles for railway signalling, the Signalling Design Tool (SDT) suite. Figure 3 gives an overview of the architecture.

It comprises a *Track Layout Editor* [16,17] to manually edit track layouts, a *Control Table Generator* [18] for automatically generating all entries of the table that can be inferred from the layout, a *Control Table Editor* [19] for manually editing control tables, and a *Counter-example Interpreter* [20] which automatically interprets counter-examples output by the verification tool, as well as the *Control Table Verification* itself which is the focus of the following sections.

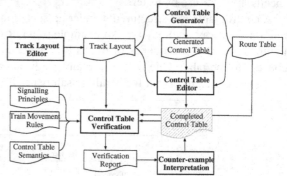

Fig. 3. Architecture of the Signalling Design Tools

2.2 Modelling Control Tables

We target an automated verification of the completed control tables utilising the model checker NuSMV [21]. This requires to provide a formal model of the control table. To this end we designed a *generic* formal model that captures the control table semantics using ASMs [22] as a vehicle. For each particular control table to be verified the generic model is to be instantiated with the data from the accompanying track-layout, the route table, and the control table itself. This instance constitutes the formal model of the control table to be checked. It is automatically translated into the model checker's input notation, here the NuSMV language [23]. The ASM model serves as a useful tool to communicate, formalise and document (our understanding of) the control table semantics. More detail on the model can be found in [11,24].

At later stages of the project we omitted the "intermediate" ASM model as we derived a generic NuSMV model from the NuSMV code that was generated by the ASM-to-NuSMV translator. The generic NuSMV model is to be instantiated similarly to the ASM model used earlier. The instantiation process has been automated within the SDT suite [25,1]. In the following we sketch the simplifying assumptions of our control table model as these have an impact on the scope of our analysis.

Train Movement. Unlike other approaches our model also includes (one or two) trains moving along the tracks. As a consequence, the safety requirements become generic and very easy to validate. They are modelled in terms of train *collision* and *derailment*. It could be shown through tests that even a very simplistic model of train movement suffices to show missing entries in the control table. The train data is limited to an identifier, which route the train is on, and which track it is occupying. The simplifications are carried by the following assumptions: (a) Trains move at a constant speed or stop (i.e., we do not model the speed of a train or its braking capacity). (b) We assume that trains always stop at red signals (excluding possible overruns). (c) Trains move according to the conditions given by the state of points and signals from track to track. (d) Trains can stop at any time. (e) The direction of a train is determined through its position, which is a particular track segment each of which carry direction information.

It suffices to consider only two trains in the system to check for collision, and only one train to detect possible derailment. The reasoning for this simplification, which is in agreement with the railway engineers, is based on the fact that the more trains are running through a particular verification area the more the movement of other trains is restricted. Moreover, trains can appear on the tracks of the verification area in an arbitrary fashion in our model. Therefore, every possible combination of two potentially colliding trains is investigated. Considering only two trains at maximum limits the additional complexity that stems from adding trains to the model to a tolerable level.

Aspect Sequencing. Signals can show only two aspects, stop and proceed. This reduces the specified aspect type (two values instead of three) but it does prevent us from checking the aspect sequencing of the interlocking design. Aspect sequencing ensures that the train driver will see a yellow aspect before a red one. This mechanism, however, can also be checked statically within the Control Table Editor [1].

Approach Locking. One part of the control table logic describes the functionality of approach locking. Approach locking prevents a route that has been set for a train from changing until it is deemed safe to do so. We decided to restrict our verification to a smaller problem without approach locking in order to decrease the model's state space and behaviour. This also allowed us to simplify the train movement and signal model as described above. Approach locking is a safety concern, but the corresponding entries in the table can be checked statically by the Control Table Editor.

Shunt Routes. Our initial model did not distinguish between normal routes and shunt routes. Shunting is a low speed operation in which trains are joined together. In terms of our initial model, however, the scenario of shunting equals a train collision since we do not consider the speed of a train. For simplicity, the shunting behaviour of trains was then ignored. As justification we used the fact that shunting does not provide a high risk safety concern due to the low speed that is involved. At a later stage of the project however it was found that the models can be extended to include shunt routes as distinguished instances. This required to change the some of the rules for train movement as well as the specification of the safety requirements for train collision.

Overlaps. Overlaps are tracks behind a signal and are introduced as a safety buffer for trains that overrun a red signal. Since the trains in our model always stop at a red signal (see above), missing overlaps in the control table cannot be detected in our initial model. Moreover, including the concept of overlaps into our model would also allow us to check for certain liveness conditions on setting signals and routes. A later version of the model included the model of overlapping tracks and it could be shown that the modification extended the scope of the verification sufficiently.

Level Crossings. Level crossings also carry a safety concern. They are not present in every area but when they are, the corresponding part of the control table should be checked. These checks require to introduce new concepts, such as gates and gate movement, as well as the notion of time into the model. This can be supported by either the use a modelling framework that supports time (e.g., timed automaton and UPPAAL [26] or timed CSP [27]), or to integrate an explicit timer variable into a "standard" model like ours. The latter approach has been proposed in [28].

Keeping the model of the interlocking design at a more abstract and more simplified level reduces the complexity of the checking process. However, it comes at a cost of retrieving counterexamples that are less intuitive for the railway engineer for whom the formal model is an internal representation he/she is not familiar with. Although revealing real errors in the control table the given path might show unusual behaviour for the trains due to our simplified model of train movement. To alleviate this problem the project designed a Counter-example Interpretation which provides the user with hints as to which entry in the table is missing [20].

All the simplifications on our model were thoroughly discussed with our industry partners from QR. The modelling decisions and their impact are well documented, especially the scope of the verification that is provided by the model checking process.

3   Symbolic Model Checking

Simplifying the model as described in the previous section helped to scale-up the verification to some extend but the improvement was not sufficient to target medium- or large-sized models. Therefore we aimed at optimising the model checking process itself.

3.1 Variable Ordering

Central to symbolic model checking is the idea of internally representing the model (i.e., its states and state transitions) using Bryant's *Binary Decision Diagrams* (BDDs) [29]. BDDs are a graph structure that allows the canonical representation of Boolean functions. In most cases a BDD representation is substantially more compact than other canonical representations in normal form, and it furthermore allows for signification reductions avoiding the representation of duplicate information.

A BDD consists of a set of nodes that are labelled with a variable. Each node is linked via two directed edges to its successor nodes. These edges represent the evaluation of the variable to *false* and *true*, respectively. The leaf nodes of the BDD are labelled with the truth values. If the labels of the nodes in the BDD are ordered then we call the graph an *ordered* BDD (OBDD).

The possible reduction of an OBDD depends on its structure which is determined by the ordering of its node variables. An OBDD for the same function but with the changed variable ordering has a different shape and consequently reduces differently.

It is infeasible to compute an optimal variable ordering in general, however, much research effort has been focused on heuristics for finding a good variable ordering automatically. These heuristics are based on dependencies between variables and early evaluation of the represented formula. When a formula represents a transition that updates one variable we refer to it as *single transition*. It will reference variables on which the transition depends. We call these variables *support variables* of the transition. Variables that are referenced by all transitions are called *global variables*. The following guidelines help finding a good ordering:

1. Declare closely related variables together. In the variable ordering, each variable should be close to the support variable of its transition [30,31].
2. For each transition, having the support variables closer to the top of the order than the variable being transformed, gives the smallest ROBDD [30].
3. Place global variables at the top of the order [31].

3.2 Transition Orderings

Due to the nature of the application our model is similar to synchronous hardware circuits. The transition relation is described as the conjunct of single transitions of which each describes the update of one state variable. That is, the value for a state variable v can be given as $v = f(v_1, \ldots v_n)$ where f is a function that captures the logical dependencies between variable v and the support variables $v_1, \ldots, v_n$. All transitions are fired simultaneously which leads to a *next state* in which some variables have changed their values while others have not. Therefore, we can use results that originated in the domain of synchronous circuit verification, in particular [32].

If we assume a set V of n state variables, $v_1, \ldots v_n$, we denote a state of the model as $S(v_1, \ldots v_n)$ and abbreviate this as $S(V)$. The transition relation, modelling the transition from current state to next state, is captured by a function N which depends on variables in V as well as their primed counterparts, V', capturing the evaluation in the next state. The function $N(v_1, \ldots, v_n, v'_1, \ldots, v'_n)$ is abbreviated as $N(V, V')$.

In symbolic model checking the state space is explored by iteratively applying the transition relation to the state. This is done in a forward fashion starting with the initial state and is called *image computation*. The operation on ROBDDs used for image computation is called *relational product*. For synchronous systems (as in our case) it is defined as

$$S'(v_1', \ldots, v_n') = \exists v_1 \in V[\ldots \exists v_n \in V[S(v_1, \ldots, v_n) \wedge N(v_1, \ldots, v_n, v_1', \ldots, v_n')] \ldots]$$

We abbreviate this formula using the notion from [32] as follows

$$S'(V') = \exists_{v \in V}[S(V) \wedge N(V, V')] \tag{1}$$

where V' is the set of primed state variables and $S'(V')$ describes the set of next states reachable from $S(V)$ via one transition step.

The transition relation $N(V, V')$ can be applied to the state as one big transition or it can be envisaged as a conjunct of smaller *partitions* of N, $N_i(V, V')$, where each partition is either a single transition (that updates one variable) or a conjunct of several single transitions, referred to as *cluster* in the following. In practise each $N_i(V, V')$ can often be represented by a small BDD whereas the whole of $N(V, V)$ becomes very large. The aim is to compute the image without building the whole of $N(V, V')$ by using the following formula:

$$S'(V') = \exists_{v \in V}[S(V) \wedge N_0(V, V') \wedge \ldots \wedge N_{n-1}(V, V')]. \tag{2}$$

Unfortunately, existential quantification (e.g., $\exists_{v \in V}$ in the formula above) does not distribute over conjunction and we cannot simply split up the operation into single steps. Burch et al. in [32], however, developed a method to overcome this problem. It is based on two observations. Firstly, our model of interlockings exhibits locality (in a similar fashion to circuits), that is, most single transitions will depend on only a small number of variables in V and V'. Secondly, sub-formulas from the relational product can be moved out of the scope of the quantification if they do not depend on the variables being quantified. Therefore, it is beneficial to conjoin the $N_i(V, V')$ with $S(V)$ one at a time moving out those variables from the scope of the quantification that none of the remaining partitions depends on. To do so we want to *order* the partitions $N_i(V, V')$ in such a way that the number of variables that can be eliminated early is maximised. This will lead to smaller intermediate results of the image computation.

Assume the chosen order of clusters is given by the permutation p that permutes the indices $\{0, \ldots, n-1\}$. That is, cluster $N_{p(i)}(V, V')$ will be applied in the ith step of the image computation. Let $D_{p(i)}$ be the variables that $N_{p(i)}(V, V')$ depends on and E_i the set of variables that can be eliminated after the ith step. That is, E_i is the subset of $D_{p(i)}$ that is not contained in any of the other dependency sets. Then $S'(V')$ can be computed in a number of steps each eliminating the variables in E_i when building the corresponding *intermediate products* $S_{i+1}(V, V')$:

$$
\begin{aligned}
S_1(V, V') &= \exists_{v \in E_0}[S(V) \wedge N_{p(0)}(V, V')] \\
S_2(V, V') &= \exists_{v \in E_1}[S_1(V, V') \wedge N_{p(1)}(V, V')] \\
&\quad \ldots \\
S'(V') &= \exists_{v \in E_{n-1}}[S_{n-1}(V, V') \wedge N_{p(n-1)}(V, V')]
\end{aligned}
\tag{3}
$$

The chosen order p has an impact on how early variables can be quantified out and therewith affects the size of the BDDs constructed. The aim is to group those transitions together into one cluster that have the same support variables. Selective grouping of transitions into clusters, and the order p of application of the clusters leads to smaller and fewer intermediate products that are manipulated faster [33]. The following heuristics can be proposed: Transitions that are supported by the maximal number of variables should be grouped together in a cluster and applied first. Subsequent transitions that are supported by fewer variables should be grouped into clusters so that as many of their support variables as possible do not support transitions in clusters yet to be applied. This enables some of the support variables to be quantified out progressively from the intermediate products giving smaller intermediate products.

If transitions do not naturally fall into clear-cut divisions, the grouping of transitions within clusters and the order of application of the clusters should be such that early elimination of support variables is maximised. We will see in the next section how a good ordering for the transitions can be generated for the domain of railway interlockings.

4 Optimised Orderings for Railway Interlockings

Checking medium-sized control tables utilising the standard user options provided by NuSMV [23] would in many cases lead to memory overflow and a non-acceptable runtime of the process. The approach needed to be taylored for the application domain.

Three optimisation were taken into consideration: (1) Generating the variable ordering on the basis of domain knowledge. (2) Computing an ordering in which the transition clusters are to be applied to maximise the early quantification of support variables. (3) Determining the threshold size for clusters based on experimental results. The following subsection report on our findings.

The domain knowledge on which our approach is based stems from the following characterisation of the domain data. Variables in our model can be divided into three groups: global, local and input variables. Similarly, single transitions can be characterised as global transitions if they update a global variable or local transitions if they update local variables.

Global Variables represent train attributes like the current position (given in terms of a track) and the currently used route. In the SMV code this is modelled by four variables of enumerated type. Typically 30 -130 different values, depending on the number of tracks and routes in the interlocking, are required. The larger and more complex the verification area, the larger becomes the set of Booleans necessary to represent the values. Typically five to seven Booleans are required for each attribute in the implementation (see [30] for details on implementing enumerated types efficiently).

Local Variables model the lie of the individual points, the current aspect of the signals, and the lock and usage of routes. Mostly, this information can be represented by simple Booleans (e.g., points are set normal or reverse, signals are set proceed or stop, routes are locked normal or reverse), only the route usage is encoded by a typically small enumerated set.

Input Variables represent signalling and train control commands (i.e., requests). They are not controlled by the interlocking but change their values randomly (to capture every possible behaviour). This can be modelled using a number of simple Booleans variables and one variable of enumerated type. The number of enumerated values again depends on the size of the verification area (number of routes, signals, etc.). The implementation of the enumerated input variable typically requires 5 to 7 Booleans.

Transitions in our context are modelled using the next operator of the SMV input language [34,23]. For each variable the evaluation in the next state is modelled depending on the previous values of the support variables. The size of the ROBDD representing the transition for each variable depends on the variable ordering (see Section 3.1).

Global transitions are supported by all the variables. Local transitions depend on a limited number of variables. Specifically they are supported by the global variables, the input variables and some of the local variables, e.g., only the occupation of nearby tracks and the input command variable are relevant to the movement of a point.

Generally, the transitions are such that if $\{v_1, v_2, v_3\}$ is the set of support variables for transition $N_{v_1}(V_1, v_1')$ then the set of support variables for transition $N_{v_3}(V_2, v_3')$ is likely to include v_1. That is, there is a cross-dependency between transitions. An analysis of the dependencies between all the variables using a dependency matrix (see [35]) resulted in a very dense matrix. This made the application of the standard heuristics which are based on the characteristics of a less dense dependency matrix unsuccessful in finding a good ordering.

Size of the Verification Area. An increase in the complexity of models (more signals, points and tracks), introduces more local variables, and maintains the same number of global and input variables but adds more values to the enumerated types. Adding more values to the enumerated types does not impact significantly on the number of Booleans used to implement them but does impact on the size of the ROBDD used to distinguish particular values of the variables.

Let $Var = \{v_1, \ldots, v_{m+n+p}\}$ be the set of state variables in our model with $\{g_1, \ldots, g_m\} \subset Var$ the set of global variables, $\{l_1, \ldots, l_n\} \subset Var$ the set of local variables and $\{req_1, \ldots, req_p\} \subset Var$ the set of input variables. Let $N_{v_i}(V, v_i')$, $1 \leq i \leq (m + n)$, be the transitions, local or global, that changes (local or global) variable v_i dependent on the support variables $V \subseteq Var$.

4.1 Optimising the Variable Ordering

We have implemented an algorithm that performs an ordering of local, global and input variables using the available data from the track layout. The strategy, and the reasoning for this strategy, on which the algorithm is based are explained in detail in the following.

Local Variables. Single transitions which model the update of signals, points, etc. depend on the support of signalling equipment that is in the close vicinity on the track-layout graph. The dependencies between the state variables are therefore related to the *geographical* arrangement that can be read from the track layout (see, for example, Figure 2).

Mechanical interlocking design suggests further considerations for this ordering strategy. Building the relays for the mechanical interlockings starts usually with points, followed by the signals whose routes crossed those points. Typically each signal is associated with routes from that signal. This leads to a strategy which associates the signals and routes with a particular point. The associated entities form a *group*.

However, there are several different ways of associating signals and points if a route comprises several in-route points. It was noted that moving a signal and its routes from a group with its first in-route *trailing* point to a group with its first in-route *facing* point made a significant difference to the model checking time and the memory used.

These consideration led to the following first ordering heuristics:

a) A signal and its routes are associated with the first facing point in the route or
b) with the first trailing point in-route if this is the only point.

While variables within groups are related by the transition relations, there is significant cross dependencies between the groups e.g. routes are related to routes that oppose them and the opposing routes are likely to be associated with different points. This leads us to the second ordering heuristics:

c) The groups are best ordered according to their arrangement on the track layout rather than in a random order.

The heuristics a) to c) form the basis of our ordering strategy, called *geographic order* which defines a permutation γ on the *local* variables. The layout is viewed as a grid and the signals and points are read in order from left to right. Where signals or points are in the same vertical grid, elements are ordered from top to bottom.

Ordering the local variables $\{l_1, \ldots, l_n\} \subset Var$ according to the geographic order following the heuristics above leads to an ordering of local variables of the form $l_{\gamma(1)} < \ldots < l_{\gamma(n)}$. For each local variable $l_{\gamma(j)}$, $1 \leq j \leq n$, the corresponding transition $N_{l_{\gamma(j)}}(V, l'_{\gamma(j)})$ then depends on local variables in reasonably close proximity to $l_{\gamma(j)}$ in the order, e.g., $l_{\gamma(j-1)}$ and $l_{\gamma(j+1)}$, etc.

Global Variables. The local transitions also depend on the global variables. Experimentation shows that putting the global variables higher in the variable order than all the local variables gives the smallest local transitions (i.e., those transitions that update local variables) supporting heuristics 3 in Section 3.1. The global transitions for the four global variables of enumerated type depend on all the variables and are large.

Input Variables. Placement of the input variables in the variable order is problematic. Input variables are in the support variables for all transitions. When they are placed at the beginning of the order, the ROBDDs representing the transitions $N_{v_i}(V, v'_i)$, $1 \leq i \leq (m + n)$, are smaller than ROBDDs for an order in which the input variables are placed lower in the order. However, this does not necessarily lead to smaller intermediate products. Experimentation has shown that placing the large input variable lower in the order increases the size of the local transitions and the size of the clusters. However, this gives smaller intermediate products and uses less memory overall. There are time and memory efficiency penalties for manipulating large transitions, large clusters, and large intermediate products and for our data, experimentation has shown that the best results are obtained by placing the large input variable about 2/3 down the order. For a detailed discussion see [13].

4.2 Improving the Transition Ordering

NuSMV did not have provision for the user to supply a transition order at the time we started our project. It has its own generic algorithm for estimating the *affinity* of transitions [35] (which describes their degree of similarity) and by default progressively builds clusters based on this affinity. A cluster is closed off when its size reaches a threshold (defined by the user or a default value) which results in evenly sized clusters.

For railway interlockings the dependency matrix on which the affinity is based is very dense. Therefore, computing the affinity between variables by itself does not provide the necessary information to improve efficiency. However, examining the railway interlocking model and its semantics has enabled us to define an order in which transitions can be conjoined and the points in the order at which to cut the conjunctions to form clusters. When these clusters are applied in turn in the image computation, the variables are quantified efficiently from the intermediate product.

We use the same argument of vicinity of symbols on the track layout that is used for finding a good variable ordering for ordering the partitioned transition relation. The global transitions, $N_{g_1}, \ldots, N_{g_m}$, are supported by all the other variables including the input variables. This suggests that global transitions should be applied first. The local transitions, $N_{l_1}, \ldots, N_{l_n}$, depend on global variables and other local variables associated with nearby symbols in the track layout. A transition order that reflects the geographic order of variables γ for the local transitions results in a permutation $N_{l_{\gamma(1)}} < \ldots < N_{l_{\gamma(n)}}$ of local transitions which then can be progressively grouped into clusters with some overlap of support variables.

Eliminating variables that are at the leaf end of an ROBDD (lowest in the variable order) favours BDD reduction and results in smaller diagrams than removing variables from the middle or root end of the diagram (higher in the variable order). Therefore, we order the local transition in such a way that transitions for variables of lower order will be applied first. If the local variables indexed progressively by $\gamma(1), \ldots, \gamma(n)$ using the geographic order γ then the aim is that the transition for the $\gamma(n)$th variable is applied before the transition for the $(\gamma(n - 1))$th variable to facilitate early elimination of the $\gamma(n)$th variable. While the $\gamma(n)$th variable may not be eliminated immediately after application of its transition, it should be soon after since all transitions using it will be within close range. This leads to an ordering of local transitions that is reverse to the ordering of local variables as introduced in Section 4.1.

In summary, a good order of application of transitions is the global transitions followed by the local transitions in the order $\gamma(n)$ to $\gamma(1)$. That is, assuming the NuSMV principle of prepending the cluster list and applying the transitions from the back to the front of the list, a good transition order for railway interlockings is the local transitions in the order $\gamma(1)$ to $\gamma(n)$, followed by the global variable transitions:

$$N_{l_{\gamma(1)}} < \ldots < N_{l_{\gamma(n)}} < N_{g_1} < \ldots < N_{g_m} \tag{4}$$

The NuSMV code was extended so that the user could provide a transition order in terms of an ordered list of the corresponding variables, $l_{\gamma(1)} < \ldots < l_{\gamma(n)} < g_1 < \ldots < g_m$.

4.3   Clustering

Transitions are conjoined in order according to the transition order. Having defined a good transition order that supports the elimination of variables as early as possible, the question becomes where to cut the transition conjunction and form a cluster. If all transitions are in one cluster, no elimination of variables can occur and the ROBDD representing the cluster becomes very large. If the clusters are too small then many intermediate products $S'(V')$ (see equation 3 in Section 3.2) have to be computed. The issue is to find the balance between size and number of clusters and intermediate products.

Using a transition order and the default threshold to form the clusters resulted in between ten and fourteen clusters for our models. This number is too large and we had to re-define the cut-off points for the clusters.

The global transitions are applied first and it is logical to put all of these into the first cluster. After application of the global cluster the *next* values for the global variables can be quantified out.

When clustering the remaining local transitions, which are ordered using the geographical ordering, we used the insight that by referencing the track layout it is possible to nominate where in the transition order the dependencies change. This observation was confirmed by the railway engineers. For example, Figure 2 shows us that variables related to symbols to the right of signal *HE1* will be supported mostly by variables lower in the transition order than the variable for signal *HE1* since we ordered the variables inspecting the track layout from left to right. Similarly, variables related to symbols to the left of signal *HE1* will be mostly supported by variables higher in the variable ordering than the variable for signal *HE1*. Thus, for this verification area the local transitions fall naturally into two clusters at this point. Including the global cluster gives three clusters for this track layout.

From our experimentation it is clear that with a good transition order, few clusters are required. We found that often the models fell naturally into three or four clusters. However, for large models these clusters can become very big and the model checker spent significant time building them. In this case the performance was best using a clustering based on the threshold.

Another way to achieve few clusters is to specify a large threshold. The clusters will not be cut as precisely as before but because the order is good, progressive elimination of variables will occur. This approach is not as efficient as the customised formation of clusters described above, but is a worthwhile improvement on the default threshold used by standard NuSMV. The result (shown in Table 1 in Section 4.4) suggest that this approach is a reasonable alternative as it requires no specialist knowledge of the model or the application domain.

4.4   Experimental Results

We conducted our experiments with real data provided by QR. Table 1 compares our results for three different sized models: The large model consists of 41 routes, 9 points, 19 signals, and 31 track circuits. The medium model comprises 29 routes, 9 points, 13 signals, and 22 tracks. The small model comprises 12 routes, 2 points, 8 signals, and 8 tracks. The experiments were conducted using the options as indicated below.

Table 1. Comparison of various sized models using the discussed options

	User Options	5 Time(s)	Memory
Small model	1	4081	655Mb
	2	651	98Mb
	3	124	42Mb
	4	61	29Mb
	5	88	36Mb
Medium model	1	9620	1098Mb
	2	734	114Mb
	3	321	78Mb
	4	152	49Mb
	5	222	63Mb
Large model	1	N/A	N/A
	2	N/A	N/A
	3	68872	3.6Gb
	4	33641	980Mb
	5	29357	1160Mb

Option 1: using NuSMV defaults for variable and transition orders and clustering

Option 2: using user-defined variable order with default transition order and clustering

Option 3: using user-defined variable ordering and user-defined transition orders with default clustering

Option 4: using user-defined variable ordering, user-defined transition order and clusters selected by user

Option 5: using user-defined variable order, user-defined transition order and clusters selected by threshold.

The figures show that a significant improvement of run-time and memory usage was achieved by choosing a good variable ordering that was based on geographical information from the track layout, i.e., domain knowledge over the dependencies. This result is not surprising as this correlation is often stated in the literature. Improvements of similar scale could also be achieved by customising the order of transition partitions and by forming the clusters. Both parameters were chosen using the same reasoning as was used for choosing the variable ordering — in our case geographic order of dependencies.

The NuSMV tool (from version 2.4.1) has been extended by the user option -t <tv_file> which allows the user to specify an alternative variable ordering to be used for clustering of the transition relation [23]. The grammar of the ordering file is the same as for the variable ordering file.

5   Conclusion

In this paper we provide a strategy for improving efficiency of symbolic model checking when applied in the domain of railway interlockings. Based on domain knowledge we show how to compute optimised variable and transition orderings and report on our findings of how to set the threshold for clusters. The results from our experiments are encouraging and render the approach feasible for use in industrial practise.

For future work it would be interesting to include an *optimised* symbolic model checking approach into a comparative study as it has been done in [10]. Moreover, we would like to apply the proposed strategies to a model on the level of code or a geographical data model of an interlocking system to confirm whether similar improvements as for the control table model can be achieved.

Acknowledgements. The work has been conducted in close cooperation with Queensland Rail, in particular we would like to thank George Nikandros, David Barney and David Tombs. The domain expertise of Neil Robinson helped to shape the model and its simplifications, and the persistence of Wendy Johnston when analysing BDD size and structures was essential in producing the ordering strategies. This work was supported by Australian Research Council (ARC) Linkage Grant LP0882479 and the Australian Safety Critical Systems Association (aSCSa).

References

1. Robinson, N., Barney, D., Kearney, P., Nikandros, G., Tombs, D.: Automatic generation and verification of design specification. In: Proc. of Int. Symp. of the International Council on Systems Engineering, INCOSE 2001 (2001)
2. Gnesi, S., Lenzini, G., Latella, D., Abbaneo, C., Amendola, A., Marmo, P.: An automatic SPIN validation of a safety critical railway control system. In: Procs. of IEEE Conference on Dependable Systems and Networks, pp. 119–124. IEEE Computer Society (2000)
3. Bernardeschi, C., Fantechi, A., Gnesi, S., Mongardi, G.: Proving Safety Properties for Embedded Control Systems. In: Hlawiczka, A., Simoncini, L., Silva, J.G.S. (eds.) EDCC 1996. LNCS, vol. 1150, pp. 321–332. Springer, Heidelberg (1996)
4. Cleaveland, R., Luettgen, G., Natarajan, V.: Modeling and Verifying Distributed Systems Using Priorities: A case Study. In: Margaria, T., Steffen, B. (eds.) TACAS 1996. LNCS, vol. 1055, pp. 287–297. Springer, Heidelberg (1996)
5. Groote, J., Koorn, J., van Vlijmen, S.: The safety guaranteeing system at station Hoorn-Kersenboogerd. In: Proceedings 10th IEEE Conference on Computer Assurance (COMPASS 1995), pp. 131–150. IEEE Computer Society Press (1995)
6. Eisner, C.: Using Symbolic Model Checking to Verify the Railway Stations of Hoorn-Kersenboogerd and Heerhugowaard. In: Pierre, L., Kropf, T. (eds.) CHARME 1999. LNCS, vol. 1703, pp. 97–109. Springer, Heidelberg (1999)
7. Eisner, C.: Using symbolic CTL model checking to verify the railway stations of Hoorn-Kersenboogerd and Heerhugowaard. Software Tools for Technology Transfer 4(1), 107–124 (2002)
8. Simpson, A., Woodcock, J., Davies, J.: The mechanical verification of solid state interlocking geographic data. In: Groves, L., Reeves, S. (eds.) Proc. of Formal Methods Pacific (FMP 1997). Discrete Mathematics and Theoretical Computer Science Series, pp. 223–243. Springer (1997)
9. Huber, M., King, S.: Towards an Integrated Model Checker for Railway Signalling Data. In: Eriksson, L.-H., Lindsay, P.A. (eds.) FME 2002. LNCS, vol. 2391, pp. 204–223. Springer, Heidelberg (2002)
10. Ferrari, A., Magnani, G., Grasso, D., Fantechi, A.: Model checking interlocking control tables. In: Schnieder, E., Tarnai, G. (eds.) Proceedings of Conference on Formal Methods for Automation and Safety in Railway and Automotive Systems (FORMS/FORMAT 2010), vol. 2, pp. 107–115. Springer (2011)
11. Winter, K., Robinson, N.J.: Modelling large railway interlockings and model checking small ones. In: Oudshoorn, M. (ed.) Proc. of Australasian Computer Science Conference, ACSC 2003 (2003)
12. Winter, K., Johnston, W., Robinson, P., Strooper, P., van den Berg, L.: Tool support for checking railway interlocking designs. In: Cant, T. (ed.) Proc. of the 10th Australian Workshop on Safety Related Programmable Systems (SCS 2005), vol. 55, pp. 101–107. Australian Computer Society, Inc. (2005)

13. Johnston, W., Winter, K., van den Berg, L., Strooper, P., Robinson, P.: Model-Based Variable and Transition Orderings for Efficient Symbolic Model Checking. In: Misra, J., Nipkow, T., Sekerinski, E. (eds.) FM 2006. LNCS, vol. 4085, pp. 524–540. Springer, Heidelberg (2006)
14. Winter, K.: Symbolic Model Checking for Interlocking Systems. In: Railway Safety, Reliability, and Security: Technologies and Systems Engineering, pp. 298–315. IGI Global (2012)
15. Robinson, N.: Operation concept document. SigTools-004, version 1.9 (May 2002)
16. Robinson, N.: Design specification – Track Layout Editor. SigTools-032, version 1.1 (April 2004)
17. McComb, T., Robinson, N.J.: Assuring graphical computer aided design tools. Technical Report TR02-18, Software Verification Research Centre, University of Queensland (2001)
18. Tombs, D., Robinson, N.J., Nikandros, G.: Signalling control table generation and verification. In: Proc. of Conf. on Railway Engineering (CORE 2002). Railway Technical Society of Australasia (2002)
19. Johnston, W.: Design specification – Control Table Editor. SigTools-044, version 0.1 (January 2003)
20. van den Berg, L., Strooper, P., Johnston, W.: An automated approach for the interpretation of counter-examples. In: Bloem, R., Roveri, M., Somenzi, F. (eds.) Proceedings of 1st Workshop on Verification and Debugging, pp. 6–25 (2006)
21. Cimatti, A., Clarke, E., Giunchiglia, E., Giunchiglia, F., Pistore, M., Roveri, M., Sebastiani, R., Tacchella, A.: NuSMV 2: An OpenSource Tool for Symbolic Model Checking. In: Brinksma, E., Larsen, K.G. (eds.) CAV 2002. LNCS, vol. 2404, pp. 359–364. Springer, Heidelberg (2002)
22. Egon Börger, R.S.: Abstract State Machines: A Method for High-Level System Design and Analysis. Springer (2003)
23. Cavda, R., Cimatti, A., Jochim, C.A., Keighren, G., Olivetti, E., Pistore, M., Roveri, M., Tchaltsev, A.: NuSMV 2.5 User Manual (2010), http://nusmv.irst.itc.it
24. Winter, K.: Model checking control tables: the ASM-NuSMV approach. SigTools.039, version 0.1 (October 2002)
25. Johnston, W.: Design specification - Verification Manager and NuSMV Driver. SigTools-051, version 0.4 (April 2004)
26. Alur, R., Dill, D.L.: A theory of timed automata. Theoretical Computer Science 126(2), 183–235 (1994)
27. Schneider, S.: An operational semantics for timed CSP. Information and Computation 116(2), 193–213 (1995)
28. van den Berg, L., Strooper, P., Winter, K.: Introducing Time in an Industrial Application of Model-Checking. In: Leue, S., Merino, P. (eds.) FMICS 2007. LNCS, vol. 4916, pp. 56–67. Springer, Heidelberg (2008)
29. Bryant, R.E.: Graph-based algorithms for boolean function manipulation. IEEE Transactions on Computers C-35(8) (August 1986)
30. Clarke, E., Grumberg, O., Peled, D.: Model Checking. MIT Press (2000)
31. Lewis, G., Comella-Dorda, S., Gluch, D., Hudak, J., Weinstock, C.: Model-based verification: Analysis guidelines. Technical Report CMU/SEI-2001-TN-028, Carnegie Mellon Software Engineering Institute (2001)
32. Burch, J., Clarke, E., Long, D.: Symbolic model checking with partitioned transition relations. In: Int. Conf. on Very Large Scale Integration (1991)
33. Geist, D., Beer, I.: Efficient Model Checking by Automated Ordering of Transition Relation. In: Dill, D.L. (ed.) CAV 1994. LNCS, vol. 818, pp. 299–310. Springer, Heidelberg (1994)
34. McMillan, K.: Symbolic Model Checking. Kluwer Academic Publishers (1993)
35. Moon, I.-H., Hachtel, G.D., Somenzi, F.: Border-Block Triangular Form and Conjunction Schedule in Image Computation. In: Johnson, S.D., Hunt Jr., W.A. (eds.) FMCAD 2000. LNCS, vol. 1954, pp. 73–90. Springer, Heidelberg (2000)

Automated Generation of Safety Requirements from Railway Interlocking Tables

Anne E. Haxthausen

DTU Informatics, Technical University of Denmark, DK-2800 Lyngby, Denmark
ah@imm.dtu.dk

Abstract. This paper describes a tool for extracting formal safety conditions from interlocking tables for railway interlocking systems. The tool has been applied to generate safety conditions for the interlocking system at Stenstrup station in Denmark, and the generated conditions were then checked to hold by the SAL model checker tool.

Keywords: railways, interlocking systems, formal methods, safety, verification, model checking, interlocking tables, signal control tables.

1 Introduction

With more than 170 million passengers going by train on a yearly basis in Denmark, the safety of the railway traffic is a top priority for Railnet Denmark. As in other countries railway interlocking systems are used to prevent trains from colliding and derailing. Many interlocking systems in Denmark are still relay based, i.e. implemented by complex electrical circuits containing relays. These systems are documented by track layout diagrams, relay circuit diagrams and interlocking tables (also sometimes called signal control tables or train route tables). The interlocking tables serve as design specifications for relay circuit implementations[1], and the latter are verified to satisfy the design requirements by manual inspection of the circuit diagrams and the tables. Such a manual verification is very challenging, time consuming, and error prone. For these reasons Railnet Denmark asked us to research a better verification method.

Our solution has been to develop a set of tools [10] supporting automated formal verification of relay interlocking systems. We decided that the verification method should be *formal* as formal verification has been recognised as one of the best ways of avoiding errors and is for that reason strongly recommended by the CENELEC standards for railway control systems. Furthermore we decided that the method should be *automated* as much as possible to reduce the time consumption. We chose the model checking approach [6] to formal verification as this allows for full automation. However, the model checking approach requires as input a formal model of the system behaviour and a formal specification of the required properties, and it is not a trivial task to create this input. To overcome this problem, we decided also to create tools for generating verifiable formal models and for generating formal requirements, respectively.

---

[1] They are also used for some computer based interlocking systems.

T. Margaria and B. Steffen (Eds.): ISoLA 2012, Part II, LNCS 7610, pp. 261–275, 2012.

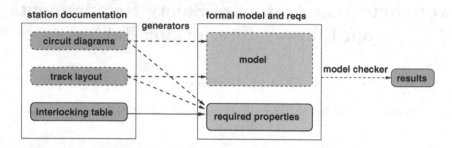

Fig. 1. Overview of generator tools. The tool described in this paper is shown by a solid arrow.

The tools are centred around a domain-specific language (DSL) for digitised representations of track layout diagrams, interlocking tables, and circuit diagrams used for documenting a relay interlocking system. We chose to centre the tools around a domain-specific language rather than a general purpose modelling language, as it is easier for railway engineers to use a language that facilitates concepts already known and used in the railway domain.

The tools comprise:

- *data validators* for checking that the documentation (in DSL) follows certain general wellformedness rules,
- *generators* that from a DSL description produce input to a model checker:
  - a formal, behavioural model (state transition system) of the described interlocking system and its environment and
  - required properties expressed as formulae in the temporal logic LTL.

Fig. 1 shows an overview of the generator tools. As it can be seen the model is generated from the circuit diagrams and the track layout diagram. Additional generators can be used to derive required properties from the circuit diagrams, the track layout diagram, and the interlocking table, respectively. The generated properties include: (1) conditions expressing desired internal model consistency properties (used for model validation), (2) high-level safety conditions expressing that there are no derailments and no collisions, and (3) low-level safety conditions expressing that general signalling rules of Railnet Denmark are obeyed, respectively. Prototypes of the generator tools have been developed using the RAISE formal method [15,16] due to previous good experience in using that method. Details on these tools and their development can be found in [2,4,11].

The whole collection of tools can be used to verify an interlocking system in the following number of steps:

- Write a DSL description of the interlocking system.
- Validate the description using the data validators.
- Apply the generators to generate input to a model checker.
- Apply the model checker to that input to investigate whether the model satisfies the required properties.

The current paper describes how one of the property generators takes interlocking tables as input and generates low-level safety conditions expressing that the signalling rules of Railnet Denmark are obeyed. This generator utilises the fact that interlocking tables serve as design specifications and contain data that can be used to instantiate generic signalling rules to concrete instances that can serve as safety requirements. More details on the tool and its development can be found in [2].

Related Work. The railway domain has been identified as a grand challenge for computer science, and the modelling, development and verification of interlocking systems has been investigated by many researchers. Different types of interlocking systems (e.g. relay based versus computer based, functional versus geographical, etc) have been modelled using different modelling formalisms and verified using different verification techniques (e.g. theorem proving and model checking). It is out of the scope of this paper to give a complete list of related work. An overview of results and trends in 2003 can be found in [3], and more recent results can be found in proceedings like [14] and book chapters like [8,17].

Several other research groups [18,13,9,12,5] have also investigated interlocking systems having interlocking tables as design specifications. They are among others concerned with the verification of the interlocking tables. Their approach for verification is to translate the tables into execution/design models for interlocking systems (typically by instantiating generic models with data from the tables) and verify by model checking that these models satisfy high-level safety requirements such as no collisions and no derailments. Furthermore, [9] studies the applicability bounds for the NuSMV and SPIN model checkers when applied to such verification problems.

Hence, a main difference between their and our verification approach is that their interlocking models are derived from the interlocking tables (i.e. from the design specification) while our models are derived from the relay circuit diagrams for the implementation. Instead of using interlocking tables for generating interlocking models, we use them for generating requirements (LTL formula) in terms of signalling. Like the others, we also check for no collisions and no derailments.

Eriksson [7] has also formally verified relay based interlocking systems by deriving a model from the relay circuits, but he used theorem proving and not model checking for the verification.

Paper Overview. First, in Section 2, an informal introduction to train route based interlocking is given. Then, in section 3, the state space of the formal models is stated, and in Section 4 the condition generator tool is described. Section 5 reports on how the tool has been applied in the verification of the interlocking system for Stenstrup station in Denmark, and finally, in Section 6 some conclusions are drawn.

2   Train Route Based Interlocking Systems

In this paper we consider a class of interlocking systems (DSB type 1954) used for many Danish stations. These systems are based on a concept of train routes and

implemented by relay based electrical circuits. In this section a short introduction
to these systems is given.

2.1   The Physical Domain of a Station

The physical domain under control consists of the railway tracks, points and
signals. The tracks are divided into sections, each having a track circuit for
detecting whether or not it is occupied by a train. The points can be switched
between two positions: plus (i.e. straight) and minus (i.e. branching), and the
signals can give proceed and stop indications by lights in coloured lamps.

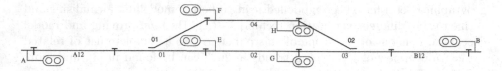

Fig. 2. Track layout diagram for Stenstrup station

Fig. 2 shows a (simplified) track layout diagram for a typical station (Stenstrup station in Denmark). The track layout diagram outlines the geographical
arrangement of the tracks and track-side equipment such as track circuits, points,
and signals. From the diagram it can be seen that Stenstrup has six track circuits
(named A12, 01, 02, 03, 04, and B12), two points (named 01 and 02), and six
signals (named A, B, E, F, G, and H).

2.2   Train Route Based Interlocking

The task of an interlocking system is to control points and signals such that
train collisions and derailments are avoided. The interlocking systems we are
considering use a *train route based* approach to achieve do that. The basic ideas
of this approach are:

- Trains should drive on predefined *routes* through the network.
- Each route is covered by an entry signal that indicates whether it is allowed
  for a train to enter the route or not. Trains are assumed to respect the
  signals.
- Two trains must never be allowed to drive on conflicting (e.g. overlapping)
  routes at the same time. *(To prevent collisions.)*
- Before a train is allowed to enter a route, the points in the route must be
  locked in positions making the route connected (i.e. it is physically possible
  to go from one end of the route to the other end without derailing), and
  the route must be empty (i.e. there are no trains on the route). *(To prevent
  derailments and collisions, respectively.)*
- The points of a route must not be switched while a train is driving on the
  route. *(To prevent derailments.)*

2.3   Interlocking Tables

For each station an *interlocking table* specifies the train routes of the station and for each of these routes (1) the conditions for when the train route can be locked (reserved), (2) the conditions for when the entry signal of the route is set to show a proceed aspect, (3) the conditions for when the entry signal of the route is set back to show a stop aspect, and (4) the conditions for releasing the train route again.

The interlocking table serves as a design specification of the interlocking system. Hence, it is used by the engineers who design the electrical circuits of the interlocking system, and it is used by the test team who tests that the implicit requirements of the table hold for the implemented interlocking system.

The aim of the generator tool we describe in this paper is to derive explicit, formal requirements from an interlocking table such that they can be formally verified to hold for a formal model of the behaviour of the implemented interlocking system. The formal model is generated from the circuit diagrams by other generators (see [11]) of our tool set.

Fig. 3 shows a (simplified) interlocking table for Stenstrup station. The interlocking table has one row for each train route. For each route

- the **Route** sub-columns contain basic information about the train route such as its identification number,
- the **Signals** sub-columns state (1) which signals (the entry signal and any distant signal for this) should be set to a proceed aspect when the conditions for entering the route are met, and (2) which signals must be set to a stop

Route			Signals						Track isolations						Points		Stop	Route release	
Id	From	To	A	B	E	F	G	H	A12	01	02	04	03	B12	01	02		Init	Final
2	A	G	gr			re	re		↑	↑	↑		↑	↑	+	+	A:A12	↓01,↑02	↓02,↑01
3	A	H	gr		re			re	↑	↑		↑	↑	↑	-	-	A:A12	↓01,↑04	↓04,↑01
5	B	E		gr	re			re	↑	↑	↑		↑	↑	+	+	B:B12	↓03,↑02	↓02,↑03
6	B	F		gr		re	re		↑	↑		↑	↑	↑	-	-	B:B12	↓03,↑04	↓04,↑03
7	E	A		gr	re				↑	↑					+		E:01	↓01,↑A12	↓A12,↑01
8	F	A		re	gr				↑	↑					-		F:01	↓01,↑A12	↓A12,↑01
9	G	B					gr	re					↑	↑	+		G:03	↓03,↑B12	↓B12,↑03
10	H	B					re	gr					↑	↑	-		H:03	↓03,↑B12	↓B12,↑03

Route Conflicts							
2							
3	○ 3						
5	○	○ 5					
6	○	○	○ 6				
7	○	○		○ 7			
8	○	○	○		○ 8		
9		○	○	○		9	
10	○		○	○			○ 10

Fig. 3. Interlocking table (divided in two parts) for Stenstrup station

aspect (to provide flank protection) before the entry signal can be set to proceed (**gr** means green light (indicating proceed) and **re** means red light (indicating stop)),

- the **Points** sub-columns state required positions of points (+ means straight position and - means branching position) for the route to be connected (and possibly also flank protected),
- the **Track isolations** columns state with an ↑ which track sections must be unoccupied for the route and its safety distance to be empty,
- the **Stop** column specifies that a certain signal (the entry signal of the route) should be switched to a stop aspect when a certain track section (the first section of the route) becomes occupied,
- the **Route release** columns define conditions for when the train route can be released (to be explained in section 4), and
- the **Route conflicts** marks with the symbol ∘ which routes are conflicting.

One of our data validator tools can be used to check that such an interlocking table contains suitable data, e.g. that overlapping routes are marked as being conflicting.

3   State Space

3.1   States of Relays

The relays in the circuits implementing an interlocking system change state over time as reaction to input from the environment. The possible states of a relay are: drawn or dropped.

In the relay circuits there are relays monitoring the states of the track side equipment:

- For each point P, there are two relays $plusP$ and $minusP$ that are true when and only when P is in the plus and the minus position, respectively.
- For each track section t, there is a relay t that is drawn when and only when the track section is unoccupied.
- For each signal signal S, there are two relays $RedS$ and $GreenS$ that are drawn when and only when there is a red light and a green light in S, respectively.

There are also relays storing the internal state of the interlocking system. For instance, there are relays keeping track of which routes are locked. For some interlocking systems, there is one locking relay for each route, however, for systems of DSB type 1954, some routes share a relay. We will use the notation $l(x)$ to denote the locking relay associated with a route x. A locking relay l is dropped, when and only when one of the train routes x associated with l is locked. Which of the routes is locked is determined by the point settings: Route x is locked, when $l(x)$ is dropped and the points settings are as required for route x according to the interlocking table.[2]

---

[2] Note: two routes can only share a locking relay when at least one point is required to be set in different positions for the two routes.

As an example, for Stenstrup station there are four locking relays, ia (for routes 2 and 3), ib (for routes 5 and 6), ua (for routes 7 and 8), and ub (for routes 9 and 10).

3.2 State Variables

The safety requirements that will be formalised in this paper can be expressed in terms of the states of the relays mentioned above.

As a relay can be in one of two states, drawn or dropped, we introduce

– a Boolean variable r for each relay r in the circuit diagrams

When a relay variable r is **true/false**, it models that the associated relay is drawn/dropped.

Furthermore, we introduce a Boolean variable $idle$. When it is true, it models that the interlocking system is in an idle state waiting for new input.

The formal model generated from the circuit diagrams and track layout diagram describes the possible state changes of all the introduced variables.

4 Safety Requirements

This section describes which formal requirements the generator tool derives from an interlocking table (that has been checked by the data validator tool). The formal requirements are formulae in LTL, expressed as conditions on the relay variables keeping the state of points, track sections, signals, and route lockings. They express safety conditions at the design level (i.e. concrete instances of the general signalling principles) that an interlocking system must satisfy.

In each subsection below, first a general signalling principle is stated informally, then it is explained how formal, concrete instances of this can be generated by instantiating a formal condition pattern with data from a given interlocking table, and finally an example of this is given for the interlocking table for Stenstrup in Fig. 3.

In the formal condition patterns the following notation will be used for a route x:

– $RouteLocked_x = \neg l(x) \wedge PointsSet_x$
– $PointsSet_x$: a condition expressing that the points of x are set as required according to the "Points" fields for x in the interlocking table.
– $TracksFree_x$: a condition expressing that the track sections of x are unoccupied as required according to the "Track isolations" fields for x in the interlocking table.
– $SignalsSet_x$: a condition expressing that the covering signals of x are set to a stop aspect as required according to the "Signals" fields for x in the interlocking table.

4.1 Locking of Conflicting Routes

Principle: *When a train route x is locked, none of its conflicting routes y must be locked.*

For each route x, this is expressed by a condition of the following form:

$$G(RouteLocked_x \Rightarrow \bigwedge_{y \in ConflictingRoutes(x)} \neg RouteLocked_y) \tag{1}$$

where $ConflictingRoutes(x)$ is the set of routes that are in conflict with x according to the interlocking table.

Example. Applying this principle to train route 2 for Stenstrup, the generated condition will be in the following form as the route is in conflict with train routes 3, 5, 6, 7, 8 and 10 according to the interlocking table for Stenstrup:

$G(RouteLocked\_2 \Rightarrow$
$\quad \neg\ RouteLocked_3 \land$
$\quad \neg\ RouteLocked_5 \land$
$\quad \neg\ RouteLocked_6 \land$
$\quad \neg\ RouteLocked_7 \land$
$\quad \neg\ RouteLocked_8 \land$
$\quad \neg\ RouteLocked_{10})$

Expanding each of the expressions $RouteLocked_y$ using the data in the interlocking table, this gives

$G(\neg\ ia \land plus01 \land plus02 \Rightarrow$
$\quad \neg\ (\neg\ ia \land minus01 \land minus02) \land$
$\quad \neg\ (\neg\ ib \land\ plus01 \land plus02) \land$
$\quad \neg\ (\neg\ ib \land\ minus01 \land minus02) \land$
$\quad \neg\ (\neg\ ua \land\ plus01) \land$
$\quad \neg\ (\neg\ ua \land\ minus01) \land$
$\quad \neg\ (\neg\ ub \land minus02)$
$)$

which can be reduced to[3]:

$G(\neg\ ia \land plus01 \land plus02 \Rightarrow ib \land ua)$

4.2 Locking and Points Positions

Principle: *When a locking relay l is dropped, one of the routes x, which is controlled by l, must have the points of that route set as required for route x according to the interlocking table.* (This implies that a route can't be locked before its points are set.)

---

[3] We can make this reduction as we are also verifying $G(\neg\ (plusP \land minusP))$ for each point P.

For each locking relay l, this is expressed by a condition of the following form:

$$G(\neg l \Rightarrow \bigvee_{x \in Routes(l)} PointsSet_x) \tag{2}$$

where $Routes(l)$ is the set of routes x controlled by l, i.e. for which $l(x) = l$.

Example. Applying this principle to locking relay ia for Stenstrup, the following condition is generated as routes 2 and 3 are the routes controlled by ia:

G($\neg$ ia $\Rightarrow$ (plus01 $\wedge$ plus02) $\vee$ (minus01 $\wedge$ minus02))

The condition expresses that when ia is dropped, points 01 and 02 are either both set in the plus position or both set in the minus position as required by the interlocking table for routes 2 and 3, respectively.

4.3   Signal Aspects

Only certain combinations of lights are allowed aspects of the signals.

Principle: *A signal must never display a red light and green light at the same time.*

For each signal S, this is expressed by a condition of the following form:

$$G(idle \Rightarrow \neg(RedS \wedge GreenS)) \tag{3}$$

Example. Applying this principle to signal A for Stenstrup, the following condition is generated:

G(idle $\Rightarrow$ $\neg$ (RedA $\wedge$ GreenA))

Principle: *When the green light is turned off in a signal S, the red light must be turned on.*

For each signal S, this is expressed by a condition of the following form:

$$G(idle \wedge \neg GreenS \Rightarrow RedS) \tag{4}$$

Example. Applying this principle to signal A for Stenstrup, the following condition is generated:

G(idle $\wedge$ $\neg$ GreenA $\Rightarrow$ RedA)

4.4 Proceed Signal

Principle: *When a signal S shows a proceed aspect, one of the routes x, starting from S, must be ready for use, i.e. (1) the route x must be locked, (2) all the track sections of the route must be unoccupied as stated in the interlocking table, and (3) all covering signals of the route must show a stop aspect as stated in the interlocking table.*

For each signal S, this is expressed by a condition of the following form:

$$G(idle \wedge GreenS \Rightarrow \bigvee_{x \in Routes(S)} RouteLocked_x \wedge TracksFree_x \wedge SignalsSet_x) \quad (5)$$

where $Routes(S)$ is the set of routes starting from signal S.

From the condition, it can be derived that the green light must be turned off when the right-hand side becomes false. As it takes time for the system to turn the green light off, *idle* has been included on the left-hand side of the implication.

Example. Applying this principle to signal A, a condition of the following form is generated as train routes 2 and 3 start from signal A:

G(idle $\wedge$ GreenA $\Rightarrow$
  $(RouteLocked_2 \wedge TracksFree_2 \wedge SignalsSet_2) \vee$
  $(RouteLocked_3 \wedge TracksFree_3 \wedge SignalsSet_3))$

Expanding each of the sub-formulae using the data in the train route table, this gives:

G(idle $\wedge$ GreenA $\Rightarrow$
  $((\neg$ia $\wedge$ plus01 $\wedge$ plus02) $\wedge$
    (A12 $\wedge$ 01 $\wedge$ 02 $\wedge$ 03 $\wedge$ B12) $\wedge$
    (RedF $\wedge$ RedG)
)
  $\vee$
  $((\neg$ia $\wedge$ minus01 $\wedge$ minus02) $\wedge$
    (A12 $\wedge$ 01 $\wedge$ 04 $\wedge$ 03 $\wedge$ B12) $\wedge$
    (RedE $\wedge$ RedH)
)
)

4.5 Stop Signal

Principle: *When the track section, $StopIsolation_x$, specified in the "Stop" field for route x in the interlocking table, is occupied in an idle state, the signal S_x in the same field must show a stop aspect.*

For each route x, this is expressed by a condition of the following form:

$$G(idle \land \neg\, StopIsolation_x \Rightarrow RedS_x) \tag{6}$$

In the condition it is necessary to include *idle* on the left-hand side of the implication in order to give the system time to change the setting of the signal as a reaction on the occupation of $StopIsolation_x$.

Example. Applying this principle to route 2 for Stenstrup, the following condition is generated:

G(idle $\land \; \neg$ A12 $\Rightarrow$ RedA)

It expresses that when track section A12 (the first section of the route) is occupied by a train (or another object), then the entry signal, A, must show a stop aspect.

Principle: *When the setting of the entry signal S of a locked route x is changed from proceed (green) to stop (red), it must keep this setting at least until the train route has been released.*

For each signal S and route $x \in Routes(S)$, this is expressed by a condition of the following form:

$$G(idle \land \neg\, L_x \land GreenS \land X(RedS) \Rightarrow X(U(RedS, L_x))) \tag{7}$$

where $L_x = l(x)$ is the locking relay of x.

The generation of the latter kind of conditions has not yet been implemented in the generator tool, but we have verified that the conditions are trivially true for Stenstrup station.

4.6   Train Route Release

Before a locked train route can be released, the two last sections $t1$ and $t2$ of the route must first have been in a state (called the *release start state*) where $t1$ is occupied and $t2$ is unoccupied, and then in a state (called the *release end state*) where $t1$ is unoccupied and $t2$ is occupied. This sequence of states is called the release sequence. This sequence will happen when a train passes the second last track section and ends on the last track section of the route. The "Route release" columns of the interlocking table states the release start and end states for each train route.

Principle: *When a train route has been locked, the route must not be released before the release sequence for the route has taken place.*

For each route x, this is expressed by a condition of the following form:

$$G(L_x \wedge X(RouteLocked_x \wedge F(L_x)) \Rightarrow$$
$$X($$
$$\quad U(\neg L_x,$$
$$\quad\quad \neg L_x \wedge Init_x \wedge$$
$$\quad\quad\quad X(U(\neg L_x, \neg L_x \wedge End_x))$$
$$\quad)$$
$$\quad)$$
$$)$$

where $L_x = l(x)$ is the locking relay of x, $Init_x$ is a condition expressing the release start state for x, End_x is a condition expressing the release end state for x, U is the LTL until operator and X is the next state operator.

Example. Applying this principle to train route 2 for Stenstrup Station, the following condition is generated:

$$G(ia \wedge X((\neg ia \wedge plus01 \wedge plus02) \wedge F(ia)) \Rightarrow$$
$$X($$
$$\quad U(\neg ia,$$
$$\quad\quad \neg ia \wedge (\neg 01 \wedge 02) \wedge X(U(\neg ia, \neg ia \wedge (01 \wedge \neg 02))))$$
$$\quad)$$
$$)$$

The left hand side of the implication says that route 2 is not locked (i.e. ia is true) in the current state, it becomes locked (i.e. ¬ ia ∧ plus01 ∧ plus02) in the next state and later on it becomes released (unlocked) again. The right-hand side says that in the next state the route will stay locked at least until the release start state (where track section 01 is occupied and track section 02 is unoccupied) and in the state after this release start state, the route will continue being locked until the release end state where track section 01 is again unoccupied and track section 02 has been occupied.

5   Experiments

We applied the developed condition generator to the interlocking table (shown in Fig. 3) for Stenstrup station in Denmark. In this way 46 conditions were generated. We also applied other condition generators from our tool set to generate 152 other desired properties from the station documentation. Furthermore, we applied yet other generator tools from our tool set to generate a transition system model for the behaviour of the implemented relay interlocking system (described by 18 circuit diagrams) and its environment (allowing operator input and an arbitrary number of trains driving according to the traffic rules). This model had 71 Boolean variables and 141 transition rules. We then used the SAL model checker [1] to verify that the generated model satisfied the 198 generated conditions. All conditions turned out to be valid.

The total execution time for model checking the 46 interlocking table conditions and the 152 other conditions were 132 seconds and 1485 seconds, respectively, when measured with the LinuxMint12 `time` command on a Lenovo T410.

According to the signalling engineers it would last about a month to validate the circuit diagrams for Stenstrup station by their traditional manual inspection, and they would only check a small part of our 198 conditions. So it is really much faster to use our tools.

We also tried to introduce some design flaws in the relay circuits to demonstrate that these can be found by using our tools. E.g. we introduced flaws such that a signal could reach a state where both the red light and the green light were turned on at the same time. In this case the model checker detected that the signal aspect condition in formula (3) was broken for that signal.

6 Conclusions

Summary. This paper has described a tool component of a tool set that supports formal verification of relay interlocking systems.

Given the interlocking table of a relay interlocking system, the tool can automatically generate formal safety requirements for the implementation of the relay interlocking system. The requirements express that the signalling rules are followed. Other tool components of the tool set can be used to generate a formal model of an implemented interlocking system and its environment. Having generated the requirements and the model, a model checker can be used to verify that these requirements always hold for the formal model.

To use such an automated, formal verification approach is a great improvement compared to manual inspections of interlocking tables, track layout diagrams and circuit diagrams: It is much faster and less error prone, it is much more complete wrt. what is being checked, and the checking it-self is exhaustive considering all possible scenarios. The approach has successfully been applied to the relay interlocking system for Stenstrup station.

Although the condition generator tool has been developed for a certain type of interlocking systems (the relay based DSB type 1954), it is expected that it can easily be adapted to other DSB types of interlocking systems that are based on similar interlocking tables as the safety conditions for these systems are basically the same.

Future Work. The current tool set has been used for a proof-of-concept. To be used in industry, further development needs to be done, e.g. a better user interface should be provided.

We plan to apply the tools to larger stations to test to which extent the method is scalable without state space explosion problems. In case of state space explosion, techniques such as compositional reasoning and induction to avoid that should be investigated. One idea could be to combine bounded model checking with inductive reasoning, as done in [12].

We also plan to make a similar tool set for the new ERTMS based signalling systems that are going to be implemented in Denmark over the next decade.

Acknowledgements. I would like to thank Kirsten Mark Hansen for providing the initial idea for this project and for many valuable discussions when she was employed at Railnet Denmark. Special thanks go to my former students Morten Aanæs and Hoang Phuong Thai who developed the first version of the generator tool described in this paper in their master thesis project supervised by me. The functionality of the tool was inspired by another master thesis made by my former students Marie Le Bliguet and Andreas A. Kjær. Finally, I would like to thank the reviewers for valuable comments to a previous version of this paper.

References

1. Symbolic Analysis Laboratory, SAL, home page (2001), http://sal.csl.sri.com
2. Aanæs, M., Thai, H.P.: Modelling and Verification of Relay Interlocking Systems. Technical Report IMM-MSC-2012-14, DTU Informatics, Technical University of Denmark, Master thesis supervised by Anne Haxthausen, ah@imm.dtu.dk (2012)
3. Bjørner, D.: New Results and Current Trends in Formal Techniques for the Development of Software for Transportation Systems. In: Proceedings of the Symposium on Formal Methods for Railway Operation and Control Systems (FORMS 2003), Budapest, Hungary, May 15-16, L'Harmattan Hongrie (2003)
4. Bliguet, M.L., Kjær, A.A.: Modelling Interlocking Systems for Railway Stations. Technical Report IMM-M.Sc.-2008-68, DTU Informatics, Technical University of Denmark, Master thesis supervised by Anne Haxthausen, ah@imm.dtu.dk (2008)
5. Cao, Y., Xu, T., Tang, T., Wang, H., Zhao, L.: Automatic Generation and Verification of Interlocking Tables Based on Domain Specific Language for Computer Based Interlocking Systems (DSL-CBI). In: Proceedings of the IEEE International Conference on Computer Science and Automation Engineering (CSAE 2011), pp. 511–515. IEEE (2011)
6. Clarke, E.M., Grumberg, O., Peled, D.: Model Checking. MIT Press (1999)
7. Eriksson, L.-H.: Using Formal Methods in a Retrospective Safety Case. In: Heisel, M., Liggesmeyer, P., Wittmann, S. (eds.) SAFECOMP 2004. LNCS, vol. 3219, pp. 31–44. Springer, Heidelberg (2004)
8. Fantechi, A.: The Role of Formal Methods in Software Development for Railway Applications. In: Railway Safety, Reliability and Security: Technologies and System Engineering, pp. 282–297. IGI Global (2012)
9. Ferrari, A., Magnani, G., Grasso, D., Fantechi, A.: Model Checking Interlocking Control Tables. In: Schnieder, E., Tarnai, G. (eds.) Proceedings of Formal Methods for Automation and Safety in Railway and Automotive Systems (FORMS/FORMAT 2010)), Braunschweig, Germany. Springer (2011)
10. Haxthausen, A.E.: Towards a Framework for Modelling and Verification of Relay Interlocking Systems. In: Calinescu, R., Jackson, E. (eds.) Monterey Workshop 2010. LNCS, vol. 6662, pp. 176–192. Springer, Heidelberg (2011)
11. Haxthausen, A.E., Kjær, A.A., Le Bliguet, M.: Formal Development of a Tool for Automated Modelling and Verification of Relay Interlocking Systems. In: Butler, M., Schulte, W. (eds.) FM 2011. LNCS, vol. 6664, pp. 118–132. Springer, Heidelberg (2011)

12. Haxthausen, A.E., Peleska, J., Kinder, S.: A Formal Approach for the Construction and Verification of Railway Control Systems. Formal Aspects of Computing 23(2), 191–219 (2011), The article is also available electronically on SpringerLink, http://www.springerlink.com/openurl.asp?genre=article &id=doi:10.1007/s00165-009-0143-6
13. Mirabadi, A., Yazdi, M.B.: Automatic Generation and Verification of Railway Interlocking Control Tables using FSM and NuSMV. Transportation Problems, 103–110 (2009)
14. Schnieder, E., Tarnai, G. (eds.): Proceedings of Formal Methods for Automation and Safety in Railway and Automotive Systems (FORMS/FORMAT 2010), Braunschweig, Germany. Springer (2011)
15. The RAISE Language Group. The RAISE Specification Language. The BCS Practitioners Series. Prentice Hall Int. (1992)
16. The RAISE Method Group. The RAISE Development Method. The BCS Practitioners Series. Prentice Hall Int. (1995)
17. Winter, K.: Symbolic Model Checking for Interlocking Systems. In: Railway Safety, Reliability and Security: Technologies and System Engineering, pp. 298–315. IGI Global (2012)
18. Winter, K., Johnston, W., Robinson, P., Strooper, P., van den Berg, L.: Tool Support for Checking Railway Interlocking Designs. In: Proceedings of the 10th Australian Workshop on Safety Critical Systems and Software, SCS 2005, Darlinghurst, Australia, Australia, vol. 55, pp. 101–107. Australian Computer Society, Inc. (2006)

Distributing the Challenge of Model Checking Interlocking Control Tables

Alessandro Fantechi

DSI - University of Florence

Abstract. Railway interlocking systems represent a challenge for model checkers: although encoding interlocking rules as finite state machines can be quite straightforward, and safety properties to be proved are easily expressible, the inherent complexity related to the high number of variables involved makes the verification of such systems typically incur state space explosion problems.

Domain-specific techniques have been adopted to advance the size of interlocking systems that can be successfully proved, but still not reaching the size needed for large deployment cases.

We propose a novel approach in which we exploit a distributed modelling of an interlocking system and a careful selection of verification scenarios, so that parallel verifications conducted on multiple processors can address systems of a large size. Some experiments in this direction are presented and new directions of research according to this proposal are discussed.

1 Introduction

In the railway signaling domain, an *interlocking* is the safety-critical system that controls the movement of trains in a station and between adjacent stations. The interlocking monitors the status of the objects in the railway yard (e.g., points, switches, track circuits) and allows or denies the routing of trains in accordance with the railway safety and operational regulations that are generic for the region or country where the interlocking is located. The instantiation of these rules on a station topology is stored in the part of the system named *control table*, that is specific for the station where the system resides [22] [21]. Control tables of modern computerized interlockings are implemented by means of iteratively executed software controls over the status of the yard objects.

Verification of correctness of control tables has always been a central issue for formal methods practitioners, and the literature counts the application of several techniques to the problem, namely the Vienna Development Method (VDM) [10], property proving [5, 9], Colored Petri Nets (CPN) [1] and model checking [24] [17, 19]. This last technique in particular has raised the interest of many railway signaling industries, being the most lightweight from the process point of view, and being rather promising in terms of efficiency. Nevertheless, application of model checking for the verification of safety properties has been successfully conducted only on small case studies, often requiring the application of domain-related heuristics based on topology decomposition. The literature is

T. Margaria and B. Steffen (Eds.): ISoLA 2012, Part II, LNCS 7610, pp. 276–289, 2012.

however quite scarce on data concerning the size of interlocking systems that have been successfully proved with model checking techniques. This because of confidentiality reasons, and because the reported experiences refer to specific case studies, with a limited possibility of scaling the obtaining results to larger systems. In a previous work [8], we investigated more systematically the actual applicability bounds for widely used model checkers on this class of systems, by studying the typical characteristics of control tables and their size parameters, by comparing the performances of two popular general purpose model checkers, the symbolic model checker NuSMV [6] and the explicit model checker SPIN [13]. A test set of generic control table models of increasing complexity has been defined and translated into the input language of the two tools, and generic safety properties have been proved on them by the two model checkers. The results have confirmed that the bound on the size of the controlled yard that can be safely addressed by the two tools is still rather small, making general purpose model checking tools not usable for medium and large scale interlockings.

These results are in accordance with those obtained by several concurrent studies. Indeed, [25, 23, 24] show that specifically optimized verification techniques allow the range of verifiable systems to be expanded. SAT-based verification techniques appear to be more promising in this direction, but still large scale interlocking systems pose a big challenge.

In this paper we address the problem from a different perspective: elaborating on the geographic approach to model interlocking systems (orthogonal w.r.t. control table-based approaches, but anyway adopted by industry in several cases), we exploit a distributed modelling approach. Some verification scenarios are then defined on such models, which require a limited verification effort, while at the same time are representative enough of real verification efforts. Preliminary results obtained with an on-the-fly model checker are discussed and hints for a general strategy, employing parallel verification runs, to verify medium/large scale interlocking systems are given.

2   Interlocking Systems Representation

In Relay Interlocking Systems (RIS), still operating in several sites, the logical rules of the control tables were implemented by means of physical relay connections. With Computer Interlocking Systems (CIS), in application since 30 years, the control table becomes a set of software equations that are executed by the interlocking. Since the signaling regulations of the various countries were already defined in graphical form for the RIS, and also in order to facilitate the representation of control tables by signaling engineers, the design of CISs has usually adopted traditional graphical representations such as ladder logic diagrams [9] [15] and relay diagrams [12]. These graphical schemata, usually called *principle schemata*, are instantiated on a station topology to build the control table, that is then translated into a program for the interlocking. In Table 1 a few lines of the control table related to the reported layout are shown; such lines describe the relations between the indicated route and the different entities (track circuits, points, signals) of the layout.

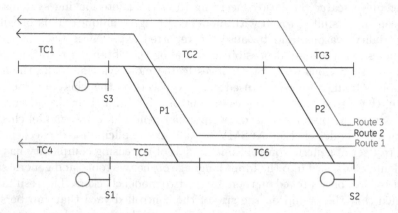

Table 1. An example Control Table

Route	S IN	S OUT	Aspect	S Ahead	Tracks	P N	P R
1	S2	S1	Y/G	R/Y	TC4 TC5 TC6	P1 P2	-
2	S2	S3	Y/G	R/Y	TC6 TC2 TC1	P2	P1
3	S2	S3	Y/G	R/Y	TC3 TC2 TC1	P1	P2

As pointed out in [9], the graphical representations and the related control tables can be reduced to a set of boolean equations of the form $x_i := x_j \wedge \ldots \wedge x_{j+k}$, where $x_j \ldots x_{j+k}$ are boolean variables in the form x or $\neg x$. The variables represent the possible states of the signalling elements monitored by the control table [20]: they might be system input, output or temporary variables. The equations are conditional checks over the current and expected status of the controlled elements.

Correctness of control tables depends also on their model of execution by the interlocking software. In building CISs, the manufacturers adopt the principle of *as safe as the relay based equipment* [1], and often the implemented model of execution is very close to the hardware behaviour. The model of execution, inherited by the typical execution of a ladder diagram, is a state machine where equations are executed one after the other in a cyclic manner and all the variables are set at the beginning of each cycle and do not change their actual value until the next cycle.

In this way, the equations can be seen as interpreted by a reasoner engine. The reasoner engine is the same for every plant; the control table is coded as data, actually boolean equations, for the reasoner. Behind this choice is the minimization of certification efforts: the reasoner is certified once for all, the data are considered "easier" to certify if they can be related in some way to the standard principle schemata adopted by railway engineers in the era of relay-based interlockings. For this reason, this approach is also referred as "data-driven". We want to stress anyway that looking at equations as data may induce the false consideration that certification of such data is easy. However, such data is actually a program interpreted by the reasoner, hence certification of this kind of data is no different from certification of a program. If we adopt formal verification, it is actually the complexity of the control table that gives the complexity of the problem.

In order to give a metric to the dimension of the problem in terms of parameters of the control tables, [8] defines the *size* of a control table as the couple (m, n), where m is the maximum number of inter-dependent equations involved, that means equations that, taken in pairs, have at least one variable in common, and n is the number of inputs of the control table. Another used metric is just the size of the layout, given as the number of physical entities that constitute the layout (points, track circuits, signals,..) and the number of routes that are established on the layout.

It is not easy to relate the two metrics, since the style of definition of the control tables, the characteristics of the physical entities and the regional/national signalling rules can make the number of equations considerably vary for similar layouts.

A very rough classification can be given between *small layouts* (in the order of a few tens of entities and ten routes, which correspond to a few tens of equations with tens of inputs), *medium layouts* (in the order of one hundred entities and a few tens of routes, which correspond to hundreds of equations with one hundred of inputs) and *large layouts* (several hundreds of entities, tens of routes, which correspond to thousands of equations with a thousand inputs). Systems of the latter size are often addressed, even in the system design phase, by slicing them into (still quite large) subsystems related to different zones of the layout. Indeed, slicing algorithms specifically aimed at optimization of formal verification have been described in [23]. Clearly, slicing can be applied only if the actual topology of the tracks layout and the interlocking functionality do separate concerns about different zones of the layout, with little interactions among them.

3 Safety Requirements

Safety requirements of signaling principles are typically expressed in the principle schemata or in the regulations. This kind of properties have shown to be representable in Computation Tree Logic (CTL) in the CTL-AGAX form: $AG(p \rightarrow AXq)$, where p and q are predicates on the variables of our model [11]. Intuitively, they represent fail-safe conditions, i.e., events that should happen on the next state if some unsafe condition occurs [7]. One of the typical safety properties that is normally required to be verified is the *no-derailment property*: while a train is crossing a point the point shall not change its position. This typical system level requirement can be easily represented in the AGAX form [24]:

$$AG(occupied(tc_i) \wedge setting(p_i) = val \rightarrow AX(setting(p_i) = val))$$

"whenever the track circuit tc_i associated to a point p_i is occupied, and the point has the proper setting val, this setting shall remain the same on the next state".

Another typical safety property for interlockings is *no-collision*: two routes that conflict on a track circuit cannot both be reserved at the same time (possibly allowing two trains to collide), expressed in the classic AG form:

$$AG \sim (reserved(route_i) \wedge reserved(route_j))$$

To check that safety properties are verified represents the worst case for a model checker: explicit and symbolic model checkers are challenged by verification of safety properties [23], since, in order to show their correctness, they have to explore the entire state space, or its symbolic representation.

We can note that certification of the correctness of a control table is the aim of this effort, and not bug-hunting, that is, finding counterexamples. Indeed control tables built by a competent signalling engineer rarely contain bugs, but it is the absolute certainty that bugs are not there which is sought for certification.

4   Limits of Model Checking

In a previous work [8], we investigated more systematically the actual applicability bounds for widely used model checkers on this class of systems, studying the typical characteristics of control tables and their size parameters, and comparing the performances of two popular general purpose model checkers, the symbolic model checker NuSMV [6] and the explicit model checker SPIN [13]. A test set of generic control table models of increasing complexity has been defined and translated into the input language of the two tools, and generic safety properties, such as the *no-collision* and *no-derailment* properties shown in Sect. 3, have been proved on them by the two model checkers.

The experiments have shown that NuSMV with the BDD-based verification algorithms succeeds in verifying systems defined at most by 70 equations with 15 inputs. SPIN behaves slightly better, reaching 80 equations and 20 inputs without using any memory oriented optimization. The usage of such optimization increases the limit of applicability to about 100 equations and 60 inputs.

In conclusion, traditional model checking tools hardly scale to verify medium size interlocking systems.

The better results reported in [22–25] are achieved within NuSMV by customising the ordering of state variables occurring in the BDD. The BDD variable ordering strategies adopted exploit *locality* exhibited by correlations of variables according to a pattern that follows the topology of the track layout information. The improvements obtained with such variable ordering strategies allow an interlocking with 41 routes, 9 points, 19 signals, and 31 track circuits to be verified, a size that was not tractable with standard variable orderings.

Another direction of improvement can be the use of different verification algorithms, such as the SAT-based ones: unpublished results of experiments conducted along the lines of [8] show that the NuSMV SAT-based solver behaves much better than that of the BDD-based one, so that a size of 200 equations with 20 inputs can be addressed. The SAT-based solver is used in a Bounded Model Checking scheme which cannot prove safety properties unless the bound is deep enough to cover all the cycles of the model. The depth for the conducted experiments has been limited to 60, on the basis of memory capacity problems for the most complex equation systems.

A few experiments conducted within General Electric Transportation Systems on Stateflow models of real medium scale interlocking systems with Mathworks' Design Verifier (based on a SAT engine by Prover Technology) show this tool is able to deal with such models, although apparently at the limits of its capacity. Actual figures are not available.

Indeed Prover Technology has launched a commercial solution (Ilock) for the production of interlocking software, that includes formal proofs, by means of a SAT solving engine, of safety conditions. Bounds on the addressable size of the controlled yard and strategies used to address large state spaces are not known. [18] reports the use of such solution on a quite complex system, part of the Paris Metro. Several difficulties in addressing such a complex case are reported, although size and evaluation time figures are not disclosed.

Anyway, there is still much space for improvements of SAT-based verification of interlockings: for example, an optimized problem-tailored boolean encoding of the equations and of the execution model should be investigated.

5   An Alternative Approach

We have seen that CISs are traditionally seen as centralized systems, that manage a whole station, or a part of it in case of large ones: the interlocking logic, based on control tables, is configuration dependent, but is seen as a monolithic set of equations interpreted by a reasoner engine.

5.1   Geographic Approach

A completely opposed approach is the geographic approach: the interlocking logic is made up by composition of small elements that take care each of the control of a physical element (point, track circuit, signal) and are connected by means of predefined composition rules, mimicking the topology of the specific layout. The global interlocking logic therefore comes out as the result of the composition of the elementary bricks. A known example of this approach is the EURIS language [4] developed in the Netherlands, and later adopted by Siemens, for the GRACE toolset of Siemens [14]. EURIS (European Railway Interlocking Specification) assumes an object-oriented architecture, which consists of a collection of generic building blocks, representing the elements in the infrastructure such as signals and points. The building blocks, which together make up the interlocking logic, communicate with each other by means of messages called telegrams. The building blocks can also exchange telegrams with two separate entities that model the logistic layer and the infrastructure.

Also the definition of generic principles as generic statecharts made by RFF (SNCF) in 2003 goes in this direction, modeling their (relay-based) principle schemata using Statemate, by means of 90 generic statecharts to model interlocking elements [16].

Another more recent example is the formalization of interlocking rules carried out in the INESS project, where UML State Diagrams have been chosen as the modeling language [26].

Indeed, the geographic approach inherits typical modelling criteria from computer science, and can be considered as a *model-based approach*, while control tables inherit the criteria of relay-based functional definition. It is however true that the geographic approach looses the separation between the reasoner engine and the data, with its advantages w.r.t. certification. The relation between control tables and the geographical modelling has been studied in [2], where automated instantiation of geographical models from control tables has been proposed, basing on the generic statecharts developed by RFF-SNCF.

5.2   Distributed Approach

The elements of the geographic approach can be configured as a set of distributed, communicating, processes, in which each distributed process controls a given layout element. The route is instead a global notion: a route has to be established by proper cooperation of the distributed elements; the communication among processes follows the physical layout of the station/yard and a route is established by the status of the elements that lie along the route.

Some experiments have been conducted at DSI on the modelling of the logic of a (simplified) distributed interlocking, using different formalisms such as SCADE, Stateflow and UML State Diagrams, with a route establishment protocol based on the classical two-phase commit (2PC) protocol: the protocol guarantees that the route is established only if all the elements on the route are reserved and locked. The experiments were mainly aimed at evaluating the possibility of formal verification via model checking of basic interlocking safety properties (e.g. no-derailment property).

The model of the layout is composed of a set of track circuits and points (we have avoided signals and other kinds of entities to maintain the model simple), that we call nodes.

Each node is modeled by an object instantiated from a class whose behaviour is represented by a statechart. Each node has among its attributes the set of routes to which it belongs. Each node has two (in case of a track circuit) or three (in case of a point) adjacent nodes. However, for each route it belongs to, the node has only one successor and one predecessor adjacent nodes. If it is a point, for each route it belongs to, the node knows whether it belongs to the route in normal or reverse status.

A route starts in a track-circuit (*start node*) and terminates in another track circuit (*end node*) and is made of adjacent nodes.

The working of the algorithm is basically the following:

- A train is assumed to request a route at its start node. The request is propagated through adjacency by the nodes of the route, in a linear fashion.
- When the request reaches the end node, and if all the nodes are free, the acknowledge message flows back to the start node. At the end of this phase,

all the nodes are reserved for the requesting train, and the points have been commanded to the proper position.

- A second round then is started by the start node to commit the reservation, and after the agree message has flowed back through all the nodes, a consensus message is given to the train that can move safely through the route.
- Either if a node is not free or if the movement of the point does not succeed (this is modelled by simple nondeterminism) the algorithm aborts the request, again by means of an abort message flowing back through the nodes of the route, and the train receives a no go message.

This basic algorithm is then enriched by the possibility to receive a route cancellation message from the train, and by the route liberation actions that make nodes behind the passing train free again.

Figure 1 shows the state diagram model of a track circuit by means of a UML statechart; we can see that a free track circuit, at the reception of a route request, engages in the 2PC protocol in order to become reserved, passing through the sequence of states *waiting ack, waiting commit, waiting agree*. A disagree message or an abort message may prevent the track circuit to reach the *reserved* state. Trigger messages are coming from adjacent nodes (previous or next in the route, according to the relevant phase of the protocol). When reserved, the track circuit goes back to the *free* state after the requesting train has passed. Knowledge on adjacent nodes on each route is stored in arrays *prev* and *next*.

The model of a point is not much different, apart from the fact that it may be commanded in its normal or reverse states, and has three adjacent notes. The model of the complete system is obtained, in compliance with the geographic approach, by instantiating the proper number of points and track circuits, and by setting their attributes (*prev* and *next*) to reflect the network layout, both in terms of adjacency and in terms of established routes.

This modelling approach has allowed us to build several experimental interlocking models of varying size by replicated instantiations of track-circuit and point classes.

5.3   UMC

The tool adopted to evaluate the approach has been UMC [3]. UMC is a framework for formal verification of the dynamic behaviour of UML models: a UML model is defined as a set of concurrently executing UML state machines. UML state machines describe the dynamic aspects of a system component's behaviour. UMC accepts a system specification given in UML-like style as a collection of active objects, modelled by state-machines, and whose behavior is described through statecharts. On such systems UMC allows to verify properties specified in the UCTL logic, a temporal logic which enriches the classical CTL temporal logic with the possibility of expressing properties over actions, and with a rich set of state propositions.The UMC framework adopts an "on-the-fly" approach to generate a Labelled Transition System (LTS) from a UML specification, meaning

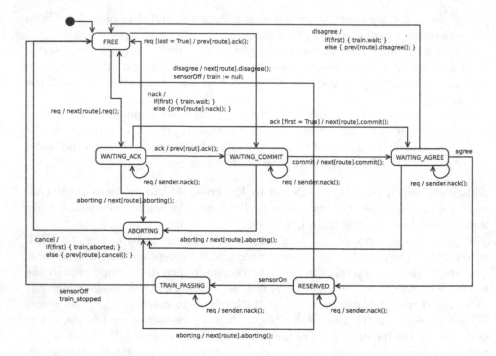

Fig. 1. UML statechart of a track circuit

that the LTS corresponding to the model is generated "on-demand", following either the interactive requests of a user while exploring the system, or the needs of the logical verification engine. However, for proving safety properties as the ones in the AGAX form, it is bound to generate the complete reachable state space.

A complete UMC model description is given by providing a set of class definitions and a set of object instantiations. Class definitions represent a template for the set of active or nonactive objects of the system. In the case of active objects a statechart diagram associated to the class is used to describe the dynamic behaviour of the corresponding objects. A state machine (with its events queue) is associated to each active object of the system.

The UMC model checker defines a textual language for describing a state diagram of a UML class, which is one to one corresponding to the UML graphical syntax. Hence, the UML state diagrams can be directly converted into UMC state machines.

In UML, the behaviour of an object, instantiated from a class to which a statechart is associated, is reactive, that is, can only be activated by triggers and by changes to variables visible through the interfaces. The former are signals exported by the class, and hence can be changed only from external objects, the latter should also be performed by external objects. If we do not include a model of such external objects, the "official" UML semantics of the model shows a null behaviour, that is, the model does not move from its initial state.

The UMC model checker follows strictly this official UML semantics, therefore simply composing the statecharts representing track circuits and points does not allow them to have a not-null behaviour. Hence no interesting properties can be checked over them. We need to add external objects that send the appropriate triggers to the state machines described by the UML state diagrams. This requires in practice to build an exhaustive simulation environment that exercises the defined state charts with all the possible sequences of triggers and variable changes.

In our case, such external objects actually need to mimic the behaviour of trains, that are positioned at input points of routes and request routes. If a route is reserved for a train, the train then moves along the tracks and points that form the route, until the end node of the route is reached. In this respect, the most general environment for our models is the one where a train is initially placed at each input point of any route, and nondeterministically requests one of the routes for which that node is an input point. Such a general environment, due to the high degree of parallelism and nondeterminism involved, is expected to exhibit an important state space explosion.

5.4 Experiments

If we include the model of just a single requesting train and we ask UMC to verify that it eventually reaches its end node, the counterexample/witness facility of UMC confirms that such a typical success computation, related to the establishment of a route and the movement of the train along the route, traverses a number of states which is linear in the length of the route. A source of nondeterministic choice along such a linear sequence of states is the possibility that a command to a point is not completely actuated, so that a disagree message flows back to the train.

If we run experiments with two trains, notwithstanding the quadratic state space size required by the interleaving, and the explicit state space representation of UMC (which in the case of AG properties is not taking advantage from the on-the-fly construction), we are still able to prove safety properties on models in the low end of the "medium" size. Table 2 reports a few results on different models (one of them is the full model built along the criteria listed above, the other ones are simplified in the sense that they do not consider cancellation of a route requests).

Table 2. Some UMC verification results

		nodes	nodes on routes	diameter	property	generated states	time (sec.)
Model A	Simplified	30	18	354	no-collision	35293	0.00003
Model B	Simplified	90	45	827	no-collision	>19941626	> 3 days
Model C	Full	9	7	394	no-collision	72052	15.693425
					no-derailment	72052	20.177162

We can see that Model B hits the limits of the tool, that we found are currently around $2 * 10^7$ states, not succeeding in proving no-collision. On this model, the computation of a successful path has required the generation of ten million states in a hour of execution time.

The length of a successful computation that lets the two conflicting trains to establish a route by serializing their requests gives actually the *diameter* of the state space, that is, the maximal depth of any cycle. This length is computed as the length of the witness of a formula asking that both trains reached their destination. It is this parameter that drives the state space growth, since non-determinism of adverse events is spread along the length of this computation, and interleaving the actions of the two trains contribute with quadratic growth. Adopting partial order reduction techniques should make it possible to deal at least with the latter. In particular, UMC has a prioritizing feature that can be used to implement a limited form of partial order reduction. At the time of writing, this feature has not yet been exploited. Obviously, using tools that include partial order reduction and that are able to deal with larger state spaces enlarges even further the tractability limits.

Hence, we can conclude that medium size interlockings are tractable if we limit to two trains, especially if specific state space reduction measures, such as partial order reduction, are adopted.

5.5   Parallel Verification

The preliminary results listed above indicate that even for medium size interlockings, states spaces appear to be affordable, provided few trains are modeled, due to the "locking" properties of the system. Limiting trains to two limits concurrent behaviour.

Although we have not a formal proof, we can state that proving no-collision for all conflicting pairs of routes with two trains requesting each route of the pair, is enough to prove global no-collision properties. Indeed, it appears that there is no possibility of a three train collision without a two-train collision first: hence proving that no two-train collision occur is enough.

Again, the interaction on a point from another train requesting or using a nearby, non-conflicting, route could be the only cause of violation of no-derailment: A train requesting a conflicting route is not allowed to reserve its route, and hence to circulate, due to the no-collision property. If we prove there is no such interaction, we show independency of the point from non-conflicting trains, which means also from a possible third circulating train.

In the end, in order to prove global no-collision and no-derailment properties, we need to perform several tractable verification runs. The resulting needed number of such runs is of the order of the square of the number of routes in the first case (more accurately, the number of pairs of non-conflicting routes), and in the order of the number of routes times the number of points for the second case.

The number of runs can therefore be quite big, but there is much space for parallel verification here: distributing such computations on a grid formed by all of a company's computer can achieve a big deal.

Distribution of tasks should follow criteria such as:

- for each pair of conflicting routes, verify no-collision on a model assuming two requesting trains on the input points of the two routes of the pair
- for each point, and for each route A not using the point, choose a route B that uses the point and is not conflicting with A; verify no-derailment on a model assuming two requesting trains on the input points of routes A and B (for this criterion an optimization can be applied which chooses pairs of routes such that no-derailment is verified for all points of one of the routes, in order to cover all points with a minimum set of route pairs: in this way the number of different models is minimized, although the number of verification runs is not).

6   Conclusions

The preliminary results obtained by experimenting with distributed modelling of interlockings encourage us to pursue a research activity in the direction of experimenting the parallel verification of an interlocking according to the principles discussed above, that is:

- assuming a distributed modelling of an interlocking
- using a model-checker that efficiently uses specific optimizations, such as partial-order reduction
- distributing the verification tasks on a grid, defining the tasks on the basis of the conflicting and non-conflicting route pairs, and on the list of points.

Such an activity will be aimed to evaluate the effectiveness and scalability of the parallel verification approach, assessing the maximum size of tractable systems. However, even if results will be positive, still two aspects need to be studied in order to translate such an approach in a viable alternative for industry.

A first issue is to verify whether the distributed approach is able to capture all the intricacies that real interlockings may exhibit in particular layouts or for particular local regulations. We believe it is so, since any case of condition affecting the safe establishment of a route can in principle be modelled as an ad hoc node that enters the 2-phase commit protocol to give its consensus. But we cannot exclude at the moment that some peculiarities may require a different handling.

A second issue to investigate is whether the proposed verification scheme applies to verification of Control-Table - based interlockings as well. Our reasoning on limiting the verification to two trains is based indeed on locality properties that are easily exhibited by a distributed model, while it is not as easy to show locality in a system of boolean equations, where inevitably the names of the variables have lost most of their geographic meaning.

On the other hand, the importance of relating the verification algorithms to the geographic layout were already established in the layout-related optimizing reordering of BDD variables in [25]. It would be interesting to investigate whether these two similar conclusions on so different models and verification algorithms are actually correlated.

Acknowledgements. I wish to thank A. Ferrari, D. Grasso, G. Magnani for their work in the area of formal verification of interlocking, on real examples produced at General Electric Transportation Systems. I also thank the students L. Brilli, L. Carlà, M. Paolieri, G. Rocciolo, S. Rossetto, A. Schiavelli, E. Vasarri, for their experiments with the UMC model checker.

References

1. Anunchai, S.V.: Verification of Railway Interlocking Tables using Coloured Petri Nets. In: Proceedings of the 10th Workshop and Tutorial on Practical Use of Coloured Petri Nets and the CPN Tools (2009)
2. Banci, M., Fantechi, A.: Instantiating Generic Charts for Railway Interlocking Systems. In: Tenth International Workshop on Formal Methods for Industrial Critical Systems (FMICS 2005), Lisbon, Portugal, September 5-6 (2005)
3. ter Beek, M.H., Fantechi, A., Gnesi, S., Mazzanti, F.: A state/event-based model-checking approach for the analysis of abstract system properties. Science of Computer Programming 76(2), 119–135 (2011)
4. Berger, J., Middelraad, P., Smith, A.J.: EURIS, European railway interlocking specification. In: Proceedings of the Institution of Railway Signal Engineers, IRSE 1993, pp. 70–82 (1993)
5. Boralv, A.: Formal Verification of a Computerized Railway Interlocking. Formal Aspects of Computing 10, 338–360 (1998)
6. Cimatti, A., Clarke, E.M., Giunchiglia, E., Giunchiglia, F., Pistore, M., Roveri, M., Sebastiani, R., Tacchella, A.: NuSMV 2: An OpenSource Tool for Symbolic Model Checking. In: Brinksma, E., Larsen, K.G. (eds.) CAV 2002. LNCS, vol. 2404, pp. 359–364. Springer, Heidelberg (2002)
7. Eriksson, L.: Use of Domain Theories in Applied Formal Methods. Technical Report, Uppsala University, Dept. of Information Technology, 2006-029 (2006)
8. Ferrari, A., Magnani, G., Grasso, D., Fantechi, A.: Model checking interlocking control tables. In: Proc. 8th FORMS/FORMAT Symposium, pp. 98–107 (2010)
9. Fokkink, W., Hollingshead, P.: Verification of Interlockings: from Control Tables to Ladder Logic Diagrams. In: 3rd FMICS Workshop, pp. 171–185 (1998)
10. Hansen, K.M.: Formalizing Railway Interlocking Systems. In: Proceedings of the 2nd FMERail Workshop (1998)
11. Haxthausen, A.E., Le Bliguet, M., Kjær, A.A.: Modelling and Verification of Relay Interlocking Systems. In: Choppy, C., Sokolsky, O. (eds.) Monterey Workshop 2008. LNCS, vol. 6028, pp. 141–153. Springer, Heidelberg (2010)
12. Haxthausen, A.E.: Developing a Domain Model for Relay Circuits. International Journal of Software and Informatics, 241–272 (2009)
13. Holzmann, G.J.: The SPIN Model Checker: Primer and Reference Manual. Addison-Wesley Professional (2003)

14. Jung, B.: Die Methode und Werkzeuge GRACE. In: Formale Techniken für die Eisenbahn-sicherung (FORMS 2000), Fortschritt-Berichte VDI, Reihe 12, Nr. 441. VDI Verlag (2000)

15. Kanso, K., Moller, F., Setzer, A.: Automated Verification of Signalling Principles in Railway Interlocking Systems. Electronic Notes in Theoretical Computer Science (ENTCS) 250, 19–31 (2009)

16. Le Bouar, P.: Interlocking SNCF functional requirements description. Euro-Interlocking Project, Paris (May 2003)

17. Mirabadi, A., Yazdi, M.B.: Automatic Generation and Verification of Railway Interlocking Control tables using FSM and NuSMV. Transport Problems: an International Scientific Journal 4, 103–110 (2009)

18. Mota, J.M.: Safety formal verification of metro railway signalling systems. Presentation at I-Day, FM 2011, Limerick, Ireland (June 2011)

19. Pavlovic, O., Ehrich, H.: Model Checking PLC Software Written in Function Block Diagram. In: 3rd International Conference on Software Testing, Verification and Validation, pp. 439–448 (2010)

20. Simpson, A.: Model Checking for Interlocking Safety. In: Proceedings of the 2nd FMERail Seminar (1998)

21. Tombs, D., Robinson, N., Nikandros, G.: Signalling Control Table Generation and Verification. In: Proceedings of the Conference on Railway Engineering (2002)

22. Winter, K.: Model Checking Railway Interlocking Systems. In: Proceedings of the 25th Australasian Conference on Computer Science, vol. 4, pp. 303–310 (2002)

23. Winter, K., Robinson, N.J.: Modeling Large Railway Interlockings and Model Checking Small Ones. In: Proceedings of the 26th Australasian Computer Science Conference, vol. 35, pp. 309–316 (2003)

24. Winter, K., Johnston, W., Robinson, P., Strooper, P., van den Berg, L.: Tool Support for Checking Railway Interlocking Designs. In: Proceedings of the 10th Australian Workshop on Safety Critical Systems and Software, pp. 101–107 (2006)

25. Winter, K.: Symbolic Model Checking for Interlocking Systems. In: Flammini, F. (ed.) Railway Safety, Reliability, and Security: Technologies and Systems Engineering. IGI Global (May 2012)

26. FP7 Project INESS - Deliverable D.1.5 Report on translation of requirements from text to UML (2009)

Quantitative Modelling and Analysis

Joost-Pieter Katoen[1,2] and Kim Guldstrand Larsen[3]

[1] University of Twente, Formal Methods and Tools, The Netherlands
[2] RWTH Aachen University, Software Modeling and Verification Group, Germany
[3] Center for Embedded Software Systems, Aalborg, Denmark

Quantitative models and quantitative analysis in Computer Science are currently intensively studied, resulting in a revision of the foundation of Computer Science where classical yes/no answers are replaced by quantitative analyses. The potential application areas are huge, e.g., performance analysis, operations research or embedded systems. This field covers extended automata-based models that permit to reasons about quantities. Over the past, one has mainly distinguished between real-time and stochastic extensions of automata.

Timed Models. The model of timed automata introduced by Alur and Dill in 1989 [2] has by now established itself as a universal formalism for describing real-time systems. In the first publications a number of problems known from the finite state systems were considered with respect to decidability and complexity. In particular reachability and model checking wrt timed extensions of CTL were shown decidable whereas (timed) languages inclusion was shown undecidable. Later other behavioral relationships like simulation and bisimulation were shown decidable. Here, the universal tool underlying the above decidability results has been the notion of regions, providing a finite partitioning of the uncountable infinite state-space which is exact with respect to the above problems.

Whereas the notion of region provides the key to decidability in many cases it is completely impractical from the point of view of making tools that perform efficiently in practice. The (coarser) notion of zone has lead to a number of tools – e.g. BIP, Kronos, UPPAAL – which support efficient analysis (reachability and model checking) of timed automata, quickly following the introduction of the timed automata formalism.

Later the more expressive formalism of hybrid automata was introduced and popularized by Henzinger et al. and the introduction of the tool HyTech providing a semi-decision algorithm for analyzing so-called linear hybrid systems. Whereas in timed automata the continuous part of a model is restricted to be clocks (which always evolve with rate 1), linear hybrid automata allow more general continuous variables with evolution rates in arbitrary intervals. Despite undecidability being a consequence of this extended expressive power the HyTech tool has been successfully applied to the verification of several hybrid systems.

The notion of priced (or weighted) timed automata was introduced independently by Alur et al and Larsen et al in 2001, with the surprising result that cost optimal reachability is decidable. Since these initial results, efficient tools exist and a number of more challenging questions has been considered including multi-priced timed automata, optimal infinite scheduling (both wrt mean

T. Margaria and B. Steffen (Eds.): ISoLA 2012, Part II, LNCS 7610, pp. 290–292, 2012.
© Springer-Verlag Berlin Heidelberg 2012

pay-off and discounting), priced timed games and model checking for priced timed automata. The last two questions are in general undecidable (if more than 2 clocks) but in the setting of 1-clock not only has decidability been obtained but complexity is also polynomial. The setting with 2 clocks remains open.

Stochastic Models. Stochastic models have a long tradition in Mathematics, starting with the work by Markov in the early 20th century and by Bellman around 1950 who introduced the basic principles of Markov chains and Markov decision processes, respectively. Nowadays, Markovian models and related stochastic models are central in many application areas, such as queuing theory, reliability and performance analysis, systems biology, social science, operational research, and control theory, to mention just a few.

In their seminal work, Hart, Sharir and Pnueli (1983, [4]) and Vardi (1985, [5]) were the first who modelled (distributed) randomized systems by finite-state automata with discrete transition probabilities and presented algorithms to prove that a given linear-time property holds with probability 1 by means of automata- and graph-based algorithms. These basic principles for model checking probabilistic systems have been extended in various ways. Modelling languages and process calculi with stochastic features were introduced with an operational semantics based on some probabilistic variant of transition systems, with behavioral equivalences and implementation relations for stochastic models, and with probabilistic branching-time logics. Another interesting extension was the combination of known model checking techniques with numerical methods for a quantitative system analysis (e.g., to compute the probabilities for certain events or expected values of certain random variables). Also, stochastic games were studied as an operational model for multi-agent systems.

The ISOLA Session. Driven by new needs in areas such as cyber physical systems, a series of recent works have tried to combine real-time with stochastic aspects, leading to new models such as timed stochastic automata.

In this ISOLA session, the main objective will be to study quantitative models and discuss their practical usage. New techniques such as statistical model checking, a simulation-based approach that allows to verify properties that cannot be expressed in classical temporal logic formalisms will be presented, and applied to a satelite system [3]. This is complemented with a paper on how to use priced timed automata to check the correctness of service-aware systems [1]

References

1. Čaušević, A., Seceleanu, C., Pettersson, P.: Checking Correctness of Services Modeled as Priced Timed Automata. In: Margaria, T., Steffen, B. (eds.) ISoLA 2012, Part II. LNCS, vol. 7610, pp. 309–323. Springer, Heidelberg (2012)
2. Alur, R., Dill, D.: Automata for Modeling Real-Time Systems. In: Paterson, M. (ed.) ICALP 1990. LNCS, vol. 443, pp. 322–335. Springer, Heidelberg (1990)

3. David, A., Larsen, K.G., Legay, A., Mikučionis, M.: Schedulability of Herschel-Planck Revisited Using Statistical Model Checking. In: Margaria, T., Steffen, B. (eds.) ISoLA 2012, Part II. LNCS, vol. 7610, pp. 294–308. Springer, Heidelberg (2012)
4. Hart, S., Sharir, M., Pnueli, A.: Termination of probabilistic concurrent programs. ACM Transactions on Programming Languages and Systems 5(3), 356–380 (1983)
5. Vardi, M.Y.: Automatic verification of probabilistic concurrent finite-state programs. In: 26th IEEE Symposium on Foundations of Computer Science (FOCS), pp. 327–338. IEEE Computer Society Press (1985)

Schedulability of Herschel-Planck Revisited Using Statistical Model Checking [*]

Alexandre David[1], Kim Guldstrand Larsen[1],
Axel Legay[2], and Marius Mikučionis[1]

[1] Computer Science, Aalborg University, Denmark
[2] INRIA/IRISA, Rennes Cedex, France

Abstract. Schedulability analysis is a main concern for several embedded applications due to their safety-critical nature. The classical method of response time analysis provides an efficient technique used in industrial practice. However, the method is based on conservative assumptions related to execution and blocking times of tasks. Consequently, the method may falsely declare deadline violations that will never occur during execution. This paper is a continuation of previous work of the authors in applying extended timed automata model checking (using the tool UPPAAL) to obtain more exact schedulability analysis, here in the presence of non-deterministic computation times of tasks given by intervals [BCET,WCET]. Considering computation *intervals* makes the schedulability of the resulting task model undecidable. Our contribution is to propose a combination of model checking techniques to obtain some guarantee on the (un)schedulability of the model even in the presence of undecidability.

Two methods are considered: symbolic model checking and statistical model checking. Symbolic model checking allows to conclude schedulability – i.e. absence of deadline violations – for varying sizes of BCET. However, the symbolic model checking technique is over-approximating for the considered task model and can therefore not be used for *dis*proving schedulability. As a remedy, we show how statistical model checking may be used to generate concrete counter examples witnessing non-schedulability. In addition, we apply statistical model checking to obtain more informative performance analysis – e.g. expected response times – when the system *is* schedulable.

The methods are demonstrated on a complex satellite software system yielding new insights useful for the company.

1 Introduction

Embedded systems involve the monitoring and control of complex physical processes using applications running on dedicated execution platforms in a resource constrained manner in terms of for example memory, processing power, bandwidth, energy consumption, as well as timing behavior.

[*] Work partially supported by VKR Centre of Excellence MT-LAB, the Sino-Danish basic research center IDEA4CPS, the regional CREATIVE project ESTASE, and the EU projects DANSE and DALI.

T. Margaria and B. Steffen (Eds.): ISoLA 2012, Part II, LNCS 7610, pp. 293–307, 2012.
© Springer-Verlag Berlin Heidelberg 2012

Viewing the application as a collection of (interdependent tasks) various scheduling principles may be applied to coordinate the execution of tasks in order to ensure orderly and efficient usage of resources. Based on the physical process to be controlled, timing deadlines may be required for the individual tasks as well as the overall system. The challenge of schedulability analysis is now concerned with guaranteeing that the applied scheduling principle(s) ensure that the timing deadlines are met.

The classical method of response time analysis [JP86,Bur94] provides an efficient means for schedulability analysis used in industrial practice: by calculating safe upper bounds on the worst case response times (WCRT) of tasks (as solutions to simple recursive equations) schedulability may be concluded by a simple comparison with the deadlines of tasks. However, classical response time analysis is only applicable to restricted types of task-sets (e.g. periodic arrival patterns), and only applicable to applications executing on single processors. Moreover, the method is based on conservative assumptions related to execution and blocking times of tasks [BHK99]. Consequently, the method may falsely declare deadline violations that will never occur during execution.

Process algebraic approaches [BACC+98,SLC06] have resulted in many methods for specification and schedulability analysis of real-time systems. Timed automata frameworks are also combined with other tools [BHK+04,BHM09] for schedulability and schedule assessment in realistic settings.

In this paper, we continue our effort in applying real-time model checking using the tool UPPAAL to obtain more exact schedulability analysis for a wider class of systems, e.g. task-sets with complex and interdependent arrival patterns of task, multiprocessor platforms, etc [DILS10]. In particular, we revisit the industrial case study of the Herschel-Planck [MLR+10] satellite system. The control software of this system – developed by the Danish company Terma A/S – consists of 32 tasks executing on a single processor system with preemptive scheduling, and with access to shared resources managed by a combination of priority inheritance and priority ceiling protocols. Unfortunately, though falling into the class of systems covered by the classical response time analysis, this method fails to conclude schedulability for the Herschel-Planck application.

In our previous work [MLR+10], we "successfully" concluded schedulability of the Herschel-Planck application using a more exact analysis based on the timed automata modeling framework for schedulability problems of [DILS10] and the tool UPPAAL. However, the analysis in [MLR+10] is based on the strong *assumption*, that each task has a given and specific execution time (ET). Clearly this is an unrealistic assumption. In reality, it can only be guaranteed that the execution time for (each execution of) task i is in some interval $[BCET_i, WCET_i]$. In particular, classical response time analysis aims at guaranteeing schedulability for intervals $[0, WCET_i]$, though unfortunately inconclusive for the Herschel-Planck control software. On the other hand the guarantee of schedulability in [MLR+10] only applies to (unrealistic) singleton intervals $[WCET_i, WCET_i]$.

Both works consider systems with preemptive scheduling and our timed automata models are using stop-watches. In addition this work deals with

Table 1. Summary of schedulability of Herschel-Planck concluded using symbolic and statistical model checking

$f = \frac{BCET}{WCET}$:	0-71%	72-86%	87-90%	90-100%
Symbolic MC:	maybe	maybe	n/a	**Safe**
Statistical MC:	**Unsafe**	maybe	maybe	maybe

non-deterministic computation times as well as dependencies between task due to resources, thus schedulability of the resulting task model is undecidable [FKPY07]. Our solution will be to consider a combination of well-known model checking techniques to obtain some guarantee on schedulability even in the presence of undecidability. Concretely, we revisit the schedulability problem for the Herschel-Planck software, with execution time intervals of the general form $[BCET_i, WCET_i]$, with $BCET_i \leq WCET_i$. Two model checking methods of UP-PAAL are applied for the schedulability analysis: classical (zone-based) symbolic model checking (MC) and statistical model checking (SMC). The core idea of SMC [LDB10,YS06,SVA04,KZH+09] is to randomly generate simulations of the system and verify whether they satisfy a given property. The results are then used by statistical algorithms in order to compute among others an estimate of the probability for the system to satisfy the property. Such estimate is correct up to some confidence that can be parameterized by the user. Several SMC algorithms that exploit a stochastic semantics for timed automata have recently been implemented in UPPAAL [DLL+11a,DLL+11b,BDL+12].

Symbolic MC allows to conclude schedulability – i.e. absence of deadline violations – for varying sizes of BCET, though with the size of the (symbolic) state-space and the overall verification time increasing significantly with an increase in the size of the intervals $[BCET_i, WCET_i]$. Moreover, the symbolic MC technique is over-approximate due to the presence of stop-watches needed to encode pre-emption. Thus, symbolic MC can not be used for *dis*proving schedulability. As a remedy, we show how statistical MC may be used to generate concrete counter examples witnessing non-schedulability. The new results obtained for Herschel-Planck are rather interesting as can be seen from the summary Table 1: when $\frac{BCET}{WCET} \geq 90\%$ symbolic MC confirms schedulability, whereas statistical MC disproved schedulability for $\frac{BCET}{WCET} \leq 71\%$. For $\frac{BCET}{WCET} \in (71\%, 90\%)$ both methods are inconclusive either due to the over-approximation induced by the symbolic approach or to a burden in computation time. In addition, we apply statistical MC to obtain more informative performance analysis, e.g. expected response times when the system is schedulable as well as estimation of the probability of deadline violation when the system is not schedulable.

2   Modeling

This section introduces the modeling framework that will be used through the rest of the paper. We start by presenting the generic features of the framework through a running example. Then, we briefly indicate the key additions in modeling the Herschel-Planck application, leaving details to be found in [MLR+10].

We consider a *Running Example*, that builds on instances from a library of three types of processes represented with timed automata templates in UPPAAL: (1) preemptive CPU scheduler, (2) resource schedulers that can use either priority inheritance, or priority ceiling protocols, and (3) periodically schedulable tasks. In what follows, we use broadcast channels in entire model which means that the sender cannot be blocked and the receiver can will ignore it if it is not ready to receive it. Derivative notation like x'==e specifies whether the stopwatch x is running, where e is an expression evaluating to either 0 or 1. By default all clocks are considered running, i.e. the derivative is 1.

For simplicity, we assume periodic tasks arriving with period Period[id], with initial offset Offset[id], requesting a resource R[id], executing for at least best case execution time BCET[id] and at most worst case execution time WCET[id] and hopefully finishing before the deadline Deadline[id], where id is a task identifier. The wall-clock time duration between task arrival and finishing is called response time, it includes the CPU execution time as well as any preemption or blocking time.

Figure 1a shows the UPPAAL declaration of the above mentioned parameters for three tasks (number of tasks is encoded with constant NRTASK) and one resource (number of resources is encoded with constant NRRES). The task_t type declaration says that task identifiers are integers ranging from 1 to NRTASK. Similarly the res_t type declares resource identifier range from 1 to NRRES. Parameters Period, Offset, WCET, BCET, Deadline and R are represented with integer arrays, one element per each task. Figure 1b shows a simple periodic task template which starts in Starting location, waits for the initial offset to elapse and then moves to Idle location. The task arrival is marked by a transition to a Ready location which signals the CPU scheduler that it is ready for execution. Then location Computing corresponds to busy computing while holding the resource and Release is about releasing the resources and finishing. The periodicity of a task is controlled by constraints on a local clock p: the task can move from Idle to Ready only when p==Period[id] and then p is reset to zero to mark the beginning of a new period. Upon arrival to Ready, other clocks are also reset to zero: c starts counting the execution time, r measures response time and ux is used to force the task progress. The invariant on location Ready says that the task execution clock c does not progress (c'==0) and it cannot stay longer than zero time units (ux<=0) unless it is not running (ux'==runs[id]). The task also cannot progress to location Computing unless the CPU is assigned to it (runs[id] becomes true). When the CPU is assigned, the task will be forced to urgently request a resource and move on to Computing, where the computation time (valuation of c) increases only when it is marked as running (runs[id] is true). The task can stay in Computing for at most worst case execution time (c<=WCET[id]), cannot leave before best case execution time (c>=BCET[id]), but can be preempted by setting runs[id] to 0. If the resource is not granted then the resource scheduler is responsible for blocking the task from using the

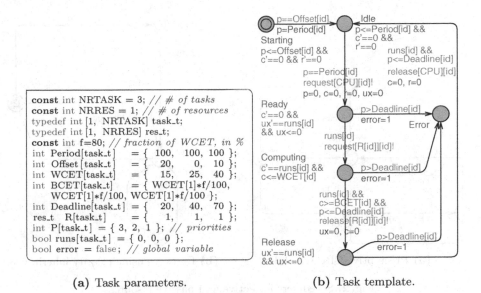

```
const int NRTASK = 3; // # of tasks
const int NRRES = 1; // # of resources
typedef int [1, NRTASK] task_t;
typedef int [1, NRRES] res_t;
const int f=80; // fraction of WCET, in %
int Period[task_t]   = { 100,  100, 100 };
int Offset[task_t]   = {  20,    0,  10 };
int WCET[task_t]     = {  15,   25,  40 };
int BCET[task_t]     = { WCET[1]*f/100,
   WCET[1]*f/100, WCET[1]*f/100 };
int Deadline[task_t] = {  20,   40,  70 };
res_t R[task_t]      = {   1,    1,   1 };
int P[task_t] = { 3, 2, 1 }; // priorities
bool runs[task_t] = { 0, 0, 0 };
bool error = false; // global variable
```

(a) Task parameters.   (b) Task template.

Fig. 1. Task parameter declaration and its stop-watch automaton template

CPU. If the deadline is not violated (p<=Deadline[id]) then the task can move on to Release and similarly complete to Idle. Notice that task competes for resources in locations Ready, Computing and Release and it will move to Error location if the deadline is exceeded (p>Deadline[id]).

The CPU scheduler is equipped with a task queue q sorted by task priorities P[t], where t is a task identifier and task variable holding the currently running task identifier. Function front(q) always returns the highest priority task identifier in the q queue. Figure 2a shows a CPU template which alternates between Free and Occupied locations.

When a request[CPU][t] arrives, the requesting task t is put into the queue and the CPU is being rescheduled. This is done either by immediate grant[CPU][task] and marking that the task is running runs[task]=true, or via preemption of the currently running task of lower priority, or simply returning to Occupied if the highest priority task in the queue is not higher than currently running. When a release[CPU][t] arrives, the requesting task t is de-queued, marked as not running (runs[t]=false), and the CPU is granted to the next highest priority task in the queue (if the queue is not empty). We use UPPAAL committed locations (encircled with C) for uninterrupted (atomic) transitions, thus Free and Occupied are the only locations where the time can pass. In addition, the scheduler is equipped with usage stop-watch: usage is stopped by invariant usage'==0 at location Free and is running with default rate of 1 in location Occupied, hence its valuation computes the CPU usage.

A resource scheduler shown in Fig. 2b is equipped with its own waiting queue w. It operates in a similar way as CPU scheduler, that is by alternating between Free and Occupied. The main difference is that a resource cannot be preempted once it is locked. The locking operations follow the priority inheritance protocol

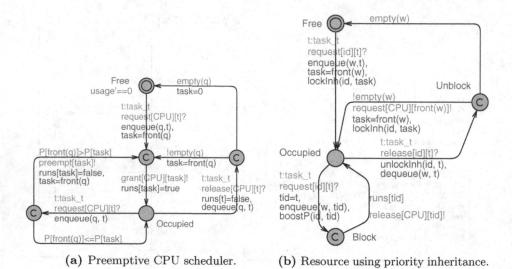

(a) Preemptive CPU scheduler.   **(b)** Resource using priority inheritance.

Fig. 2. Schedulers for active and passive resources

implemented in functions `lockInh(res,task)`, `unlockInh(res,task)`. Operation `boostP(res,task)` raises the priority of the resource `res` owner to higher level than the requesting `task`. Figure 3 shows the listing of UPPAAL code implementing the priority inheritance protocol.

```
/** Boost the priority of resource owner based on priority inheritance protocol: */
void boostP(res_t res, task_t task) {
    if (P[owner[res]] <= defaultP(task)) {
        P[owner[res]] = defaultP(task)+1;
        sort(q); // sorts the queue by descending priorities
    }
}
/** Lock the resource based on priority inheritance protocol: */
void lockInh(res_t res, task_t task) {
    owner[res] = task; // mark the resource as occupied by the task
}
/** Unlock the resource based on priority inheritance protocol: */
void unlockInh(res_t res, task_t task) {
    owner[res] = 0; // mark the resource as released
    P[task] = defaultP(task); // return to default priority
}
```

Fig. 3. Data and function declarations

Similarly to priority inheritance scheduler, we can also model priority ceiling protocol by suitable modification of the locking functions.

Herschel. In this paper, we will also consider a large, industrial case study: the schedulability analysis of the control software of the Herschel satellite. This case study, which will seriously challenge the capabilities of UPPAAL, uses the same basic stop-watch modeling principles as in the *Running Example* described above. The Herschel model consists of 32 tasks sharing 6 resources using two

Table 2. Summary of schedulability of the *Running Example* example concluded using symbolic and statistical MC for varying sizes of computation time intervals

$f = \frac{BCET}{WCET}$	0-79%	80-83%	84-100%
Symbolic MC:	maybe	maybe	**Safe**
Statistical MC:	**Unsafe**	maybe	maybe

protocols (priority inheritance and priority ceiling). Among these tasks, 24 are periodic, while 8 are triggered in a sequence. Additionally, tasks use multiple resources in a sequence, thus the sequence between `Idle` and `Release` of acquiring and releasing resources is more refined. As an optimization, the resource sharing and blocking is built into tasks to alleviate the need for task queues. We refer the reader to [MLR+10] for more details.

3   Symbolic Safety Analysis

In this section we apply the classical zone-based symbolic reachability engine of UPPAAL to verify schedulability. As we are considering systems with preemptive scheduling our models will be using stop-watches. With the addition of having non-deterministic computation times – i.e. computation *intervals* – as well as dependencies between task due to resources, schedulability of the resulting task model is undecidable as a consequence of the results of [FKPY07]. In this case, the analysis provided by UPPAAL is over-approximate, guaranteeing that safety properties established are valid properties of the system but leaving reachability properties to be possibly spurious.

Running Example As detailed in Section 2, our running example consists of three tasks with WCET times being $15, 25, 40$, deadlines $20, 40, 70$ and with one single resource shared by the three tasks. In Table 2 the result of applying symbolic MC with respect to the safety property

```
A[]   !error
```

is given. Here `error` is a Boolean being set whenever a task misses its deadline (see Figure 1b). Thus this property expresses absence of deadline violations (i.e. schedulability), and is confirmed (within 0.06s) for computation intervals $[f \cdot WCET, WCET]$ with $f \geq 84\%$. For $f < 84\%$, the over-approximate analysis of UPPAAL returns symbolic counter-example traces indicating possible deadline violations for task `T(1)`. However, these may be spurious.

In addition to schedulability, we may obtain upper bounds on the WCRTs of the three tasks by posing the the query

```
sup:  T(1).r, T(2).r,  T(3).r
```

where T(i).r is a stopwatch running whenever the task T(i) is not idle. Again the results fall in two classes: for computation intervals $[f \cdot \text{WCET}, \text{WCET}]$ with $f \geq 84\%$ the WCRTs are $20, 40, 70$ and for $f < 84\%$ the WCRTs are $55, 40, 70$, again indicating the possibility of deadline violation for task T(1).

Finally, using an additional stopwatch usage, which is only stopped when the CPU is free (and reset for each 2000 time-units) the query sup: usage returns the value 1600, providing 80% ($= 1600/2000$) as an upper bound of the CPU utilization.

Herschel. Applying in a similar manner symbolic MC to the Herschel case seriously challenges the engine of UPPAAL, due to the the explosion in the size symbolic state-space with the increase of the size of the computation time intervals. In fact, to avoid the analysis to run out of memory we have applied the so-called sweep-line method.

Table 3 provides a summary of the effort spent in verifying the model. We started verification with model-time limited instances to get an impression of resources need to verify the model and once we gained enough confidence we increased the limit, thus the results are sorted by the model-time limit. The deterministic case of $f = 100\%$ is relatively cheap and even unlimited case is verifiable within three hours. Important insight here is that the verification time correlates linearly with the limit and the unlimited case seems to correlate with 156 cycles which is the least common multiple of all task periods. So given enough time we managed to verify down to $f = 90\%$ where the resource consumption is increased drastically to more than 6 days. Finally, the model-checker indicate a (possibly spurious) deadline violation for the case $f = 86\%$ after a little bit more than 4 days.

Table 3. Verification statistics for different task execution time windows and exploration limits: the percentage denotes difference between WCET and BCET, limit is in terms of 250ms cycles (∞ stands for no limit, i.e. full exploration), memory in MB, time in hours:minutes:seconds

| limit | $f = 100\%$ | | | $f = 95\%$ | | | $f = 90\%$ | | | $f = 86\%$ | | |
cycle	states	mem	time	states	mem	time	states	mem	time	states	mem	time
1	0.001	51.2	1.47	0.5	83.0	15:03	1.5	124.1	1:22:43	3.3	186.9	6:39:47
2	0.003	53.7	2.45	0.8	96.8	27:00	2.4	139.7	2:09:15	5.3	198.7	9:14:59
4	0.005	54.5	4.62	1.5	97.2	48:02	4.4	138.3	3:48:40	9.2	274.6	14:12:57
8	0.010	54.7	8.48	2.8	97.8	1:28:45	9.1	156.5	8:38:42	18.2	364.6	28:35:32
16	0.020	55.3	16.11	5.4	112.0	2:45:52	17.8	176.0	16:42:05	35.4	520.4	44:06:57
∞	0.196	58.8	2:39.64	52.7	553.9	27:05:07	181.9	1682.2	147:23:25	**pos.unsafe**		99:07:56

Since symbolic MC proves that $f = 90\%$ case is safe, we also computed WCRT upper bounds. Table 4 compares the UPPAAL bounds on WCRTs with the bounds from classical response time analysis performed by Terma A/S. In particular Terma A/S found that PrimaryF task (#21) might violate its deadline even though this violation has never been observed neither in simulations nor in system deployment, whereas the bound provided by UPPAAL is still within the deadline, thus (re)confirming schedulability.

Table 4. Specification and worst-case response-times of individual tasks

ID	Task	Specification			WCRT			
		Period	WCET	Deadline	Terma	$f = 100\%$	$f = 95\%$	$f = 90\%$
1	RTEMS_RTC	10.000	0.013	1.000	0.050	0.013	0.013	0.013
2	AswSync_SyncPulseIsr	250.000	0.070	1.000	0.120	0.083	0.083	0.083
3	Hk_SamplerIsr	125.000	0.070	1.000	0.120	0.070	0.070	0.070
4	SwCyc_CycStartIsr	250.000	0.200	1.000	0.320	0.103	0.103	0.103
5	SwCyc_CycEndIsr	250.000	0.100	1.000	0.220	0.113	0.113	0.113
6	Rt1553_Isr	15.625	0.070	1.000	0.290	0.173	0.173	0.173
7	Bc1553_Isr	20.000	0.070	1.000	0.360	0.243	0.243	0.243
8	Spw_Isr	39.000	0.070	2.000	0.430	0.313	0.313	0.313
9	Obdh_Isr	250.000	0.070	2.000	0.500	0.383	0.383	0.383
10	RtSdb_P_1	15.625	0.150	15.625	4.330	0.533	0.533	0.533
11	RtSdb_P_2	125.000	0.400	15.625	4.870	0.933	0.933	0.933
12	RtSdb_P_3	250.000	0.170	15.625	5.110	1.103	1.103	1.103
13	(no task, this ID is reserved for priority ceiling)							
14	**FdirEvents**	250.000	5.000	230.220	7.180	5.553	5.553	5.553
15	**NominalEvents_1**	250.000	0.720	230.220	7.900	6.273	6.273	6.273
16	**MainCycle**	250.000	0.400	230.220	8.370	6.273	6.273	6.273
17	HkSampler_P_2	125.000	0.500	62.500	11.960	5.380	7.350	8.153
18	HkSampler_P_1	250.000	6.000	62.500	18.460	11.615	13.653	14.153
19	**Acb_P**	250.000	6.000	50.000	24.680	6.473	6.473	6.473
20	**IoCyc_P**	250.000	3.000	50.000	27.820	9.473	9.473	9.473
21	**PrimaryF**	250.000	34.050	**59.600**	**65.47**	54.115	56.382	58.586
22	**RCSControlF**	250.000	4.070	239.600	76.040	53.994	56.943	58.095
23	Obt_P	1000.000	1.100	100.000	74.720	2.503	2.513	2.523
24	Hk_P	250.000	2.750	250.000	6.800	4.953	4.963	4.973
25	StsMon_P	250.000	3.300	125.000	85.050	17.863	27.935	28.086
26	TmGen_P	250.000	4.860	250.000	77.650	9.813	9.823	9.833
27	Sgm_P	250.000	4.020	250.000	18.680	14.796	14.880	14.973
28	TcRouter_P	250.000	0.500	250.000	19.310	11.896	11.906	14.442
29	**Cmd_P**	250.000	14.000	250.000	114.920	94.346	99.607	101.563
30	**NominalEvents_2**	250.000	1.780	230.220	102.760	65.177	69.612	72.235
31	**SecondaryF_1**	250.000	20.960	189.600	141.550	110.666	114.921	122.140
32	**SecondaryF_2**	250.000	39.690	230.220	204.050	154.556	162.177	165.103
33	Bkgnd_P	250.000	0.200	250.000	154.090	15.046	139.712	147.160

4 Statistical Analysis

In the previous section, we observed that symbolic MC can be used to conclude schedulability, but not to disprove it. This is reflected in the first line of Table 1 where there is a wide range of values of f for which symbolic MC cannot conclude due to the potential presence of spurious counterexamples. In this section, we introduce SMC, a technique that we consider here to be the dual of symbolic MC. Namely, SMC can be used to disprove schedulability, but not to conclude it.

Concretelly, SMC is a simulation-based approach whose core objective is to estimate the probability for a system to satisfy a property by simulating and observing some of its executions, and then apply statistical algorithms to obtain the result. SMC is parameterized by two parameters: a *confidence interval size* on the estimate of the probability and a *confidence level* on the probability that the answer returns by methodology is correct. In terms of schedulability, SMC will thus be useful to generate concrete counterexample but cannot be used to conclude schedulability.

Several SMC algorithms have recently been implemented in UPPAAL [DLL+11b]. In this section, we will show how this implementation can be used not only to prove schedulability, but also to observe and reason on the execution of tasks. The latter will be done by exploiting the simulation engine and various informations displayed by the GUI of the tool.

SMC relies on the assumption that the dynamic of the system is entirely stochastic. In [DLL+11a,DLL+11b], we have proposed a refined stochastic semantic for timed automata that associates probability distributions to both the time-delays spend in a given state as well as to the transition between states. In this semantics timed automata components repeatedly race against each other, i.e. they independently and stochastically decide on their own how much to delay before outputting, with the "winner" being the component that chooses the minimum delay. Our stochastic schedulability model exploits the semantic of [DLL+11a,DLL+11b] as it assumes the execution time of the task 4 to be picked uniformly in the interval $[f \cdot \text{WCET}_i, \text{WCET}_i]$.

In the rest of this section, we shall see how the SMC approach can be used to generate a witness traces when concluding that the system is not schedulable with a probability greater than 0. We will also illustrate how the SMC engine of UPPAAL can evaluate the probability to reach a state violating a deadline. Finally, and not to be underestimated, we will show how the GUI of the UPPAAL tool can be exploited to give quantitative feedback to the user on, e.g., blocking time, CPU usage, distribution of response time.

Running Example. Table 5 shows the query used to evaluate the probability of violating a deadline for runs bounded by 200 time units and the results for different values of f. We check only for cases when the symbolic model-checker reports that deadlines *may* be violated to generate a witness with SMC. The SMC technique gives results with certain levels of confidence and precision, i.e., the actual result is an interval. However, if the lower bound is strictly positive, it guarantees that the checker did find witnesses. The case $f = 80\%$ is interesting because it seems to be a spurious result from the symbolic model-checker. In fact we can do hypothesis testing to get a more precise result more cheaply. The model-checker accepts the hypothesis Pr[<=200](<> error) <= 0.00001 with 1% significance level in 25s. As summarized in line 2 of Table 1 SMC allow to conclude unschedulability for $f \leq 79\%$.

Table 5. Probability of error estimation with 1% level of significance

f		50%	70%	79%	80%
Pr[<=200](<> error)		[0.847,0.858]	[0.604,0.615]	[0.301,0.312]	[0,0.005]

We can visualize traces (and inspect witnesses of deadline violation) by asking the checker to generate random simulation runs and visualize the value of a collection of expressions as a function time in a Gantt chart. In addition, we can filter these runs and only retain some that reach some state, here the error state. This is done with the following query producing the plot in Fig. 4b:

```
simulate 1000 [<=300] {
  (T(1).Ready+T(1).Computing+T(1).Release+runs[1]-2*T(1).Error)+6,
  (T(2).Ready+T(2).Computing+T(2).Release+runs[2]-2*T(1).Error)+3,
  (T(3).Ready+T(3).Computing+T(3).Release+runs[3]-2*T(1).Error)+0
} :1: error
```

If the filtering ("`:1:error`") is omitted, the plot contains all the runs, and for clarity just a single of them is displayed in Fig. 4a. As a result the plot encodes the

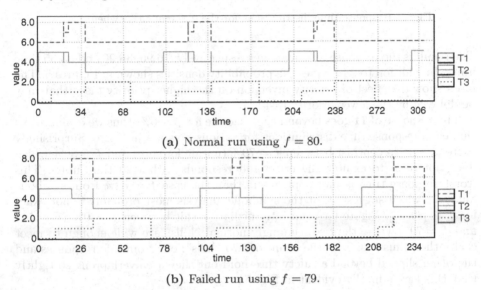

(a) Normal run using $f = 80$.

(b) Failed run using $f = 79$.

Fig. 4. Visualization of runs as a Gantt chart. The chart shows an encoding of the state with different weights corresponding to steps of different heights.

task states (idle, ready, running or error) in the level of the curve. For example, Figure 4a shows that T2 becomes ready and running starting from 0 time. At 10 task T3 becomes ready, but is not running. Then at 20 task T1 becomes ready and becomes running by preempting T2 but then it immediately gives up the running status (due to resource blocking) and resumes by preemption when T2 releases the resource. At this point T2 is not finished yet and will be able to finish only when T1 finishes and releases the CPU, hence there is a small spike just before going to idle state. The lowest priority task T3 has a chance to run and finish only when both T1 and T2 are done. Figure 4b is interpreted similarly, where the task T1 violates its deadline because T3 managed to get the resource before T1 and thus T1 was blocked from finishing.

More insight on the behavior of the tasks is gained by estimating expected response times using the queries:

```
E[<=200; 50000] (max: T(1).r)
E[<=200; 50000] (max: T(2).r)
E[<=200; 50000] (max: T(3).r)
```

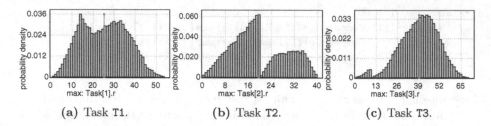

(a) Task T1.   (b) Task T2.   (c) Task T3.

Fig. 5. Response time distributions for the different tasks when $f = 0$

The result is the response time averages respectively: 16.96, 36.96 and 63.65 time units. In addition tool provides the probability densities shown in Figures 5. The plots show the effect of priority inversion on the higher priority tasks that may be delayed by the lower priority task.

The response of T1 goes beyond the deadline for $f = 0\%$, thus we evaluate the shapes of response time distributions for various f values in Fig. 6. Surprisingly there is a sharp contrast between $f = 79\%$ (unsafe for sure) and $f = 80\%$ which does not seem to exhibit the error and responds within 20 time units. This worst response time is more optimistic than the case $f = 83\%$ from symbolic analysis, which suggests that the symbolic analysis most probably is not exact for $f \in [80, 83]$. Figure 6a is an intermediate result between $f = 0\%$ (Fig. 5a) and $f = 79\%$ where the two seemingly normal "hills" are wide enough to meet each other, thus Fig. 5a is the result of two "hills": one from safe responses and the other slipped beyond a safety threshold but they are overlapping so tightly that this fact is hardly evident in Fig. 5a.

Herschel. We generalize this methodology to our more complex Herschel case-study to confirm deadline violations and to study performance.

Table 6 shows the results when we vary the execution time to be in the interval $[f \cdot \text{WCET}, \text{WCET}]$. The table shows the probabilities in function of this factor f and statistical parameters α ($1 - \alpha$ is the confidence level) and ε the size of the confidence interval of the probability. Asking for more precise results yields more traces at the cost of time. At first we limited the search to just one cycle of 250ms, but then at the point of $f = 62\%$ the errors are rarely found even with high confidence and many runs. Then we increased the limit which increased our

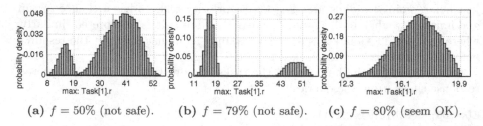

(a) $f = 50\%$ (not safe).   (b) $f = 79\%$ (not safe).   (c) $f = 80\%$ (seem OK).

Fig. 6. Response time distributions for Task T1 using various f ratios

Table 6. Results of Herschel statistical model-checking

Limit cycles	f %	SMC parameters α	ε	Total traces, #	Error traces #	Probability	Earliest cycle	Error offset	Verification time
1	0	0.0100	0.005	105967	1928	0.018194	0	79600.0	1:58:06
1	50	0.0100	0.005	105967	753	0.007106	0	79600.0	2:00:52
1	60	0.0100	0.005	105967	13	0.000123	0	79778.3	2:01:18
1	62	0.0005	0.002	1036757	34	0.000033	0	79616.4	19:52:22
160	63	0.0100	0.05	1060	177	0.166981	0	81531.6	2:47:03
160	64	0.0100	0.05	1060	118	0.111321	1	79803.0	2:55:13
160	65	0.0500	0.05	738	57	0.077236	3	79648.0	2:06:55
160	66	0.0100	0.05	1060	60	0.056604	2	82504.0	2:62:44
160	67	0.0100	0.05	1060	26	0.024528	1	79789.0	2:64:20
160	68	0.0100	0.05	1060	3	0.002830	67	81000.0	2:67:08
640	69	0.0100	0.05	1060	8	0.007547	114	80000.0	12:23:00
640	70	0.0100	0.05	1060	3	0.002830	6	88070.0	12:30:49
1280	71	0.0100	0.05	1060	2	0.001887	458	80000.0	25:19:35

chances of finding the errors, we were lucky to find some errors as early as in the first cycle. Most of the errors are found quite early (cases where $f < 68$), but for smaller time-windows it is much harder to find and the few found ones are quite far in the run. Eventually the search took more than a day to find only a few error instances for $f = 71\%$, hence we stopped here.

Similarly to Fig. 5, response times for the most stressed task `PrimaryF` are estimated by generating 2000 probabilistic runs limited to 156 cycles for the safe case of $f = 90\%$. The vast majority (1787) of instances responded before 51093.3 and the rest is distributed about evenly (see Fig. 7). The worst found response time was of 52851.2 which is significantly lower than bound of 58586.0 found by symbolic MC in Table 4. The computation for this model took 17.6 hours.

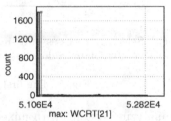

Fig. 7. Response times

Fig. 8a shows an overview chart of all 32 tasks during the first 85ms. Each task can be identified by its base level 3*ID, thus `PrimaryF` with ID=21 is at 63. `PrimaryF` starts with an offset of 20ms and it has to finish before a deadline of 59.6ms. Under safe conditions of $f = 90\%$ `PrimaryF` finishes before $70500\mu s$ (Fig. 8a) but with $f = 50\%$ it fails at $79828.3\mu s$ (Fig. 8b).

5   Conclusion

In this paper, we have applied both symbolic MC and statistical MC to schedulability analysis. In particular, we have demonstrated that the complementary qualities of the two methods allow to conclusively confirm as well as disprove schedulability for a wide range of cases. This is an impressive result as the problem is known to be undecidable. In addition we have illustrated how the user can benefit from the UPPAAL features in plotting, observing and reasoning about task executions, and hence improving the modeling process. We also believe that the combination of symbolic MC and statistical MC will prove highly useful in

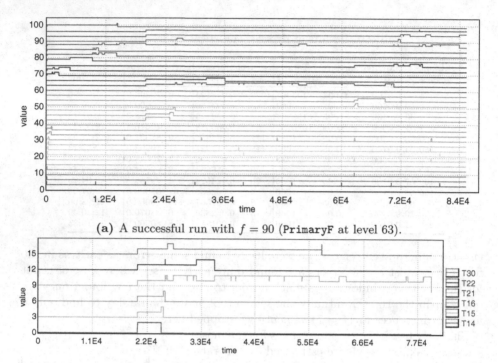

(a) A successful run with $f = 90$ (PrimaryF at level 63).

(b) Selected processes of a simulation run with $f = 50\%$, where PrimaryF (task T21 at level 9) violates a deadline.

Fig. 8. The first 85ms of Herschel model simulation runs

analyzing systems with mixed critically, i.e. systems containing tasks with hard timing constraints as well as soft, where the timing constraints are permitted to be violated occasionally.

References

BACC+98. Ben-Abdallah, H., Choi, J.-Y., Clarke, D., Kim, Y.S., Lee, I., Xie, H.-L.: A process algebraic approach to the schedulability analysis of real-time systems. Real-Time Systems 15, 189–219 (1998), doi:10.1023/A:1008047130023

BDL+12.   Bulychev, P., David, A., Guldstrand Larsen, K., Legay, A., Mikučionis, M., Bøgsted Poulsen, D.: Checking and Distributing Statistical Model Checking. In: Goodloe, A.E., Person, S. (eds.) NFM 2012. LNCS, vol. 7226, pp. 449–463. Springer, Heidelberg (2012)

BHK99.   Bradley, S., Henderson, W., Kendall, D.: Using timed automata for response time analysis of distributed real-time systems. In: Systems in 24th IFAC/IFIP Workshop on Real-Time Programming, WRTP 1999, pp. 143–148 (1999)

BHK⁺04.   Bohnenkamp, H.C., Hermanns, H., Klaren, R., Mader, A., Usenko, Y.S.:
Synthesis and stochastic assessment of schedules for lacquer production.
In: Proceedings of the First International Conference on the Quantitative
Evaluation of Systems, QEST 2004, pp. 28–37 (September 2004)

BHM09.   Brekling, A., Hansen, M.R., Madsen, J.: Moves – a framework for modelling and verifying embedded systems. In: International Conference on
Microelectronics, ICM 2009, pp. 149–152 (December 2009)

Bur94.   Burns, A.: Preemptive priority based scheduling: An appropriate engineering approach. In: Principles of Real-Time Systems, pp. 225–248. Prentice
Hall (1994)

DILS10.   David, A., Illum, J., Larsen, K.G., Skou, A.: Model-Based Framework for
Schedulability Analysis Using UPPAAL 4.1. In: Nicolescu, G., Mosterman,
P.J. (eds.) Model-Based Design for Embedded Systems, pp. 93–119. CRC
Press (2010)

DLL⁺11a.   David, A., Larsen, K.G., Legay, A., Mikučionis, M., Bøgsted Poulsen, D.,
van Vliet, J., Wang, Z.: Statistical Model Checking for Networks of Priced
Timed Automata. In: Fahrenberg, U., Tripakis, S. (eds.) FORMATS 2011.
LNCS, vol. 6919, pp. 80–96. Springer, Heidelberg (2011)

DLL⁺11b.   David, A., Larsen, K.G., Legay, A., Mikučionis, M., Wang, Z.: Time for
Statistical Model Checking of Real-Time Systems. In: Gopalakrishnan, G.,
Qadeer, S. (eds.) CAV 2011. LNCS, vol. 6806, pp. 349–355. Springer, Hei-
delberg (2011)

FKPY07.   Fersman, E., Krcal, P., Pettersson, P., Yi, W.: Task automata: Schedulability, decidability and undecidability. Information and Computation 205(8),
1149–1172 (2007)

JP86.   Joseph, M., Pandya, P.K.: Finding response times in a real-time system.
Comput. J. 29(5), 390–395 (1986)

KZH⁺09.   Katoen, J.-P., Zapreev, I.S., Moritz Hahn, E., Hermanns, H., Jansen, D.N.:
The ins and outs of the probabilistic model checker MRMC. In: Proc. of
6th Int. Conference on the Quantitative Evaluation of Systems (QEST),
pp. 167–176. IEEE Computer Society (2009)

LDB10.   Legay, A., Delahaye, B., Bensalem, S.: Statistical Model Checking: An
Overview. In: Barringer, H., Falcone, Y., Finkbeiner, B., Havelund, K.,
Lee, I., Pace, G., Roşu, G., Sokolsky, O., Tillmann, N. (eds.) RV 2010.
LNCS, vol. 6418, pp. 122–135. Springer, Heidelberg (2010)

MLR⁺10.   Mikučionis, M., Larsen, K.G., Rasmussen, J.I., Nielsen, B., Skou, A., Palm,
S.U., Pedersen, J.S., Hougaard, P.: Schedulability Analysis Using Uppaal:
Herschel-Planck Case Study. In: Margaria, T., Steffen, B. (eds.) ISoLA
2010, Part II. LNCS, vol. 6416, pp. 175–190. Springer, Heidelberg (2010)

SLC06.   Sokolsky, O., Lee, I., Clarke, D.: Schedulability analysis of aadl models. In:
20th International Parallel and Distributed Processing Symposium, IPDPS
2006, p. 8 (April 2006)

SVA04.   Sen, K., Viswanathan, M., Agha, G.: Statistical Model Checking of Black-
Box Probabilistic Systems. In: Alur, R., Peled, D.A. (eds.) CAV 2004.
LNCS, vol. 3114, pp. 202–215. Springer, Heidelberg (2004)

YS06.   Håkan, L., Younes, S., Simmons, R.G.: Statistical probabilistic model
checking with a focus on time-bounded properties. Inf. Comput. 204(9),
1368–1409 (2006)

Checking Correctness of Services Modeled as Priced Timed Automata

Aida Čaušević, Cristina Seceleanu, and Paul Pettersson

Mälardalen Real-Time Research Centre (MRTC),
Mälardalen University, Västerås, Sweden
{aida.delic,cristina.seceleanu,paul.pettersson}@mdh.se

Abstract. Service-Oriented Systems (SOS) have gained importance in different application domains thanks to their ability to enable reusable functionality provided via well-defined interfaces, and the increased opportunities to compose existing units, called services, into various configurations. Developing applications in such a setup, by reusing existing services, brings some concerns regarding the assurance of the expected Quality-of-Service (QoS), and correctness of the employed services. In this paper, we describe a formal mechanism of computing service guarantees, automatically. We assume service models annotated with pre- and postconditions, with their semantics given as Priced Timed Automata (PTA), and the forward analysis method for checking the service correctness w.r.t. given requirements. Under these assumptions, we show how to compute the strongest postcondition of the corresponding automata algorithmically, with respect to the specified precondition. The approach is illustrated on a small example of a service modeled as Priced Timed Automaton (PTAn).

1 Introduction

The complexity of software systems has been continuously increasing during the last decade. One of the reasons underlying such a phenomenon is a new trend that aims to integrate and connect heterogeneous applications and available resources while aiming at improved software reusability. Service-oriented systems (SOS), which have emerged as context independent component-based systems (CBS), are becoming one of the dominant paradigms for developing large scale systems out of self-contained and loosely coupled services. Among the main benefits of the approach, the most appealing are: the reusable functionality via well-defined interfaces, the service infrastructure that enables services to be published, discovered, invoked, and, if needed destroyed on demand, as well as the fast application development by employing existing services.

In systems built up in such a setup, it becomes essential to ensure a satisfying level of the system's Quality-of-Service (QoS). Sometimes, based on the QoS, one simply needs to decide which service to select out of a number of available services that offer similar functionality. To deliver guarantees on provided QoS, some SOS approaches [3, 15, 19, 21] support formal analysis; however, in most cases building the formal system model, out of formalized services, is far from straightforward.

T. Margaria, B. Steffen, and M. Merten (Eds.): ISoLA 2012, Part II, LNCS 7610, pp. 308–322, 2012.

Once a model is created, it becomes crucial to be able to check the fulfilment of requirements of the employed services, both in isolation, as well as in the context of the newly created system that involves service compositions. An important aspect, often ignored, is the service's resource usage. Any analysis approach that abstracts from service resource constraints might produce analysis results that are insufficiently correct, or reliable.

For instance, let us consider a three shuttle system, previously modeled and analyzed in the Priced Timed Automata (PTA) formal framework [5]. In brief, the system provides transportation services to three different locations. We assume a scenario in which two out of three shuttles are supposed to stay in a convoy and reach the common final location. Considering energy to be the most critical resource in the system (i.e., each shuttle operates on batteries with a limited capacity), it would be beneficial to be able to formally check if the current energy level in each shuttle is sufficient to reach the final destination, before the actual convoy is created. In addition, each shuttle has timing constraints, which should be in accordance with the deadline of the convoy.

To tackle the above concerns, in this paper, we focus on computing functional and extra-functional service guarantees, automatically. The service model is time- and resource-aware, being described in REMES [23], a behavioral language intended for modeling and analysis of interacting embedded components and services. The system is obtained by composing REMES models, via operators that we have defined previously [6].

In our recent work, we have shown how service correctness can be checked using Hoare triples, and strongest postcondition semantics technique, described in Section 3.1. However, the postcondition calculation, on which the verification relies, is not currently automated, thus hindering the applicability of the method. Here, we address this deficit by presenting algorithms for computing strongest postconditions (service guarantees) automatically, by applying minimum/maximum reachability analysis on PTA [17] translations of the REMES service models (Section 3).

We consider the service resource usage in REMES as a cost variable in PTA, and we include the computation of the minimum and maximum reachability costs of a final PTA location in our algorithms, alongside with calculating the strongest postcondition of reaching such location, over symbolic states. The approach, described in Section 3, is accompanied by an illustrative example of a simple model of a PTA service. Last but not least, we compare our approach with some relevant work in Section 4 before concluding the paper in Section 5.

2   Preliminaries and a Simple Example

2.1   REMES Modeling Language

To model functional and extra-functional behavior such as timing and resource usage of SOS, in this paper, we use the dense-time state-based hierarchical modeling language called REMES [23]. The language has been initially intended as a meaningful basis for modeling and analysis of embedded systems in a component-based fashion. To make it suitable for modeling SOS too, we have recently extended REMES with constructs fit for an SOS description [6]. To enable formal analysis, REMES models can be transformed into Timed Automata (TA) [1], or PTA [2], depending on the analysis type [13].

REMES is appropriate for describing the behavior of SOS, as it is well-suited for abstract modeling, since it is a language well-suited for abstract modeling, supports hierarchical modeling, has an input/ouput distinction, a well-defined formal semantics, and tool support [14] [1].

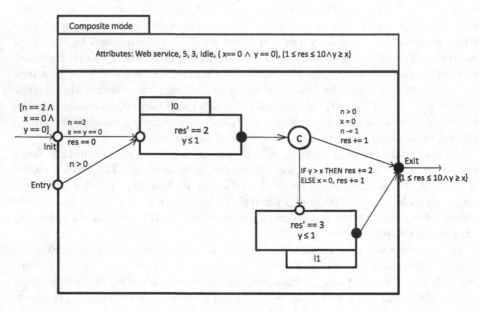

Fig. 1. An example of a REMES service

Let us assume a simple example of a composite mode that models a web service depicted in Fig. 1. The composite mode contains two submodes, i.e., *atomic* modes I0 and I1. The mode has a special Init entry point, visited when the service executes first, and where all variables are initialized.

In REMES one may model timed behavior and resource consumption. Timed behavior is modeled by global continuous variables of specialized type *clock* evolving at rate 1 (x, y in Fig. 1). Each (sub)mode can be annotated with the corresponding continuous resource usage, if any, modeled by the first derivative of the real-valued variables that denote resources that evolve at positive integer rates (res' == 2 in Fig. 1). Discrete resources are allocated through updates, e.g., res += 1 in Fig. 1.

The REMES service shown in Fig. 1 contains a list of attributes (i.e., service type is Web service, capacity is 5, time-to-serve is 3, status is Idle, service precondition is $(x == 0 \land y == 0)$, and postcondition $(1 \leq res \leq 10 \land y \geq x)$) exposed at the interface of the REMES service. A service precondition is a predicate that constrains the start of service execution, and must be true at the time a REMES

---

[1] The REMES tool-chain is available at http://www.fer.hr/dices/remes-id

service is invoked. A postcondition must hold at the end of a REMES service execution and it can be the same or included into the user defined requirement, also modeled as a predicate.

To verify the service correctness, we use the forward analysis technique based on the computation of the strongest postcondition of a REMES service w.r.t. a given precondition. To prove the correctness of a REMES service in isolation, we check that the calculated strongest postcondition is no more than the given requirement. Since REMES models can be automatically transformed to PTA via a well-defined set of rules [13, 14, 20], in this paper, we propose an algorithmic technique of strongest postcondition calculation on the PTAn description of a service, in order to provide automation to our REMES verification procedure.

The service composition correctness check reduces to discharging similar boolean implications, as we have shown in our recent work [6]. Therefore, automating the strongest postcondition calculation of services is central to the applicability of our analysis method.

For a more thorough description of the REMES language, we refer the reader to our previous work [6, 23].

2.2 Priced Timed Automata

In the following, we recall the model of PTA [2, 4], an extension of TA [1] with prices on both locations and edges.

Let us assume a finite alphabet Act ranging over a, b etc., a finite set of all data (i.e., boolean, integer or array) variables V, a finite set of real-valued clocks χ and $\mathcal{B}(\chi)$ the set of formulas obtained as conjunctions of atomic constraints of the form $x \bowtie n$, where $x \in \chi$, $n \in \mathbb{N}$, and $\bowtie \in \{<, \leq, =, \geq, >\}$. The elements of $\mathcal{B}(\chi)$ are called *clock constraints* over χ. Similarly, we use $\mathcal{B}(V)$ to stand for the set of non-clock constraints that are conjunctive formulas of $i \sim j$ or $i \sim k$, where $i, j \in V$, $k \in \mathbb{Z}$ and $\sim \in \{<, \leq, =, \neq, \geq, >\}$. We use $\mathcal{B}(\chi, V)$ to denote the set of formulas that are conjunctions of clock constraints and non-clock constraints. Additionally, $\mathcal{P}(\chi)$ represents the powerset of χ.

Definition 1. *A linearly Priced Timed Automaton (PTAn) over clocks χ and actions Act is a tuple (L, l_0, E, V, I, P), where L is a finite set of locations, $l_0 \in L$ is the initial location, $E \subseteq L \times \mathcal{B}(\chi, V) \times Act \times \mathcal{P}(\chi) \times L$ is the set of edges, V is a finite set of data variables, $I : L \to \mathcal{B}(\chi)$ assigns invariants to locations, and $P : (L \cup E) \to \mathbb{N}$ assigns prices (or costs) to both locations and edges.* ∎

In the case of $e = (l, g, a, r, l') \in E$, we also write $l \xrightarrow{g,a,r} l'$. For an edge e we refer to l as the source of e, to l' as the target of e, to g as the guard of e, to a as the action of e, and to r as the reset set i.e., data- or clock assignment of e. Fig. 2 depicts the PTAn description of the REMES service introduced in Fig. 1. We omit the REMES interface from the model, so only the internal behavior is represented. The PTA description consists of three locations: l_0, l_1, and l_2 (with l_0 as the initial location), and edges, which are directed lines connecting locations. The timing behavior is controlled by two clock variables, x and y. For

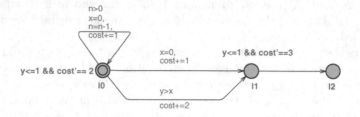

Fig. 2. The PTAn model of the REMES service of Fig. 1

each location, it is possible to assign an invariant that must hold in order to stay in that location (e.g., invariant $y \leq 1$), which enforces a location change in case it ceases to hold. Further, each edge, may be decorated with guards, that is, boolean expressions that must hold in order for an edge to be taken (e.g., $y > x$). For simplicity, to prevent infinite looping in l_0, in this example we use the integer variable n. To model, simulate and verify our example we use the UPPAAL CORA tool. The tool extends Definition 1 with data variables of different types, arrays of data variables, constants, and records.

The semantics of PTA is defined in terms of priced transition systems over states of the form (l, u), where l is a location, $u \in \mathbf{R}^X$ are clock valuations, and the initial state is (l_0, u_0), where u_0 assigns all clocks in χ to 0. In this model, there are two kinds of transitions: delay transitions and discrete transitions. In delay transitions,

$$(l, u) \stackrel{d,p}{\to} (l, u \oplus d),$$

where $u \oplus d$ is the result obtained by incrementing all clocks of the automata with delay d, and $p = P(l) * d$ is the cost of performing the delay (the cost of staying in location l_0 is described by $cost' == 2$). Discrete transitions

$$(l, u) \stackrel{a,p}{\to} (l', u')$$

correspond to taking an edge $l \stackrel{g,a,r}{\to} l'$ for which the guard g is satisfied by u. The clock valuation u' of the target state is obtained by modifying u according to updates r. The cost $p = P((l, g, a, r, l'))$ is the price associated with the edge (the cost of taking a self loop in location l_0 is annotated as $cost+ = 1$).

A timed trace σ of a PTAn is a sequence of alternating delays and action transitions

$$\sigma = (l_0, u_0) \stackrel{a_1,p_1}{\to} (l_1, u_1) \stackrel{a_2,p_2}{\to} \ldots \stackrel{a_n,p_n}{\to} (l_n, u_n)$$

A network of PTA $A_1, \ldots, A_n$ over χ and Act is defined as the parallel composition of n PTA $A_1 \parallel \ldots \parallel A_n$ over χ and Act. Semantically, a network again describes a timed transition system obtained from those components, by requiring synchrony on delay transitions, and requiring discrete transitions to synchronize on complementary actions (i.e., a? is complementary to a!) [4]. Next, we recall the basic symbolic reachability analysis notions on which our algorithms are based.

2.3   Symbolic Optimal Reachability

The text in this subsection is an adaptation for single-cost PTA, from the one presented by Larsen and Rasmussen, for dual-priced PTA [17]. Symbolic techniques are required in the analysis of infinite state systems. They provide effective ways to describe and manipulate sets of states simultaneously. To enable cost-optimal analysis, such techniques are enriched with cost information annotated to each individual symbolic state [16].

A priced transition systems with a structure $\tau = \langle S, s_0, \Sigma, \rightarrow \rangle$, where S is a set of states, $s_0 \in S$ is the initial state, Σ is a finite set of labels, and $\rightarrow$ is a partial function from $S \times \Sigma \times S$ into the non-negative reals, $\mathbb{R}_{\geq 0}$, defines all possible systems transitions with their respective costs. An execution of τ is a sequence $\gamma = s_0 \xrightarrow{a1,p1} s_1 \xrightarrow{a2,p2} \ldots \xrightarrow{an,pn} s_n$. The cost of γ with respect to some goal state $G \subseteq S$, is defined as:

$$COST_G(\gamma) = \begin{cases} \infty, & \text{if } \forall \ i \geq 0 \ : \ s_i \notin G \\ \sum_{i=1}^{n} p_i, & \text{if } \exists \ n \geq 0 \ : \ s_n \in G \ \wedge \ \forall \ 0 \leq i < n \ : \ s_i \notin G. \end{cases}$$

For a given goal state s, the minimum cost of reaching s is the infimum of the costs of the finite traces ending in the s. Dually, the maximum cost of reaching the goal state s is the supremum of the costs of the finite traces ending in s. Similarly, the minimum/maximum cost of reaching a set of states $G \subseteq S$ is:

$\inf \{COST_G(\gamma) : \gamma \in \Gamma\}$, and

$\sup \{COST_G(\gamma) : \gamma \in \Gamma\}$,

where Γ is the set of all executions in the priced transition system τ.

To effectively analyze priced transition systems, priced symbolic states of the form (A, π) are used, where $A \subseteq S$ is a set of states, and $\pi : A \rightarrow 2^{\mathbb{R}_{\geq 0}}$ assigns non-negative costs to all states of A. The reachability of the priced symbolic state (A, π) assumes that all $s \in A$ are reachable with all costs in $\pi(s)$. To express successors of priced symbolic states, e.g., all states that can be reached from the current state $s \in A$, we use a Post-operator $Post_a(A, \pi) = (post_a(A), \eta) = (B, \eta)$ expressed as follows:

$$B = \{s' \mid \exists \ s \in A : s \xrightarrow{a} s'\}$$

$$\eta(s) = \inf\{\pi(s') + p \mid s' \in A \wedge s' \xrightarrow{a,p} s\}$$

Here η provides the cheapest cost for reaching states of B via states in A, assuming that these may be reached with costs according to π.

A symbolic execution of a priced transition system τ is a sequence $\beta = (A_0, \pi_0), \ldots, (A_n, \pi_n)$, where for $i < n$, $(A_{i+1}, \pi_{i+1}) = Post_{a_i}(A_i, \pi_i)$ for some $a_i \in \Sigma$ and $A_0 = \{s_0\}$ and $\pi_0(s_0) = 0$. The relation between executions and symbolic executions is expressed as follows:

– For each execution γ of τ ending in s, there is a symbolic execution β ending in (A, π) such that $s \in A$ and $COST(\gamma) \in \pi(s)$.

– Let β be a symbolic execution of τ ending in (A, π); then, for each $s \in A$ and $p \in \pi(s)$, there is an execution $\gamma \in s$ such that $COST(\gamma) = p$.

From the statements above, one can notice that symbolic states accurately capture the cost of reaching all states in the state space.

3   Algorithms for Calculating Strongest Postconditions of Services

To provide constructs for the correctness check of a REMES service, as described in Section 2 and introduced in [6], we assume that the service is described by a Hoare triple, on which we apply the forward analysis technique. The latter relies on computing the strongest postcondition of the REMES service w.r.t. the given precondition. Proving the correctness of a REMES service in isolation reduces to simply checking the Boolean implication between the calculated strongest postcondition and the given user requirement.

Previously [6], we have focused on less complex systems and employed the Guarded Command Language (GCL) [9] to prove service correctness by manual computation of the strongest postconditions needed in the process. In this paper, we aim for a more automated mechanism to check service correctness, focusing on developing algorithms that facilitate such computation for REMES services formally described as PTA. We can perform maximum/minimum resource-usage trace computation on the corresponding PTA, while accumulating the strongest postcondition during the analysis. The algorithms for strongest postcondition calculation, presented in this paper, rely on the symbolic reachability algorithms for computing the minimum and the maximum reachability cost, respectively, proposed by Larsen and Rasmussen [17].

In the following, we recall the notion of strongest postcondition, as introduced by Dijkstra and Sholten [10], and the program correctness check based on it. Next, we introduce two algorithms that compute the strongest postcondition of a REMES service formally described as PTA, together with the maximum/minimum cost reachability analysis, respectively.

3.1   Strongest Postcondition

Assume that $\{p\}S\{q\}$ is a Hoare triple denoting the partial correctness of service S with respect to precondition p and postcondition q. According to Dijkstra and Sholten [10], the strongest postcondition transformer, denoted by $(sp.S.p)$, is the set of final states for which there exists a computation controlled by S, which belongs to class "initially p". Assuming that p holds, the execution of a service S results in $sp.S.p$ true, if S terminates. Proving the Hoare triple, that is, proving the correctness of service S, reduces to showing that $(sp.S.p \Rightarrow q)$ holds.

To illustrate the strongest postcondition calculation on a simple statement, let us assume that a service performs a simple subtraction operation $(x := x - 5)$ and that the provided precondition is $p = (x > 15)$, while the requirement is $q = (x > 10)$. Then, calculating the strongest postcondition reduces to the following:

$$sp.(x := x - 5).(x > 15) = (\exists x_0 \cdot x = x_0 - 5 \wedge (x_0 > 15))$$

where x_0 is the initial value of x. Verifying the correctness of S, with respect to p, and q above, reduces to showing that:

$$\exists x_0 \cdot x = x_0 - 5 \wedge (x_0 > 15) \Rightarrow (x > 10)$$

In the following, we show how to compute $sp.S.p$ automatically, assuming S is the PTA semantic translation of a REMES service.

3.2 Strongest Postcondition Calculation and Minimum Cost Reachability

In this section, we show the algorithm that computes the strongest postcondition, and the minimum cost of resource consumption for a given REMES service, formally described as a PTAn.

Let us assume (A, π) and (B, η) as our priced symbolic states. If $A \subseteq B$ and $\eta(s) \leq \pi(s)$, for all $s \in A$, we denote by $(B, \eta) \sqsubseteq_{inf} (A, \pi)$ the preorder expressing that (B, η) is "at most as big and cheap" as (A, π) [16].

Algorithm 1 employs two data-structures, WAITING (initially containing the initial priced symbolic state (A, π_0)) and PASSED (initially empty) to hold the priced symbolic states waiting to be examined, and those that are already explored, respectively. At each iteration, the algorithm selects a priced symbolic state (A, π) from WAITING. If (A, π) is a goal state [2] not contained in a goal state previously stored in SP (strongest postcondition), it is added to the calculated postcondition SP. Otherwise, if it is not a goal state and not contained in a symbolic state previously stored in PASSED, it is added to PASSED, and all its successor states are added to WAITING. When WAITING is empty, the strongest postconditions calculated for each path reaching the goal state are returned. We define Final (A, π) as follows:

$$\text{Final}\,(A, \pi) = \begin{cases} true, & \text{if } (A, \pi) \in F \\ false, & \text{otherwise.} \end{cases}$$

where F denotes the final priced symbolic state.

The algorithm terminates when WAITING is empty, that is, when no further priced symbolic state is left to be examined. The algorithm results in a set of strongest postconditions SP. Termination of the algorithm is guaranteed, provided that $\sqsubseteq_{inf}$ is a well quasi-ordering on symbolic states [16].

In addition, information about the cost of service execution is carried within the calculated strongest postcondition. The cost is assumed to be initially set to ∞ and updated whenever a goal state is found, which can be reached with the lower cost than the current one.

---

[2] Note that, in a PTAn describing a REMES service, the goal state is determined by a unique location and hence, if Final (A, π) holds, then the whole of (A, π) is a goal state, assuming that every symbolic state (A, π) satisfies the property that all states in A are in the same location.

```
00  SP := {}
01  PASSED := {}
02  WAITING := {({A₀}, π₀)}
03  while WAITING ≠ {} do
04    select (A, π) from WAITING
05    if (Final (A, π) ∧ ∀ (B, η) ∈ SP : (B, η) ⋢ᵢₙf (A, π))
06    then SP := SP ∪ (A, π) else
07      if ∀ (B, η) ∈ PASSED : (B, η) ⋢ᵢₙf (A, π) then
08        PASSED := PASSED ∪ {(A, π)}
09        WAITING := WAITING ∪ ⋃ₐ∈Σ Postₐ(A, π)
10      end if
11    end if
12  end while
13  return SP
```

Algorithm 1. Abstract algorithm for computing the service strongest postcondition and the minimum cost of reaching the goal state.

As stated, the algorithm provides a set of strongest postconditions calculated for distinctive paths that reach the goal state (location) in the PTAn. Finally, to get the actual strongest postcondition, we simplify the set SP. The strongest postcondition can be simplified as follows:

$$\forall\ (A, \pi)_i \in \text{SP}\ :\ \bigcup_{j \neq i} (A, \pi)_j \not\sqsubseteq_{inf} (A, \pi)_i$$

The simplification assumes that each symbolic priced state that is not included into the reunion of all other symbolic priced states is subtracted. For more details regarding simplification, we refer the reader to [7, 12].

Example Revisited. To illustrate our approach, we recall the simple service shown in Fig. 2. In the automaton, it is possible to delay either in location l_0 or l_1. Location l_2 is assumed to be the final location. From l_0, it is possible to take a self-loop, for maximum two times (integer n is initially set to two) and then take one of the available edges, or directly take one of the edges that lead to location l_1, and finally end up in location l_2. Staying in locations l_0 or l_1 or taking any of the available edges increases the accumulated cost, modeled by cost variable. We are interested in calculating the minimum cost for reaching the final location (l_2) and the respective strongest postcondition.

Let us now assume that our service is annotated with precondition p, which we assume satisfied, and postcondition q, which represents the service requirement, as follows:

$$p = (x = 0 \wedge y = 0)$$

$$q = (1 \leq res \leq 10 \wedge x \leq y)$$

In the above, x and y are clock variables, n is an integer variable that bounds the number of loop iterations in location l_0, and res is the variable modeling the resource usage of the original service. In the corresponding PTAn representation, res translates into the automaton's cost variable. By verifying q, within the minimum cost reachability context, we want to check whether our service consumes at least 1 unit of resource, for the system to be considered correct.

Proving correctness of the PTAn w.r.t. this requirement relies on the strongest postcondition computation, for minimum cost, according to Algorithm 1.

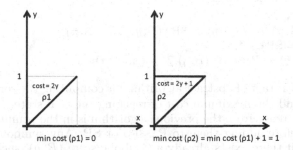

Fig. 3. Symbolic states for minimum reachability cost

In Fig. 3, we illustrate one trace of the minimum cost reachability analysis that reaches the goal location l_2. Note that in the minimum cost case, it is optimal to reach l_2 in zero time units, via location l_1. The accumulated cost is then 1. In case of the total accumulated delay 1, it is optimal to delay in l_0 with cost 2, hence the cost of reaching l_2 is $2y + 1$ and the strongest postcondition *of this trace* is $\mathsf{cost} = 2y + 1 \wedge y \leq 1 \wedge x \leq y$.

There are four more traces reaching l_2. The total SP becomes

$$(\mathsf{cost} = 2y + 1 \wedge y \leq 1 \wedge x \leq y) \vee$$
$$(\mathsf{cost} = 2y + 2 \wedge y \leq 1 \wedge x \leq y) \vee$$
$$(\mathsf{cost} = 2y + 3 \wedge y \leq 1 \wedge x \leq y) \vee$$
$$(\mathsf{cost} = 2y + 3 \wedge y \leq 1 \wedge x < y) \vee$$
$$(\mathsf{cost} = 2y + 4 \wedge y \leq 1 \wedge x < y)$$

After simplifying according to our definition, the total SP can be reduced to the following:

$$(\mathsf{cost} = 2y + 4 \wedge y \leq 1 \wedge x < y)$$

It is easy to prove that the above strongest postcondition implies the following predicate:

$$v = (1 \leq \mathsf{cost} \leq 6 \wedge x \leq y),$$

which in turn implies q, if cost is replaced by *res*. It then follows that the minimum-cost strongest postcondition implies q, which completes our correctness proof in this case.

3.3 Strongest Postcondition Calculation and Maximum Cost Reachability

Algorithm 1 can be modified to provide the strongest postcondition calculation together with the maximum reachability cost. At the service level, this would translate into checking whether, in the worst-case of service resource-usage, the latter does not exceed a prescribed upper bound. We here briefly sketch the required modifications of Algorithm 1. As previously, we assume that all paths eventually reach the goal state. The modification concerns the lines 05 to 07 of Algorithm 1, which become as follows:

```
05     if (Final (A, π) ∧ ∀ (B, η) ∈ SP : (B, η) ⋢_sup (A, π))
06     then SP := SP ∪ (A, π) else
07         if ∀ (B, η) ∈ Passed : (B, η) ⋢_sup (A, π)) then
```

Algorithm 2. Extract of abstract algorithm for computing the service strongest postcondition and the maximum cost of reaching the goal state.

The only difference from the previous algorithm is in the pruning of symbolic priced states before adding them to Passed or SP. Any symbolic state $(A, π)$ can be pruned if there exists already a symbolic state $(B, η)$, such that $A \subseteq B$ and $π(s) \leq η(s)$ for all states $s \in A$. Similarly, the strongest postcondition can be simplified as follows:

$$\forall (A, π)_i \in SP : \bigcup_{j \neq i} (A, π)_j \not\supseteq_{sup} (A, π)_i$$

Example Revisited. The PTAn depicted in Fig. 2 is again used to illustrate the approach described above. According to our methodology, to verify the correctness of the service w.r.t. p and q, we need to first compute the strongest postcondition of the corresponding PTAn, under the assumption of worst-case resource usage, that is, maximum cost in PTA terms.

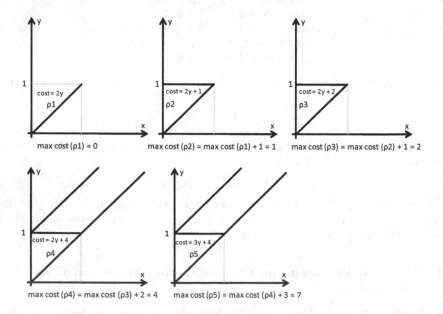

Fig. 4. Symbolic states for maximum reachability cost

Fig. 4 depicts a trace of the reachability analysis, assuming the maximum cost of reaching the goal location. In this case, the trace includes two self-loops in l_0, and then a jump to l_1 via the lower of the two possible edges. The costs are $2y$, $2y + 1$, and $2y + 2$ in l_0, and then $3y + 4$ in l_1 (and in l_2). The strongest postcondition w.r.t. the maximum cost of the trace becomes $\mathsf{cost} = 3y + 4 \wedge y \leq 1 \wedge x < y$. The total SP of the whole PTAn w.r.t. maximum cost becomes

$$(\mathsf{cost} = 3y + 1 \wedge y \leq 1 \wedge x \leq y) \vee$$
$$(\mathsf{cost} = 3y + 2 \wedge y \leq 1 \wedge x \leq y) \vee$$
$$(\mathsf{cost} = 3y + 3 \wedge y \leq 1 \wedge x \leq y) \vee$$
$$(\mathsf{cost} = 3y + 3 \wedge y \leq 1 \wedge x < y) \vee$$
$$(\mathsf{cost} = 3y + 4 \wedge y \leq 1 \wedge x < y)$$

The calculated SP can now be simplified according to our definition and reduced to the following:

$$(\mathsf{cost} = 3y + 4 \wedge y \leq 1 \wedge x < y)$$

By applying simple rules of logic, we can verify that the above SP with maximum cost implies the following predicate:

$$w = (1 \leq \mathsf{cost} \leq 7 \wedge x \leq y)$$

Next, after replacing cost by res in w, it follows straightforwardly that $w[\mathsf{cost} \leftarrow res] \Rightarrow q$, which entails that the strongest postcondition for maximum cost implies the requirement q. This actually proves the correctness of our original service, including its feasibility w.r.t. worst-case resource usage.

4   Discussion and Related Work

Beek et al. [24] give an exhaustive survey of several popular approaches [3, 15, 19, 21] that provide means for service modeling, service composition, and service correctness check. While all the described approaches offer a rich environment for service modeling and composition, neither of them has included direct support for service correctness check. To overcome this limitation, recently, in some of these approaches [8, 18, 22] formal methods have been employed with the intention to provide guarantees for web-service compositions.

Diaz et al. describe how BPEL and WS-CDL services can be automatically translated to timed automata and verified by UPPAAL model checker [8]. However, the described approach is limited to checking service timing properties. Narayanan et al. show how semantics of OWL-S, described using first-order logic, can be translated to Petri-nets and then analyzed as such [18]. The analysis includes reachability and liveness properties, and checking if the given service or service compositions are deadlock free. Weber et al. introduce a formalism to check control-flow correctness [25]. They first verify whether the given process is sound, meaning that the control-flow of interest guarantees proper completion and that there are no deadlocks. Further, they consider process models in which the individual activities are annotated with logical preconditions and postconditions. In the last step, the authors aim to determine whether the interaction of control flow and logical states of the process is correct. Gilmore et al. present a model-driven approach for the development of SOS that facilitates the specification of extra-functional properties [11]. The benefit of this approach is support for reliability and performance analysis i.e., performance estimates based on the timed process algebra PEPA.

Compared to these approaches, REMES services can be both mechanically reasoned about [6], and also, translated to PTA [2] where one can apply algorithmic computation of the strongest postcondition of PTA, as presented in this paper. Moreover, REMES services formally described as PTA can be analyzed with UPPAAL , or UPPAAL CORA tools[3], for functional but also extra-functional behaviors, in particular, timing and resource-wise behaviors.

5   Conclusions

In this paper, we have presented an approach that facilitates the automated correctness check for services, formally described as PTA, by providing forward analysis algorithms that compute the most precise postcondition (strongest postcondition) that is guaranteed to hold upon termination of the service execution, which corresponds to reaching a final location of the given PTAn service description. The approach serves as the alternative algorithmic verification method for services modeled as REMES modes, complementary to the deductive method that uses Hoare triples and the strongest postcondition semantics to prove service correctness [6].

In our previous work, we show that proving the correctness of a REMES service reduces to showing that the calculated strongest postcondition of that particular service is at least as strong as the user-defined requirement. The algorithms that we propose here extend the existing maximum, minimum cost reachability algorithms [17], with strongest postcondition calculation. In our case, the cost variable models the service's accumulated resource-usage. Consequently, the computed strongest postcondition of a service modeled as a PTAn could contain both functional, but also timing and resource-usage information, observable at the end of the service execution.

The approach is illustrated on a small example, on which we also show resource usage/cost calculation using symbolic states. However, the complexity of our algorithms, and their applicability on larger examples have not been investigated yet. We plan to validate our approach on a more complex case study in which the direct application of the method on SOS will be emphasized.

As future work, we plan to address the above issues, by first implementing the strongest postcondition algorithms in the UPPAAL CORA tool. We also intend to extend the REMES tool-chain with a postcondition calculator that would run UPPAAL CORA as a back-end.

---

[3] For more information about the UPPAAL and UPPAAL CORA tool, visit the web page www.uppaal.org.

References

[1] Alur, R., Dill, D.L.: A theory of timed automata. Theoretical Computer Science 126(2), 183–235 (1994), citeseer.nj.nec.com/alur94theory.html

[2] Alur, R., La Torre, S., Pappas, G.J.: Optimal Paths in Weighted Timed Automata. In: Di Benedetto, M.D., Sangiovanni-Vincentelli, A.L. (eds.) HSCC 2001. LNCS, vol. 2034, pp. 49–62. Springer, Heidelberg (2001)

[3] Andrews, T., Curbera, F., Dholakia, H., Goland, Y., Klein, J., Leymann, F., Liu, K., Roller, D., Smith, D., Thatte, S., Trickovic, I., Weerawarana, S.: BPEL4WS, Business Process Execution Language for Web Services Version 1.1. IBM (2003)

[4] Behrmann, G., Fehnker, A., Hune, T., Larsen, K.G., Pettersson, P., Romijn, J., Vaandrager, F.: Minimum-Cost Reachability for Priced Timed Automata. In: Di Benedetto, M.D., Sangiovanni-Vincentelli, A. (eds.) HSCC 2001. LNCS, vol. 2034, pp. 147–161. Springer, Heidelberg (2001)

[5] Causevic, A., Seceleanu, C., Pettersson, P.: Formal reasoning of resource-aware services. Technical Report ISSN 1404-3041 ISRN MDH-MRTC-245/2010-1-SE, Mälardalen University (June 2010)

[6] Čaušević, A., Seceleanu, C., Pettersson, P.: Modeling and Reasoning about Service Behaviors and Their Compositions. In: Margaria, T., Steffen, B. (eds.) ISoLA 2010, Part II. LNCS, vol. 6416, pp. 82–96. Springer, Heidelberg (2010)

[7] David, A., Håkansson, J., Larsen, K.G., Pettersson, P.: Model checking timed automata with priorities using DBM subtraction. In: Asarin, E., Bouyer, P. (eds.) FORMATS 2006. LNCS, vol. 4202, pp. 128–142. Springer, Heidelberg (2006)

[8] Díaz, G., Pardo, J.-J., Cambronero, M.-E., Valero, V., Cuartero, F.: Automatic Translation of WS-CDL Choreographies to Timed Automata. In: Bravetti, M., Kloul, L., Zavattaro, G. (eds.) EPEW/WS-EM 2005. LNCS, vol. 3670, pp. 230–242. Springer, Heidelberg (2005)

[9] Dijkstra, E.W.: Guarded commands, nondeterminacy and formal derivation of programs. Commun. ACM 18(8), 453–457 (1975)

[10] Dijkstra, E.W., Scholten, C.S.: Predicate calculus and program semantics. Springer-Verlag New York, Inc., New York (1990)

[11] Gilmore, S., Gönczy, L., Koch, N., Mayer, P., Tribastone, M., Varró, D.: Nonfunctional properties in the model-driven development of service-oriented systems. Software and Systems Modeling 10, 287–311 (2011), doi: 10.1007/s10270-010-0155-y

[12] Hsiung, P.-A., Lin, S.-W.: Model checking timed systems with priorities. In: Proceedings of the 11th IEEE International Conference on Embedded and Real-Time Computing Systems and Applications, RTCSA 2005, pp. 539–544. IEEE Computer Society Press, Washington, DC (2005)

[13] Ivanov, D.: Integrating formal analysis methods in PROGRESS IDE. Master of science thesis, Malardalen Research and Technology Centre, Vasteras, Sweden (June 2011)

[14] Ivanov, D., Orlic, M., Seceleanu, C., Vulgarakis, A.: Remes tool-chain - a set of integrated tools for behavioral modeling and analysis of embedded systems. In: Proceedings of the 25th IEEE/ACM International Conference on Automated Software Engineering, ASE 2010 (September 2010)

[15] Kavantzas, N., Burdett, D., Ritzinger, G., Fletcher, T., Lafon, Y., Barreto, C.: Web services choreography description language version 1.0. World Wide Web Consortium, Candidate Recommendation CR-ws-cdl-10-20051109 (November 2005)

[16] Larsen, K.G., Behrmann, G., Brinksma, E., Fehnker, A., Hune, T., Pettersson, P., Romijn, J.: As Cheap as Possible: Efficient Cost-Optimal Reachability for Priced Timed Automata. In: Berry, G., Comon, H., Finkel, A. (eds.) CAV 2001. LNCS, vol. 2102, pp. 493–505. Springer, Heidelberg (2001), http://portal.acm.org/citation.cfm?id=647770.734117

[17] Larsen, K.G., Rasmussen, J.I.: Optimal reachability for multi-priced timed automata. Theor. Comput. Sci. 390, 197–213 (2008), http://portal.acm.org/citation.cfm?id=1330765.1330861

[18] Narayanan, S., McIlraith, S.A.: Simulation, verification and automated composition of web services. In: WWW 2002: Proceedings of the 11th International Conference on World Wide Web, pp. 77–88. ACM, New York (2002)

[19] Object Management Group (OMG): Business Process Modeling Notation (BPMN) version 1.1 (January 2008), http://www.omg.org/spec/BPMN/1.1/

[20] Orlić, M.: Resource usage prediction in component-based software systems. Phd thesis, Faculty of electrical engineering and computing, University of Zagreb (November 2010)

[21] Roman, D., Keller, U., Lausen, H., de Bruijn, J., Lara, R., Stollberg, M., Polleres, A., Feier, C., Bussler, C., Fensel, D.: Web service modeling ontology. Applied Ontology 1(1), 77–106 (2005)

[22] Salaün, G., Bordeaux, L., Schaerf, M.: Describing and reasoning on web services using process algebra. In: ICWS 2004: Proceedings of the IEEE International Conference on Web Services, p. 43. IEEE Computer Society Press, Washington, DC (2004)

[23] Seceleanu, C., Vulgarakis, A., Pettersson, P.: Remes: A resource model for embedded systems. In: In Proc. of the 14th IEEE International Conference on Engineering of Complex Computer Systems (ICECCS 2009). IEEE Computer Society (June 2009)

[24] Ter Beek, M.H., Bucchiarone, A., Gnesi, S.: Formal methods for service composition. Annals of Mathematics, Computing & Teleinformatics 1(5), 1–10 (2007), http://journals.teilar.gr/amct/; In: Annals of Mathematics, Computing & Teleinformatics, vol. 1(5), pp. 1–10. Technological Education Institute of Larissa (TEIL), Greece (2007)

[25] Weber, I., Hoffmann, J., Mendling, J.: Beyond soundness: on the verification of semantic business process models. Distrib. Parallel Databases 27, 271–343 (2010), http://dx.doi.org/10.1007/s10619-010-7060-9

Software Aspects of Robotic Systems

Jens Knoop and Dietmar Schreiner

Institute of Computer Languages,
Vienna University of Technology,
1040 Vienna, Austria
{knoop,schreiner}@complang.tuwien.ac.at
http://www.complang.tuwien.ac.at

The development of autonomous robotic systems has experienced a remarkable boost within the last years. Away from stationary manufacturing units, current robots have grown up into autonomous, mobile systems that not only interact with real world environments, but also fulfill mission critical tasks in collaboration with human individuals on a reliable basis. Typical fields of application are unmanned vehicles for exploration but also for transportation, reconnaissance and search-and-rescue in hazardous environments, and ambient assisted living for elderly or disabled people.

Hence, algorithms in cognition, computer vision, and locomotion have become hot-spots of research and development. In addition, modern concepts like evolutionary and bio-inspired design have entered the stage to tackle open issues in robotics and to cope with domain specific properties like inherent indeterminism.

The back-side of this boost is an even larger increase in complexity of modern robotic systems. Numerous actuators and sensors have to be controlled simultaneously. Complex actions have to be performed via timed parallel execution of multiple instruction streams on distinct electronic control units. Autonomy, especially long term autonomy as required by deep-sea or space exploration missions, necessitates features of fault-tolerance, error recovery, or at least well-defined fallbacks. Due to the physical interaction of robots with the real world, safety violations are extremely harmful, in the worst-case they might lead to severe damage and even to casualties.

This track continues the *1st International ISoLA Workshop on Software Aspects of Robotic Systems* that has been held in October 2011 in Vienna. It brings together researchers and practitioners who are interested in the software aspect of robotic systems and stretches from robot programming, to languages and compilation techniques, real-time and fault tolerance, dependability, software architectures, computer vision, cognitive robotics, multi-robot-coordination, simulation, bio-inspired algorithms to machine-learning.

T. Margaria and B. Steffen (Eds.): ISoLA 2012, Part II, LNCS 7610, p. 323, 2012.
© Springer-Verlag Berlin Heidelberg 2012

Process-Oriented Geoinformation Systems and Applications

Hartmut Asche

FG Geoinformatik, Universität Potsdam (Germany)
gislab@uni-potsdam.de

It is a well-accepted truism that the vast majority of digital data have a geographical reference. In the past decades geodata have been processed and visualised by dedicated software products of the geoinformation systems (GIS) type for a limited range of scientific and professional applications. However, For more than a deacade, however, both geodata and GIS functionalities are having an increasing, by now almost ubiquitious impact on various fields of everyday life. Against this background space-related, process-orientend software environments will play a decisive role in the development and delivery of a variety of geoinformation and geovisualisation products and services for a wide range of scientific and practical applications alike. This track aims at providing an update on current as well as emerging issues and applications in ubiquitious geoinformation and geovisualisation.

This track contains four papers concerning

- *Concepts, processes and techniques of 3d online atlases*, by René Sieber, Livia Hollenstein, and Remo Eichenberger (ETH Zürich),
- *Process Control based on Data Usability for Deriving Remote Sensing Value Added Data Products*, by Erik Borg and Bernd Fichtelmann (DLR Neustrelitz), and Hartmut Asche (Univ. Potsdam),
- *Comparison of topical machine learning algorithms (random forest, artificial neural network, support vector machine) with maximum likelihood for supervised crop type classification*, by Ingmar Nitze and Urs Schulthess (Department of Geography, University College Cork), and Hartmut Asche (Univ. Potsdam),
- *Web-based on-demand service for the generation of quality maps: concept and processing pipeline*, by Hartmut Asche and Rita Engemaier (FG Geoinformatik, Universität Potsdam).

T. Margaria and B. Steffen (Eds.): ISoLA 2012, Part II, LNCS 7610, p. 324, 2012.
© Springer-Verlag Berlin Heidelberg 2012

Concepts and Techniques of an Online 3D Atlas – Challenges in Cartographic 3D Geovisualization

René Sieber, Livia Hollenstein, and Remo Eichenberger

Institute of Cartography and Geoinformation, ETH Zurich, Switzerland
{sieber,hollenstein,eichenberger}@karto.baug.ethz.ch

Abstract. During the last two decades numerous interactive atlas and mapping systems have been developed, offering a variety of mainly statistical 2d map types like choropleths, point symbols and diagrams but scarcely also some 3d map types like panoramic views and block diagrams. These systems include a bundle of atlas functionality for spatial and temporal navigation, map visualization, and layer handling.

Today, atlas systems have to compete with a multiplicity of freely available map services, geoportals and virtual globes; thus, atlases have to strive for new horizons. At the same time, the big popularity of geodata and geo-applications is offering a unique chance to digital atlas products in order to activate new user groups and to animate them for collaboration.

Results of a detailed survey on current products of geovisualization are pointing out that the majority of up-to-date's applications is originally dedicated and conceived for web and mobile use. The attractiveness of such applications is primary based on the immediate benefit in everyday life, on the up-to-dateness of the data offered, and on their integrative possibilities. In addition, applications using 3d concepts and virtual globes are persuading users by their intuitive navigation and spatial clarity. However, these applications are rather heterogeneous concerning content handling and cartographic quality.

Therefore, the main challenge for future digital atlases will be to merge the big trends of *3d mapping, online and mobile applications* with *cartographic design and atlas-specific functionality*. Research and development should focus on cartographic 3d visualization and interactivity for different user groups and applications.

The Swiss Atlas Platform (APS) project, launched in 2011, is dealing with these aspects of online 3d cartography in order to set up a basic 3d atlas configuration. Based on this APS, the new product line of ATLAS OF SWITZERLAND and affiliated atlases will be developed.

During the first project phase, the concept of a 3d atlas platform has been defined, having the potential to realize a unique combination of interactive thematic cartography and 3d atlas technology. From the point of view of system design, the Swiss Atlas Platform consists of extensible modules for *spatial navigation, map visualization and information retrieval*, unified under a flexible *graphical user interface*. These modules contain a large number of cartographic and general functions; *core functionality* will be implemented first which in a later phase can be extended according to user needs.

T. Margaria and B. Steffen (Eds.): ISoLA 2012, Part II, LNCS 7610, pp. 325–326, 2012.
© Springer-Verlag Berlin Heidelberg 2012

Currently, work is done on the *visualization core module*, allowing for 2d and 3d mapping by means of osgEarth – a dedicated virtual globe engine. This visualization engine is capable of handling large amounts of geographical data and web services. Essentially, the system offers 2d and 3d visualization of raster data (DTMs, grids, map sheets, aerial and satellite images) and vector data (choropleths, univariate symbols and diagrams, POIs), and even solid 3d objects. Moreover, it allows for intuitive spatial navigation, layer management, information query, and labeling.

Future core development will be necessary to refine cartographic 3d representation techniques and to implement interactive methods. Concurrently, a flexible GUI for different platforms has to be set up and a lot of cartographic and editorial work has to be done to realize an online 3d atlas application.

Handling Heterogeneity in Formal Developments of Hardware and Software Systems

Yamine Ait-Ameur[2] and Dominique Méry[1]

[1] Université de Lorraine, LORIA CNRS UMR 7503, Vandœuvre-lès-Nancy, France
mery@loria.fr
[2] Ecole Nationale Supérieure d'Electrotechnique, d'Electronique, d'Informatique,
d'Hydraulique et des Télécommunications (ENSEEIHT), IRIT
2, rue Charles Camichel, B.P. 7122, 31071 Toulouse Cedex 786961
yamine@enseeiht.fr

Nowadays, the formal development of hardware and/or software systems implies the design of several models on which properties are expressed and then formally verified. Moreover, these models may be expressed in different modeling languages [1] and semantics. As a consequence, this development process leads to heterogeneous developments. Heterogeneity may appear in two different forms.

The first one is related to the large variety of formal development techniques and to the semantics and proof systems carried out by these techniques. Several formal descriptions may be associated to a given system with different semantics.

The second type of heterogeneity results from the modeling domain [2–4] chosen for formalizing the described system. Usually, this domain is not explicitly described nor formalized. Most of the knowledge related to this domain is hardly encoded by the formal system description. The last decade has made use of ontologies [5] as an explicit formalization of such modeling domains. Expressing, in formal models, references to ontological concepts contribute to reduce such a heterogeneity. It also allows developers to address specific properties related to interoperable, adaptive, reconfigurable and plastic systems.

This thematic track is considering two technical papers, which are included into this proceedings and a presentation talk of the related topics by the organizers.

A first paper [6], entitled *Leveraging formal verification tools for DSML users: a process modeling case study*, provides a nice case study on the problems of model driven development, where a translational semantics is used to link the client oriented (business) models with the engineer oriented (formal) models. The key issue is one of feedback - once the client oriented models are translated to formal models then how to feedback the results of running formal methods tools to the clients in a language that they can understand.

A second paper [7], entitled *An Ontological Pivot Model to Interoperate Heterogeneous User Requirements*, proposes a conceptual ontology-driven approach to facilitate the interoperability and to reduce the heterogeneity among different formalisms using a pivot- model-based approach; it provides a final model, which encapsulates the different stakeholders requirements.

The two papers highlight the recent advances in this research field and encourage further research and prospective activities to tackle questions related to

T. Margaria and B. Steffen (Eds.): ISoLA 2012, Part II, LNCS 7610, pp. 327–328, 2012.
© Springer-Verlag Berlin Heidelberg 2012

multi-modeling and meta-modeling formal techniques, the definition of unified theories and heterogeneous reasoning, the validation and verification methods for heterogeneous formal models, specification, design and architecture languages, ontology based formal modeling, domain ontologies and explicit model annotation, ontology based reasoning for formal verification, formal models for ontologies and formal models annotation.

Moreover, we are concerned with the separation of concerns when reasoning about properties of models. An intrinsic property is a property that a model has of itself, independent of other models, including its context. An extrinsic (or relational) property of a model depends on that models relationship with other models, including its context. Without a more formal software engineering development approach, based on separation of implicit and explicit, the composition of software components in common contexts risks compromising correct operation of the resulting system. This is a significant problem when software systems are constructed from heterogeneous components that must be reliable in unreliable contexts[8]. As an example, mass is an intrinsic property whereas weight is an extrinsic property that depends on the contextual gravitational field. Development of a software control system for a space craft will, very likely, need models of both mass and weight in order for the system to be verified to function correctly. Thus, we conjecture the need for separation of intrinsic and extrinsic concerns by building explicit formal models of contextual semantics. Although the concerns need to be cleanly separated, the models need to be tightly integrated: achieving both is a significant challenge.

References

1. Bjorner, D., Henson, M.C. (eds.): Logics of Specification Languages. EATCS Textbook in Computer Science. Springer (2007)
2. Bjorner, D.: Software Engineering 1 Abstraction and Modelling. Texts in Theoretical Computer Science. An EATCS Series (2006) ISBN: 978-3-540-21149-5
3. Bjorner, D.: Software Engineering 2 Specification of Systems and Languages. Texts in Theoretical Computer Science. An EATCS Series (2006) ISBN: 978-3-540-21150-1
4. Bjorner, D.: Software Engineering 3 Domains, Requirements, and Software Design. Texts in Theoretical Computer Science. An EATCS Series (2006) ISBN: 978-3-540-21151-8
5. Gruber, T.R.: A translation approach to portable ontology specifications. Knowl. Acquis. 5(2), 199–220 (1993)
6. Zalila, F., Crégut, X., Pantel, M.: Leveraging Formal Verification Tools for DSML Users: A Process Modeling Case Study. In: Margaria, T., Steffen, B. (eds.) ISoLA 2012, Part II. LNCS, vol. 7610, pp. 330–344. Springer, Heidelberg (2012)
7. Boukhari, I., Bellatreche, L., Jean, S.: An Ontological Pivot Model to Interoperate Heterogeneous User Requirements. In: Margaria, T., Steffen, B. (eds.) ISoLA 2012, Part II. LNCS, vol. 7610, pp. 345–359. Springer, Heidelberg (2012)
8. Garlan, D., Schmerl, B.: Model-based adaptation for self-healing systems. In: Proceedings of the First Workshop on Self-healing Systems, WOSS 2002, pp. 27–32. ACM, New York (2002)

Leveraging Formal Verification Tools for DSML Users: A Process Modeling Case Study

Faiez Zalila, Xavier Crégut, and Marc Pantel

Université de Toulouse, IRIT – France
firstname.lastname@enseeiht.fr

Abstract. In the last decade, Model Driven Engineering (MDE) has been used to improve the development of safety critical systems by providing early Validation and Verification (V&V) tools for Domain Specific Modeling Languages (DSML). Verification of behavioral models is mainly addressed by translating domain specific models to formal verification dedicated languages in order to use the sophisticated associated tools such as model-checkers. This approach has been successfully applied in many different contexts, but it has a major drawback: the user has to interact with the formal tools. In this paper, we present an illustrated approach that allows the designer to formally express the expected behavioral properties using a user oriented language — a temporal extension of OCL —, that is automatically translated into the formal language; and then to get feedback from the assessment of these properties using its domain language without having to deal with the formal verification language nor with the underlying translational semantics. This work is based on the metamodeling pattern for executable DSML that extends the DSML metamodel to integrate concerns related to execution and behavior.

Keywords: Domain specific modeling languages, Model formal verification, Behavioral properties, Translational semantics, Verification feedback.

1 Introduction

TOPCASED[1] is a project[2] started in 2005 in the French "Aerospace Valley" cluster that gathers academic and industrial partners [1]. TOPCASED is dedicated to the development of an open source Computer Assisted Software Engineering (CASE) tool for the development of safety critical aeronautics, automotive and space embedded systems. Such developments will range from system and architecture specifications to software and hardware implementation through equipment definition.

TOPCASED provides modeling languages, both domain specific (SAM, EAST-ADL, SAE AADL, SDL[3] and xSPEM[4]) and general purpose (SYSML, UML, etc.) and

---

[1] *Toolkit In OPen source for Critical Applications & SystEms Development*, www.topcased.org

[2] This work was funded by the French ministries of Industry and Research and the Midi-Pyrénées regional authorities through the FUI TOPCASED, ANR OpenEmbedd, ITEA SPICES and ITEA2 OPEES projects.

[3] *Specification and Description Language: is an object-oriented formal language developed and standardized by The International Telecommunication Standardization Sector (ITU-T).*

[4] *OMG SPEM extended for execution.*

T. Margaria and B. Steffen (Eds.): ISoLA 2012, Part II, LNCS 7610, pp. 329–343, 2012.

associated tools like graphical and textual editors, documentation generators, validation through model animation, verification through model checking, version management, traceability, etc. TOPCASED relies on MDE generative technologies to define the languages and build all these tools for all these languages. It is thus an MDE platform both for building system models and for building the platform itself. MDE technologies used in TOPCASED for defining and tooling languages are centered around Ecore[5] and configuration models taken as inputs by generative or interpretative tools.

Because the TOPCASED toolkit addresses safety critical systems, Validation and Verification activities are of primary importance and should be performed as early as possible at design time on the various models, both to reduce the development costs and to provide higher quality systems.

Validation is performed through model animation [2]: the designer builds a model using a graphical editor and can execute it according to scenarios. The runtime data produced by these executions is displayed as decorations of the graphical representation of the model or thanks to a dedicated view. Model animation is thus very similar to source level debugging for software. Scenario driven model execution runs through a single path in the set of all possible executions for the model. The use of several scenarios provides a coverage of the various possible executions but this validation is usually not exhaustive.

On the contrary, verification aims to check whether a property holds for all possible executions of the model. Model-checkers are dedicated tools for that purpose. These tools usually rely on two formal verification languages: one to model the behavior of the system and one to express the properties to check. For example, the TINA toolbox [3], available in TOPCASED, relies on Time Petri nets (TPN) for the behavior and State-Event Linear Temporal Logic (SE-LTL) for the properties. Thus, the use of such model checking tools requires to translate the system business domain model into an equivalent behavior model in the considered formal verification language and to express the system requirements as properties. Furthermore, results are obtained on the formal side as execution traces and have to be translated back into the system domain. This is a well-known technique called *translational semantics*. Nevertheless, even if the translations are automated, they are often defined in an ad hoc way, specific to the considered business domain. Furthermore, system requirements are most of the time directly written as formal properties, in the verification tool domain and not in the system domain. Thus, the designer must have a good understanding of: a) the various domain languages; b) the behavior and property languages from the various tools; and c) on the translation scheme used to go from one to the other in both directions. Verification is thus a difficult activity requiring many abilities that are generally not available to the casual business domain designer. Our purpose is to provide methods and tools in order to ease the integration of model checking in MDE toolchain. This integration will provide seamless verification facilities to the business domain designer without requiring him to deal with target verification language and associated model-checkers. We will describe a partly automated MDE driven tool chain for expressing the system requirements in the business domain language, translating the requirements to model checking tools property languages, and translating the failure execution traces back to the designer's world.

---

[5] Ecore is the metalanguage of Eclipse Modeling Framework,

`www.eclipse.org/modeling/emf`

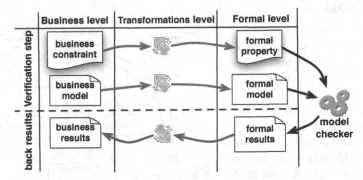

Fig. 1. General approach of a translational semantics with feedbacks

Our contribution consists in reifying elements involved in the semantics of a DSML in order to ease, and partially automate, the different translations that are summarized in Figure 1. More precisely, it includes:

1. the use of MDE technologies on both sides, business and formal verification domains based on a metamodel architecture that combines concerns related to model execution, including runtime information and the stimuli that make the model evolve. This metamodel guides the definition of the translational semantics and simplifies the production of business domain feedback to the end-user.
2. a user dedicated language for the expression of business properties.
3. automatic translation of business properties into formal verification domain properties based on the translational semantics.
4. automatic translation of the verification results obtained in the verification domain to the business domain. When a property does not hold, the obtained counter example is presented to the user either as a business domain scenario or a snapshot of the model completed with runtime information.

The approach is illustrated on a case study which concerns modeling of process using a process description language derived from the SPEM OMG Standard [4].

The paper is organized as follows. Section 2 presents the case study from the end-user viewpoint. It defines some constraints to assess and the expected feedback. Section 3 describes the formalism used for modeling processes, the language of expression of temporal constraints and extensions made on the DSML to be able to capture verification results. Section 4 presents the formal language and tools. Section 5 describes all required transformations for process verification and verification feedbacks. Section 6 considers related works and the last section concludes.

2   End-User Concerns

This section presents the business domain – process modelling – considered in the case study and the concerns of end-users. We first present the kind of process models the end-user wants to build. Then we explain the kind of properties he wants to check on his models. Finally we describe the feedback the end-user expects from verification tools in order to get insight on the errors the models may contain.

2.1 Business Models

Figure 2 shows an example of a
process model. It corresponds to
a simplified development process
composed of four activities, each
represented in an ellipse: *Programming*, *Designing*, *Test case writing*
and *Documenting*. Arrows between
activities indicate dependencies: the
target activity depends on the source
activity. The label specifies the kind
of dependency. The word before the
"To" is the state that should have
been reached by the source activity
in order to perform the action on the
target activity, action which appears

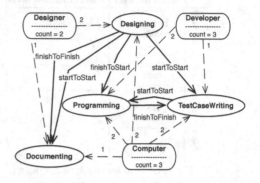

Fig. 2. A business development process

after the "To". For example, the "finishToStart" dependency between *Designing* and
Programming means that *Programming* can only be started when *Designing* has been
finished. *Documenting* and *TestCaseWriting* can start once *Designing* is started (*start-
ToStart*) but *Documenting* cannot finish if *Designing* is not finished (*finishToFinish*).
The dependencies put between *Programming* and *TestCaseWriting* enforces a test
driven development: programming can only starts when test cases are already started
and, obviously, test case writing can only be finished when programming is finished in
order to take into account test coverage.

Rounded rectangles represent the number of available resources (2 *Designers*, 3 *Developers* and 3 *Computers*). Dashed arrows indicate how many resources an activity
requires. *Programming* needs two developers and two computers. Resources are allocated when an activity starts and freed when it finishes.

These processes are deliberately simplified to avoid overloading this presentation but
time constraints or hierarchical decomposition of activities could be added.

2.2 User Verifications

To validate or to verify a model, the user may check that properties derived from the
system requirements hold on that model. We focus on *behavioral properties*, properties
that concern the evolution of the model over time. Static properties are also important
for the end user but they can easily be included in the editing tool using for example an
OCL checker.

The user may be interested in general properties not specific to a given process
model. For example, he may want to check whether a process model may finish or
not (P_1). A process finishes if all its activities finish while respecting constraints imposed by dependencies and resource allocation. If these properties hold, the user may
want to get a terminating scenario and use it to pilot the process execution.

The user may also want to verify properties that are specific to a particular process
model. As an example, he might want to know if in all cases *Documenting* is finished
before *Designing* is finished (P_2).

2.3 Verification Feedback

Once the end user has defined his model and expressed his requirements through properties, he wants to have feedback on the assessment of those properties. If a property evaluates to true, then the requirement is fulfilled. But if a property evaluates to false, the user expects to have feedback in order to understand why the property does not hold. For example, a counter example may be exhibited. Obviously, this counter example should be expressed at the business domain level.

For instance, using the example shown in Figure 2, property P_1 does not hold and there is indeed a deadlock during process execution. The user can be provided with a counter example that explains the deadlock as a scenario like the one of Figure 3 which lists the actions (start or finish) applied on activities. The deadlock is due to the fact that *Programming* cannot be started because a *Computer* is missing. If a computer was added, then the P_1 requirement would hold. The property P_2 does not hold. Indeed, it is possible to finish *Designing* before *Documenting* is finished. A possible scenario is shown on Figure 4 (counter-example). The user may want to play those scenarios using a model animator like the one developed in the TOPCASED project [5].

```
Start Designing
Finish Designing
Start Documenting
Finish Documenting
Start TestCaseWriting
```

```
Start Designing
Finish Designing
Start Documenting
Start TestCaseWriting
Finish Documenting
```

Fig. 3. A scenario from P_1 **Fig. 4.** A scenario from P_2

3 Business Metamodeling

Metamodels generally focus on business domain concerns and do not take into account other elements required to execute a model. As model execution may be of interest for most of the modeling languages, especially in the context of safety critical systems, we have defined a general solution to describe all the data required to define an execution semantics for any executable modeling language [6]. It is a kind of *metamodeling pattern* that may be used from design time to run time. This pattern has been applied in the TOPCASED project to build animators [2] that allow validation of SysML/UML State Machine and Activity diagrams or SAM (an automate-based language used by Airbus) models. It is also helpful to ease the definition of forward and backward transformations toward verification languages in order to get back failure scenarios from model checkers.

The pattern advocates to structure an executable DSML metamodel in such a way that the different concerns are stressed: the business domain, the queries a user may ask on a model to assess it satisfies its requirements (i.e. the model business properties), the stimuli that make the model evolve. The corresponding xSPEM metamodel is shown on Figure 5 and detailed in the next paragraphs.

3.1 xSPEM Domain Definition Metamodel (DDMM)

A metamodel defines the concepts (metaclasses) of the business domain addressed by the DSML and the relationships between them (references). In the executable metamodel pattern defined in TOPCASED, this reference metamodel is called the *Domain Definition MetaModel*, DDMM . The DDMM of XSPEM is shown on Figure 5 (package named DDMM at the bottom). It defines the concepts of process (*Process*) composed of a set of (1) workdefinitions (*WorkDefinition*) that model the activities (described in section 2.1) performed during the process, (2) worksequences (*WorkSequence*) that define dependency relationships between workdefinitions and (3) resources (*Resource*) allocated to activities (*Parameter*).

Obviously, this metamodel could be extended with well-formedness rules for example using OCL to express constraints not captured by the metamodel definition (names of workdefinitions have to be unique, worksequences should not be reflexive, resources counts should be positive, etc.). This aspect related to the static semantics of the DSML is not in the scope of this paper.

3.2   XSPEM Query Definition Metamodel (QDMM) and Formal Expression of Requirements

End users' behavioral properties usually rely on information that is not directly available in the DDMM because they only exist when the model is executed (runtime information). For example, the previous properties rely on the state of a workdefinition: started or finished. As usual, this information has to be reified. Thus, we have chosen to extend the DDMM with a new metamodel which describes the queries the user can conduct on his models. We call it QDMM (Query Definition MetaModel). For XSPEM, queries such as *isStarted* and *isFinished* can be applied on a *WorkDefinition* (see top right of Figure 5). A query *isFinished* is defined on *Process* in order to model the end-user business requirement, (P_1), defined in section 2.2.

To be checked, requirements of section 2.2 have to be formally expressed. OCL is not well suited for that purpose because it only allows the specification of structural properties and some Floyd-Hoare behavioral properties for methods. Nevertheless, it is now a widely known language and a few temporal extensions of OCL have been proposed in order to specify event-based behavioral properties whereas OCL only targets function-based properties. We have chosen to rely on Temporal OCL and especially on the proposal from [7] as the syntax of this extension is quite natural for OCL users. It introduces usual future-oriented temporal operators such as *always*, *sometimes*, *next*, *existsNext* as well as their past-oriented duals.

Here-after are the expression of the P_1 and P_2 requirements identified in section 2.2. They rely on the DDMM but also on the queries defined in the QDMM.

```
context Process        -- P₁ requirement
inv isFinished:
    eventually (self.workDefinitions->
        forAll(a: WorkDefinition | a.isFinished())))
context Process        -- P₂ requirement
    inv: always self.(getWD("Documenting").isFinished()
        precedes self.getWD("Designing").isFinished());
context Process
    def: getWD(WDName: String): WorkDefinition =
        self.workDefinitions
            ->select(wd: WorkDefinition | wd.name = WDName)
            ->asList->first()
```

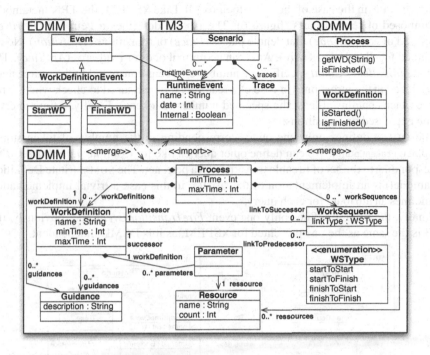

Fig. 5. xSPEM Metamodels

We have build a TOCL text editor dedicated to the end-user thanks to the xText tool from Eclipse Textual Modeling Framework (TMF) and the TOCL grammar of [7].

3.3 xSPEM Event Definition and Trace Management Metamodels (EDMM & TM3)

The DDMM and QDMM allow to express the requirements but we also need to show to the user the results obtained in the formal verification domain. A Snapshot can be expressed using QDMM because it represents all runtime information of interest to the user. To express the scenario corresponding to a counter example (like the one shown in Figure 4) we define two other metamodels that also extend the DDMM. The first one is the Trace Management Metamodel (TM3). It allows definition of a scenario as a sequence of runtime events — a stimulus that makes the model evolve. The TM3 is independent of any DSML. On the contrary, the Event Definition Metamodel (EDMM) is specific to a DSML and defines its runtime events. For instance, runtime events for xSPEM include "start a workdefinition" and "finish a workdefinition".

4 Formal Level Metamodeling

In order to represent the semantic data and ease the exchange of verification results with business domain models, the metamodeling pattern is also applied on the formal language, TPN in the case of the TINA toolbox [3]. Like xSPEM, the TPN metamodel is composed of several parts (figure 6). The DDMM describes a Petri net (*PetriNet*) composed of nodes (*Node*) that denote places (*Place*) or transitions (*Transition*). Nodes are linked together by arcs (*Arc*). Arcs can be normal ones or read-arcs (*ArcKind*). The attribute *initialtokenCount* specifies the number of tokens consumed in the source node or produced in the target one (in case of a read-arc, it is only used to check whether the source place contains at least the specified number of tokens). Finally, a time interval can be expressed on transitions.

The QDMM defines only one query corresponding to the number of token stored in a place (tokenCount). We can define other queries like for example *fireableTransition* corresponding to the set of fireable transitions in a petri net. The SDMM (State Definition Metamodel) is an implementation of the QDMM, in this case a trivial implementation that defines an attribute for each query.

Finally, the EDMM defines only one event *FireTransitionEvent* and, obviously, the TM3 is the same as the one presented for xSPEM, as it is DSML-independent.

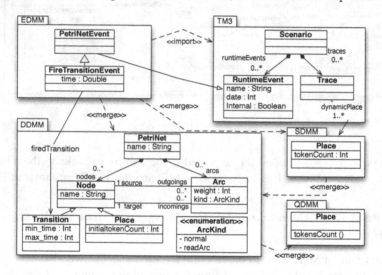

Fig. 6. PETRINET metamodels

5   The Transformation Level

The last steps concern the transformation level of Figure 1. It consists first in defining the translational semantics, that is translating an xSPEM model into a Petri net one. Then, TOCL properties have to be translated into LTL formulae so that they can be checked by the TINA toolbox. Finally, results obtained on the formal verification domain have to be translated back into the business domain. One can notice that business metamodel (or model) TOCL invariants may be expressed to assert that they are preserved by the translational semantics.

All these transformations are defined at the metamodel level. They have thus only to be defined once by DSML and formal domain experts and the end-user can use them for any of the xSPEM models.

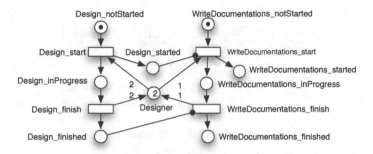

Fig. 7. Generated Petri net for parts of Figure 2

5.1 Translation XSPEM 2petrinet

Several translational semantics may be defined for XSPEM according to the level of details in the execution that we want to model and the kind of properties we want to assess. Thus, we advocate in [8] that defining the translational semantics should be *property-driven* to favor the definition of a *minimal* semantics, that will allow to answer to the questions the user may ask about his models.

As the QDMM metamodel records all the aspects of interest to the end user, the expert has to verify that all the queries may be expressed using the formal language translation. Thus, the QDMM can be used as a guide to write the translation. For example, in the formal language, one should be able to determine if a workdefinition is started or finished as these queries are part of the QDMM. A *WorkDefinition* is thus translated into four places characterizing its state (*notStarted*, *started*, *running* and *finished*) linked by two transitions. These transitions model the actions that we want to observe on a workdefinition: one can *start* a workdefinition and then *finish* it. A workdefinition is considered *started* if it is either running or finished. This is recorded by the place named *started*.

A *WorkSequence* becomes a *read-arc*[6] from one place of the source workdefinition (either *started* or *finished*) to a transition of the target workdefinition (either *start* or *finish*) according to the kind of *WorkSequence* (*linkKind* attribute). A resource becomes a place whose initial marking (*initialtokenCount*) corresponds to its *count*. Each *Parameter* element is translated into two arcs, the first one to take resources when the concerned workdefinition starts and the second one to release them when the workdefinition finishes.

Figure 7 contains the Petri net model resulting from the application of the translational semantics on a part of the XSPEM model from Figure 2 (*Designing* and *Documenting* workdefinitions and worksequences between them as well as the *Developer* resource).

The ATL transformation language [9] has been used to implement this translational semantics. First, an ATL module describes the transformation from an XSPEM model to a Petri net model [10] (not shown here[7]). Then, an ATL query[8] generates the textual

---

[6] A read-arc only checks that there is enough tokens in the input place but those tokens are not withdrawn when the transition is fired.

[7] http://combemale.svn.enseeiht.fr/proto/fr.irit.acadie.xspem2tina/

[8] This query is obviously independent of the translational semantics.

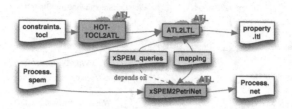

Fig. 8. Architecture of the ATL transformations

syntax used by the TINA tools from a Petri net model. This part could be implemented with any model to text language but it was simpler to rely on the same tool.

5.2   Translating TOCL to SE-LTL

Translating TOCL properties into LTL implies dealing with three main aspects. First, temporal operators have to be translated. It is straightforward since LTL provides the same kind of temporal operators. Second, OCL operators have to be evaluated, especially those that query the model. Finally, queries specified in xSPEM QDMM have to be translated into LTL. The meaning of these queries obviously depends on the previously defined translational semantics. Thus, while defining the translational semantics, the expert has to provide an ATL library called xSPEM_*queries* which defines all queries as helpers returning the appropriate LTL formulae. For example the WorkDefinition query "isFinished" becomes a helper "isFinished()" that computes the string "self.name + "_finished"".

The TOCL to LTL transformation is composed of two stages (top of Figure 8). The first one is a Higher Order Transformation (HOT-TOCL2ATL) that takes as input a TOCL model and generates an ATL transformation, which is the one executed in the second stage. This second transformation takes as input the business domain model (conforming to xSPEM in our case study) upon which the TOCL properties handled in the first stage will be run to generate the LTL formulae.

This transformation strategy results from two points. First, it is not possible in the first stage to use the xSPEM_queries library because there is no reflexivity in ATL. Second, several TOCL operators can be applied to each element of an input model. So, ATL iteration rules must be generated to traverse the model.

One strong point is that the TOCL2LTL transformation is generic and automated. It is only parametrized by the ATL module that provides the definitions of the QDMM queries for the target formal property language.

Applied on P_1, the TOCL2LTL transformation produces the following formulae:

```
<> (Designing_finished /\ Programming_finished
    /\ TestCaseWriting_finished /\ Documenting_finished)
```

The formulae corresponding to P_2 is:

```
[] ([] (- Designing_finished) U Documenting_finished)
```

5.3   Checking SE-LTL Properties

Once the Petri net and the LTL formulae have been generated, the selt model checker from the TINA toolbox is used. If the LTL formulae does not hold, it exhibits a counter-example: a specific execution of the model that leads to a state where the property is not satisfied. Figure 9 shows the counter example corresponding to the P_1 property. It consists of a sequence of states. A state is a snapshot of the model showing the places marking. After each state, there is the transition fired to go to the next state. The example shows a deadlock (last transition).

```
FALSE
 state 0: Programming_notStarted Designing_notStarted Documenting_notStarted TestCaseWriting_notStarted computer*3
         designer*2 developer*3
 -Designing_start->
 state 1: Programming_notStarted Designing_inProgress Designing_started Documenting_notStarted
         TestCaseWriting_notStarted computer developer*3
 -Designing_finish->
 state 2: Programming_notStarted Designing_finished Designing_started Documenting_notStarted
         TestCaseWriting_notStarted computer*3 designer*2 developer*3
 -Documenting_start->
 state 3: Programming_notStarted Designing_finished Designing_started Documenting_inProgress Documenting_started
         TestCaseWriting_notStarted computer*2 designer developer*3
 -Documenting_finish->
 state 4: Programming_notStarted Designing_finished Designing_started Documenting_finished Documenting_started
         TestCaseWriting_notStarted computer*3 designer*2 developer*3
 -TestCaseWriting_start->
 * [accepting] state 5: Programming_notStarted Designing_finished Designing_started Documenting_finished
         Documenting_started TestCaseWriting_inProgress TestCaseWriting_started computer designer*2 developer*2
 -deadlock->
 state 5: Programming_notStarted Designing_finished Designing_started Documenting_finished Documenting_started
         TestCaseWriting_inProgress TestCaseWriting_started computer designer*2 developer*2
 [accepting all]
0.001s
```

Fig. 9. Selt output for P_1 checked on example of Figure 2

5.4   Designer Dedicated Feedback

Model verification based on a translational semantics provides a significant advantage: the reuse of existing sophisticated model checkers. But there is one significant drawback: results are obtained at the verification level and have to be translated back to the business domain level. This section explains this translation.

Generating PETRINET Scenario and Trace. Using xText, we analyze the output of the selt model-checker and produce a PETRINET scenario and trace using the PETRINET metamodels and the TM3 presented in sections 3 and 4. The PETRINET scenario corresponding to the counter example of Figure 9 is the following.

```
FireTransitionEvent Designing_start
FireTransitionEvent Designing_finish
FireTransitionEvent Documenting_start
FireTransitionEvent Documenting_finish
FireTransitionEvent TestCaseWriting_start
```

The same tool builds the PETRINET models that corresponds to each states of the counter-example (not shown here).

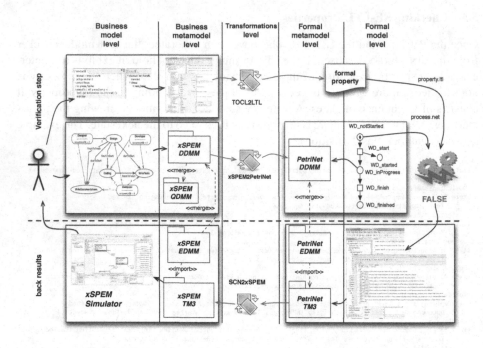

Fig. 10. General approach illustrated with the XSPEM case study

Translating PETRINET Scenario to XSPEM Scenario. The PETRINET Scenario is then transformed to an XSPEM Scenario. This transformation converts transition firing events *FireTransitionEvent* to XSPEM events, either start (*StartWD*) or finish (*FinishWD*) a *WorkDefinition*. The naming convention defined in the *Mapping* ATL library are used to decode the fired transition names and produce the corresponding XSPEM events and their target workdefinitions. The XSPEM scenario corresponding to the previous PETRINET one is the one shown on Figure 3. To obtain the scenario of figure 4, we have to check the negation of P_2 because we want an example which satisfies P_2.

The same approach is used to translate PETRINET snapshots (that is PETRINET models) into XSPEM ones. It could be automated using traceability data between source and target models generated during the transformation step.

6   Related Work

Translational semantics with feedbacking verification results: The main advantage of translational semantics is the reuse of existing tools from the target technical space like model-checkers. Its major issue is that it provides results in the target space that must be translated back to the business domain space. Hegedus et al. [11] propose a method based on a traceability mechanism of model transformations. It relies on a relation between elements of the source (BPEL) and the target (PETRINET) metamodel, implemented by means of annotations in the transformation's source code. The authors propose a technique for the back-annotation of simulation traces based on change-driven model transformations from traces generated by SPIN model checker to the specific animator named BPEL Animation Controller. However, in our approach, we try to generate a scenario (a set of events) that will be animated by a generic animator. In [12], authors use traceability links of the transformation which generates Alloy models from UML. The back-annotation transformation is automatically generated based on these traceability links using a QVT-based implementation. Here, the back-annotation is supported for static model instances, and not for execution traces of Executable DSML models like in our case. In [13], the authors define an approach named Arcade that uses SPIN model checker for evaluating safety and liveness properties of a Domain Reference Architecture that is translated to Promela language. Arcade interprets SPIN counter-example and generates an Architecture Trace Diagram (ATD) that has two dimensions: a vertical dimension that represents time and a horizontal dimension representing SPIN processes. Nevertheless, they do not define a high-level abstraction between business level and formal level. Contrary to our work, we separate the two domains (DSML and formal verification ones) and we hide all formal aspects by translating formal results to business ones. In [14], Pelliccione *et al.* present a software tool platform for the model-based design and validation of software architectures, named CHARMY, that offers an extension called SASIM deriving from Theseus approach [15]. Both translate the violation trace from SPIN model checker on a generated sequence diagram and an animated UML state diagrams. vUML [16] also use the same approach. CHARMY, Theseus and vUML are based on a very ad hoc approach that uses UML diagrams and SPIN model checker. On the contrary, we rely on a generic approach that can be applied to other DSML.

All the above approaches aim at verifying a specific DSML through formal tools by translating business semantics into formal one and by feedbacking formal verification results to the initial business level. However, our work provides a generic approach for the verification of executable DSML. It is based on the explicit definition of the different concerns involved in model execution (runtime information expressed as queries, events) thanks to the executable DSML metamodelling pattern. Based on this pattern and the translation semantics, generic transformations allow to translate user properties to logical formulae and verification results back to business level.

Behavioral property Patterns: To verify BPEL service composition schemas, [17] proposes a property specification language based on ontologies and named PROPOLS which allows composition of the patterns defined in [18]. These patterns are close to TOCL temporal operators and composition corresponds to OCL operators. Rather than relying on a Query Definition MetaModel, a one to one mapping has to be defined for each property item to the corresponding BPEL operation.

In [19], the authors provide a graphical tool named PSC (Property Sequence Chart), to specify temporal properties as an extended notation of a selected subset of the UML 2.0 Interaction Sequence Diagrams. Theseus approach [15] uses SPIDER to translate natural language properties to the property specification language of the targeted analysis tools. Both, PSC and SPIDER are specific approaches used in a specific domain between UML and SPIN. User-oriented property languages, graphical or not, are an important point to make formal verification accessible to end users. TOCL is certainly not the best-suited language despite it is an extension of OCL, a well accepted language in MDE. Nevertheless, we consider it can be used as a pivot language for more user-oriented languages.

7   Conclusion

Using the XSPEM case study, this paper has illustrated a method to ease the integration of verification tools for safety and liveness properties on executable models. It relies on the executable DSML metamodeling pattern using a translation to the Time Petri nets as formal verification language providing the semantics. This could be applied to any other kind of formal language providing automated verification tools. We have recently applied it to the FIACRE intermediate verification language [20], that abstracts several existing verification toolsets such as TINA and CADP in order to factorize common aspects and avoid redefining transformations for all toolsets. This experiment results will be presented in a forthcoming paper. The integration is provided through QDMM extension to the pattern and automated translations on the property side.

This approach has been designed for domain specific languages and this is a key point to keep it simple. It is currently being experimented for several significantly different DSMLs (and sub-languages from general purpose languages) such as data flow models, SAE AADL, SDL, UML and SYSML class, state machine, activity and composite structure diagrams. But, it is still to be shown if it can scale up to more complex languages or to languages that combine different models of computation.

These preliminary experiments allowed a first validation of our proposal for the systematic construction of verification tools for behavioral properties expressed on a DSML. We have chosen to rely on TOCL to express properties at the business domain level because it is close to OCL. However, some early feedback have shown that it is still not well suited to many end users. Therefore, we might need to investigate new user-oriented language for expressing behavioral constraints. It is a problem that has already been identified in [21]: the authors have defined a new dialect of linear temporal logic more suitable for control engineers.

Finally, we propose to ease the feedback of verification results. We currently rely on naming conventions. We are investigating the explicit construction of the links between the business domain and verification models elements during the downward translation so that they can be used during the upward feedback.

References

1. Farail, P., Gaufillet, P., Canals, A., Camus, C.L., Sciamma, D., Michel, P., Crégut, X., Pantel, M.: The TOPCASED project: a toolkit in open source for critical aeronautic systems design. In: Embedded Real Time Software (ERTS), Toulouse, France (January 2006)
2. Crégut, X., Combemale, B., Pantel, M., Faudoux, R., Pavei, J.: Generative Technologies for Model Animation in the TOPCASED Platform. In: Kühne, T., Selic, B., Gervais, M.-P., Terrier, F. (eds.) ECMFA 2010. LNCS, vol. 6138, pp. 90–103. Springer, Heidelberg (2010)

3. Berthomieu, B., Ribet, P.-O., Vernadat, F.: The tool TINA – Construction of Abstract State Spaces for Petri Nets and Time Petri Nets. International Journal of Production Research 42(14), 2741–2756 (2004)
4. Software & Systems Process Engineering Metamodel (SPEM) 2.0, Object Management Group, Inc. (October 2007)
5. Combemale, B., Crégut, X., Giacometti, J.-P., Michel, P., Pantel, M.: Introducing Simulation and Model Animation in the MDE TOPCASED Toolkit. In: Proceedings of the 4th European Congress EMBEDDED REAL TIME SOFTWARE (ERTS), Toulouse, France (2008)
6. Combemale, B.: Simulation et vérification de modèle par métamodélisation exécutable, E. U. Européennes, ed. (June 2010)
7. Ziemann, P., Gogolla, M.: An Extension of OCL with Temporal Logic. In: Jürjens, J., Cengarle, M.-V., Fernandez, E., Rumpe, B., Sandner, R. (eds.) Critical Systems Development with UML – Proceedings of the UML 2002 Workshop, vol. TUM-I0208, pp. 53–62, Université Technique de Munich, Institut d'Informatique (September 2002)
8. Combemale, B., Crégut, X., Garoche, P.-L., Thirioux, X., Vernadat, F.: A property-driven approach to formal verification of process models. In: ICEIS, Selected Papers (2007)
9. Jouault, F., Kurtev, I.: Transforming Models with ATL. In: Bruel, J.-M. (ed.) MoDELS 2005. LNCS, vol. 3844, pp. 128–138. Springer, Heidelberg (2006)
10. Bendraou, R., Combemale, B., Crégut, X., Gervais, M.-P.: Definition of an executable spem 2.0. In: APSEC, pp. 390–397. IEEE Computer Society (2007)
11. Hegedus, A., Bergmann, G., Rath, I., Varro, D.: Back-annotation of simulation traces with change-driven model transformations. In: IEEE International Conference on Software Engineering and Formal Methods, vol. 0, pp. 145–155 (2010)
12. Shah, S.M.A., Anastasakis, K., Bordbar, B.: From UML to Alloy and back again. In: Proceedings of the 6th International Workshop on Model-Driven Engineering, Verification and Validation (MODEVVA 2009). ACM International Conference Proceeding Series (2009)
13. Barber, K.S., Graser, T., Holt, J.: Providing early feedback in the development cycle through automated application of model checking to software architectures. In: Proceedings of the 16th IEEE International Conference on Automated Software Engineering, ASE 2001 (2001)
14. Pelliccione, P., Inverardi, P., Muccini, H.: Charmy: A framework for designing and verifying architectural specifications. IEEE Trans. Soft. Eng. 35(3), 325–346 (2009)
15. Goldsby, H.J., Cheng, B.H.C., Konrad, S., Kamdoum, S.: A Visualization Framework for the Modeling and Formal Analysis of High Assurance Systems. In: Wang, J., Whittle, J., Harel, D., Reggio, G. (eds.) MoDELS 2006. LNCS, vol. 4199, pp. 707–721. Springer, Heidelberg (2006)
16. Lilius, J., Paltor, I.: vuml: a tool for verifying uml models. In: 14th IEEE International Conference on Automated Software Engineering, pp. 255–258 (October 1999)
17. Yu, J., Manh, T., Han, J., Jin, Y., Han, Y., Wang, J.: Pattern Based Property Specification and Verification for Service Composition, pp. 156–168 (2006)
18. Dwyer, M., Avrunin, G.S., Corbett, J.C.: Property specification patterns for finite-state verification. In: Proceedings of the Second Workshop on Formal Methods in Software Practice, pp. 7–15. ACM Press (1998)
19. Autili, M., Inverardi, P., Pelliccione, P.: Graphical scenarios for specifying temporal properties: an automated approach. Automated Software Engg. 14, 293–340 (2007)
20. Berthomieu, B., Bodeveix, J.-P., Filali, M., Farail, P., Gaufillet, P., Garavel, H., Lang, F.: FIACRE: an Intermediate Language for Model Verification in the TOPCASED Environment. In: 4th European Congress EMBEDDED REAL TIME SOFTWARE (ERTS) (January 2008)
21. Ljungkrantz, O., Akesson, K., Fabian, M., Yuan, C.: A formal specification language for plc-based control logic. In: 2010 8th IEEE International Conference on Industrial Informatics (INDIN), pp. 1067–1072 (July 2010)

An Ontological Pivot Model to Interoperate Heterogeneous User Requirements

Ilyès Boukhari, Ladjel Bellatreche*, and Stéphane Jean

LIAS - ISAE-ENSMA - Futuroscope, France
{ilyes.boukhari,bellatreche,jean}@ensma.fr

Abstract. With the globalisation, the development of advanced applications and complex systems requires the implication of a large number of designers that may come from different fields, departments, research laboratories, etc. Usually, they are free to use their favourite vocabularies and formalisms to express the requirements related to their assigned parts of a given project. Various formalisms exist to express user requirements: informal (interviews), semi-formal (UML use case, goal oriented, etc.) and formal (B-Method, etc.). The concepts and properties used by these formalisms may belong to different alphabets. This situation makes the interoperability between user requirement formalism models difficult. In this paper, we propose a conceptual ontology-driven approach to facilitate this interoperability and to reduce the heterogeneities between formalisms. We first present the concepts related to conceptual ontologies and their connection with the user requirement formalisms. Secondly, a pivot model allowing the integration of different semi-formal models is described, through a case study. Finally, an implementation based on model driven approach (MDA) is given.

Keywords: Requirement Engineering, Ontologies, Goal-oriented, MDA.

1 Introduction

The collection, the representation and the analysis of user requirements ($\mathcal{UR}$) are the core phases ensuring the success of projects and applications [1]. $\mathcal{UR}$ are used on each stage of the life cycle of information based-applications: *conceptual*, *logical* and *physical*. They allow constructing conceptual models of applications by the means of *properties* (attributes) identified through $\mathcal{UR}$ analysis. At the logical phase, they facilitate the determination of *important* properties and *constraints* such as *primary keys* of a database schema. In the physical phase, they are used for benchmarking and simulating the target applications[1]. Their omnipresence of $\mathcal{UR}$ generates a design approach called *user-centred design approach* ($\mathcal{UCDA}$) [1]. It allows an interactive development of systems and focuses specifically on making systems usable and safe for their users. It also empowers users and motivates them to learn and explore new system solutions.

---

* Corresponding author.
[1] Queries are usually exactracted from the $\mathcal{UR}$.

T. Margaria and B. Steffen (Eds.): ISoLA 2012, Part II, LNCS 7610, pp. 344–358, 2012.

Databases [2], data warehousing [3], data integration systems [4] are examples of applications developed according the $\mathcal{UCDA}$.

Usually, most of studies developed according the $\mathcal{UCDA}$ assume the presence of one or several *homogenous designers*. By *homogenous*, we mean that designers use the *same formalism* to express their $\mathcal{UR}$ and the *same vocabulary*. Usually, the process of designing complex systems and applications needs to decompose them into *several sub-systems*. According the *ANSI-EIA-632* Standard (Processes For Engineering a System)[2], a system is a set of products required to achieve a goal or function. With the globalization, the process of making a system requires the involvement of various designers from different departments, research laboratories, countries, etc. Two successful projects are examples of such a situation: (i) the project of the *jumbo Airbus A380* involving four sites in different countries: *Toulouse (France), Madrid (Spain), Hamburg (Germany)* and *Filton (England)*. The European project *Health-e-Child* initiated in 2006 aiming at developing a platform for prevention of health children (www.health-e-child.org/).

Designing such a project represents a big challenge and is time-consuming for large scale companies. Several factors increase its complexity: (a) *the large number of designers involved in developing the target system*, (b) the *diversity of formalisms* used by designers, (c) the *used vocabularies are heterogeneous* and (d) the *autonomy of designers*. **(a)** The large number of designers: developing complex applications for very large scale companies requires the presence of various designers and experts. Each designer has her/his habitudes; she/he uses her/his favourite formalism to express $\mathcal{UR}$. **(b)** The diversity of the used formalisms: designers may use different formalisms to express $\mathcal{UR}$ that may be classified into three main categories: (i) *informal* (linguistic) formalisms: they are based on natural languages with or without structuring rules. They may generate *ambiguities* because neither their syntaxes, nor their semantics are perfectly defined. Among these techniques, we can quote *questionnaires* and *interviews*. (ii) *Semi-formal* formalisms are proposed, especially for domains, with structured knowledge and expertises. We can cite for example, engineering, medicine, environment, etc. These models are generally based on graphical notations with a specified syntax. They offer a clear vision of the system and their use facilitates the communication between project's designers. UML notations, *KAOS* (Knowledge Acquisition in autOmated Specification) [5], the *MERISE* method [6] are examples of this class of formalisms. (iii) *Formal formalisms*: are based on mathematical or logical notations which provide a precise and no ambiguous framework for requirements modelling. They allow automatic verification of $\mathcal{UR}$ (ex., *B-method* [7]). **(c)** The diversity of the used vocabularies: each designer uses her/his vocabulary to express application requirements. This may generate semantic and syntax conflicts between designers. Structural heterogeneity exists because designers may use different structures and/or different formats to express requirements. The criterion concerns the three categories of $\mathcal{UR}$. The autonomy of the sources significantly increases the heterogeneity between generated $\mathcal{UR}$

---

[2] http://www.geia.org/

models. Indeed, the designers may work independently, and usually the interaction between them is done *at the end* of the requirement process phase. The semantic heterogeneity is due to different interpretations of real world objects, generating several categories of conflicts (*naming conflicts, scaling conflicts, confounding conflicts* and *representation conflicts* [4]). Several suggest proposed the use of *ontologies* to reduce different conflicts that may exists between actors [8]. They play the role of global conceptual models. Conceptual ontologies can be defined as explicit, formal descriptions of concepts and their relationships that exist in a certain universe of discourse, together with a shared vocabulary to refer to these concepts [9]. They may offer the alphabet on which designers pick their concepts and properties.

Based on the above discussion, we claim that to interoperate different designer's models, an *integration solution is more feasible*. Generally, integration technology becomes a big industry, where solutions were proposed for integrating various objects: *information sources* (called *Enterprise Information Integration*), *application integration* (Enterprise Application Integration), *Services* (Service Integration), *workflows*, etc. Unfortunately, integrating user requirements does not get more attention compared to other objects, except the research efforts performed by Lopez et al. [10], where a genetic meta-model (a priori defined) is proposed. It allows designers expressing their requirements and representing them by their favourite formalisms. The main drawbacks of this work are: (1) it does not offer *autonomy* to designers; (2) designers need to understand the generic model to express their requirements and (3) it ignores semantic and syntax heterogeneities that may exist between the expressed requirements. In this paper, we present an ontology-based integration solution that reduces the heterogeneity between vocabularies and formalisms using a model driven architecture.

The rest of this paper is organized as follows: section 2 reviews the related work. Section 3 describes the different heterogeneities that may occur when interoperating user requirements. Section 4 describes the case used to illustrate the steps of our proposal. Section 5 presents our proposal. Section 6 concludes the paper and suggests some future issues.

2   Related Work

Nowadays, ontologies are largely used in several research and industrial domains such as Semantic Web [9], data integration [4], e-commerce, data warehousing [3], natural language processing, data mining, etc. Several industrial and academic Database Management Systems offer solutions for managing and storing ontological instances (Oracle, IBM Sor). Ontologies have been incorporated in the field of requirement engineering since 80s. They contribute largely in specifying, unifying and reasoning on $\mathcal{UR}$ [11],[12],[13],[14],[2]. [11] proposed an ontological method for analyzing requirements, where a mapping between specified requirements and ontological elements is established. This ontology consists of a thesaurus and inference rules. [14] proposed an approach to improve the natural language for specifying requirements by the use of linguistic ontologies. The authors propose a tool, called RESI *(Requirements Engineering Specification Improver)* to support requirement analysts working with textual specifications. RESI identifies the linguistic defection and offers a dialog-system suggesting improving the quality of the requirements by marking the ambiguous specifications. [13] dealt with the problem of expressing $\mathcal{UR}$ and their refinement. To do so, the authors propose the use of goal-oriented analysis language to describe each requirement that can be refined into sub-goals. A tool called AGORA (Goal-Oriented Requirements Analysis) supporting this approach is developed. It is based on domain ontology. [2] proposed the use of linguistic ontologies for facilitating the collection and the expression of $\mathcal{UR}$ to develop conceptual models of traditional databases. The majority of these studies dealt with the heterogeneity of vocabularies, but they ignore the heterogeneity of the used formalisms, except the work of Lopez et al. [10].

3 Heterogeneity Types

In this section, we present the two heterogeneity types that occur when expressing requirements that concern vocabularies and formalisms.

3.1 Heterogeneity of Vocabularies

The autonomy of designers generates vocabulary heterogeneity. This heterogeneity is more classical and has been identified in the context of multi-databases and data source integration. [4] identified the following conflicts: naming conflicts, scaling conflicts, confounding conflicts and representation conflicts.

- *Naming conflicts*: occur when naming schemes of concepts differ significantly. The most frequently case is the presence of synonyms and homonyms. For example, a naming conflict occurs when actor use *Student* to express requirements for the England university, other actor uses *Scolar* to express requirements for the French university.
- *Scaling conflicts*: occur when different reference systems are used to measure a value (for example, marks of a student can be given on 20 or on 10).
- *Confounding conflicts*: occur when concepts seem to have the same meaning, but differ in reality due to different measuring contexts. For example, the weight of a student depends on the date where it was measured.
- *Representation conflicts*: arise when two formalisms describe the same concept in different ways. For example, in one formalism, student's information is represented by four elements (Name, Marks, Weight, Age) and in another one it is represented by three elements (Name, Marks, Weight).

Figure 1 illustrates these conflicts. Another problem involved in the requirements engineering is the risk of presence of inconsistencies and ambiguities between requirements at semantic level. These conflicts may be detected by the use of ontologies [8].

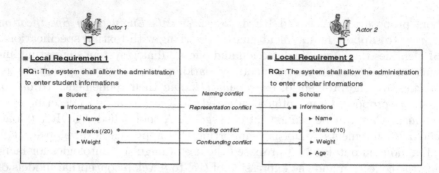

Fig. 1. Types of semantics conflict

3.2 Heterogeneity of Formalisms

The heterogeneity of vocabularies may impact the formalisms, since they are defined on these vocabularies. As we said before, several types of formalisms exist and in each type, various models exist. This generates schematic and representations conflicts between formalisms. Sometimes it is hard for a designer to move from formalism to another; even they share the same knowledge and terminology (actors, actions, results, etc.).

To reduce the heterogeneity between vocabularies and formalisms, their homogenisation is required. For the vocabulary homogenisation, we propose the use of conceptual ontologies allowing designers to pick their concepts and properties to express their requirements. For formalisms, a pivot model facilitating their interoperability is proposed. These homogenisations are described in the next sections.

3.3 Ontologies: Concepts and Formalisms

Several definitions have being proposed for ontology [15,16,9]. [9] defines a domain ontology as *a domain conceptualization in terms of classes and properties that is formal, consensual and referencable*. This definition emphasizes the three criteria that distinguish ontologies from all other models used in Computer Science such as Conceptual Models. An ontology is:

- *Formal*: an ontology is a conceptualization based on a formal theory which allows to check some level of consistency and to perform some level of automatic reasoning over the ontology-defined concepts and individuals. In our context, ontologies offer reasoning capabilities that can be used either to detect incompleteness and inconsistency included in a requirements specification.
- *Consensual*: the consensual aspect that characterizes ontologies allows designer to share/exchange their models with other project groups referencing the same ontologies.
- *Capability to be referenced*: each concept in the ontology (i.e., class and property) has the capability to be referenced through a universally unique identifier. This mechanism allows defining the semantic of requirements.

Two main categories of ontologies have emerged in the literature [9]. *Conceptual Ontologies* (CO) and *Linguistic Ontologies* (LO):

- *Conceptual Ontologies (CO)* represent object categories and properties that exist in a given domain whereas.
- *Linguistic Ontologies (LO)* define the terms that appear in a given domain. LOs include relationships between terms such as synonymous-of or homonymous-of. They are useful for system-user communication as well as providing the terms used in a given domain in different natural languages. Wordnet[3] is a well-known example of such ontologies.

With the increasing use of ontologies, a number of ontology models and languages with different formalisms have been proposed: PLIB [9] for engineering applications or semantic web languages like RDFS [17] and OWL [18]. We focus in our study on conceptual ontologies, whose schema can be formally defined as follows: [8]: $\mathcal{O} :< \mathcal{C}, \mathcal{P}, \mathcal{S}ub, \mathcal{A}pplic >$:

- $\mathcal{C}$ is the set of classes describing the concepts of a given domain.
- $\mathcal{P}$ is the set of properties describing the instances of $\mathcal{C}$.
- $\mathcal{S}ub : \mathcal{C} \rightarrow 2^{\mathcal{C}}$ is the subsumption function, which associates each class C_i its direct subsumed classes. Two subsumption relationships are introduced in our framework: (i) OOSub: describes the usual subsumption of inheritance relationship, where the whole set of applicable properties is inherited. (ii) OntoSub: describes a subsumption relationship without inheritance, where a part of the whole applicable properties may be imported from a subsuming class to the subsumed one. OntoSub is the formal operator. OntoSub is formalized by 'case-of' relationships in the PLIB formalism [9]. A similar mechanism exists in OWL ontologies, where an ontology can refer another ontology by using different namespaces.
- $\mathcal{A}pplic : \mathcal{C} \rightarrow 2^{\mathcal{P}}$ is a function that associates to each ontology class, the properties that are applicable for each instance of this class.

3.4   Pivot Model as a Solution for Formalism Heterogeneity

Let $\mathcal{D} = \{D_1, D_2, ..., D_n\}$ be the set of designers involved in the development of a given application. Each designer D_i ($1 \leq i \leq n$) has to express her/his requirements $\mathcal{UR}^{D_i}$ using her/his favourite formalism $\mathcal{F}_i$ and terminology (alphabet) $\mathcal{T}_i$. To interoperate different requirements, a naive solution may exist. It consists in establishing ($\frac{n \times (n-1)}{2}$) different mappings between n formalisms. This solution is costly, since it requires considerable efforts to map them, especially, if the number of used formalisms is large. To reduce this complexity, the pivot model is suitable. It offers a generic representation of different formalisms. More precisely, when using a pivot model the number of mapping is reduced to n mappings.

More formally, a $\mathcal{UR}$ integration system according a pivot approach is represented as a triple: $< P; \mathcal{UR}; M >$, where P is a pivot schema (generic), expressed

---

[3] http://wordnet.princeton.edu/

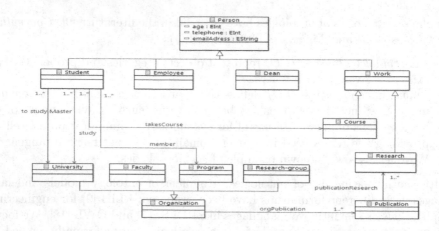

Fig. 2. A partial view of LUBM benchmark ontology

in a given formalism $\mathcal{F}^P$ over an alphabet $\mathcal{T}^P$; $\mathcal{UR}$ is the set of all $\mathcal{UR}$, expressed in different formalisms and terminologies and M is the mapping between P and $\mathcal{UR}$.

To facilitate the understanding of our heterogeneity of formalisms, we judge that it is helpful for readers to consider a case study.

4   Case Study

In this study, we suppose the existence of a global domain ontology that represents University activities. The ontology of the *Lehigh University Benchmark* (LUBM) is used [19] (Figure 2). Three designers from three countries (UK, Spain and France) express their requirements using three different semi-formal formalisms: the U*ML use cases* (UK), the *Goal-Oriented language* (Spain) and *MERISE* (Process Conceptual Model, MCT) (France). Next sections briefly describe the three formalisms.

4.1   UML Use Case Model

Use Case modelling is a technique which was developed to define requirements more than for capturing them [20]. A use case model consists of *actors*, use cases and relationships between them. It is used to represent the environment by actors and the scope of the system by use cases. An actor is an external element to the system (e.g. a user, another system) that interacts with the system. According to Jacobson [20], a use case is "*a description of a set of sequence of actions, including variants, that a system performs that yields an observable result of value to a particular actor*". Formally, a use case model may be defined as follows:

UC_{model}:$< Actor,$ $UseCase,$$Relationship,$ $ExtentionPoint,$ $Constraint >$, where:

- *UseCase*: is the set of use cases, where each one is described by $< \mathcal{A}, \mathcal{R} >$, where:

- $\mathcal{A} = \{a_1, a_2, ..., a_n\}$, a set of actions that a system performs that yields an observable result. For each $a \in \mathcal{A}$, $a: f(P)$, such as $P = \{p_1, p_2, ..., p_n\}$, a set of properties satisfied by the system.
- $\mathcal{R} = \{r_1, r_2, ..., r_n\}$, a set of results realized by the system.

Figure 3 shows an example of use case model used by the *UK designer*.

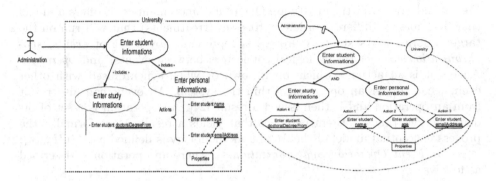

Fig. 3. Example of Use Case   **Fig. 4.** Example of a Goal Model

4.2   Goal-Oriented Model

A goal is an objective the system under consideration should achieve. Goal-oriented requirements engineering is concerned with the use of goals for eliciting, elaborating, structuring, specifying, analyzing, negotiating, documenting, and modifying requirements [5]. Goal-oriented produces the so called goal graphs, which represent goals and their logical relationships in an *AND-OR* graph form. According to the definition of *Goal Question Metric* (GQM) [21] *'A goal is defined for an object, for a variety of reasons, with respect to various models of quality, from various points of view, relative to a particular environment'*. Note that this formalism has been used to designing *relational data warehouse* applications [22]. Goal formulations thus refer to intended properties to be ensured, they are optative statements as opposed to indicative ones, and bounded by the subject matter [23]. Based on the previous definitions and *i* framework*[4], the goal oriented formalism model may be represented as follows:

$Goal_{model}$: $<$ *Actor, Goal, Relationship, AND/OR decomposition* $>$, in which:

- *Goal*: is the set of goals, where a goal is defined by $< \mathcal{A}, \mathcal{R}, \mathcal{O}, \mathcal{Q}, \mathcal{C} >$, such that:
  - $\mathcal{A} = \{a_1, a_2, ..., a_n\}$, a set of actions that achieve a goal; For each $a \in \mathcal{A}$, $a: f(P)$, such as $P = \{p_1, p_2, ..., p_n\}$, a set of properties;
  - $\mathcal{R} = \{r_1, r_2, ..., r_n\}$, a set of results (reasons) achieved by a goal;
  - $\mathcal{Q} = \{q_1, q_2, ..., q_n\}$, a set of models of quality (parameters) are entities possibly influencing a goal result;

---

[4] Is a framework using notions of Goals and Agents.

- $\mathcal{O}$: the goal object;
- $\mathcal{C}$: the goal context (environment).

Figure 4 gives an example of goal model used by the *Spanish designer*.

4.3 Process Conceptual Model

MERISE is an information system design methodology and developed by the French Industry Ministry in 70's [6]. One of its functionalities, it offers a model that describes the different ordered processes (treatments) that will run on the target information system. A process is represented by a set of *events, synchronisation criteria* (using logical connectors between events) and *operation*. An event is an activity which, on its own or when synchronised with other events, can trigger an operation within the system. An event can also result from an operation and is then issued a result [24]. An operation is a set of ordered actions that a system performs that yields a result. More formally, the process conceptual model of the *Merise* methodology is defined as: MCT_{model}: $<$ *Actor, Event, Operation, Synchronization* $>$, where an operation is described as follows:

- *Operation*: is the set of operations. An operation is defined as:$< \mathcal{A}, \mathcal{E}, \mathcal{R} >$, such as:
  - $\mathcal{A} = \{a_1, a_2, ..., a_n\}$, a set of actions that a system performs in response to an event that yields an observable result. For each $a \in \mathcal{A}$, a: $f(P)$, such as $P = \{p_1, p_2, ..., p_n\}$, a set of properties satisfied by the system to be designed.
  - $\mathcal{E} = \{e_1, e_2, ..., e_n\}$, a set of emission rules.
  - $\mathcal{R} = \{r_1, r_2, ..., r_n\}$, a set of results achieved by an operation.

Figure 5 shows an example of the MERISE diagram of the *French designer*.

This case study allows us identifying different objects manipulated by the three formalisms which facilitates the definition of our pivot model.

5   Our proposal

Before presenting in details our proposal, some hypotheses are required:

1. we assume the existence of a shared global ontology GO :$< \mathcal{C}, \mathcal{P}, Sub, Applic >$.
2. each designer references that ontology "as much possible" and locally, she/he may extend it by other concepts and properties to fitfully her/his local requirements. As consequence, each designer will have her/his own ontology (called local ontology). The designers may communicate through the common used concepts. This hypothesis is feasible in the context of major contractors (e.g., Airbus company), where they may impose to their designers to follow a global ontology. The presence of ontologies significantly reduces the vocabulary heterogeneity. Each designer may pick her/his properties and concepts from those ontologies (Figure 6).

Based on this reasoning, each local ontology shall then be connected to the used formalism model as shown in next section.

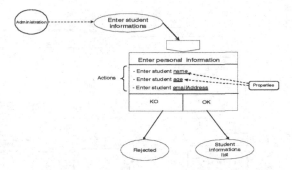

Fig. 5. Example of process model

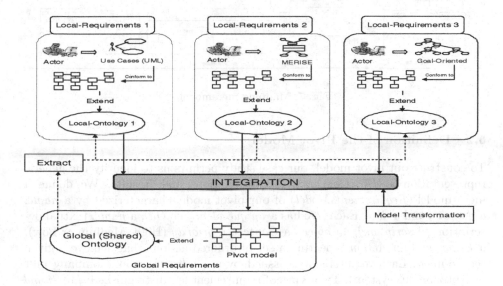

Fig. 6. Approach overview

5.1 Connection of Ontology Meta Model to Local $\mathcal{UR}$ Meta Model

We propose to connect each local formalism to its local ontology. To make this connection more generic, we propose the use of a *meta-modelling approach* [25]. This means that each meta-model of a local formalism is connected to the meta-model of the used formalism.

Example 1. Let us consider the meta-model of the goal oriented language. Its objects (Action, Result, Object and Parameter) are connected to the ontological concepts (classes and properties). Figure 7a represents a fragment of the *OWL* ontology meta-model [18] extended by our goal meta-model (Figure 7b). Each requirement expressed by the goal oriented language becomes an instance of this merged meta-model.

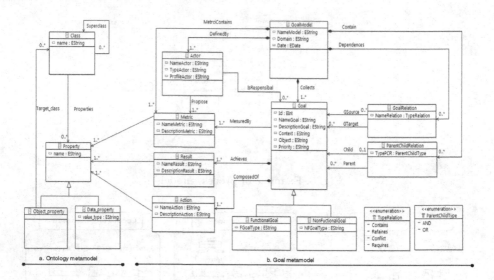

Fig. 7. Mapping metamodel

5.2 Definition of the Pivot Model

To construct our pivot model, our case study permits us to identify the generic representation a $\mathcal{UR}$: Concepts, Actors, Actions and Results. We define a meta-model (*RequirementsModel*) of our pivot model characterized by a *name*, a *domain*, and a *date*. Each $\mathcal{UR}$ has a *unique identifier (Id)*, a *name*, textual description *(description)*, an *object*, a *Context*, a *priority* (High, Medium or Low), a *Result* and an *Action* reflecting a set of ordered actions that achieve a given requirement. Each requirement is issued by an *Actor* (Person, Company unit or Autonomous system). Two types of requirement are distinguished: *functional* and *non-functional*. A non-functional requirement is defined as an attribute or constraint of the system (such as security, performance, flexibility, etc) [26]. Each requirement involves one or more actors that interact with the system to fulfil the requirement. Requirements can be related with each other through one of the following relationships: (*Requires, Refines, Contains, Equivalence* and *Conflicts*). The presence of these relationships may help the reasoning on requirements.

The actions are the most important part of our pivot model. According to [27], a $\mathcal{UR}$ can be viewed as a description of a system property or properties which need to be fulfilled. According to this, we define formally a requirement as follows: *Requirement*:$< \mathcal{A}, \mathcal{R}, \mathcal{S} >$, in which:

- $\mathcal{A} = \{a_1, a_2, ..., a_n\}$, a set of sequence of actions that a system performs that yields an observable result. For each $a \in \mathcal{A}$, $a\colon f(P)$, such as $P = \{p_1, p_2, ..., p_n\}$, a set of properties that may belong to a given local ontology.
- $\mathcal{R} = \{r_1, r_2, ..., r_n\}$, a set of results realized by the system.
- $\mathcal{S} = \{s_1, s_2, ..., s_n\}$, a set of systems that are satisfied by the $\mathcal{A}$.

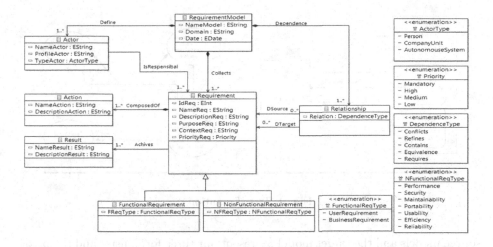

Fig. 8. Pivot metamodel

Since an action of a $\mathcal{UR}$ may be expressed by the means of concepts and properties of its local ontology, we first need to connect that to its $\mathcal{UR}$ model. We also use the meta-modeling approach to handle these connections. Four types of meta-models need to be defined: (1) one for each local ontology, (2) one for each $\mathcal{UR}$ formalism, (3) one for the pivot model and (4)and one for the global ontology. Note that the meta-models of local and global ontologies are similar[5].

Similarly to the previous connection, a link between the global ontology metamodel and the pivot meta-model is established. The merged meta-model, called *OntoPivot* is defined as: $< GO, Pivot >$, such that:

- GO: $< \mathcal{C}, \mathcal{P}, Sub, Applic >$: the global ontology.
- *Pivot*: a pivot model of requirements.

The Model *Pivot* is defined as follows: $Pivot = < C_p, P_p >$, such that:

- C_p: represents the set of classes of the pivot model.
- P_p: represents the set of properties of each requirement are expressed by using the ontological properties: $P_p \in 2^{P_{go}}$

5.3   Mapping between Local Formalisms and the Pivot Model

To ensure the mapping between local formalisms (Goal-Oriented ontology, Use Cases ontology and MCT ontology) and the pivot model, we use transformation model techniques [28]. For our proposal, we use the ATLAS Transformation Language (ATL) (http://www.eclipse.org/atl/). It consists of a set of model-to-model transformation tools integrated into Eclipse framework. ATL provides ways to produce a set of target models from a set of source models. In our case,

---

[5] Local ontologies are extracted from the global one.

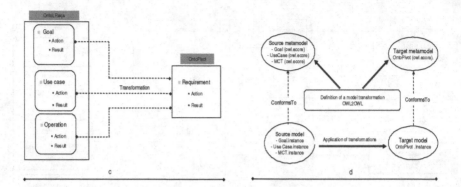

Fig. 9. Transformation

source models and the target model represent our three formalisms and the pivot model, respectively. We have defined two types of rules to ensure the mappings: one for concept mapping (classes, properties) and another for individual mapping (Figure 9 c,d).

To illustrate our transformations, let us consider the mapping between the Goal oriented ontology and the pivot model where class-to-class and instance-to-instance are defined as follows:

```
rule Goal2Requirement {
from  s: GoalModel!Goal  -- source classe (Goal)
to    t: PivotModelRequirement!Requirement(-- target classe
      uriRef  <-s.uriRef,            -- mapping properties
      IdReq   <-s.Id,
      NameReq <-s.NameGoal,
      DescriptionReq <-s.DescriptionGoal,
      ContextReq  <-s.Context,
      PurposeReq  <-s.Purpose,
      PriorityReq <-s.Priority
         )
}
```

6   Conclusion

User requirements represent the heart of developing applications and systems. With the globalisation, various systems are developed by the participation of a large number of designers; each one uses her/his vocabulary and favourite formalism to express requirements. This situation give raises two complementary problems: heterogeneity of vocabularies and heterogeneity of formalisms. In this paper, we presented an approach for dealing with both heterogeneities. For the first one, we propose the use of conceptual models and each designer picks her/his concepts and properties from that ontologies. This may be feasible for several domains, where concepts are highly formalised and structured (engineering, industrial, medicine, etc.). To deal with the second heterogeneity, we use a pivot model connected to the ontologies. A mapping is done between the meta-models representing the pivot model formalisms. A case study developed by considering three formalisms belonging to the category of semi formal formalism: UML use case, goal oriented language and Merise. Our proposal is validated by a tool using ATLAS Transformation Language (a model driven architecture).

This work leads to many other tasks currently in progress including: (i) evaluating our approach for large scale case study by considering other classes of formalisms (formal and informal), (ii) reasoning about requirements in order to detect conflicts and (iii) studying of the impact of requirements evolution on our proposal.

References

1. Golfarelli, M., Rizzi, S.: Data Warehouse Design: Modern Principles and Methodologies. McGraw Hill (2009)
2. Sugumaran, V., Storey, V.C.: The role of domain ontologies in database design: An ontology management and conceptual modeling environment. ACM Transactions on Database Systems (ACM-TODS) 31(3), 1064–1094 (2006)
3. Khouri, S., Bellatreche, L.: DWOBS: Data Warehouse Design from Ontology-Based Sources. In: Yu, J.X., Kim, M.H., Unland, R. (eds.) DASFAA 2011, Part II. LNCS, vol. 6588, pp. 438–441. Springer, Heidelberg (2011)
4. Goh, C.H., Bressan, S., Madnick, S., Siegel, M.: Context interchange: new features and formalisms for the intelligent integration of information. ACM Trans. Inf. Syst. 17, 270–293 (1999)
5. van Lamsweerde, A.: Goal-oriented requirements engineering: A guided tour. In: Proceedings of the Fifth IEEE International Symposium on Requirements Engineering, RE 2010, pp. 249–263. IEEE Computer Society (2001)
6. Rochfeld, A.: Merise, an information system design and development methodology, tutorial. In: Proceedings of the Fifth International Conference on Entity-Relationship (ER), pp. 489–528 (1986)
7. De Sousa, T., Almeida Jr., Viana, S., Pavón, J.: Automatic analysis of requirements consistency with the b method. ACM SIGSOFT Software Engineering Notes 35(2), 1–4 (2010)
8. Bellatreche, L., Xuan, D.N., Pierra, G., Dehainsala, H.: Contribution of ontology-based data modeling to automatic integration of electronic catalogues within engineering databases. Computers in Industry Journal Elsevier 57(8-9), 711–724 (2006)
9. Pierra, G.: Context representation in domain ontologies and its use for semantic integration of data. Journal of Data Semantics (JODS), 173–210 (2008)
10. López, O., Laguna, M.A., Peñalvo, F.J.G.: A metamodel for requirements reuse. In: VII Jornadas de Ingeniería del Software y Bases de Datos (JISBD), pp. 427–428 (2002)
11. Kaiya, H., Saeki, M.: Ontology based requirements analysis: Lightweight semantic processing approach. In: Proceedings of the Fifth International Conference on Quality Software, pp. 223–230. IEEE Computer Society (2005)
12. Dzung, D.V., Ohnishi, A.: Ontology-based reasoning in requirements elicitation. In: IEEE International Conference on Software Engineering and Formal Methods (SEFM), pp. 263–272 (2009)

13. Saeki, M., Hayashi, S., Kaiya, H.: A tool for attributed goal-oriented requirements analysis. In: 24th IEEE/ACM International Conference on Automated Software Engineering, pp. 674–676 (2009)
14. Körner, J.S., Torben, B.: Natural language specification improvement with ontologies. Int. J. Semantic Computing 3(4), 445–470 (2009)
15. Gruber, T.: A translation approach to portable ontology specification. Knowledge Acquisition 5(2), 199–220 (1993)
16. Guarino, N., Poli, R.: Formal ontology in conceptual analysis and knowledge representation. Special Issue of the International Journal of Human and Computer Studies 43(5-6), 625–640 (1995)
17. Connolly, D., Guha, R.: Rdf vocabulary description language 1.0: Rdf schema. w3c (2002), http://www.w3.org/TR/rdf-schema/
18. Bechhofer, S., van Harmelen, F., Hendler, J., Horrocks, I., McGuinness, D., Patel-Schneider, P., Stein, L.: Owl web ontology language reference. w3c (2004), http://www.w3.org/TR/owl-ref/
19. Guo, Y., Pan, Z., Heflin, J.: Lubm: A benchmark for owl knowledge base systems. Journal of Web Semantics, 158–182 (2005)
20. Jacobson, I., Bittner, K., Spence, I.: Use Case Modeling. Addison Wesley Professional (2002) ISBN 0-201-70913-9
21. Victor, R., Gianluigi, C.R.H.D.: The goal question metric approach. computer science technical report series cs-tr-2956. Computer Science Technical Report Series CS-TR-2956 (1992)
22. Bonifati, A., Cattaneo, F., Ceri, S., Fuggetta, A., Paraboschi, S.: Designing data marts for data warehouses. ACM Transactions on Software Engineering and Methodology 10(4), 452–483 (2001)
23. Zave, P., Jackson, M.: Four dark corners of requirements engineering. ACM Trans. Softw. Eng. Methodol. 6(1), 1–30 (1997)
24. Rochfeld, A., Tardieu, H.: Merise: An information system design and development methodology. Information and Management, 143–159 (1983)
25. Nissen, H.W., Jeusfeld, M.A., Jarke, M., Zemanek, G., Huber, H.: Managing multiple requirements perspectives with metamodels. IEEE Software 13(2), 37–48 (1996)
26. Glinz, M.: On non-functional requirements. In: 15th IEEE International Requirements Engineering Conference, RE 2007, pp. 21–26 (2007)
27. Goknil, A., Kurtev, I., Berg, K., Veldhuis, J.W.: Semantics of trace relations in requirements models for consistency checking and inferencing. Softw. Syst. Model. 10, 31–54 (2011)
28. Kleppe, A.G., Warmer, J., Bast, W.: MDA Explained: The Model Driven Architecture: Practice and Promise. Addison-Wesley Longman Publishing Co., Inc., Boston (2003)

Author Index